Hypnosis in the Realm of De-Sign

Maurício S. Neubern

Hypnosis in the Realm of De-Sign

 Springer

Maurício S. Neubern
Clinical Psychology Department
Institute of Psychology, University of Brasília
Brasília, Brazil

ISBN 978-3-031-81295-8   ISBN 978-3-031-81296-5 (eBook)
https://doi.org/10.1007/978-3-031-81296-5

© The Editor(s) (if applicable) and The Author(s), under exclusive license to Springer Nature Switzerland AG 2025

This work is subject to copyright. All rights are solely and exclusively licensed by the Publisher, whether the whole or part of the material is concerned, specifically the rights of translation, reprinting, reuse of illustrations, recitation, broadcasting, reproduction on microfilms or in any other physical way, and transmission or information storage and retrieval, electronic adaptation, computer software, or by similar or dissimilar methodology now known or hereafter developed.

The use of general descriptive names, registered names, trademarks, service marks, etc. in this publication does not imply, even in the absence of a specific statement, that such names are exempt from the relevant protective laws and regulations and therefore free for general use.

The publisher, the authors and the editors are safe to assume that the advice and information in this book are believed to be true and accurate at the date of publication. Neither the publisher nor the authors or the editors give a warranty, expressed or implied, with respect to the material contained herein or for any errors or omissions that may have been made. The publisher remains neutral with regard to jurisdictional claims in published maps and institutional affiliations.

This Springer imprint is published by the registered company Springer Nature Switzerland AG
The registered company address is: Gewerbestrasse 11, 6330 Cham, Switzerland

If disposing of this product, please recycle the paper.

To Elias B. Neubern, my son, and
To Miguel Neubern, my father, with Love.

Foreword

It was early March of 2021 when I received an unexpected but interesting email. The email included a formal letter and two other attachments from Maurício S. Neubern, an Associate Professor who teaches hypnosis at the Institute of Psychology, University of Brasília (UnB), Brazil. Neubern expressed his fascination with the concepts contained in my 2019 book: *De-sign in the Transmodern World: Envisioning Reality Beyond Absoluteness*. He anticipated formulating some new knowledge and authentic ideas that would embody the beautiful and agapistic practices of hypnosis. Maurício conveyed his intention of fulfilling his desire to undertake a post-doctoral fellowship with me under the auspices of Antioch University Seattle, where I taught.

Indeed, Maurício Neubern delved deeply into his post-doctoral inquiry project at Antioch University Seattle during the period from January 16, 2022, to January 16, 2023. His project was accepted by Dr. Colin Ward, Chair of the School of Applied Psychology, Counseling, and Family Therapy and was conducted in consultation with a Post-Doctoral Committee composed of the following members: Professor Emeritus Dr. Farouk Y. Seif (Chair), Professor Emeritus Dr. Randy Morris, and Professor Emerita Dr. Ann Blake. Maurício Neubern successfully completed his post-doctoral research project in February 2023. During this post-doctoral study, Maurício Neubern and I often met virtually to collaborate and review his ongoing project. In addition, the entire Committee met monthly to review Dr. Neubern's conceptual and practical applications of his intellectual inquiry. Neubern worked on an impressive list of presentations, seminars, and published articles, which are included in the references here. Due to the restrictions caused by the coronavirus pandemic and the logistics of traveling during it, Maurício and I met via Zoom numerous times to review and discuss the progress, scope, and content of this book, which has come to be entitled: *Hypnosis in the Realm of De-Sign*.

From the outset, I wondered (for two differing reasons) whether or not my own involvement in Neubern's inquiry would be beneficial to him. First, I questioned why someone would approach *me* about hypnosis? This area of knowledge or subject matter has never been on my academic radar, and I, consequentially, know very little about it. Second, I wondered in what ways could someone teaching and practicing hypnotherapy utilize the notion of *De-sign* to advance his work on hypnosis. Neubern, however, through reading my book *De-sign in the Transmodern World* and other articles I have published, had uncovered interesting connections between the notion of hypnosis and the interdisciplinary perspective of *De-sign* as being a meaningful way of thinking and acting in the world. After all, hypnosis is a phenomenological experience that involves using intention to alter the state of human consciousness in order to seek imaginative enactment for desired outcomes. Such a way of life requires a different mode of inquiry—one including abductive reasoning and intimate dialoguing—in order to free humans from self-entrapment in an otherwise absolute reality.

Neubern has sought throughout this work to substantiate his hypothesis regarding the intimate connection between *De-sign* and hypnosis. He has creatively integrated semiotic systems, pragmatism, and *De-sign* principles into the act of hypnosis. He has validated his ideas by sharing actual hypnotherapeutic experiences—both those of his own, as well as those of other hypnotherapists—that have occurred while working with patients. By exploring these concepts as interrelated, Neubern has discovered striking affinities between therapeutic hypnosis and *De-sign* intention. He has, via combining their principles, seen a way in which self-rebirth and renewal can be attained by their co-joined use.

Reflecting on the contributions of the American hypnotist/psychiatrist Milton Hyland Erickson and the Brazilian spiritualist medium Chico Xavier, Neubern herein argues that the notion of *De-sign*, while not communicated explicitly in hypnosis, is nevertheless (surprisingly) at the core of hypnotic therapy. As with every *De-sign* situation, each patient requires a unique therapeutic strategy and approach that is individually appropriate for them. Neubern thereby encourages therapists to become *de-signers*, working *with*—not *for*—their subjects. He feels hypnotherapists must strive to create a context within which their subjects can awaken their therapeutic potential. By doing so, patients can then bring into focus that which *could be*, rather than focusing on that *which is*. Neubern also draws our attention to the paradoxical challenges that are commonly associated with both *De-sign* and hypnosis, such as knowing and not-knowing, surrendering and controlling, tolerating ambiguity and feeling at ease with uncertainty. In such a manner, hypnotherapy becomes a truly legitimate process of *De-sign* whereby the outcome, while unpredictable, is a welcoming gift of rebirth and renewal.

Having had the good fortune of reviewing, discussing, and offering suggestions to Maurício for nearly three years, I have had the pleasure of not only knowing an esteemed scholar but of also (and of equal significance) learning a great deal about hypnosis and how the notion of *De-sign* can pragmatically cross boundaries of different, seemingly unrelated disciplines. Drawing on the notion of Transmodernity and the practice of "trance," Neubern's concluding chapter demonstrates an acumen for perceiving hypnotherapy as a form of "Trance-Modernity." Undoubtedly—due to making this connection between *De-sign* and hypnosis—Neubern's book, *Hypnosis in the Realm of De-sign*, validates the possibility and actuality of how the transdisciplinary framework of *De-sign* can be sensibly applied to a whole new range of disciplines and fields. Certainly, it is a significant benchmark in the ever forward motion of our transmodern lifeworld.

Professor Emeritus
Antioch University Seattle,
Seattle, WA, USA
September 2024

Farouk Y. Seif

Acknowledgments

My acknowledgments to Professor Farouk Seif, PhD, Antioch University, Seattle (USA), who was essential to this book project. His wisdom and friendship introduced me to the new universe of De-sign, leading me to a rebirth experience as a person, hypnotherapist, and researcher. I also acknowledge Ann Blake, PhD, Randy Morris, PhD, and Colin Ward, PhD, from Antioch University, who supported me during my post-doctoral studies, which was the basis of this work.

My best gratitude to my friends from Réunion Island meeting 2023 (France): Antoine Bioy, PhD, Université Paris VIII; Jean-Claude Lavaud, PhD, Ericksonian Institute Île de la Réunion; Thierry Servillat, PhD, Ipnosia, France; Teresa Robles, PhD, Centro Ericksoniano de Mexico; and Kathryn Rossi, PhD, USA. Their friendship and good attitudes had a deep impact on my thoughts and feelings, especially when I was writing this book.

My acknowledgment to my team, the CHYS research group, José Francisco Miguel Bairrão, PhD (University of São Paulo, USP); Anotine Bioy, PhD (University Paris VIII); Hugo Nogueira, PhD; Elizabeth Quintiliano, MS; Rafaela Camões Rabelo, PhD; Erica Negri, PhD; Felix Jorge Robinson, PhD student; Carlos Eduardo Soares Reis, PhD student; Felipe Monsalve, PhD student; Barbara Fontoura, Psychologist; Monalisa Oliveira, psychologist; and Talles Caiubi, undergraduate student. Without your support, friendship, and dedication, I'd never be able to develop many ideas expressed in this book. I also acknowledge Virgínia Turra, psychologist, PhD, and Bruno Costa, psychologist, MS, from our center of therapy (CAEP/IP/UnB).

I'd also like to acknowledge Marta Helena de Freitas, PhD, Catholic University of Brasília, Brazil, and my colleagues from the Ethnopsychology research group, Fabio Scorsolini-Comin, PhD, USP; José Francisco Miguel Bairrão, PhD, USP; and Ronilda Yakemi, PhD, USP. I thank CAPES (Ministry of Education) and FAP-DF (Brasília) our agencies for financial support.

To God, my ancestors, and the invisible beings of my Ethos. Because I see them in my future.

Contents

1	De-Sign and Hypnosis.	1
2	Hypnosis and Reality: About That Which Is Overlooked.	17
3	Working With.	53
4	Thinking and Doing: The Challenge of Effectiveness.	83
5	Hypnosis, De-sign & Paradoxes.	113
6	The Multiple Faces of Love.	145
7	Hypnosis and Trance-Modernity.	195
Index.		223

Chapter 1
De-Sign and Hypnosis

Hypnosis and Its Elusive Nature

On one occasion, I received a 42-year-old man called Antônio asking for help through hypnotherapy. He suffered from chronic pains caused by a sequence of surgical errors. Antônio was very depressed, with previous suicidal attempts, and saying that hypnosis was his last attempt before giving up. Before hypnosis, he had insistently undergone different types of treatment (both conventional medicine and alternative therapies) without success. During one hypnotic session, I told him how people would feel like a plume gliding in the air following the wind. They could contemplate landscapes, people, houses, mountains, trees, and rivers from the sky through angles impossible to the human eye. Subsequently, those people would become drops of water inside a great river. The drops did not lose themselves in the river but felt as part of it—they could see the most profound landscapes, fishes, boats, fishers, animals, and washerwomen. Asked by a student about the reasons for such interventions, I explained that he used Antônio's earliest experiences with fishing and nature, which were essential and pleasant for him. He also stated that becoming a plume or a drop of water to be carried by some fluid mass (such as the air or the water) was a way to suggest the changing of some references about himself in terms of matter, body, time, and space. In order for a person to deal with realities that seem insoluble, the person needs to experience the alteration of these references, as provided by the trance.

This brief clinical story has excellent therapeutic value because it indicates how a story told during a trance state can determine the reconfiguration of a subjective experience. Taking inspiration from Milton Erickson—one of the most important references to this book—this story highlights how particular experiences can be applied therapeutically. Regarding the meta-knowledge of hypnosis, it implicates a point of the highest importance: the story can be understood as a metaphor for how the obstacles to the studies on hypnosis can be overcome (Stengers, 2002). In order to be approached pertinently, hypnosis should be conceived as a subjective and elusive field of study and research. Similarly to what happened with Antônio, the characteristics of hypnosis must be recognized as potential resources in order to enable it as a field of study. In other words, the processes conceived as subjective notions in the modern scientific paradigm (Santos, 2000), such as imagination, feelings, and meanings, must be taken as the main categories for studying hypnosis.

Hypnosis is still a controversial field of study, despite the significant research since the beginning of modern science (Carroy, 1991; Mehéust, 1999). Despite the diverse and important research carried out in the last 30 years (Neubern & Bioy, 2023), hypnosis is a field with few consensus points (Facco, 2021), especially regarding the definition of its nature. What kind of reality hypnosis is; which are its methodological exigencies; and what are the potentially required methodological and conceptual changes remain as some unanswered questions. It is possible that the excessive emphasis on instrumentalist methodologies from researchers (Psillos & Zorzato, 2021) and on the part of therapists, as well as the absence of more in-depth conceptual reflections and research alternatives, have contributed to such issues. This has rendered it practically unchanged since the beginning of scientific studies in the field (Stengers, 2001). Thus, despite the interest it has received in important scientific communities worldwide, a more comprehensive understanding of it still seems far on the horizon through commonly used perspectives.

Precisely at this point that this book's proposal—an understanding of hypnosis through De-sign (Seif, 2019)—becomes relevant. De-sign is a way of thinking that integrates two traditions –design and semiotics (Seif, 2020a); it is an inquiry that appropriates the notions of subjectivity marginalized by the modern paradigm of science. In this sense, De-sign allows the study of hypnosis to be analogically compared to Antônio's story: he needs to stop trying the same things to make things happen; he needs to be himself in order to become somebody different from himself (such as the drop of water and the plume), reconnect with his subjective universe, and consequently access the ways to deal with his demands. Nevertheless, when this book appropriates notions such as the imaginary, plurality of meanings, feelings, paradoxes, and the diversity of times and spaces, it does not attempt to become a proposal of subjectivism since De-sign transcends the opposition subjectivity-objectivity (Seif, 2020b). It is rather a form of metaknowledge that is not inserted into humanities or hard sciences, proposing a dialogue with both fields while respecting their particularities and, in turn—transcending them. Regarding hypnosis, De-sign is very relevant because it promotes the dialogue and the transcendence of the typical oppositions of this field, such as clinical practice vs. research, qualitative vs. quantitative, and knowledge vs. practice.

> The Modern Paradigm of Western knowledge is organized around two main axes: subjectivity and objectivity (Santos, 2000). At first, there are notions such as the singular, love, the aesthetic, the ethical, spiritual, feelings, and the qualitative, all based on a perspective of dialogue and contemplation. Arts, philosophy, theology, law, and common sense meet on this axis. In the axis of objectivity, there is a proposal of exclusive and privileged knowledge of reality through the scientific method that, by removing appearances of phenomena, it reaches the laws that control them. From this, their prediction, explanation, and control become possible, mainly due to quantification.
>
> Contrary to what occurs in knowledge linked to subjectivity, different interpretations of the same phenomenon are not allowed due to the idea of a single reality in objectivity. The eventual differences need to be eliminated over time through the collective effort of scientists. Physics, Chemistry, Biology, and the sciences that derive from them are on the axis of objectivity. The human and social sciences are born at the intersection of these two great axes, and their different variations can lean toward either side.

The following topics will present some concepts in more detail to promote a clearer understanding of this book's proposal.

De-Sign

De-sign is a way of thinking that integrates design and semiotics (Seif, 2019). It goes beyond the mere production of objects and is conceived as a purposeful action, while semiotics is the study of signs (CP[1] 2.227). Thus, the De-sign integrates the notions of form and teleology, in which form is a system that reconfigures itself, while the semiotic offers a processual way of interpreting signs. Since De-sign is an imaginary way of inquiry, it becomes a powerful way to question the absolute categories of reality, especially modern ones. According to the ideas in De-sign, time is no longer an ordered process of past-present-future, but a circular and polychronic experience (Hall, 1969/1983), where somebody can live different time references at the exact moment. During the De-sign inquiry, the person can live and experience numerous forms of space without the obligation of adopting an exclusive space experience. Similarly, the concrete and absolute space of modern reality is replaced by the diaphanous space and the transparent vision of experience (Gebser, 1949/1985).

---

[1] CP means the Collected Papers of Charles Sanders Peirce (Hartshorne & Weiss, 1980), being the first number, the volume, and the last before the point, the paragraph. Despite its difference concerning the other citations, CP will be preserved in the present work because of its familiarity with the semioticians for whom this book is also intended. Another Peircean acronym is MS, which means the Annotated Catalogue of Papers of Charles S. Peirce (Robin, 1967).

If reality is not absolute but fluid and multifaceted in its categories, De-sign also does not allow a search for definitive results (Seif, 2020a). A De-sign inquiry is comparable to a navigation process, in which the traveler leaves a port without knowing exactly where they will arrive. Nevertheless, when following intentionality as a compass, they come across something unexpected and full of meaning—the desirable outcomes. These evade the planned and deliberated. They are subtle and commonly play a role in making the inquirer feel that their journey has reached a destination where they feel more integrated with themselves and are able to perceive life from new perspectives of meaning. The central proposal of De-sign is, therefore, not that of efficacy, technique, and cause, but that of teleology, effectiveness, and integration with oneself. In a way, this is a paradoxical proposal since an inquirer's search to know the world in its various facets leads them to become more integrated unto themselves.

> *Charles S. Peirce (CP 5.448) considered that the universe was perfused by signs, which were present in all their facets. This means that it would be impossible to think or even feel the world without signs. Hence the importance of semiotics, or logic, as the study of signs. Sign is that which replaces an object and produces an effect –the interpretant– in the mind of the interlocutor. Signs can be classified in the relationships to their objects (icons, indices, and symbols), as to themselves (quali-sign, sin-sign, legi-sign), and as to interpretants (rema, student, and argument). The first classification is the best known, it is worth highlighting what these signs are: icons represent their objects by their qualities (such as emoticons, drawings, hieroglyphs, etc.), indices represent objects by causality (such as footprints or scars) or functionality (such as the numbers in a thermometer). Symbols represent them through laws, habits, or conventions (such as words, laws, and regularities). Throughout his life, Peirce proposed various combinations between these signs generating more complex classifications which will not be explored in this work.*

As such, De-sign adopts the paradox as one of its most essential principles (Seif, 2019). If reality is not absolute and has many faces, the paradox is not a problem to be avoided or eliminated, but a component of life. Beautiful *vs.* ugly, good *vs.* evil, sacred *vs.* profane, among others, are paradoxes present in the everyday life of many people, for whom these paradoxes become important ways of personal growth. Frequently, they become a source of suffering, especially when linked to absolute notions of reality. Nevertheless, the tension of such conflicts commonly promotes new ways of teleology. As affirmed by Seif (2019), perseverance through paradoxes leads the person to a very different consciousness about the world. During the De-sign inquiry, the dimensions of a paradox leave out the logic of opposition (A against B) or exclusion (A or B) into an integrative one (A and B). The field approached by the De-signer can be simultaneously good and evil, beautiful and ugly, individual and collective, free and determined.

Hypnosis

The Notion of Self

In the present perspective, a new understanding of hypnosis must be based on a complex and semiotic notion of the self (Petrilli, 2017). In a way, the self is a great sign that makes references to a multitude of objects that are macro and collective systems (biology, the social world, culture, economy, politics, ethnicity, spirituality, gender, among others). Being a sign, or rather a configuration of signs, the self is always in motion, transforming itself from different processes of semiosis, that is, when one sign is translated into another (Short, 2009). Generally speaking, some points can be highlighted in understanding the self. In the first place, the self is a process highly crossed by the social (Colapietro, 1989), incompatible with the modern vision of an individualized psyche closed in itself (Dumont, 1983). Peirce (CP 4.69) considered that the conception of an individualized self would be a practical joke or something disappointing and distanced from the truth. In this sense, the self is essentially porous (Petrilli, 2017) by the very constitution and action of the signs; that is, each person brings the set of relationships that they experience throughout their life. Nevertheless, the idea of self does not discard individuality as some may conceive: based on the notion of haecceity by Duns Scotus[2] (cited in Raposa, 1989), it is possible to conceive it as a semiotic system, which maintains an interpenetration with the world without losing its individuality.

> *Phenomenology is a philosophical discipline fundamental to Peirce's work. It supports the Normative Sciences (ethics, aesthetics, and semiotics) and or the study of reality –metaphysics (Liszka, 1996). It is the study of what one appears to experience, which he classified into three broad categories. Firstness refers to a qualitative experience, based on feelings and images. It is an experience of what is potential, not yet existing. Secondness refers to an experience characterized by reaction, the existing, and the singular. Thirdness refers to thoughts, laws, and habits. Peirce's signs are closely related to the phenomenological categories: icons, qualisigns, and remas are signs of Firstness, while indices, sinsigns, and students relate to Secondness. Symbols, legisigns, and arguments are signs linked to Thirdness. In practical experience, phenomena always present different articulated types of signs that refer to different phenomenological categories.*

---

[2] John Duns Scotus (1266–1308) was one of the most medieval philosophers of the Middle Ages. He received intensive influence from Aristotle's legacy and is probably the author of the term 'reality'. Charles Peirce was very influenced by Scotus' work, especially his conception of reality (Boler, 1963).

Secondly, the self must be understood in relationship with the ego, which composes the dimension of everyday deliberations social, and consensual references about reality. As sustained by Peirce (CP 1.631; 7.456), much of our psychic activities are not determined by our conscious but by involuntary or unconscious processes. Thus, the ego is not the most critical center of our mental activity as the rationalistic ideal supposes. The common interpretation of people's experience does not focus on objects' signs under the focus of attention, which suggests the absence of perfect harmony between the constituent habits of the psyche and the characteristics peculiar to the object of the environment. For such reasons, the imaginary and daydreaming processes in which the inner focus seems to ignore the external signs seem to be dominant in everyday experience, which makes one closer to somnambulism than what is commonly assumed (Colapietro, 1995). Only a small portion of the outer signs receive greater attention from people, promoting a conscious exercise of this process. The very porosity that the ego maintains in the relationship with the self promotes this type of condition. However, the relationships between these two instances can't be understood deeply without the paradoxical binds of determination and freedom. Ego is comparable to a wave in the ocean of the self (CP 5.225), the latter being much wider and more complex. Thus, while this relationship implies a series of determinations, it also needs a creative dimension on the part of the ego, without which semiosis would not become possible. The relationships between ego and self are not defined by sharp boundaries, nor do they occur in linear fashion. Both present their own agency and creative possibilities that transcend a mechanistic idea of the mind.

Trance and Influence

The notion of hypnosis adopted here (Neubern, 2016) involves two basic axes—trance and influence. The elusive condition of everyday experience (Colapietro, 1995) allows that under certain conditions, there are intense modifications in the references between ego and world, which contemplate time, space, matter, body, and cause. Such changes characterize trance. In this mode of experience, one can be in the river of the family farm doing an activity at the current time while picturing a future situation, all at the same time. In such cases, time and space are largely altered. As in Antônio's case, he can perceive himself in the office chair while at the same time feeling entirely like a different object (such as the drop of water or feather) in other sensorial spaces. In summary, these changes amplify the porosity between ego and self, and a series of experiences, learnings, scenes, memories, and sensations come to the fore—all with high potential for transformation.

This plasticity linked to trance did not go unnoticed by Peirce (CP 6.228):

> Perhaps it may be thought that hypnotic phenomena show that subconscious feelings are not unified. But I maintain that those phenomena exhibit the very opposite peculiarity. They are unified so far as they are brought into one quale-consciousness; and that is why different personalities are formed. Of course, each personality is based upon a "bundle of habits", as the saying is that a man is a bundle of habits. But a bundle of habits would not have the unity of self-consciousness. That unity must be given as a center for the habits.

In this passage, Peirce highlights a variety of apparently disparate phenomena, which, in the end, find themselves under unity. This unity is linked exactly to the term "quale"–consciousness, highlighting the primacy of the qualitative and potential aspect of feelings, situating it as an experience deeply permeated by Firstness. The considerable potential for change of trance is based on this "quale" condition, mainly in the sense of undoing and remaking habits linked to signs derived by stiffened perceptions and worldviews about reality. This type of plastic, imaginary, and for many, unreal experience can favor profound changes in a person's life, as occurred with Antônio in his chronic pain and life attitudes. In a word, trance has considerable impacts on the reconfiguration of different semiotic systems at the level of agencies.

This potential for change also encompasses a fundamental type of reference in people's lives: those of the social world (Clément, 2011). When triggered, notions such as beautiful *vs.* ugly, good *vs.* evil, sacred *vs.* profane, reality *vs.* imaginary, human *vs.* divine, and masculine *vs.* feminine, among others, can be highly modified. As in the case of Antônio, a human has become part of nature and not something distinct from it. In other situations, a man can assume a female role, as in the case of Siberian tribe shamans who become the spiritual wife of the deer, the totemic animal of that group (Clément, 2011). In short, when the universe of the self is accessed through trance, the everyday logic guided by such notions can be substantially modified. Such experiences are also collective, either due to the social context of the self or a range of collective agencies and knowledge that cross the trance experience (Neubern, 2022a). This collective content of trance has two significant consequences. On the one hand, trance seems to amplify the very polyphony in the self (Morin, 2001/2015) so that many beings (which are signs) can present themselves and establish new relationships with the ego. Thus, the image of someone dear to the person's history, a "you," for example, can arise and dialogue with one about important emotional issues in the history of both. Scenes can contain a diversity of signs (places, landscapes, tastes, smells, colors, and shapes) that do not necessarily have a relationship with something that has already occurred in concrete reality but that is undoubtedly significant for the person. The collective content of the symbolic dimension, in these cases, is more linked to a person and their circle of closest relationships.

Ethnopsychology is a proposal for understanding traditional knowledge from world references. Although there are several different theoretical tendencies, some principles can be cited: a) one cannot talk about others, but only with others; b) there is no difference between those who know and those who believe; c) knowledge is built by the tension between skepticism (distance) and proximity (acceptance, affection); d) there are no "pure" people, since we are all mixed in terms of ethnic belonging. Ethnopsychology opposes the colonialism of Modern Sciences and religions while recognizing the legitimacy and specificity of traditional knowledge (Neubern, 2013, 2022a).

On the other hand, these signs may imply broader collective agencies, as in the case of knowledge that permeates the philosophical and spiritual practices in different cultures (Nathan, 2001/2014; 2004). In these cases the beings (ancestors, *orixás*, spirits, demons, angels, saints, gods) are signs formed from specific machinery[3] and devices (Deleuze & Guattari, 1980) and appear as a "we", since their message has implications of a collective order, such as the convocation of that person for a mission or the transmission of a revelation. Such cultural technologies also involve agency linked to the body itself (Csordas, 1997), which allows the expression of signs linked to corporeality (in other words, "it"), such as anesthesia and cures. In these cases, the symbolic that manages such signs encompass broader groups, linking to collective knowledge.

Hypnosis also has an axis of influence, ant its role is to trigger the trance, transmitting something to the person. The influences can be involuntary, when a therapist's own way of being and self-expressing favors the construction of the trance. They can also be deliberate, as with the diversity of techniques used by therapists and researchers, consisting of a wide variety of signs (Neubern, 2016). Imperative commands, tales of stories, truisms, word games, attention fixation, and dramatizations are some of examples of influence techniques. Roughly speaking in semiotic terms, they can have prevalence in signs of Firstness, Secondness, and Thirdness, according to the clinical need sought. They can cover more specific situations, linked to a symptom, for example, or promote deeper changes in terms of agency. In religious and spiritual contexts,[4] techniques compose devices that trigger trance and function as cultural technologies of exchange with the invisible world. They encompass the use of certain words, songs, dances, food, drinks, clothes, odors, objects, and movements that make up specific performances to achieve the objectives (Nathan, 2001/2014; 2004).

---

[3] Machineries are large collective agencies organized around knowledge (Nathan, 2001/2014). They have worldviews, theories, rules, and techniques or rituals that manipulate energies, objects, plants, *etc.*, for specific purposes. They have specialists, initiates, and many other characters who access it and use its resources. They manufacture beings from their technical devices, which are ways of questioning the types of reality to which they refer. Thus, while physics has the machinery of modern scientific knowledge, a device like a laboratory and a being like the Electron, religion has machinery (a knowledge of oral or written tradition), a ritual (as the dance and singing wheels in Umbanda) and beings (spiritual entities or *orixás*). Beings generated from machinery, such as the scientific one, do not respond to the machinery of religion and vice versa.

[4] Many people who sought hypnotherapy with me presented religious themes and were affiliated to some spiritual practice. This is very common in Brazil, where 90% of the population says they are affiliated to some religion. Such facts justify the inclusion of spiritual trances in the discussion of this work, such as the support of ethnopsychology.

Facing Challenges

The two key notions described above—De-sign and Hypnosis—are fundamental to achieve the objectives proposed here. This implies dealing with three ever-present obstacles in the study of hypnosis. The first of these is the problem of reality, which has always collaborated so that hypnosis was associated with notions despised by the modern paradigm of science, such as subjectivity and imagination (Stengers, 2001). In a way, as Peirce (1903/1997) would say, Cartesianism recognizes only elements of Secondness (such as brute force and opposition) and Thirdness (laws), leaving aside processes of Firstness. This coincides with the absence of an ontological definition of subjective experiences (Gonzalez Rey, 2019), which still brings considerable damage to contemporary psychology. Hypnosis also has a central characteristic, called hypnogenesis, in which a person tends to reproduce the expectations and theories of the authority with whom they relate, such as a researcher, a teacher, or a therapist (Chertok & Stengers, 1989). Thus, the differences between subject and object and, especially, between fact and artifact are compromised before the requirements of the modern scientific paradigm for building reliable knowledge.

Thus, the first challenge of hypnosis reading through De-sign is that of a broader and more integrative proposal of reality. It is a reflection greatly influenced by metaphysics (Ibri, 1992/2017) and by the questioning of absolute notions of reality (Seif, 2019). At the same time, this reflection proposes an integrative understanding between the dimensions of Firstness, Secondness, and Thirdness that transcends the real *vs.* imaginary opposition of the modern paradigm. In hypnosis, this point is of the highest relevance since the dominance of Firstness (Neubern, 2017) does not prevent it from producing quite concrete effects on the body, as in the case of chronic pain. In short, De-sign can favor a way of understanding where the elusive is integrated into concrete results in some form of generalization without one dimension diluting the other.

The second challenge derived from the first is the construction of an intelligibility linked to an experience as elusive as hypnosis. Not without reasons, hypnosis has historically been present in the works of writers, poets, and mystics (Bioy, 2018), not to mention its kinship with other cultural technologies such as exorcism and different expressions of shamanism (Martino, 1944/1999). Such facts bring some important considerations about the proposal of this book. They refer to the importance that the notions linked to such a field may be taken up as possible references for reflection, not as obstacles to constructing knowledge. Imaginary, sentimental, and spiritual processes, for example, should not mean adherence to mystical and spiritualistic schools but the construction of a rationality that integrates Firstness rather than despising it. Both ethnopiscology (Neubern, 2023) focused on highlighting the logical pertinence of each knowledge, and semiotics, which highlight the various ways of thinking about signs, are pertinent in this sense. By highlighting "what was left out" in terms of important notions for understanding hypnosis (Stengers, 2002), De-sign proposes a differentiated rationality for understanding this field. Terms such as imaginary, abduction, love, paradox, and desirable outcomes do not arise, therefore, as an opposition to reality, but as a broader way of understanding it.

In this sense, it is important to consider that the second challenge is not restricted to a process of thought construction. Following the very perspective of De-sign (Seif, 2019), thinking and doing are inseparable. In terms of hypnosis, this construction implies an experience together with another that leads to a deep meeting with oneself. Far beyond a collection of techniques, hypnosis from the perspective of De-sign advocates a path lived and shared by the relationship protagonists, in which the therapist is placed in a condition of service and in the process of reinvention. The therapist, as a De-signer, is not a mere applicator of techniques, but someone who exerts a creative and service role so that the other develops new attitudes towards life. Technique, therefore, is an important element, but it only comes to life from a teleological attitude of the therapist himself to his role. Therapists cannot be conceived as artists since this creation contemplates an interlocutor, with the former weaving a unique process for the latter. The aesthetic in the De-signer is therefore very much rooted in agape and the ideal of service. As such, the therapist works as a midwife who helps the interlocutor to be reborn several times, hence the notion of palingenesis (Seif, 2019).

The third challenge concerns the role of De-sign as a meta-knowledge. As pointed out (Seif, 2020a), De-sign does not consist of knowledge inserted in the humanities, since it belongs to a third culture. It approaches Peirce's cenoscopic sciences (CP 1.184), with a role of meta-knowledge, a reflective knowledge that offers references so that scientists and therapists can reflect more deeply on their fields. By offering a logic based on a constellation of specific concepts (many of them marginalized by the modern paradigm of science), De-sign does not aim to solve the problems of the scientist and therapist, but helps them think and rethink their fields, creating the conceptual and technical alternatives to the problems they face within themselves. Therefore, we do not seek the creation of a new theory or school of hypnosis but rationality around key issues of this field that are relevant to those who are interested in it. Themes such as the elusive nature of hypnosis (Neubern, 2023), hypnogenesis (Chertok & Stengers, 1989), the dilemmas between state and non-state (Ribeiro, 2023), and the methodological and clinical requirements of this field are particularly important for reflection via De-sign.

The Proposal of This Book

The proposal of this book is similar to the therapeutic path of many people who seek hypnosis, such as Antônio. For them to reach the desirable outcomes, they need to walk different paths and let themselves be carried away, both by the influence of the therapist and by their own inner wisdom. Thus, in order to make hypnosis reach a broader understanding, it is necessary to let itself be led by the agapistic reflection of De-sign (Seif, 2019) and by its very nature –populated with notions despised by the modern paradigm. Some references become fundamental so that one can recognize what one will find intending to reach this goal.

In the following paragraphs, the proposals for each chapter of this book will be presented. Each important theme related to hypnosis will be developed under the multiple conceptual lenses of De-sign (Seif, 2019, 2020a). It is worth noting that each chapter will feature some clinical illustrations of hypnotherapy cases, some of them by Milton Erickson (Erickson & Rossi, 1979, 1980), myself,[5] and other relevant authors on hypnosis.

Thus, Chap. 2 will be developed around a discussion on the absolute notion of reality present in the modern paradigm of science. A brief historical reflection on names such as Mesmer, Puységur, Bernheim, Liébeault, Charcot, and Freud will be developed in order to highlight how notions linked to Firstness have been systematically left aside in the study of hypnosis. Special emphasis will be placed on the role of Milton Erickson—the most important reference on hypnosis for this book—whose innovative work seems to have developed a broader understanding of the elusive tenor of hypnosis. His principles of utilization and indirect modes of suggestion are of considerable importance for new ways of conceiving reality. Whether in the case of a man who walked compulsively (Erickson, 1958), or in the case of Joe, the florist, in palliative care with severe pain (Haley, 1993), these principles are useful for a new way of conceiving reality. Considering hypnosis as a specific field of study, with its own characteristics and requirements, the ontological notions of chance, existent and law (Ibri, 1992/2017) will be used as references in this reflection. The De-sign will be used here as an inquiry proposal that integrates different dimensions while transcending them. Thus, it provides the integration of the phenomenological categories of Firstness, Secondness, and Thirdness, but transcends the sum of these three categories by constructing a way of investigating in which the feeling, the qualitative, the imaginary, and the present are dominant references.

It is a way of integrating the different phenomenological and ontological dimensions that make up hypnosis without dissolving them. This ranges from its elusive and qualitative aspects to concrete responses (such as measurable results) and notions of habits linked to the agendas that give some level of regularity to the processes of the self. Therefore, a trance experience centered on the present is what allows a polychronic and recursive experience of time and multiple diaphanous and transparent spaces. Hypnotic reality can be understood from a transmodern perspective (Seif, 2019) that integrates the visual and concrete content of modernity, the virtual and symbolic of post-modern under the references of the visceral, feeling, and desire.

---

[5] It is important to emphasize that the clinical cases attended by me are linked to my research group "Complexity, Hypnosis and Subjectivity" (CHYS), registered at the National Research Council (CNPq), Ministry of Science and Technology, Brazil. Thus, all cases were submitted to two ethics committees of the University of Brasilia and strictly obeyed their conditions. Therefore, the information used to portray such persons (such as their names) was altered, obeying the secrecy required by the Ethics Committees.

Chapter 3, on the other hand, will discuss the partnership between the members of the hypnotic relationship as a fundamental principle of De-sign. It is a critique of the notion of control historically present in hypnosis (Méheust, 1999), according to which hypnosis would be a unilateral process based on the authority of the therapist (or researcher) over a person whose role would only be to reproduce the commands of that authority. Even if this idea is not dominant among current therapists, its resumption is important because it promotes a discussion about the role of the members in this relationship. In the chapter, the idea that both are De-signers is defended, providing the condition of protagonists who manipulate and reconfigure the forms of experience that generate meaning according to the needs and clinical potentialities of the person. In the chapter, the phenomenological characters highlighted by Peirce (1903/1997) –the artist, the bulldog, and the mathematician, are integrated into attitudes necessary for the therapist to develop hypnosis: being with (in which the importance of being present with the other is emphasized in order to establish a deep affective connection as emphasized by existentialist and humanists therapists); dancing with (in which the role of body choreography and technique, as highlighted by behavioral and cognitive therapists); and the thinking with (in which the reflexivity and symbolic dimensions of hypnotherapy are discussed, as proposed by psychoanalysts and Jungians). For each of these attitudes, there are also the implications and counterparts of the people whose protagonism is essential for therapy. There is also a discussion in the chapter about dialogue that transcends the ordinary notion of conversation due to its teleological, collective role that advances beyond the present moment. This discussion is based on the clinical report of a young wheelchair user (Erickson & Rossi, 1979, p. 428) with strong suicidal ideas. The temporal distortions produced by hypnosis will be of great relevance to this discussion.

The effectiveness of hypnosis from the perspective of De-sign (Seif, 2019) is discussed in Chap. 4. In this chapter, the notion of outcome is criticized and conceived within a broader perspective –effectiveness– based on the perspective of desirable outcomes. It is argued that the answer should be conceived as a sign immersed in various semiotic networks, while the individualistic notion of mind needs to be redefined in terms of the semiotic self (Petrilli, 2017). It starts with a clinical discussion of my case study, in which the care of a woman with severe pain generated after a surgical accident is described. Next, a brief discussion is made on the conceptions of change in Erickson and Freud, mainly around the problem of symptom elimination. This stage is based on the clinical case of a young woman suffering from asthma with a psychological origin (Erickson & Rossi, 1979, p. 234). In both clinical cases, it is considered that efficacy should be inserted into a broader notion of effectiveness (Seif, 2019) linked to some key notions: the three Is (imagination, integration, and intentionality), the development of autonomy and the quality of relationships, as well as reinsertion into one's own Ethos (belonging niches). Such notions involve aspects such as the new modes of integration between ego and self, the reconfiguration in terms of agency, and the protagonist role that the person develops in their reconstruction. It is also emphasized that, as a De-signer, the therapist who embarks with the person on a journey such as the De-sign inquiry goes through a process of rebirth, especially regarding the teleological aspects by which one's own life is guided.

In Chap. 5, the theme of paradoxes in the hypnotic experience is explored. By its own characteristics (CP 6.228), trance consists of another version of reality, which is at the same time one and multiple. De-sign, as an inquiry associated with the hypnotherapeutic practice, allows the person to travel between such universes, persevering between the inherent tensions in reality *vs.* fiction (Seif, 2020b). The idea of persevering through the paradox (Seif, 2019) emphasizes that hypnosis seeks to provide a context of a teleological trajectory where this transition is an integrated part of the person's growth, with two central implications. On the one hand, the binomial sanity *vs.* madness stands out, especially because of trance's therapeutic and iatrogenic potential. As such, it highlights that many psychopathology frames can be resized if the cultural and relational context offers affective reception and possibilities of symbolization of such experiences. It analyses Ramakrishna (Clément & Kakar, 1993), the God's Madman, discussing how cultural trance technologies can be important for integrative processes, and Erickson's schizophrenic patient (Zeig, 1985) who demanded special techniques of hypnosis associated with a strong social net of relationship. At the same time, it emphasizes that even a technique with a great therapeutic impact, such as hypnosis, can become harmful in the absence of this affective soil and the construction of broader meanings about life. On the other hand, De-sign also allows us to consider paradoxes such as determinism *vs.* freedom or sleepwalking *vs.* being awake. Under its conceptual lens, hypnosis becomes a liberating control and a sleep promoter of consciousness, not only for the relationship of partnership and the protagonism already discussed in Chap. 3 but also because of the intentionality that springs from an integrative therapeutic context. Special emphasis will be placed on the production of amnesia in hypnosis, as in my clinical case of a woman who, in order to be cared for, needed to be commanded by the therapist.

Love, in turn, will be the central theme of Chap. 6. Starting from Peirce's evolutionary cosmology (CP 6.287), it will be somewhat equated to intentionality or a teleological search for important themes in life. The De-sign, as crossing or transcendence of worlds, allows us to conceive why the notion of agape in Peirce is closely associated with the natural tendency of signs, such as the self, to grow into multiple semiotic processes. Thus, the sign allows an inefficient relationship to become efficient or fulfill its role as a sign (CP 8.332). In clinical terms, this refers to a notion of fulfillment that can reach broader dimensions of life, such as the aesthetic and collective ideal to which the ego surrenders. The hypnotic experience, especially in spiritual and philosophical contexts, allows the person to surrender and begin to be guided to love in broader terms as a kind of life mission. This broader notion of love or agape is, in itself, hypnotic, since it causes the person to experience and reconfigure their main references and values about reality. At this point, a brief ethnopsychological discussion will be carried out on how the cultural devices that build trance can favor the experience of Agape. This point will be developed from the case study of a Brazilian medium called Chico Xavier, who is considered a saint in his country (Neubern, 2022a, b). Nevertheless, a counterpoint will also be made by emphasizing that the same cultural technologies of trance can favor the emergence of grotesque and dark trance processes, such as those linked to other Brazilian medium João de Deus, accused of various sexual cases of abuse and other crimes (Felliti, 2020).

The chapter also highlights that this realization is also present in more personal aspects of life (love relationships, sex, profession, money, friendships), where love is assumed as Eros that, based on desire, allows the resumption of dreams whose clinical impacts on a person's life are fundamental. At this point, we highlight how hypnosis can be of great relevance in clinical situations where love and destruction are intertwined in a person's life, as in the case of the young woman with several suicide attempts (Erickson & Kubie, 1941). In short, De-sign allows us to understand that there are trances in which there is a tendency of the ego to surrender to a broader ideal present in the self (agape), while in other trance modes, the ego needs to be reintegrated and strengthened together with the self and the various experiences offered by the world (Eros). Although the trances linked to Agape and Eros are complementary, start from the same source (desire), and remain open to the future, they have distinct modes of realization that need to be properly recognized.

Finally, Chap. 7 will discuss the idea of Trance-modernity, in which the polyphonic aspect of trance will be deepened in the light of De-sign and Ethnopsychology (Neubern & Nogueira, 2019; Neubern, 2022b). Trance-Modernity is a way of thinking and living derived from Transmodernity and emphasizes the idea that trance is a natural phenomenon of human beings. Trance is an essential practice to promote integration with the multiple self that inhabits human self and with the multiple dimensions of social and cultural world. Permeated by Ethnopsychology, the chapter is essentially based on a case study of a woman who denied her spiritual experiences but simultaneously couldn't deny her spiritual belonging (Ethos). This case study was compared to "The February Man", a polemic and creative Ericksons case study (Erickson & Rossi, 2009), and with AI and metaverse (Santaella, 2021), especially concerning the use of technical devices and integration. In this sense, the first axis of this chapter is related to *Ethos and Rebirth*, through which multiple senses of belonging from our lives compose a contemplative attitude towards reality, especially based on desirable outcomes and contemplation. Krenak's idea (Krenak, 2022) that life is not useful, but a cosmic dance, is central to this axis. The second axis is related to the Self and the World and considers trance as a mindset where Firstness is a main reference that fosters new ways of interpreting signs linked to the integration with the world, the different knowledges, the self, and collectiveness, especially concerning the obvious, which is commonly beyond the obvious itself.

References

Bioy, A. (2018). O pequeno teatro da hipnose: Uma leitura clínica do funcionamento hipnótico. [The little theater of hypnosis: A clinical understanding of hypnotic functioning]. In M. Neubern (Ed.), *Clínicas do transe. Etnopsicologia, hipnose e espiritualidade no Brasil* (pp. 49–68). Juruá.

Boler. (1963). *Charles Peirce and the scholastic realism. A study of Peirce's relation to John Duns Scotus.* University of Washington Press.

References

Brentano, F. (1995). *Descriptive psychology*. Routledge. (original work published in 1874).
Carroy, J. (1991). *L'hypnose et suggestion. L'invention du sujet*. [Hypnosis and suggestion. The invention of the subject] Press Universitaire de France.
Chertok, L., & Stengers, I. (1989). *Le Coeur et la raison. L'hypnose en question de Lavoisier à Lacan*. [The Heart and the reason. The hypnosis in question from Lavoisier to Lacan]. Payot.
Clément, C. (2011). *L'appel de la transe*. [The Call of the Trance]. Stok.
Clément, C., & Kaka, S. (1993). *La folle et le saint*. [The madwoman and the Saint]. Seuil.
Colapietro, V. (1989). *Peirce's approach to the self*. Suny.
Colapietro, V. (1995). Notes for a sketch of a peircean theory of the unconscious. *Transactions of Charles S. Peirce Society, 31*(3), 482–506.
Csordas, T. (1997). *The sacred self*. University of California Press.
Deleuze, G., & Guattari, F. (1980). *Mille Plateaux*. [A thousand plateus]. Minuit.
Dumont, L. (1983). *Essais sur l'Individualisme. Une perspective anthropologique sur l'idéologie moderne*. [Essays on Individualism. An anthropological Perspective on Modern Ideology]. Seuil.
Erickson, M. (1958). Naturalistic techniques of hypnosis. *The American Journal of Clinical Hypnosis, 1*, 3–8.
Erickson, M., & Kubie, L. (1941). The sucessful treatment of a case of acute hysterical depression by a return under hypnosis to a critical phase of childhood. *Psychoanalytic Quarterly, 10*(4), 122–142.
Erickson, M., & Rossi, E. (1979). *Hypnotherapy: An exploratory casebook*. Irvington.
Erickson, M., & Rossi, E. (1980). *The collected papers of Milton Erickson, MD*. Irvington.
Erickson, M., & Rossi, E. (2009). *The February man. Evolving consciousness and identity in hypnotherapy*. Routledge.
Facco, E. (2021). Hypnosis and hypnotic ability between old beliefs and new evidences: an epistemological reflection. *American Journal of Clinical Hypnosis, 64*(1), 20–35. https://doi.org/10.1080/00029157.2020.1863181
Felitti, C. (2020). *A casa. A história da seita de João de Deus*. [Home. The history of the sect of John of God]. Todavia.
Gebser, J. (1985). *The ever-present origin*. Ohio University Press. (Original work published in 1949).
Gonzalez Rey, F. (2007). *Pós-modernidade e psicoterapia*. [Postmodernity and psychotherapy]. Thomsom.
Gonzalez Rey, F. (2019). Subjectivity in debate: Some reconstructed philosophical premises to advance its debates in psychology. *Journal of Theory and Social Behavior, 49*, 1–23.
Haley, J. (1993). *Uncommon therapy*. The Psychiatric Techniques of Milton Erickson, MD. Norton.
Hall, E. (1983). *The dance of life: The other dimension of time*. Doubleday & Company. (original work published in 1969).
Hartshorne, C. & Weiss, P. (1980). *The collected papers of Charles S. Peirce (CP, 8 vol.)*. Harvard University Press.
Ibri, I. (2017). *Kósmos Noetós: The metaphysical architecture of Charles Peirce*. Springer. (original work published in 1992).
Krenak, A. (2022). *Futuro ancestral* [Ancestor future]. Companhia das Letras.
Liszka, J. (1996). *A general introduction to the semeiotic of Charles Sanders Peirce*. Indiana University Press.
Martino, E. (1999). *Le Monde Magique. Parapsychologie, Ethnologie et Histore*. [The Magical World. Parapsychology, Ethnology and History]. Synthélabo. (original work published in 1944).
Méheust, B. (1999). *Somnambulisme et Médiumnité*. [Somnambulism and Mediumship]. Synthélabo.
Morin, E. (2015). *La méthode V. L'humanité de l'humanité. L'identité humaine*. [The method V. The humanity of humanity. Human identity]. Points. (Original work published in 2001).
Nathan, T. (2004). *Du commerce avec les diables*. [Trade with the devils]. Synthélabo.
Nathan, T. (2014). *Nous ne sommes pas seuls au monde*. [We are not alone in the world]. Seuil. (Original work published in 2001).

Neubern, M. (2013). *Psicoterapia e espiritualidade*. [Psychotherapy and spirituality]. Diamante.
Neubern, M. (2016). Iconicity and complexity in hypnotic communication. *Psicologia: Teoria e Pesquisa, 32*, 1–9. https://doi.org/10.1590/0102-3772e32ne217
Neubern, M. (2017). Contribuições epistemológicas da hipnose de Milton Erickson Para a psicologia moderna. [Epistemological contributions of Milton Erickson's hypnosis to moderna psychology]. In D. Amparo, E. Lazzarini, L. Polejack, & I. Silva (Eds.), *Psicologia Clínica e Cultura 3* (pp. 684–709). Technopolitik.
Neubern, M. (2022a). Chico Xavier and the sacred experience: A semiotic and ethnopsychological perspective. *International Journal of Latin American Religions, 2*, 1–24.
Neubern, M. (2022b). When spirits become therapists. Ethnopsychology and hypnotherapy in Brazil. *International Journal of Latin American Religions, 1*, 1–26.
Neubern, M. (2023). Hypnosis, university and democracy: An emancipatory proposal. In M. Neubern & A. Bioy (Eds.), *Hypnosis in academia: Contemporary challenges in research, healthcare and education* (pp. 27–52). Springer.
Neubern, M., & Bioy, A. (Eds.). (2023). *Hypnosis in academia: Contemporary challenges in research, healthcare and education*. Springer.
Neubern, M., & Nogueira, H. (2019). Complex hypnosis contribution to clinical psychology. In C. Antloga, K. Brasil, S. Lordello, M. Neubern, & E. Queiroz (Eds.), *Psicologia Clínica e Cultura 4* (pp. 71–90). Technopolitik.
Peirce, C. (1903). Pragmatism as a principle and method of right thinking. In P. Turrisi (Ed.), *(1997). The 1903 Harvard lectures on pragmatism*. State University of New York Press.
Petrilli, S. (2017). *The self as a sign, the world, and the other*. Routledge.
Psillos, S., & Zorzato, L. (2021). Against cognitive instrumentalism. *International Studies in the Philosophy of Science, 3*, 247–257. https://doi.org/10.1080/02698595.2021.1961420
Raposa, M. (1989). *Peirce's philosophy of religion*. Indiana University Press.
Ribeiro, P. (2023). Hypnosis and academia from an Iberian perspective. In M. Neubern & A. Bioy (Eds.), *Hypnosis in academia: Contemporary challenges in research, healthcare and education* (pp. 125–152). Springer.
Robin, R. (1967). *Annotated catalogue of the papers of Charles S*. University of Massachusetts Press.
Santaella, L. (2021). *Humanos hiper-híbridos*. [hyper-hybrid humans]. Paulus.
Santos, B. (2000). *A crítica da razão indolente*. [The critique of indolent reason]. Cortez.
Seif, F. (2019). *De-sing in transmodern world*. Envisioning reality beyond absoluteness. Peter Lang.
Seif, F. (2020a). The role of pragmatism in De-Sign: Persevering through paradoxes of design and semiotics. *Cognition, 21*(1), 112–131.
Seif, F. (2020b). De-sign as a destiny of navigation: The paradox of sustaining boundaries while traversing borders. *The American Journal of Semiotics, 36*(3–4), 179–215.
Short, T. (2009). Peirce's theory of signs. .
Stengers, I. (2001). Qu'est-ce que l'hypnose nous oblige à penser ? [What does hypnosis force us to think about?]. *Ethnopsy, 3*, 13–68.
Stengers, I. (2002). *Hypnose: Entre Magie et science*. [Hypnosis: Between magic and science]. Synthélabo.
Zeig, J. (1985). *Experiencing Erickson. An introduction to the man and his work*. Brunner/Mazel.

Chapter 2
Hypnosis and Reality: About That Which Is Overlooked

The Modern Paradigm and Hypnosis

In a trance situation (Neubern, 2016), a person with a phobia of closed places can visualize a window in the wall that no one else will perceive. Under the lens of modern science, that vision should not be conceived as reality but as imagination (Chertok & Stengers, 1989). Even if this process frees them from the phobia, that window could not be evaluated from a scientific perspective as real information. However, even though it is considered a subjective process, the image of the window triggers various semiotic processes that can reconfigure a person's experience so they might normally attend open spaces. The evaluation of effectiveness to be made by the psychologist or psychiatrist can attest that the strategy has worked; perhaps they can ascertain what occurs in the person's brain; nevertheless, the image itself it cannot be considered anything. For many researchers, the signs connected to efficacy would be enough for research since one can verify that the effect of the image was real. However, as I discuss in this chapter, for hypnosis, the imaginary window is the point that should be focalized, better understood, and integrated as part of the object of investigation. Considering this process, something opposed to reality is what seems to situate hypnosis as a controversial field (Stengers, 2002). This condition has not changed after two centuries of research despite several studies in the last 30 years (Bioy & Neubern, 2023). During this chapter, De-sign (Seif, 2019) is highlighted as an essential way of thinking that can overcome the Modern Paradigm dichotomies, especially concerning the absolute notion of reality conceived by this last. The difference between things, which are mind-independent, and objects, which are mind-dependent (Deely, 2009) is one of the most relevant notions for understanding the controversial studies on hypnosis during the history of science.

One of the main roots of such controversy is found in the very formation of the great Modern Paradigm, which established boundaries of knowledge in Western civilizations for the last centuries (Santos, 2019). The division between objectivity and subjectivity is what best characterizes that paradigm. Directly speaking, there is privileged knowledge, capable of accessing reality free from fantasies and personal opinions. One moves away from appearances and reaches essences, that is, the laws governing a certain phenomenon of nature. Such a process, highly grounded by quantification, is what enables prediction, explanation, and, especially, the control of that certain phenomenon. Objectivity becomes a correlate for reality, which advocates an independent access to what people think, inaccessible to other ways of knowing. Through that proposal, science would—or should, in the future—be able to mirror reality. The term Physics, which described the main representative of objectivity, derives from the Greek *Physis*, meaning nature.

Reality would, therefore, be something capable of resisting and contradicting expectations, fantasies, and desires of the researcher, so as to become independent from them (Bachelard, 1938/1996). To be objective, a researcher should seek to state that which is closest to reality, unable to fit two or more explanations on the same phenomenon. Through a device such as the laboratory, rival explanations would be silenced, sooner or later, in the name of the one that best explained the issue in dispute (Stengers, 1995). Matter was the foremost means to understand objectivity, but it had to undergo a kind of exorcism: no spirits, animism, or gods should be able to explain it. Nature would not be governed by hidden intentions, like that of God, but by measurable mechanical laws and, by chance, itself (Reynolds, 2002). The space for creation is much more restricted, mainly mechanical laws govern and determine phenomena. The so-called "hard sciences" best adapted to objective rationality, although said adaptation was not always entirely uneventful. While astronomy and chemistry had to disentangle themselves from astrology and alchemy, biology and its derivatives, even today, still encounter difficulties regarding the mechanics imposed by objective views on qualitative notions—such as life.

The axis of subjectivity, on the other hand, is situated as opposite to objectivity (Santos, 2019); consequently, it becomes contrary to "real." It encompasses the field of fantasy, feelings, spirituality, imagination, and artistic creation. It is also the field of creation and qualitative traits, much approached by artists, mystics, poets, and philosophers. Concepts beyond matter, such as life, soul, consciousness, God, love, and language, inhabit this side of the paradigm. In subjectivity, appearances matter and are not considered chimeras, residues, or sources of error. Therefore, instead of control, which is unilateral, the proposal of knowledge is linked to contemplation and understanding. In subjectivity inhabit knowledges such as Law, Philosophy, Arts, Letters, Theology, and the great enemy of science—common sense. However, that field undergoes a process of colonization from the perspective of objectivity, under the claim that knowledge should seek rigor of method to address a single notion from reality. This impact has been more significant in fields such as law and some branches of philosophy, as both must be allied to the rigor of the scientific method to be better recognized.

However, what perhaps most characterizes the colonization of objectivity over subjectivity is the birth of the human and social sciences. Again, an exorcism occurs upon key notions of subjectivity: God, soul, spirits, beauty, life, feelings, quality—common terms in European thought until the Renaissance (Ellenberger, 1970/2003;

Koyré, 1971)—leave a scenario that would be occupied by notions more entrenched upon the mechanics of matter. Thus, while the body is no longer a field of confluence of cosmic forces, it becomes a system of organic matter, worthy of studies by biologists and doctors; the soul is detached from its transcendent and theological content to become the psyche or the mind for psychologists.

Some consequences of the division set by the Modern paradigm deserve to be highlighted for the purposes of this book. First, paraphrasing Peirce (1903/1997), that paradigm is characterized by privileging and recognizing reality as linked to Secondness and Thirdness—to the detriment of Firstness. Roughly speaking, that which exists and is opposed to the researcher's thought is linked and governed by a law that, once known, enables control, prediction, and explanation. As for scientific interest and research, phenomena linked to Firstness have only two yields: contempt, because they are considered sources of error, or subjugation to consecrated areas (such as brain, matter, and language) (Gonzalez Rey, 2019). The phenomenological reading of these phenomena is highly compromised; as a replacement for a description and comprehension of a field's ontological characteristics (Brentano, 1874/1995), there is a mechanistic, and sometimes deterministic, *a priori* thinking that holds that any form of reality must adapt to its framework. The signs to be considered are, then, selected beforehand, regardless of the importance they may have for a field (Morin, 1991/2014).

Deely's work (2009), through the study of Medieval authors, such as St. Jean de Poinsot, still adds another important contribution. Modern paradigm replaced the ecological notion of signs for representation, which is an isolated unity, which had as its main consequence the separation between ontology, then related to things, and epistemology, more related to objects. It is extremely related to the Cartesian division between objectivity and subjectivity, being the former the place of knowledge and the latter the source of error. In contrast with the Medieval philosophers, for whom objectivity was known through a close relationship between Inwelt and Umwelt, Modern objectivity was then associated with the external world, in which the objects were related through mechanical laws that could offer the researcher the possibilities of control. It was the logical field of objective data and legitimated knowledge. In the same perspective, Subjectivity, which was what is not known, became associated with human experience as something elusive and diaphanous, possessing many risks for scientific knowledge. Its influences on scientific research should be eliminated or, at least, avoided. Not without reason, hypnosis is still currently a problematic field of research since it integrates objectivity and subjectivity, internal and external, facts and artifacts (Neubern, 2023).

Peirce (1903/1997), in his conception of metaphysics, highlighted the ontological correspondents of phenomenological categories (Ibri, 1992/2017). Chance, especially in its random creations, would be linked to Firstness, and the existent, to Secondness. Moreover, laws, regularity, and habits would be part of Thirdness, sharing a capacity for intense regulation over phenomena. Thus, if there is not a single existing one not linked to some law, determination on it can be variable and never absolute, because, in its cosmology, the universe would be in evolution and, for this, the creative aspect of chance is fundamental (Reynolds, 2002). Through chance, phenomena might create new facets and escape, at some level, the determinations of laws—which, so they may continue to exercise their role as the organization of the universe, would also tend to evolve. Unlike Einstein, the God advocated by Peirce would "roll the dice," given the importance of chance in the universe that would make room to undermine deterministic laws and evolution itself (Ibri, 1992/2017). Theses conceptions find considerable affinity with contemporary ideas from the hard sciences (Prigogine, 1994): chance is incorporated as an important element of the universe and makes room for a teleological perspective on physical systems (Liszka, 1996). In terms of psychology, on the other hand, the determinism of universal laws has been imposed as a central explanatory axis to the detriment of chance, despite that being acknowledged in some theories (Gonzalez Rey, 2019).

This same tendency acted, in a hegemonic way, upon the study of hypnosis, in which conceptions of Firstness, such as chance, were considered a source of error. It matters little that icons, rema, and quali-signs are fundamental to understand hypnosis; they need, in some way, to be translated into existence and linked to some law so the study can be valid. This gap becomes problematic, as the dimension of hypnosis remains outside the modern scope. An icon, for example, cannot be taken as an *indice*, because they have distinct semiotic natures and different roles in the semiotic exchange that occurs during hypnosis. Furthermore, while *indices* are linked to reactive processes between different systems of the self, icons play a role in habit formation (CP[1] 6.228). In other words, the imaginary exercise promoted by hypnosis favors the formation of new habits in the face of different situations in a person's life, as a kind of imaginary stage anticipating the elaboration of alternatives for that person in the face of some problematic situation that might generate suffering. In terms of research, the inclusion of icons dictate that the questions guiding procedure cannot be restricted to causal perspectives (such as "what caused such an effect?") so they might encompass a broader, recursive understanding ("how does this process happen?"). In addition, research must include teleology: questions on a possible cause which cannot always be answered must give way to various implications of finality (hence the idea of meaning) in a complex system, such as the self during trance—especially with regard to future projections.

Secondly, the reality derived from this modern paradigm is conceived in absolute terms (Seif, 2019). It is true that many thinkers (Kuhn, 1962/2012) advocate a science in motion, as one scientific system can give way to another that may be more compatible with reality. However, the Modern thinking is the approximation to this reality which remains absolute in categories like time and space. Hence the notion of "fact" as something that simply reveals itself rather than constructs itself; something that is already in nature, that is simply given, regardless of the researcher's views; something that does not offer margins of interpretation, as only one should prevail as the most valid answer (Stengers, 1995). A second association with fact is control—without which the fact would not be known. To know, for a modern

---

[1] Hartshorne & Weiss (1980) is the reference of CP, which means the Collected Papers of Charles Peirce. I adopted the CP due to the fact that this is the most known reference among semioticians of Peirce's collected papers.

scientist, means to control. From the conditions of research (controlled in its variables) towards the conclusion over facts, control is considered a critical notion for the knowledge of nature. Not without reason, control is profoundly associated with efficacy, since a controlled survey should provide the expected answers. It matters little that the logic of control enacts mutilation of a field and that this brings more or less destructive consequences in systemic and ecological terms (Morin, 1991/2014).

> *Colonialism is a form of collective domination of a group or a system of ideas. In some way, Modern Sciences are colonialists because they impose their ideas on other systems of knowledge that must change their central references to reality. Human sciences, such as some schools of psychology, sociology, and economy, were deeply colonized by hard science methods, conceived by many scientific communities as the best representative practices of the Modern Sciences* (Santos, 2019). *In other circumstances, Modern Sciences attack systems that are not coherent with its concepts, such as religious systems and traditional knowledge of non-Western societies* (Nathan, 2001/2014). *In both cases, there are complicated ecological consequences since colonization frequently threatens person's ties with his sociocultural belongings.*

The science originating from this modern paradigm becomes, as a result, one of the culprits for the construction of a disenchanted world:

> Science disenchants the world; everything it describes is hopelessly reduced to a case of the application of general laws, devoid of particular interest. What for previous generations had been a source of joy or wonder dried up at their approach. [...] What classical science touches, dries, and dies. It dies to qualitative diversity, to singularity, to become the simple consequence of a general law. (Prigogine & Stengers, 1979, pp. 22, 39).

Thus, under the rule of rational knowledge and devoid of any *indices* of subjectivity, at least in theory, there would no longer be room for ideas such as God or the soul of the universe from the Renaissance (Koyré, 1971). Spirits, beings of nature, gods, demons, hermaphroditism, and constitutive polarities of the universe (Ellenberger, 1970/2003) become proscribed notions, along with the idea of a cosmic connection involving individuals with a kind of universal wisdom. As Tobie Nathan (Nathan & Stengers, 1999) would say, the modern man has become lonesome; that is, humans have become the only thinking power in the universe, devoid of beings with which their ancestors were used to negotiate. Ready-made mechanical laws govern the universe, amenable to quantification that sooner or later will reveal their mechanisms to humans. Beauty, intuition, passion, and morality should be relegated to other knowledges within subjectivity. At the same time, science aims at independence from history, society, and culture, since that reality to be revealed should be autonomous from such systems. Although this has not been embraced in the humanities and social sciences, many contemporary researchers still position themselves alongside the idea that their data is impenetrable regarding values, ideologies, and interests other than "the search for truth." These factors have guided science towards a real crusade of disqualification for other forms of knowledge (Nathan, 2007;

O'Donohue, 2013). That which does not fulfill the validity requirements of their methods should be discarded until someone proves otherwise. Especially in the fields of health and psychology, that scientific crusade did not tire of charging as charlatans those who professed systems that rebel to their demands.

Regarding hypnosis, the idea of control and efficacy is highly restrictive to the field, because efficacy says little about the set of processes that are mobilized and reconfigured throughout hypnotherapy. The emphasis on specific responses loses its ecological character. Control is also problematic in hypnosis research, as it deeply implies processes of autonomy and agency upon systems of the self (Neubern, 2023). There are two points of relevance here. On the one hand, autonomy is closely linked to internal and imaginary processes—Peirce's imaginary stage precedes habit formation (Colapietro, 1989). Peirce's thought is coherent with authors such as Milton Erickson, for whom the active condition of the subject and their power of choice is deeply marked by the elusive experience of subjectivity. On the other hand, insofar as control separates the subject from the object, the problem of hypnogenesis is excluded from research on the topic (Stengers, 2001). Again, the subject's tendency to reproduce the therapist's theory is permeated by the elusive, fleeting, and plastic processes linked to Firstness. There is, therefore, no researcher who unilaterally controls their subject's responses; instead, they establish an interaction marked by mutual influence.

Disenchanted hypnosis, in turn, refers to its detachment from a series of notions which had been present at its origin (Clément, 2011; Ellenberger, 1970/2003). Technologies in modern trance no longer aim to open a field of negotiations with collective beings and knowledge, as with their ancestors (Neubern & Nogueira, 2019). They aim to put the subject in contact with a solitary and individual world, be it psychological or neurological. In the same perspective, this modern person would not belong to a cosmos, nor would they be in an alliance with a wise universal nature, as the ancient magnetizers would say (Mehéust, 1999); their main ambitions in therapy, for example, would be individual resolution that could, in some cases, percolate across their closest social relations. In a word, hypnosis should be fitted, even if forcibly, into a mechanical, individualistic world, devoid of subjectivity and supported by the methodological criteria of science—even if this would cause it considerable mutilation.

Thirdly, the typical division of the Modern paradigm situates subjectivity as a probable source of error and associates it, to a large extent, with the human psyche (Gonzalez Rey, 2019). Although modern science stands in opposition to the medieval tyranny of the Church and places the human in the place of God as the center of knowledge, it eventually becomes impersonal, beyond limitations, errors, and human opinions. Writing in the third person is a relevant sign of that, since it suggests that the researcher does not speak from their opinions, but from what the method revealed to them when questioning reality. In historical and philosophical terms, this place of subjectivity created by the modern paradigm implies a radical change from the ideas of the medieval thinkers who preceded them. It is certain that the term reality, as something that opposes thought, was coined by Duns Scotus, a scholastic philosopher according to Peirce's thought (1903/1997). Nevertheless, as

Deely's work demonstrated (2009), for Medieval philosophers, subjectivity and objectivity had a complementary role in knowledge construction that could not be conceived without them.

The relevance of the idea that objectivity and subjectivity are not opposites, but dimensions that complement and interact with each other, is quite relevant for the study of hypnosis, especially as it highlights the need to include processes of Firstness. This has not gone unnoticed by contemporary philosophers (Hacking, 2000; Latour, 1996) when they introduce, for example, the close relationship between facts and artifacts, or between revelation and construction in science. In hypnosis, this debate has had little repercussion among researchers and therapists, despite Leon Chertok and Isabelle Stengers's efforts. Willem Wundt's idea, as highlighted by de Martino (1944/1999), still seems to be the prevailing approach among members of the psychology field and, particularly, among hypnosis researchers. For the famous German author, there would only be two types of universes: the first was composed of topics such as the projection of light and the study of particles, of interest to men like Newton and Leibnitz. The other universe, linked to supernatural phenomena, spirits, and gods, would be of interest to mystics, illusionists, and mediums, these being always hysterical. It is true that many authors, when faced with such a statement, saw Wundt's criticism as much more focused on metapsychics, the ancestor of parapsychology (Mehéust, 1999), than on hypnosis itself, mainly because the latter was clothed with scientific seriousness that brought it prestige among researchers from different universities around the world (Neubern & Bioy, 2023). Nevertheless, this criticism is undoubtedly applicable to the study of hypnosis because of its elusive and treacherous character, which has never allowed researchers to unite around central issues (Facco, 2021). Additionally, the very historical kinship of hypnosis with metapsychics (Blum, 2004) and spiritualist practices (Nathan, 2001/2014) further reinforces the idea that Wundt's criticism also turned to hypnosis as a field of subjectivity.

De-sign and Realities

For the study of hypnosis, the notion of De-sign (Seif, 2020a, b) is situated as an essential alternative to the Modern paradigm as it breaks with the disjunctions and reductionisms that characterize it. During inquiry, the emphasis it places on Firstness does not prevent it from integrating Secondness and Thirdness as well. The semiotic networks in an experience such as trance promote a recursive movement between different types of signs, demanding that they be recognized in the inquiry. If the De-sign inquiry does not propose to answer what a scientific procedure would do, such as finding a proposition, it opens way to clarifying the nuances of that terrain. Icons, remas, and quali-signs cannot be reduced to their second-rate correspondents, nor can they be undermined in research; instead, they must be considered within their respective logical conditions. The imaginary window mentioned at the beginning of this chapter would gain a special look under the lens of De-sign: in addition to its polychronic aspect and diaphanous spatiality, it would also be integrated into a teleological dimension, without which it would not be possible to understand the experience of the subject in trance and the hypnotic relationship that favored its emergence.

In this sense, the ideas of things and objects are essential for De-sign inquiry (Deely, 2009). Things are mind-independent and do not necessarily become an object. In other words, things' existence is *ens reale* or independent of mind processes such as perception, cognition, or memory. Objects, in turn, are *ens rationis*, or they are a being in perception. As described by Seif (2019), Napoleon can be a thing (because he existed, in fact) and an object since many people create representations about him; a unicorn or a medieval dragon could be only objects because nobody can affirm they once existed concretely. Nonetheless, the distinctions between things and objects apparently confirm the Cartesian division between subjectivity and objectivity, with the former being external and objective and the latter being subjective and constructed. In this way, De-sign would not be relevant to understanding hypnosis since things and objects would only confirm the Modern paradigm limitations that are dominant in hypnosis history (Stengers, 2001). Charles Peirce offers an interesting solution for this problem when he considers past experiences having the condition of *alterity* concerning ego (CP 5.459). If past experiences can be mediatized through thinking and become part of the ego, there are past experiences that work as Secondness, which press and influence the ego independently of its deliberations (CP 1.324). These kinds of Secondness experiences, frequent in clinical hypnosis (Erickson & Rossi, 1979), let us conceive of the existence of things created in human experiences, which are imaginative and the basis of desirable outcomes (Seif, 2019). However, they don't have the same semiotic characteristics as physical things, which allows the scientific approach through scientific devices, such as laboratories (Stengers, 1995). In some way, we can consider them as "quasi-realities," as we will discuss in this chapter.

An image like the window abovementioned, displayed during trance, can favor the concrete elimination of a phobic symptom, for example, and enables new ways of integrating the person with themselves, as well as with new narratives and meanings. The whole range of developments of that image can be evaluated and legitimized by research; however, the process only becomes more complete when researchers understand that, in fact, this image is a semiotic process. In short, De-sign allows it to be considered a "quasi-reality," which does not respond to scientific devices but that can be accessed and understood through De-sign inquiry.

By not adopting an absolute notion of reality, De-sign Seif, (2019) is very compatible with hypnosis as a field of study. Multiple experiences can be experienced simultaneously in a trance, which coincides with the polychronic time of De-sign. A person can be in different places at once, which demands a multiple vision of multiple facets of spatiality created in that experience, which is incoherent with an absolute perspective of reality. The De-signer must be flexible in adopting various angles and covering a broad conception of the self. In addition, De-sign requires transparency to deal with the diaphanous content of these spaces and to accompany the fluidity that characterizes them. Thus, the fact ceases to be a sign of truth as an absolute entity, fixed in space and time and becomes a relevant sign for constructing broader and procedural knowledge in a field. Similarly, control is no longer the relational condition in the field to give space to dialogue based on a partnership. Visualizing an image, such as the previously mentioned window, is much more interesting when it occurs through an active and creative attitude of the subject in a trance rather than through simple obedience to a therapist's orders. In other words, fact and control are categories that dismiss important and elusive dimensions of hypnosis, while construction and dialogue integrate those into the inquiry process (Seif, 2013).

In the same line of thought, De-sign conceives that objectivity and subjectivity are complementary dimensions of knowledge (Deely, 2009), even if, they may come into conflict on occasion. Much of this has already been explained here, in the inclusion to Firstness and broader proposal of reality in the study of hypnosis. Nevertheless, the idea of De-sign can be summarized as meta-knowledge, linked to a third culture that is not restricted to objectivity or subjectivity (Seif, 2020a). The proposal of meta-knowledge refers to the task of thinking beyond barriers that define a branch of knowledge, in order to consider, integrate, and transcend them. By proposing dialogue with each form of knowledge, like psychology and psychotherapy, the De-signer and their interlocutor acknowledge its pertinence while they also recognize its limits and potentialities. From this mutual learning, ideas can emerge for a more comprehensive perspective of these disciplines, especially with regard to reality. At the same time, the De-signer also enriches themselves in such a way as to possess broader and more complex ideas on the field of psychologists and psychotherapists. In the specific case of hypnosis, in addition to the striking similarities with De-sign, the principles of form and interpretation can favor the advancement of ideas for striking problems in the field, as the case of arguments about state and non-state (Ribeiro, 2023) or hypnogenesis itself (Chertok & Stengers, 1989).

On the other hand, as an integrative proposal, De-sign constitutes a highly relevant path for the resumption of an enchanted world (Seif, 2020b), particularly in hypnosis. Obviously, this re-enchantment of the world does not mean an adherence to mystical ideas or a return to traditional knowledges, nor does it mean the rejection of modern scientific achievements, whose historical, social, and epistemological magnitude is immeasurable. It is a proposal of dialogue with systems and notions of subjectivity, some present in human sciences and traditional knowledges, which becomes relevant for a comprehensive understanding of hypnosis. Principles like a multifaceted reality, in terms of time and space, of the primacy of Firstness, of paradox, of the relationships between logic, ethics, and aesthetics, as well as dialogue itself, are fundamental in this sense. A dialogical proposal like De-sign (Seif, 2013) implies acknowledging each piece of knowledge, its limits and potentialities, and in their transcendence, contributions can be integrated into broader constructions.

However, before explaining this proposal, it is necessary to approach the historical and epistemological controversies concerning the studies on hypnosis, especially the experiences that were ignored or despised by the Modern paradigm.

Historical and Epistemological Controversies

Mesmer and the Battle of Methods

> *Franz Anton Mesmer (1734–1815), Austrian physician, was the creator of a therapeutic method called animal magnetism or mesmerism. For him, there would be a kind of magnetic fluid in the universe linking all things, and its variation among living beings would be responsible for health or disease. Mesmer has taken the idea from Renaissance authors (Ellenberger, 1970/2003), but perhaps he was the first to attribute scientific reliability to it. In his practice, people gathered around a wooden tub filled with water (the* baquet*) and were magnetized by the doctor and his assistants through the imposition of hands and other element, such as music. Some patients even had convulsions and seizures, which were conceived as a sign of healing. With the negative assessment of the scientific commission appointed by ling Louis XVI, Mesmer sought self-exile near his homeland. The designation of other agents than animal magnetism—such as imagination—overthrew his thesis. However, even if he did not revolutionize Medicine and become a rich man, as he meant to, Mesmer eventually became pivotal to the history of Psychology. From the judgment of his method, movements that discussed the role of imagination gained momentum and that practice became the basis for further formation of that science.*

In 1784, Louis XVI, King of France, appointed two commissions of scientists to evaluate the validity of a therapeutic method called animal magnetism or mesmerism (Chertok & Stengers, 1989), created by the Austrian physician Franz Anton Mesmer. After a series of controversies and pressure from institutions such as the Faculty of Medicine of Paris and the French Academy of Sciences, the king commissioned Guillotin, Jussieu, Bailly, and Benjamin Franklin, among others, to evaluate the scientific provenance of animal magnetism in order to legitimize it or to dismiss it as a medical practice on French territory. Departing from his own doctoral thesis in 1776 and from Renaissance ideas (Méheust, 1999), Mesmer advocated there was a kind of magnetic fluid linking all things in the universe and that the circulation of it in the human body would be responsible for states of health and disease. Thus, the commission members asked Charles D'Eslon, former student, Mesmer's dissident, and doctor of the high nobility, to serve as the subject of the experiments aimed at attesting the existence and actions of said fluid. In a sequence of experiments, a person who was supposedly sensitive to fluid perception was asked to identify, for example, which glass of water on a tray had been magnetized or which tree in an orchard had also been magnetized.

Mesmer's method was somewhat unusual for the time (Ellenberger, 1970/2003). Patients gathered around a large tub of water (the *baquet*), holding small cords that came out of it. In this tub, there was water which had been previously magnetized by the team of doctors, and the fluid would be transmitted through ropes, but also through doctors' hands or even metal rods that they used to manipulate the fluid more precisely. On more than a few occasions, a small orchestra played music that, according to the mesmerists, could aid the fluidic treatment. Many patients had seizures during treatment which was conceived as an expression of healing. Nevertheless, Mesmer (1779/2005) was clear in asserting that animal magnetism, though sometimes perceptible, could only be attested through its effects, given its highly subtle nature. The committee reached an unfavorable verdict to Mesmer's basic thesis. For them, the influence and the cures attributed to mesmerism would occur due to imitation, friction, touch, and imagination. Bailly, head of one of those committees, also sent the king a secret report (Bailly, 1784/2004), warning about the risks that female patients, the majority of the public of mesmerism, could be sexually abused by unscrupulous doctors given their passivity during the procedure.

However, Laurent de Jussieu, a naturalist, broke with the committee and chose to produce an independent study with field observation (Jussieu, 1784/2004). The esteemed naturalist corroborated the causes noted by the committee but made an important caveat: for him there would still be another factor named as "animal heat" in the animal magnetism sessions, which was a possible agent of cure. In some field sessions, he could notice repeatedly that some blind patients seemed to react every time he pointed his metal rod against their bodies from a distance. Even though he was not unconditional in stating that such an agent was the cause of the cure, he strongly recommended its study and claimed that he still did not see any problem with doctors in the practice of mesmerism, as long as they presented systematic data from their work to the academic community.

The consequences of committee's work were tragic for animal magnetism, which was banned in France (Bertrand, 1826/2004; 1826/2010). Any member of the medical profession who practiced it would be expelled and have his registration as a doctor revoked. The only acceptable interest for such a practice would be of a historical nature. Conservative sectors from French society celebrated these decisions, mainly so that women would not be exposed to perverted doctors. Mesmer, disappointed by the whole endeavor, seen by him as inconsistent from the start, retired in voluntary exile to a region near his homeland, Lake Constance, in Switzerland. Thereafter, his public appearances were rare, and he preferred to enjoy a quiet retirement. As for Jussieu, even though his report was extolled by the practitioners of mesmerism, he simply did not present the slightest echo among the authorities of the government and academia, who ignored him. The situation became somewhat complex due to the delicate political moment—on the verge of the French Revolution. Mesmerism had strong connections within various social sectors, ranging from the high nobility to workers and peasants. Driven by institutions such as Freemasonry, it infiltrated French culture and influenced other countries. The ideas of animal magnetism, regardless of Mesmer's intentions, became political elements for tension in France at that time.

Therefore, the committee episode also pointed to a number of problems in the methodological and philosophical fields (Chertok & Stengers, 1989). If Imagination was seen as one of the factors for the possible cures, it should be isolated as a variable to verify its modes of action—which the committee did not do. In such a position, their work became a disconcerting contradiction because, instead of being conclusive, as per the initial proposal, it was a mere hypothesis. Given the controversies at stake in the French sovereign's request and in methodological coherence, the verification should have been done, but committees decided not to proceed. The scientific question was whether imagination and other factors could or could not produce the same effects as animal magnetism if the experimental circumstances were reproduced, so they could discard it as a variable. Nevertheless, the institutional, political, and skeptic members of the committees seemed to have weighed more heavily, so both the royals and the institutions involved decided to consider hypothesis accurate. For them, even a researcher of the stature of Laurent de Jussieu should not be considered since the conclusions brought seemed to be satisfied.

The first issue to raise is the methodological choice for evaluating the field. Mesmer (1779/2005) was adamant in his criticism by asserting that animal magnetism, given its subtlety, could only be verified via its effects. From a metaphysical point of view, in a field permeated by Firstness, subtle and elusive, that terrain is inaccessible to experimental procedures and focused essentially on existing phenomena and laws. Mesmer's critique was also limited; without the necessary and compatible categories, there is a severe risk of never conceiving of such a dimension, as it often happens with contemporary methodologies. The chosen method was brutally imposed on the field without any regard for its characteristics and requirements as reality. Such a methodological choice could be the departure for a broader reflection, providing *indices* of a first approximation to the field. However, if this were the case, the continuity of the studies would be mandatory, as opposed to the silence that was imposed on any related initiative. At the same time, the choice of such a controversial term as imagination was a sign of several obscure issues. If a subtle phenomenon such as imagination could be capable of so many effects, why should its study not be recommended rather than prohibited? If Mesmer's fame crossed borders and a significant number of patients attested to the efficacy of his treatments, studies on imagination could open paths of great relevance to Medicine research. If imagination were pointed out as probable cause, it would be up to that field to investigate its nature. Whether merely an expression of the brain or a subtle field of experience connected with Firstness, that was a pertinent question that could not be silenced.

The trial of mesmerism thus became a landmark for the establishment of a disenchanted world. Without any previous observation of the field as reality, an observation capable of describing its nuances and pointing out the influences of different ontologies (Peirce, 1903/1997), the committee opted for the imposition of an *a priori* method, centered on the idea of controlling variables, blind research subjects, and obtaining answers. Methodological imperialism was born (Gonzalez Rey, 2019). The qualitative dimension *par excellence*—imagination—has become an *indice* for contradiction in this method, pointed out simultaneously as fallacy and as cause. A brief semiotic and metaphysical reading of reality conveyed by that methodological choice would point to a mechanical world, governed by deterministic laws and accessible by methods that obtained static and finished signs, *indices* of access to an absolute reality. A radical break with the Renaissance was required so that modern science could establish itself: no integration of humanity with the cosmos, no ethereal notions such as fluid.

Jussieu's attitude was important in the sense of conceiving an alternative path to that research problem. The famous naturalist adopted a procedure related to phenomenology: when trying to enter the field, he observed and described its various facets. It was not that his conclusions mattered: even if he did not manage to do a longer and more detailed descriptive and categorical work, Jussieu developed an important process of description that could perfectly set himself at the beginning of a broader investigation. It is even possible to consider that he started as Pierce's artist (1903/1997) but did not have (perhaps for a while) ways to implement the bulldog and the mathematician. Whether or not he had the conditions for such a refined process is a point that remains open. However, by refusing methodological imperialism, Jussieu illuminated paths that led him to the door of the phenomenon, even if he did not enter it.

Thus, the committees were a landmark for a set of decisive, but fragile and contradictory, ideas and procedures for the study of hypnosis. A method is chosen and raised to a universal level, as if there were a single version of the scientific method. The characteristics of the field are ignored due to an *a priori* definition of how such a reality should behave and, consequently, satisfy the methodological requirements of researchers, without any consideration to the possible ontological requirements of that same reality. The mere outline of a phenomenological attitude like Jussieu's is ignored and rendered irrelevant for reflection on the field. Imagination becomes a means for disqualifying mesmerism, which became vulgar for other moments of social exchange, as when someone's ideas or experiences are taken as "mere imagination." At the same time, mesmerism is associated with serious ethical risks of control over the other, rendering it a morally controversial topic—that tone follows hypnosis to the present day (Dimsdale, 2021). Defending the sexual integrity of women serves as a kind of scapegoat that imposes silence on a field with vast potential for study, as if other health practices, in the past and present, were not also permeated by the risk of harassment.

In short, the judgment of mesmerism brought with it a logic of disqualification (Chertok & Stengers, 1989) that contradicts the expectations of the researcher. Like a child who does not understand the logic of a toy and prefers to break it, the committees and the institutions that sponsored them chose to disqualify a field they knew little about and that seemed threatening to them. That attitude refers much more to a posture of protection than to the desire to learn. Silence was imposed, under various forms of threat, and the contradictions of the procedures themselves could not serve any kind of criticism and reflection. Ignoring was necessary; the verb 'ignore' serves as an attitude in which the researcher places themselves above the field, unable to see themselves in the face of the difficulties that this brings. Nevertheless, the contradictions linked to that field and the ways of approaching it could be hidden, but only for a certain time. In the manner of repression that erupts from darkness, magnetism and its successor, hypnosis, would soon return, bringing new reflections and controversies to the scientific world.

The mesmerism's judgment is an illustrative process when considering a De-sign inquiry (Seif, 2020a). The committees understood that the studied field could be approached through physical phenomena as if a subject could perceive animal magnetism physically—a conception that led them to deny the field. Nevertheless, De-sign is pertinent to this point in two ways. On the one hand, its approach is not dependent on physical events, which are signs of Secondness composing an ecological and semiotic world in which Firstness and Thirdness are also pertinent. Thus, the physical sensations during Mesmer's treatment would not be the only source of signs relevant to the inquiry, since the imaginary and feeling processes, as well as the new habit configurations, would be equally necessary. Human healing, as highlighted in some studies (Neubern, 2018), does not obey a mechanical law perspective, being permeated by several forms of semiotic exchange: the relational context, social insertion, confidence in treatment, spiritual beliefs, and support, affective relationships, and economic safety are some of the dimensions that influence healing processes. On the other hand, De-signing is not about a discipline; it integrates many disciplines into a dialogic process. Facing the committees, the De-signer would invite Jussieu to engage in dialogue with his colleagues since he had relevant ideas to share. But not only him, because many other researchers and patients should also have important angles to add to the discussion. The De-sign inquiry would give these other representatives a voice, intending to create a risk for the inquiry: the transcendence of its own limits (Seif, 2020a). Imagination, beliefs, feelings, desires, and paradoxes would coexist with the objective results searched by the committees. In short, if the inquiry of animal magnetism found an unexpected and uncommon sense, it could be more coherent with the field studied.

Puységur, Somnambulism, and the Birth of Hypnosis

The revolutionary climate of France at the end of the nineteenth century would soon revive quarrels around animal magnetism, now explicitly linked to subversive ideas. Armand Marie-Jacques de Chastenet, the Marquis de Puységur, was one of the most notable characters in that process. The celebrated Colonel of Artillery of the French Army was of aristocratic origin, affiliated with Freemasonry and a practitioner of philanthropy—a habit inherited from his family. For his libertarian ideals, he was imprisoned with his family, saw his brothers exiled and lost a large portion of their assets (Méheust, 1999). Even so, he remained an ardent adept of animal magnetism, especially after giving it a new version through artificial somnambulism. In this distinguished state, a simple and uneducated person could present paranormal abilities and knowledge far beyond their degree of formal education. His writings on animal magnetism (Puységur, 1784/2003), published after the silence imposed by the authorities, are at the same time an act of resistance and a precious set of reports on the experiences of somnambulists used by him for treating different ailments.

In a somnambulistic state, the subject, usually a woman,[2] had different capacities for healing, ranging from diagnosis, magnetic intervention, and the prescription of medications, including herbs (Puységur, 1784/2003). They could intervene in their own health issues or assist other patients during treatment. The somnambulist could predict how many days she would remain sick, when she would be in crisis—through which her 'evil' would be expelled from the body. She could also make diagnoses, in the presence of the patient or remotely, without any medical information on the patient—only through a kind of extrasensory vision. Puységur dispensed with the use of the *baquet*, being perhaps the first great mesmerist to propose the individualization of treatments based on magnetic passes. He was also different from Mermer in other things, though he had been his student: the treatment and teaching of magnetism should be free and have as its sole motivation the firm desire to do good. With this way of thinking, the wisdom of the universe, expressed through the somnambulistic state, would come to the aid of the magnetizer, assisting them in their healing purposes. The clientele that entered his estate in Buzancy was formed by various types of people, men and women, peasants, the bourgeoisie, and nobles, as well as atheists and religious people. Another important idea which arose in response to the criticisms of the commission of 1784 was given by the somnambulists themselves: in a somnambulistic state, the magnetizer could never induce a person to do something that was contrary to one's morals. Even so, Puységur adopted the habit of, when treating a female patient, always having someone she trusted in the same room.

Armand Marie-Jacques de Chastenet (1751–1825), the Marquis de Puységur, was one of the most celebrated magnetizers of his time. A disciple of Mesmer, this Colonel of the French Army developed different work from his master, either by individualizing treatment or by seeing patients without requiring pay. His most important contribution was in artificial somnambulism, that is, a state of deep trance accessed via magnetism, in which people displayed unusual abilities. His work was also strongly influenced by the Renaissance (Méheust, 1999), especially in ethical terms: if a doctor had the firm desire to do good, the cosmic wisdom of the universe would come to meet them through means such as the somnambulistic state. Of aristocratic origin, he was given to philanthropy and Freemasonry, which facilitated the spread of animal magnetism in France and other countries. In addition to the solid humanist influence that, in a way, is verified in authors such as Milton Erickson, his work influenced later movements, such as Allan Kardec's Spiritism and metapsychics, the precursor of parapsychology.

---

[2] In Puységur's work, the woman commonly had a special role as somnambulistic subjects (Méheust, 1999). Culturally, people considered they were more sensitive than men, being more available for spiritual experiences and mediumship. During the animal magnetism age, their performances were socially conceived as subversive by conservative institutions such as the Church and the State because they would demonstrate abilities of medicine or philosophy commonly attributed to men. The social norm for women was the domestic space, including marriage and maternity, being marginalized the women who adopted other forms of social life (Edelman, 1995).

Unlike the first judgments by the committees, the following evaluations on animal magnetism seem to have adopted more political and ideological criteria than scientific ones (Méheust, 1999). In 1831, Husson, president of the French Academy of Sciences, decided not to publish the results of his favorable evaluation to magnetism to avoid great conflict between the members of the institution who were favorable and opposed to such treatment. Shortly thereafter, Dubois d'Amiens takes on the role of sabotaging several attempts to verify the procedures through experiments and disrupted any attempts at independent study of the field. If the committees from 1784 contradicted each other mostly around methodological problems, those from the nineteenth century used force to avoid more accurate investigation. Furthermore, the hypotheses around intense pressure from conservative sectors and institutions of society became very plausible (Neubern, 2009). Magnetism, and especially this new version—artificial somnambulism—gave great visibility to the figure of the woman who, in a state of trance, could display superior knowledge to many men. In a highly patriarchal society, as women were expected to keep to domestic spaces as wives, or in the convent, that movement was a scandal (Edelman, 1995). Animal magnetism, as ritualized by Puységur, was also very similar to a perspective of equality, opposed to the hierarchical society that defended person's merit originated from their moral values—and not from their social origin. Progressive bourgeois people and nobles, as well as peasants and proletarians, were attracted by that concept. Magnetism also advocated healing power was in nature, whether cosmic or personal, in an affront to the influential medical power in the society of the time. Another institution that opposed him was the Catholic Church, very exasperated by a series of spiritualist movements linked to it that infiltrated the population and questioned its power.

The animal magnetism in Puységur's somnambulists was thus somewhat problematic in scientific and social terms. In particular, somnambulists bore marks of an enchanted universe, typical of German Romanticism (Ellenberger, 1970/2003; Koyré, 1971), such as the relationship with the cosmos, the exaltation of the feminine, and a notion of healing associated with the harmonization of fluidic elements and people's moral stance. In some versions, like Jean-Baptiste de Villermoz's (Bergé, 1995), there was an explicit association with spiritual beings which increased the ideal of union between religion and science. In scientific terms, if Mesmer's original magnetism had already presented itself as a highly contradictory problem, artificial somnambulism seemed to bring something unthinkable: the resumption of fluids, an original relationship with the universe that was present there and, in some cases, fostered interaction with the spiritual world. It was a marginalized movement for subverting notions of modern reality that were already beginning to strengthen through science (Martino, 1944/1999). In addition to the social implications described here, it would be difficult or even impossible for such institutions to consider it an exemption and proceed towards a more focused study on the knowledge of the field. From this cultural broth, movements that were also quite contested did not fail to emerge, but they enjoyed a certain space in European societies, such as metapsychics, ancestor of parapsychology (Blum, 2004), and Allan Kardec's Spiritism (Sharp, 2006).

What happened with the passage of time is that magnetism, as a way of explaining the field, was extinguished and provided space to other alternatives. The young doctor Alexandre de Bertrand, Abbot de Faria's disciple, developed a line of thought based on the "medicine of the imagination," one of the first references to psychology (Carroy, 1993). This perspective was perpetuated until the end of the nineteenth century and did not fail to present strong associations with the School of Nancy, headed by Bernheim and Liébeault, for whom hypnosis was a process of acceptance of suggestions from the brain. Despite Bertrand's influences and even the ancient magnetizers', imagination itself became a phenomenon subjugated to the speech of suggestion and the functioning of the brain. Another dominant perspective was provided by James Braid when seeking to explain these phenomena through physiological means, that is, through nervous sleep or hypnosis. Even if the term "hypnosis" had already been adopted twenty years earlier by magnetizers (Méheust, 1999), it now seemed coated by something more reliable: the functioning of the brain. Braid's ideas went on to support the next generations and established strong dealings with the School of Paris, whose leading name was Jean-Martin Charcot and for whom hypnosis was a matter of psychic and pathological states associated with hysteria.[3]

The same idea of disenchantment is striking in this new stage for the origins of hypnosis. The term hypnosis, even if previously used, was then associated with two existing fields that produced visible signs as a response: the brain and words (Neubern, 2009). Imagination, if it were to be of interest, should be translated into a semiotics of existents and laws, detached from its qualitative nature. Chance, of course, should be controlled and reduced to laws so that it ceased being a source of error. The notion of fluid should be banned, given its elusive content and its prospect of mixing subject/object. For reality to reveal itself, separation should prevail between the researcher and their object of study, without admitting any sort of continuity. Even if that notion appealed to the study of phenomena linked to hypnosis, like rapport and hypnogenesis (Roustang, 2015), it should be thrown into oblivion. However, the notion of subject changes drastically in this new stage. Even if Puységur's somnambulist did not have a consistent conceptual framework, he referred to an active and creative subject, at the same time individual and a sign of collective influence from the Cosmos. Unlike them, the subject of hypnosis, mostly linked to Charcot, became an automaton, detached from any belonging or collective connection and destined to offer good answers to the researcher. He was a member of the mechanical and absolute universe of modernity.

---

[3] Hysteria was a clinical diagnosis widely studied at the end of the nineteenth century (Carroy, 1991), characterized, above all, by intense symptoms of anguish and conversion. The term was derived from the Greek system, meaning uterus (*hysteron*), although Charcot demonstrated that they also occurred in men. A few years after his internship at Charcot, Freud associated it with the repression of sexual desires.

Freud and Psychoanalysis

By claiming to discover the unconscious, capable of resisting the patient's and the therapist's will, Sigmund Freud (1856–1939) believed he had created a method, in the clinical field, as reliable as the method for Natural Sciences (Stengers, 1996). If this unconscious resisted human interference, it could offer facts, fleeing from the great fear that seemed to characterize hypnosis—the artifacts. In other words, it would not be possible to know whether what the person presented in trance was reliable or an attempt to lie or to please the therapist. Failures, gaps, forgetfulness fits that could occur during free association pointed towards a dimension beyond that person's deliberations, with its own functions and contrary to the therapist's expectations. Freud, in a way, inaugurated a clinical field apart from the Natural Sciences, in which notions such as desire, fantasy, libido, and sexuality appeared, and which also presented meanings of symptoms as linked to non-biological causes. It was a memorable resumption of the Humanities that already seemed to be born at war with the Natural Sciences. At the same time, Freud did not dispense with a typically modern notion of reliability, as if the psychoanalytic method of interpreting resistance and transfer might allow for a privileged form of access to that person's truth.

> *Sigmund Freud (1856–1939), Austrian physician and creator of psychoanalysis. Through his interest in hysteria, he developed the idea that a physical symptom (such as conversion) originated from symbolic themes linked to sexual repression. He was an adept of hypnosis for a time, but eventually became disappointed with it. It seemed ineffective to him, as the symptoms could return or be replaced. So, he developed a method—psychoanalysis—for transforming the unconscious into the conscious in order to arrive at what he believed to be more credible cures (Chertok & Stengers, 1989). If hypnosis was a cosmetic and superficial procedure, psychoanalysis was surgical and profound, which made it a superior form of treatment. At the end of his life (Freud, 1937/1996), Freud considered that the same problems that occurred in hypnosis (return and replacement of symptoms, worsening of the patient) also occurred in psychoanalysis, which did not award the latter any superiority. Nevertheless, most of his followers did not delve into these statements by Freud and remained connected to the ancient opposition between hypnosis (superficial) and psychoanalysis (deep and capable of reaching the root of problems.*

Posing as an heir of Copernicus, Freud (1916/1996) claimed that psychoanalysis would cause a narcissistic wound to modern man. If for Copernicus the Earth was not the center of the universe but a modest planet revolving around the sun and, in Darwin, man was not set apart from animal evolution, in psychoanalysis the human would not be governed by reason, but by the unconscious. Placing himself in this powerful line of succession and under a supposedly modern methodological proposal, Freud was not slow to disqualify hypnosis, even though it was responsible for opening the field of the unconscious. In a large portion of his texts (Freud, 1905, 1912, 1917) hypnosis is presented as something superficial and cosmetic, while psychoanalysis as a method would be able to push away appearances and reach the nuclei of conflict. Consequently, while in hypnosis, dubious in nature, the risk of substitution or return of symptoms was higher, in psychoanalysis the cure would be more convincing and lasting. In short, although his theoretical interest persisted throughout his career (Freud, 1921/1996), most of his works were firm in maintaining this opposition. However, at the end of his life, Freud (1937/1996) made an important revision to his stance on hypnosis. The return and replacement of symptoms, as well as the worsening of patients in many cases, did not prove psychoanalysis was superior to other methods, both in the sense of cure and truth. More importantly, he stated that no substitute had been found for suggestion and even that the works of names such as Sandor Ferenczi, an important psychoanalyst dedicated to hypnosis, had not evolved to the point of standing out from others. It would not be possible, therefore, to disqualify rival approaches since psychoanalysis did not present anything different from them in terms of privileged access to real and therapeutic efficacy. His old idea compared psychoanalysis to surgery and hypnosis to a cosmetic procedure (Freud, 1905/1996) lost its sense. Despite Freud's courageous attitude, such ideas did not bring great repercussions in the psychoanalytic movement that remains, until today, linked to Freud's initial opposition to hypnosis (Stengers, 2002). The teaching and diffusion of psychoanalysis, in different countries of the world, are still based on this opposition, as the problems that led Freud to reject this technique as a therapeutic procedure are highlighted.

Freud's ideas were great contributions for understanding subjective experience as a field of study. Imagination, desire, fantasy, dreams and others are notions permeated by Firstness in their qualitative and sentimental content. Psychoanalysis has also contributed significantly to a methodological alternative that is coherent with the field, characterized by the interpretation of resistances and transfers and in the construction of concepts that can dialogue with that reality. In a way, Freud was innovative in treating experience as a kind of reality, linked to psychic life, symptoms, suffering, and desire. Approaching the humanities, he strove to maintain the modern tone of privileged knowledge—so that he might disqualify rival perspectives.

Therefore, hypnosis remained a serious problem for his constructions, which he came to admit in lengthy and endless analyses (Freud, 1937/1996). One of the main problems that became his epistemological nightmare was complacency (Stengers, 1996) which, reissuing hypnogenesis, did not expose the difference between fact and artifact. This obstacle constitutes a serious problem for their claims; without the possibility of obtaining facts, privileged access to reality would not be possible—nor more convincing cures. Freud's curious conclusion in 1937 could be translated thus: hypnogenesis is also present in psychoanalysis, and this does not distinguish it from other therapeutic and research methods. Perhaps Freud sought to attribute to such a field a role of existent, much like existent materials. It is not that an image or a dream cannot have some existent elements that might operate a certain opposition to thought, but these processes differ greatly from the opposition that emerges from a chemical reaction or from a concrete object in a laboratory experiment.

Hypnogenesis, then, remained an epistemological nightmare for Freud, because subjective processes, even at some level, were still highly permeated by signs of Firstness and Thirdness. Therefore, an elusive experience would not involve, at least according to the psychoanalytic method, a concrete dimension to be revealed, that is, a fact, but it had to be something intertwined and transformed by the researcher's influence—an artifact. The modern idea of validity (Hacking, 2000; Stengers, 2001) becomes unsustainable since fact and artifact would be inseparable in the hypnotic process. Possibly because of the era in which he lived (Hacking, 2000; Lyotard, 1979), as points of contact between revelation and construction were discussed and deepened, the dilemma between fact and artifact remained insoluble and problematic for Freud. Despite his emphasis on the importance of relationships and transferential processes, notions such as the opposition between nature and culture and an individualistic psyche not only advanced psychoanalysis to an absolute perspective but also hindered any understanding of the elusive and treacherous phenomena linked to hypnogenesis.

Freud believed that psychoanalysis would have the same reliability as a natural science (Stengers, 1996). He conceived that, through the psychoanalytic method, psychological experiences could be as objective as the electron in the Physics laboratory, which could confer to psychoanalysis a superior condition in comparison with other therapeutic methods, including hypnosis. Nevertheless, he committed a crucial error when he understood psychological experiences things as if they were of the same nature of physical things. He ignored that hypnogenesis could influence and frame psychological experiences, which would be essential for establishing differences between psychological and physical things and their particular forms of resistance, while Secondness phenomena.

In other words, Freud tries to assign a role of existent to subjective and imaginary processes permeated by Firstness. These would need to oppose the therapist's thought, as a physical object is capable of doing. In a way, Freud seeks to expand modern logic towards a elusive field, so that it might be seen as a form of reality, rather than something opposite to it. In the name of validity, subjective processes eventually empty themselves of their qualitative content and become things, as if they were material objects. Despite the relevance of his work, reification was one of his strategies to mischaracterize the processes of Firstness, either in phenomenological terms, as with feelings, or in metaphysical terms, with chance. As a result, both the elusive dimension of experience and the multiplicity of chance are emptied and, to some extent, resemble the material world. Soon, phenomena like trance as quale-consciousness become inaccessible from the psychoanalytic perspective.

Similarly, the notion of law gradually occupied a hegemonic aspect in Freud (Gonzalez Rey, 2007). Despite its profound interpretation of the complexity of human experience, the search for universals became a problem for understanding the diversity of phenomena from Firstness (Ibri, 1992/2017). Notions such as the

Oedipus complex, both as the founder of the psyche and as a clinical complex, become problematic, as they lead towards the homogenization of human diversity and its ways of generating processes and constructing changes. Thus, as the processes permeated by Firstness are reified, psychic and human diversity become submissive to Freud's universals. While this idea approached a modern scientific proposal for the subjective field, it demonstrated its collapse. Freud's own clinical experience (1937/1996) did not corroborate the influence of universals, since psychoanalytic results were not superior to other methods. Firstness, in the form of quality and chance, needed to be taken up again and considered a constituent in hypnotic processes. This mission would be resumed a few decades later by Milton Erickson.

Milton Erickson: Innovation and Hope

Milton Hyland Erickson, American psychiatrist, was a relevant alternative in terms of understanding hypnosis. He was not only one of the most extraordinary therapists of the twentieth century but also a clinician-researcher whose reflections, to some extent, rescue essential elements from that field, as well as point out possible ways for its study (Neubern, 2023). One of the main pillars of his work is naturalism, according to which trance is a natural phenomenon in people (rather than an anomalous experience), which would also carry a whole potential, capable of helping them in the face of difficulties (Erickson, 1958). The proximity to Puységur at this point is surprising. At the same time, contrary to the obsessive tendency towards universals in modern science, Erickson conceived each subject in their singularity, proposing, as no therapist seems to have achieved it, particular therapeutic contexts, appropriate to individuals (Erickson, 1959). The same psychiatric condition, like depression, with similar symptoms in two different people, was treated very differently for each of them. While for one he could adopt task prescriptions and involvement of the social network, in the other, he might proceed with an age regression work, aiming to promote reconstruction of identity. In such cases, the interest in minimal signs (Erickson, 1964) was the basis for a distinct mode of clinical research with the idea of particularized law for each person. In other words, instead of searching for universals in each subject, as his contemporaries had done (Foschi & Inammoratti, 2020), Erickson was more interested in the "personal laws" of each patient. This perhaps explains why he was never interested in constructing a theory in the modern sense of the term, or even in founding a school of psychotherapy and hypnosis.

Another fundamental principle of Erickson's work was the way he conceived suggestions (Erickson & Rossi, 1979). In terms of therapeutic principles, he opposed direct suggestions from classical hypnosis, although he might use them at times. A direct order or prescription would have many limitations for him, such as mobilizing resistance, restricting the spectrum of responses, or setting the person towards greater passivity or obedience to the therapist. Indirect suggestions, on the other hand, might invite people to more active and motivated participation, the exploration of their potential for change, and a considerable range of options for new paths. Short stories, wordplay, truisms, interpersal phrases, and dramatizations were some of the ways Erickson applied, established relationships, and mobilized his clients for therapy. Advocating an idea of session control, for which he actively worked, the context created by indirect suggestions positioned subjects in a free and participatory way. Thus, while complying with one of the modern methodological assumptions—control—his relationships were based on partnership, mainly because they valued autonomy and creative potential. As a De-signer (Seif, 2020b), he conceived hypnosis as a paradox in which control would promote freedom.

> *Milton Hyland Erickson (1901–1980) was one of the most important names in the renewal of hypnosis in the twentieth century. American psychiatrist, he proposed a rather innovative approach to hypnosis: instead searching for general laws, he conceived the uniqueness of each person; instead of direct suggestions, he proposed indirect modes of communication such as storytelling; instead of pathology, he emphasized the potentiality within each person. His naturalistic approach meant that each person has their own way of experiencing trance, and many did not fit the general patterns of theories and scalability. His techniques advocated different characteristics and expressions from the person (symptoms, resistances, ways of thinking and relating etc.) could be used in favor of therapy. Erickson did not seem imbued with the modern search for truth, as he understood the distinctive nature of hypnosis and the great diversity in people. Despite the few inquiries about his legacy on a philosophical and epistemological level, Erickson's ideas have great potential for approaching and comprehending hypnosis in a different way, considering clinical practices and metaphysics.*

The principle of utilization—another central basis for his work—also reinforces that humanistic perspective (Erickson, 1958). According to him, the therapist should create a context in which the person could exercise some of their characteristics (such as symptoms, resistances, ways of thinking, relating, perceiving) in favor of therapy. In that perspective, what might be a defect or something undesirable for therapy, for Erickson, could be something used by the person to awaken their therapeutic potential and deal with the demands worked in session. Based on the naturalistic principle, his practice was a way of promoting, via experience, new forms of connection with oneself in order to facilitate the integration between concrete action, thinking, and feeling—close to Pierce's pragmatism (1903/1997) and De-sign thinking (Seif, 2020a). The experience of doing, in this case, becomes a powerful therapeutic instrument for knowing the self. At the same time, it requires capacity for empathy and acceptance of others (Erickson & Rossi, 1979), since the expressions used are often reasons for reproach and accusation from professionals and people who are close to the patient. Using, therefore, does not mean manipulation or arbitrary play on the part of the therapist, but their adaptation to a person's uniqueness, with their multiple and complex forms of expression. More importantly, the therapy thus proposed is not limited to intellectual or narrative exercises, but to a continuous act of their own way of being, linked to their daily life.

Erickson's a-theoretical attitude (Haley, 1985) is a great contribution to a new way of understanding and researching hypnosis. On the one hand, the explicit denial of theory is a clear warning on the limitations of theorizing forms in modern sciences, grounded in universalism (laws) that encompasses and mischaracterizes singularity, and in the reactivity of the real (existent), which despises the subtle processes of subjectivity. On the other hand, his work is not limited to technical applications of acknowledged efficacy; on the contrary, the principles developed by him constitute important research references for the complex and elusive universe of hypnosis. His preference for indirect suggestions, naturalism, the emphasis on potentiality, and the search for solutions, as well as the pragmatic value given to this complex, elusive and diaphanous field, with its specific and distinct modes of organization of raw matter, differ from modern science extracts in much of its logic. Hypnotic trance becomes a plastic field of great potential, revealing itself far beyond the ordinary capacities of the waking state. Nevertheless, the intent reader should wonder why Erickson's ideas could make more accurate references to hypnosis as a field of study, given that many other authors preceded him. Additionally, if so many authors are subject to hypnogenesis, why could Erickson differentiate himself from the others? After all, his ideas also tended to reproduce themselves with their interlocutors.

To answer this question, it is often assumed that Erickson had a compatible attitude with Eidos[4] (Ibri, 1992/2017) to build his knowledge about hypnosis. Hypnogenesis does not guarantee, in itself, proximity to the field, because an emphasis on control, as proposed by methodologies of the past and present, can impose limitations on how the hypnotic field presents itself to the researcher, preventing them from developing a broader vision that contemplates multiple facets. Both the principle of utilization and indirect suggestion allow us to assume that Erickson captured semiotic systems from the subjects and proposed something like them, like a mirror. Then, in a therapeutic perspective, it was not a simple mirror, as it added systems of signs that instilled differences aimed at potentiality and change. In semiotic terms, this mirroring is based on the principle that any sign has, in some way, an icon and establishes a basic relationship of similarity with its object (CP 4.531). Somehow, Erickson seems to have grasped this principle and used it to develop a detailed and complex understanding of hypnosis as a large semiotic field, with its many objects. If similarity is a typical quality of Firstness, Erickson's mirroring would be a way of confronting the state of quale-consciousness characteristic of trance, with its one-multiple paradox and its considerable creative power.

---

[4] The platonic term *Eidos* refers to the structure of the real and its intelligibility. According to Ibri (1992/2017), Peirce's evolutionism raises a consequence of making the emergence of laws identify with the tendency to acquire habits, as it occurs with the mind. This idea anticipates an objective idealism and is what, in a way, enables the mind to know the world.

Therefore, by developing a context for the man who walked compulsively when anxious, Erickson (1958) allowed him to walk compulsively in the office and added some commands to direct the number of steps and their direction. Approaching and moving away from the chair repeatedly, the man accused by other therapists of being uncooperative eventually sat down and went into a trance, beginning his therapy. In this curious example of utilization, the therapist created a similar but different context, precisely because he was able to capture the subtlety of his different semiotic systems or configurations and placed them in the form of technique. It is as if, from a phenomenological attitude, Erickson captured and reflected on these systems, with their internal logic and created something new and pertinent in terms of meaning for his patient. In short, he assumed an eidetic attitude by "absorbing" pertinent semiotic configurations into his own experience to reproduce the subject's complex systems and to propose some alternatives of change to them.

In his own way, Erickson developed a phenomenological attitude towards hypnosis, adopting the artist's, the bulldog's, and the mathematician's postures. His artist had a nearly incomparable level of precision, especially as he could capture diverse signs that were hidden in most ordinary people. Not without reason, his ability to capture people's uniqueness soon became legendary. That Firstness with which he connected with the patient allowed Erickson to be inserted in a state of receptivity or even trance, which rendered him sensitive in this process of capturing what comes from the other. The artist's feeling in Erickson becomes the basis for his construction of experiences. His bulldog was tenacious and made him stop for hours or days on the same clinical situation so he might understand it and propose a therapeutic path. It is a sign of the perseverance necessary to carry out fruitful investigation (Seif, 2019). His mathematician, fleeing from universalist temptations, was adept at capturing the regularities or "personal laws" for each one, in a version of the self close to Peirce's (Colapietro, 1989). Though he did not use habit as a concept, as there is a disposition for certain actions under given circumstances, Erickson's mathematician fostered an understanding of such general dispositions of individual particular universes that were fundamental for therapeutic planning and intervention. Without more pronounced determinisms from law, habit opens more possibilities for creation (Ibri, 1992/2017), restoring the interaction with the artist, as Erickson well understood.

The case of Joe the florist is illustrative of that (Haley, 1993). When Erickson tells the story of a tomato seedling to a mature man who had been overtaken by metastases and with pain that no longer responded to medications in palliative care, he promoted more than a comfortable trance with a strong anesthetic influence. In the tale, there is considerable emphasis on the sensitivity of the stems of the little tomato plant. Thus, Erickson refers to a complex universe of experiences that involve a series of semiotic systems that permeate mind-body relationships. First, he uses a relevant and familiar theme for the subject—the growth of a plant. The tomato seedling becomes a focus of attention and a theme full of meanings. Because of the man's resistance to psychiatrists and hypnosis, Erickson, at the insistence of family members, decided to see him, but introduced himself as a friend who would like to talk about plants. Thus, a strange but friendly man who introduces himself as a friend (whom he did not know) but talks about something interesting becomes a powerful sign for holding his attention, mainly because of the stranger's ability to tell stories. There begins a rapport, that is, a relationship of mutual responsiveness, in which those involved have the feeling of receiving the other in their worlds of experience (Melchior, 1998). This focus of attention, based on the subject's symbolic interest but also on other signs linked to the figure of the therapist and that context, initially conceive some indices on the hypnotic universe. What holds the subject's attention to initiate a rapport and trance is not a stimulus-response relationship, but a semiotic process with various signs. Such immersion of the subject in this focus seems to be what leads the ego to undergo changes in its references of relationship with the world (time, space, body, cause, and matter), favoring the emergence of the self with other potential for experience reconfiguration, starting with anesthesia.

Secondly, storytelling carries considerable semiotic complexity, not only because the theme and words are taken from a vocabulary that is familiar to the subject, but mainly because of the capacity for semiosis present in trance. On the one hand, the richness in the story has a great affinity with the subject's vocabulary and with his bodily sensitivity—one of the objectives pursued by Erickson. The constant use of *interpersal* phrases throughout the context are also noteworthy, since different emphases in tone of voice and rhythm for certain parts of the sentence (which characterizes this technique) become signs with suggestive potential. On the other hand, this web of signs launched in the relationship with the subject in the format of diagrams favors multiple processes of semiosis that occur beyond the subject's deliberation. Roughly speaking, part of them is transformed by different forms of agency into various anesthetic processes. There is an important consideration regarding quale-consciousness: words can become images and sensations and might even contribute to new habits, in the case, dealing with pain. Then, what seemed the broader semiosis is the metaphor created as an interpretant of the tale: Joe's body image is closely associated with the tomato plant. The sensitivity of the transparent stems is linked to the internal and external sensitivities of the body, as well as branches and leaves are parallel to limbs, the stem to the trunk, and possibly the fruits to organs or tumors. In short, the tomato plant as a feeling body is a kind of mirror for the subject's body, as he interacts with the image and it teaches him new sensations.

Instead of a direct order to reduce pain, Erickson told a story to a subject in critical condition. That universe required indirect ways for approach, and that in turn involves different requirements. The first is symbolic relevance of the signs, that is, they must have a similar or familiar meaning to the signs from his experience. That applies to words, gestures, and broader constructions, such as the roles taken and the story told. The second is the freedom implied in the story that can propose certain themes (such as growth and sensitivity) in a broad way, so that the creation of solutions is favored, involving the reconfiguration of pain systems. It is a way of inserting the subject as an autonomous being, but not only in terms of ego: the story addresses different sectors of experience, like the body, organs, skin, and the self, most of which are beyond conscious deliberations. It is as if Erickson dialogues, through the story told in trance, with different modes of agency from Joe's experience.

In terms of hypnogenesis, values and ideas associated with human freedom, complexity, and uniqueness were essential so the field could present itself from its own references. There is a curious analogy here: everything happens as if the painter (the therapist) painted on a canvas (the hypnotic field), but the canvas itself was, little by little, deciding on the colors and shapes to display. The canvas would not, therefore, be a mere reproducer of the artist's intentions; depending on the freedom proposed by the latter, it might show itself according to its own reality, hidden in the potential plane of Firstness. As in De-sign inquiry (Seif, 2020b), the inquirer doesn't know which processes will emerge; he expects the unexpected, being surprised by a process in which he participated intensively. As the painter and the therapist, the De-signer works hard to construct something with others, but these constructions become alive in some way, being independent of him. This beauty of surprise permeates both De-sign and Erickson's hypnosis.

Given all these contributions, Erickson's work is a significant step towards the re-enchantment of the world regarding the study of hypnosis. At first, he does not conceive of an absolute notion of reality, mainly because of his emphasis on trance and the self as elusive experiences. Time and space become distinct, flexible, and multiple, contrasting with the closed modern notions for such categories. Erickson considered in his care the potential for creating trance, as well as the multiplicity of processes generated in this experience. In the fluid and fugue universe of hypnosis, chance and habit seemed to converge for human diversity and for the multiplicity of creative processes, which keep many similarities with De-sign (Seif, 2019): no absolute realities, polychronic time, diaphanous space and navigation thought. He claimed that:

> Your patient is one person today, quite another person tomorrow, and still another person next week, next month, next year. Five years from now, ten and twenty years from now, he is yet another person. We all have a certain general background, it's true, but we are different people each day that we live. (Rossi & Ryan, 1983, p. 3).

This excerpt refers to the considerable fluidity of human experience, close to the semiotic self (Petrilli, 2017) and De-sign navigation (Seif, 2020a). For Erickson, there would also be some level of organization in these processes that, even if subject to change, would be responsible for ordering subjectivity, as advocated in the notion of habit (Ibri, 1992/2017). Thus, there are signs that bring Erickson's ideas closer to those of contemporary scientists (Bohm, 2004; Prigogine, 1994), in which notions such as chance, history, and teleology are required for theoretical construction. There is still coherence with contemporary theories on agency (Gallagher, 2014). Although elusive, these systems that constitute the self have some form of organization, as order and disorder are articulated and define their directions. Such fluidity would not, therefore, be compatible with an *a priori* methodology, as in the judgment of mesmerism, but it should become a fundamental condition of the field to be considered by researchers interested in approaching it.

Some implications about this way Erickson understood the human experience are identified, especially in trance. There is, at least at first glance, a dissociation between healing and truth, so Erickson's work took a different direction from the Freudian proposal. In theory, if people's experiences were singular and unrepeatable, the idea of a universal law could hardly explain them. Nevertheless, his proposal for hypnotherapy would not fail to present relevant reflections for, science. At first, the confluence of the artist, the bulldog and the mathematician made him a skilled De-signer, so he could flow through complex semiotic systems of the self and obtain effective results, hardly comparable to those of other therapists. That effectiveness was not limited to obtaining a response, since it involved the reconfiguration of broader systems and brought it closer to Seif's (2019) ideas of effectiveness. The process and the totality of experience do not become superfluous or sources of error in the search for results. Instead, they are references without which the investigation and construction of knowledge become empty. The construction of therapeutic change is based on the deep and active participation of the person, which would not be possible without a teleological dimension, that is, without a construction of meanings by the person facing their future. If there is no commitment to an external and absolute truth, as the modern paradigm proposed, the truth here is deeply associated with constructions of meaning by the person. Even if fleeting, because they are always in transformation, these truths are fundamental to understand the universe of the self and promote a good therapeutic process.

Moreover, his way of understanding therapeutic relationships and hypnosis already announced a considerable break with modern individualism: through trance, the therapist was present in the person's universe and broke with the rigid limits of psychic otherness. This approach to the semiotic self (Colapietro, 1989; Petrilli, 2017) allows for two significant consequences. The first refers to the rupture with the separation between the subject and the object, mainly due to hypnogenesis. If the therapist enters and is penetrated by the person's self, they must consider this in technical, therapeutic, and, above all, ethical terms. What they bring requires reflective work, as they must consider what will be conveyed to this other and its possible implications. The second consequence concerns the notion of control that, in Erickson, acquires a paradoxical aspect. If it is correct that Erickson seemed to measure and evaluate each step of therapy, being quite directive in its conduct, it is also fair that his work has always aimed at the autonomy of people, characterized by significant enrichment of psychic life. As he regarded people in their profound diversity, the principles of utilization and indirect communication support that, for an investigation process to occur, partnership with the person, in its entirety, is a fundamental condition. Thus, the existence of control in the conduct of the process must be integrated into a broader logic of partnership, without which the results obtained would lack a person's authorial content. They would, therefore, be illegitimate if they were constructed by someone else and obeyed a unidirectional relationship that restricted the therapist to the role of providing answers.

Erickson's work also has a considerable aesthetic dimension that advocates an essential principle of re-enchantment for the construction of science. Many of his writings are marked sometimes by precise and impressive logic, sometimes by humor, drama, and poetry. He seems to embody the aesthetic ideal because of his intense dedication to a mission despite great difficulties related to his fragile health and his own setbacks in the study and clinic of hypnosis (Zeig, 1985). Erickson equally catered to people from different social levels according to their financial possibilities; he did not prioritize fame, success, and money. The stoicism of his last thirty years, as he lived as a wheelchair user, was accompanied by a strong workflow, focused on different therapeutic demands. Despite the limitations imposed by his pain and by paralysis, he continued to receive patients and students from different parts of the country. The richness of his clinical experience that benefited countless people was accompanied by a herculean dedication, as he spent long periods studying and taking notes on treatment plans. His eccentricity in everyday life was accompanied by a modest life, surrounded by family, friends, pets, patients, and students. While he maintained collaboration or even friendship with people such as Margaret Mead, Gregory Bateson, Aldous Huxley, Lawrence Kubie, and Ernst Hilgard, his care took place in his own home, adapted to his unique needs. It was also a way of criticizing the formalism of many psychotherapy practices. Changes should be linked to a person's daily life and not to the artificial space of the office.

Erickson's dedication to the aesthetic ideal linked to the creation, practice, and diffusion of hypnosis has important developments in terms of a new way of thinking about hypnosis and science itself. On the one hand, that beauty is attractive to many people, linked to the great movement of Ericksonian hypnosis around the world, even if Erickson never founded a school or a movement. This links to a rhetorical aspect (CP 2.207) for fostering a critical community, engaged in the search for knowledge. Erickson's hypnosis thus becomes a relevant alternative, either for the various facets of the experience it allows access to, or for the beauty it attributed to the field, in contrast to modern mechanicism. That engagement is, in itself, collective and teleological, since scientific research itself turns to the future. On the other hand, Erickson becomes a great symbol of the researcher who is confused by his own field, integrating life and profession (Romanyshyn, 2021). He was symbol focused on the search for meaning in what he did to embody the idea of achievement and desirable outcomes (Seif, 2018) above the achievement of academic results. Awards, titles, and the number of publications with impact become puerile compared to the personal and epistemological importance of desirable outcomes. The direct implication for a new way of thinking about science, reality, and hypnosis is that the subject is a sign of a world with multiple belonging (*ethos*) with which he seeks to reconcile (Neubern, 2023). The investigation of the world thus becomes a process in which, as the therapist gets to know the reality of the other, also comes across new facets of their own. Hypnosis, as a cultural technology, can be a way for this knowledge made in the relationship with the other, as it turns to the therapist's own *ethos*.

Many might state that Erickson, in his writings, did not weave claims such as those raised in this chapter. His work was basically done through a large set of reports on therapeutic care of his patients. However, in these reports, there are important entries about what has not yet been said or elaborated in an inquiry process. It is precisely at this point that De-sign (Seif, 2019, 2020a) becomes relevant, as it allows an investigation into the various points that have not been explored but remained significant for a more comprehensive understanding of hypnosis.

De-sign and the Challenges of Hypnosis

The intention of this book is to, through De-sign (Seif, 2019, 2020a), build an understanding of hypnosis based on the notions that were overlooked throughout its history. It is not a linear application of concepts or techniques, but rather some principles for the intelligibility of the complex and elusive field of hypnosis. In a way, this reinterpretation of hypnosis through De-sign is an idea of re-enchantment of the world, not because of an adherence to subjectivism or by abandoning the various achievements of the modern paradigm, but as a way of promoting the construction of distinct knowledge, integrated to its object of study and to the dimensions of which it has divorced in the name of privileged access to reality. In short, this book seeks to welcome and integrate the marginalized dimensions by the modern paradigm, forming the conditions for legitimate knowledge about hypnosis.

As mentioned, hypnosis is, *par excellence*, a field based on Firstness (CP 6.228), with many implications for the present investigation. The first of these is the rescue of the elusive and diaphanous dimensions of hypnosis, resuming notions like quality, imagination and feeling as constitutive of inquiry and the construction of knowledge. Without further metaphysical elaboration, this book rescues the reality of hypnosis, which becomes a fundamental point for other moments of inquiry about it as an object of study. On the one hand, each sign contains an icon (CP 2.254–2.263) that highlights some level of participation of Firstness in any phenomenon under study. In hypnosis, despite imagination being historically opposed to reality (Stengers, 2001), imaginary processes play a fundamental role in the construction of habits (CP 6.20). This is the first point of study in which the semiotic processes of icons and feelings contribute to form complex configurations of signs (design), producing meaning (semiotics) under the organization of specific modes of agency. Firstness still has the critical role of bringing, via chance and instability (Ibri, 1992/2017), modifications upon such highly elusive systems. The elusive things and objects of human experiences are predominantly linked to desirable outcomes without losing some level of concreteness through which they can influence other experience systems. Being closely linked to "what is yet to come," they are essential in the process of changing or constructing habits, acting on a Thirdness level of experience.

The dimensions of time, space, and matter undergo significant modifications. Being in multiple places and times at once, in trance, is not understood as failure to obtain objective data (Chertok & Stengers, 1989). This way of living is a matter of pertinence because, from the point of view of the living, multiplicity can be highly transformative in terms of habits and constructions of meaning. As a result, the idea of trance can be taken as a *transit* between planes of distinct and pertinent experiences to what is experienced by the person. The result of a hypnotherapeutic process is conceived as "that which is" (according to the initial question of a survey), but it is also inseparable from what "should be" and what "could be" (Seif, 2020a). At the same time, De-sign allows for a considerable expansion of the focus on what it is, moving from a perspective of response and efficacy to that of a broader and procedural understanding, focused on desirable outcomes and effectiveness (Seif, 2019). In other words, what remains of a hypnotherapeutic process for a person is not restricted to a set of responses, but to more comprehensive processes of integration between ego and self, as well as of the person with their ethos (Neubern & Nogueira, 2019).

On the other hand, this work also mentions the possibility of conceiving Firstness as an ontology beyond chance. Following the idea of the *pure play of musement* (Peirce, 1908/1991), this book explores the investigation of elusiveness from Peirce's principle, in which the interpretant of a good argument is the creation of habits. There is, at this point, an integrative content in Peirce's modes of inference[5] (Fann, 2010), as abduction becomes a connecting field for deduction and induction in a broader process of inquiry (Seif, 2019). In other words, the primacy of imaginary navigation advocated by the De-sign inquiry is not a surrender to chaos and subjectivism but a process in which abduction is the most significant reference of rationality and integrates moments of deduction and induction. The emphasis on the process, rather than the outcome, submits the idea of knowledge (something general and established) to the idea of a "knowing." From the condition of noun condition (existing and symbolic)—knowledge—inquiry becomes a verb, with its iconic characteristics (Nöth, 2015). Happening, finitude, process, vagueness, and evanescence characterize local and transitory knowledge. Erickson's idea that "your patient is someone else every day" (Rossi & Ryan, 1983) is consistent with this perspective, which implies dealing with a fluid, polychronic, and diaphanous reality. Spiritual themes will be included in some clinical studies because of trance situations from different cultures (Nathan, 2001/2014; Neubern 2022). Ethnopsychology will serve as complement to that part, mainly by highlighting how other knowledges mobilize specific devices and collective discussions for investigating trance experiences, as they are conceived as real. Although it is not the focus of this book, some ontological comparisons with the virtual universe (Santaella, 2022) will also be developed in its implications on people's daily lives.

The second implication of this proposal relates to hypnogenesis. In ontological terms, there are relevant questions to the inquiry, as hypnosis is a field that responds to what the therapist uses to interrogate it (Melchior, 1998). Historically it is possible to verify that the way of constructing trance by subjects revealed researcher

---

[5] Peirce (cited in Fann, 2010) conceived three basic forms of inference or way of constructing thought in an inquiry: abduction (construction of hypotheses), deduction (there is a work of refinement and ordering of hypotheses), and induction (characterized by the verification of them). They are respectively linked to the phenomenological categories previously raised.

beliefs (Mehéust, 1999). Thus, the subjects of Donatus, who believed in authority, resembled trained animals, while those by Charcot were modern and mechanicist automata. Those by Puységur and Erickson, humanists, were free and creative. Nevertheless, although hypnotic reality does not offer the same resistance as a physical object, the interlocutor's self is not a mere passive field for the researcher's ideas. They necessarily have active and creative roles that must be included as a conditions for inquiry. Erickson's work, at this point, is one of the most relevant because it highlights his indirect and naturalistic ways of approaching the other meet active and protagonist conditions.

In terms of De-sign inquiry, both hypnogenesis and Erickson's approach have significant consequences. The first refers to the notion of synechism that advocates a continuity between things (CP 5.4). Reality is, therefore, not apart from the researcher but intertwined with them. In the case of the hypnotic relationship, it becomes even more plastic and interpenetrating. Thus, the first challenge of inquiry becomes not obtaining data or answers in the modern sense, but the production of desirable outcomes that mark someone's authorship for what is obtained from hypnosis. Although inquiry is a joint process, it is important that hypnotherapy be an authorial and emancipatory process for the person. Partnership, instead of modern control, is what guides the relationship with reality, according to De-sign (Seif, 2020b). It is necessary that reality be implicated in the inquiry as a set of autonomous systems that may create and recreate themselves. In human terms, partnership also translates as dialogue (Seif, 2013), implying a deep consideration of the person in their autonomy, way of being, and making choices. Dialogue goes beyond a conversation mainly because of the variety of signs it assumes and incorporates in exchanges with the other and in the transcendence of time and space. Moreover, it is polyphonic because multiple voices, internal and external to the self, establish significant exchanges with each other (Neubern, 2016). If inquiry based on dialogue implies movement and process, it results, in some way, in the integration of the person with themselves or between ego and self. Consequently, trance has considerable therapeutic magnitude in the process of reconciliation with oneself, either in individual terms or in terms of *ethos* (Neubern, 2022).

De-sign (Seif, 2019) allows the inquirer to consider that knowing is born from a relationship with reality, differently from control or methodological imperialism: it springs from partnership, as participants are protagonists and reconnect with themselves through trance. By becoming a De-signer, the therapist necessarily connects with the one whom they study, whereas through De-sign, typically modern separations such as theory vs. practice, therapist vs. researcher, and subjectivity vs. objectivity are transcended. The conditions that precede and fabricate knowledge must be recognized and included in inquiry, since they do not constitute processes that are part of its execution. Similarly, information is not constituted as isolated data and reduced in the diversity of dimensions that precede them, but in signs that refer to the considerable diversity of objects, necessarily systemic and complex.

Hypnotherapy becomes a significant process through De-sign, the end of which is not a product, but a kind of rebirth of the person. Inventing and recreating oneself from one's own references (Morin, 2001/2015) is one of the characteristics of that field of inquiry. Again, there is the idea that the interpretant of a good claim is the creation of a habit (Peirce, 1908/1991), a relevant sign for understanding change. In a certain way, symbolically, there are numerous deaths and rebirths of the same person, which refers to the idea of palingenesis (Seif, 2019), which implies different moments of suffering and joy. Therefore, the hypnotherapeutic context must be based on the principles of Agape, as an evolutionary and teleological power, and Eros, advocating the desirable future (Seif, 2018) for a new position in the it. Changes, in De-sign (Seif, 2020a), follow a pragmatic perspective: they convey meanings for life, referring to the emergence of intentionality. Between the sleeping and waking of hypnosis, which symbolically reissues the idea of dying and rebirth from ancient peoples (Seif, 2019), the person is reborn as a new intentional being without ceasing to be themselves. It is a movement that can extend from a reconciliation with the *ethos* (Neubern, 2023) to a broader process of existential meaning about life (Frankl, 1959/1984). One's new perspective on life tends to have new qualitative elements linked to feeling, colors, taste, desire, and love (Seif, 2018), which do not exempt them from the vicissitudes and sufferings of life, even if provide them with another condition to deal.

Another relevant consequence linked to hypnogenesis is the reflective content that becomes inevitable to the therapist. It is crucial that they should reflect on the type of idea that they convey to their interlocutor in the hypnotherapeutic relationship. In terms of De-sign (Seif, 2020a), the emergence of the reality for the other is important because the logic of what is investigated is deeply linked to ethics and aesthetics. Respect, freedom, and integrity as values are conveyed to a person and irretrievably linked to their truth. Similarly, the very ideas of teleology and realization, also conveyed in a hypnotic process, are deeply involved with the aesthetic, that is, what is beautiful without comparison with something else (Peirce, 1903/1997). In short, hypnosis requires a way of conceiving science with other dimensions of knowledge, in a legitimate process of *religare* (Morin, 1991/2014). Consequently, if such a transmission is bound to the therapist's own self, he also wonders about that integration into their own life. De-sign provides the transformation of the other, but also involves the therapist in this process with the notion of service. It is, roughly speaking, a submission of the ego to broader and collective aesthetic ideals that are established in the self (Colapietro, 1989).

The third implication of this book is the need to include paradox in the inquiry process. The modern paradigm of science has considerable difficulties in including paradox among its conceptions, mainly because of the notion of unique access to reality. It is true that, by the very innovation of their conceptions, many studies in Physics have made important contributions, like systems far from equilibrium, in which a relationship between stability and instability is advocated (Prigogine & Stengers, 1979). Some authors on hypnosis (Benedittis, 2020; Midol, 2015) try to import current notions from the hard sciences to understand common paradoxes in this field. Nevertheless, these contributions do not consider either the specificities of hypnotic experiences or the particularities of the human self, largely distant from them. Despite the similarities between hard sciences and trance, for example, the kinds of paradoxes are different because, unlike physical systems, human systems think, feel, and are conscious. Nevertheless, from a clinical point of view, the integration or overcoming of paradoxes is not new; a large part of the therapeutic proposal consists of generating meanings about what seems irreconcilable to the person (Erickson, 1992). It is about transforming the antinomy into the paradox, becoming a powerful generator of meanings. A person who integrates into themselves what they considered "evil" can generate great benefits, as in cases when aggressiveness can be used to assertive and leave abusive relationships.

From the point of view of understanding hypnosis, the absence of an ontological conception about the psyche (Gonzalez Rey, 2019) links the various paradoxes to the self and to hypnosis as a set of antinomies. Trance, in turn, is a paradoxical field *par excellence*, integrating different sides of experience, such as internal vs external, individual vs collective, freedom vs determination, and consciousness vs unconscious. In a trance, a person can call themselves one and multiple at the same time; the determinations of different origins and the possibilities of choice can coexist within a broader logic of life; the beautiful and the ugly, as well as good and evil, can be configured in new modes of relationship, favoring arrangements of great relevance in people's lives. Therefore, De-sign provides a significant understanding for these modes of integration, either through a semiotic notion of the self (Petrilli, 2017) or because of the emergence of intentionality. Paradoxes are not a problem to be avoided, but conditions for the process of human existence, amplified during hypnosis. Design, therefore, is an appropriate lens for the reconstruction of meaningful arrangements between the facets of the paradox, as inquiry is open to the future through intentionality (Seif, 2019). Between sleeping and waking, as between dying and being born from trance, the perspective of the future is what enables the emergence of the new.

References

Bachelard, G. (1996). *La formation de l'esprit scientifique*. Puf. (Original work published in 1938).
Bailly, J.-S. (1784). Rapport des comissaires chargés par le Roy de l'examen du magnétisme animal. [Report of the commissioners entrusted by the King with the examination of animal magnetism] (2004). In A. Bertrand (Ed.), *Du magnétisme animal en France* (pp. 70–117). (Original work published in 1824).
Benedittis, G. (2020). From quantum physics to quantum hypnosis: A quantum mind perspective. *International Journal of Clinical and Experimental Hypnosis, 68*(4), 433–450.
Bergé, C. (1995). *L'Au-delà et les Lyonnais. Mages, Médiums et Francs-Maçons du XVIII siècle*. [The Afterlife and the People of Lyon. Magi, Psychics and Freemasons of the XVIII Century]. Lugd.
Bertrand, A. (2004). *Du Magnétisme animal en France*. [Animal magnetism in France]. Harmattan. (Original work published in 1826).
Bertrand, A. (2010). *Extase. De l'état d'extase considéré comme une des causes des effets attribués au magnétisme animal*. [Ecstasy. Of the state of ecstasy considered as one of the causes of the effects attributed to animal magnetism] University of Michigan Library. (original work published in 1826).

Bioy, A., & Neubern, M. (2023). Hypnosis, science and contemporary universities: An introduction. In M. Neubern & A. Bioy (Eds.), *Hypnosis in academia: Contemporary challenges in research, healthcare and education*. Springer.

Blum, D. (2004). *Ghost hunters. William James and the search for scientific proof of life after death*. Penguin Books.

Bohm, D. (2004). *Wholeness and the implicated order*. Routledge. (Original work published in 1980).

Carroy, J. (1991). *L'hypnose et suggestion. L'invention du sujet*. [Hypnosis and suggestion. The invention of the subject] Press Universitaire de France.

Carroy, J. (1993). Magnétisme, hypnose et philosophie. [Magnetism, hypnosis and philosophy]. In I. Stengers (Ed.), *Importance de l'Hypnose*. Synthélabo.

Chertok, L., & Stengers, I. (1989). *Le Coeur et la raison. L'hypnose en question de Lavoisier à Lacan*. [The heart and the reason. The hypnosis in question from Lavoisier to Lacan]. Payot.

Clément, C. (2011). *L'Appel de la Transe*. [The Call of the Trance]. Stok.

Colapietro, V. (1989). *Peirce's approach to the self*. Suny.

Deely, J. (2009). *Intentionality and semiotics. A story of mutual fecundation*. University of Scranton Press.

Dimsdale, J. (2021). *Dark Persuasion. A history of brainwashing from pavlov to social media*. Yale University Press.

Edelman, N. (1995). *Voyantes, guérisseuses et visionaires en France: 1785–1914*. [Clairvoyants, healers and visionaries in France: 1785–1914]. Albin Michel.

Ellenberger, H. (2003). *The discovery of the unconscious*. Basic Books. (Original work published in 1970).

Erickson, M. (1958). Naturalistic techniques of hypnosis. *The American Journal of Clinical Hypnosis, 1*, 3–8.

Erickson, M. (1959). Further clinical techniques of hypnosis: Utilization techniques. *The American Journal of Clinical Hypnosis, 2*, 3–21.

Erickson, M. (1964). The "surprise" and "my friend John" techniques of hypnosis: Minimal cues and natural field of experimentation. *The American Journal of Clinical Hypnosis, 6*, 293–307.

Erickson, M. (1992). Healing in hypnosis. In E. Rossi, M. Ryan, & F. Sharp (Eds.), *The seminars, workshops, and lectures of Milton Erickson, MD* (Vol. 1). Irvington.

Erickson, M., & Rossi, E. (1979). *Hypnotherapy: An exploratory casebook*. Irvington.

Facco, E. (2021). Hypnosis and hypnotic ability between old beliefs and new evidences: An epistemological reflection. *American Journal of Clinical Hypnosis, 64*(1), 20–35. https://doi.org/10.1080/00029157.2020.1863181

Fann, K. T. (2010). *Peirce's theory of abduction*. Partidrge.

Foschi, R., & Innamorati, M. (2020). *Storia critica dela psicoterapia*. [Critical history of psychotherapy]. Raffaello Curtina Editore.

Frankl, V. (1984). *Man's search for meaning*. Pocket Books. (Original work published in 1959).

Freud, S. (1905). Sobre a psicoterapia. [On psychotherapy]. In J. Salomão (1996) (Ed.), *Obras Completas de Sigumund Freud* (Vol. VII, pp. 239–252). Imago.

Freud, S. (1912). Recomendações aos médicos que exercem a psicanálise. [Recommendations to doctors practicing psychoanalysis]. In J. Salomão (1996) (Ed.), *Obras Completas de Sigumund Freud* (Vol. XII, pp. 149–162). Imago

Freud, S. (1916). Fixação em traumas. O inconsciente. [Fixation on traumas. The unconscious]. In J. Salomão (1996) (Ed.), *Obras Completas de Sigumund Freud* (Vol. XVI, pp. 323–335). Imago

Freud, S. (1917). Terapia analítica. [Analytic therapy]. In J. Salomão (1996) (Ed.), *Obras Completas de Sigumund Freud* (Vol. XVI, pp. 523–540). Imago

Freud, S. (1921). Psicologia de grupo e análise de ego. [Group psychology and ego analysis]. In J. Salomão (1996) (Ed.), *Obras Completas de Sigumund Freud* (Vol. XVIII, pp. 89–182). Imago

Freud, S. (1937). Análise terminável e interminável. [Terminable and endless analysis]. In J. Salomão (1996) (Ed.), *Obras Completas de Sigumund Freud* (Vol. XXIII, pp. 231–274). Imago

Gallagher, S. (2014). *The Oxford handbook of the self*. Ofxord University Press.

References

Gonzalez Rey, F. (2019). Subjectivity in debate: Some reconstructed philosophical premises to advance its debates in psychology. *Journal of Theory and Social Behavior, 49*, 1–23.

Hacking, I. (2000). *The social construction of what?* Harvard University Press.

Haley, J. (1985). *Conversations with Milton Erickson.* Triangle Press.

Haley, J. (1993). *Uncommon therapy.* The Psychiatric Techniques of Milton Erickson, MD. Norton.

Hartshorne, C. & Weiss, P. (1980). *The collected papers of Charles S. Peirce (CP, 8 vol.).* Harvard University Press.

Ibri, I. (2017). *Kósmos Noetós: The metaphysical architecture of Charles Peirce.* Springer. (Original work published in 1992).

Jussieu, L. (1784). Rapport des comissaires chargés par le Roy de l'examen du magnétisme animal. [Report of the commissioners entrusted by the King with the examination of animal magnetism]. (pp. 119–152). In: A. Bertrand (2004). (Ed.). *Du magnétisme animal en France.* (Original work published in 1824).

Koyré, A. (1971). *Mystiques, Spirituels, Alchimistes du XVI Siècle Allemand.* [Mystics, spiritualists, and alchemists of sixteenth-century Germany]. Gallimard.

Kuhn, T. (2012). *The structure of scientific revolution.* University of Chicago Press. (Original work published in 1962).

Latour, B. (1996). *Petite réflexion Sur le culte modern des dieux faitiches.* [A little reflection on the modern cult of the faitich gods] Synthélabo.

Liszka, J. (1996). *A general introduction to the semeiotic of Charles Sanders Peirce.* Indiana University Press.

Lyotard, J.-F. (1979). *La condition postmodern.* [The postmodern condition]. Minuit.

Martino, E. (1999). *Le Monde Magique. Parapsychologie, Ethnologie et Histore.* [The Magical World. Parapsychology, Ethnology and History]. Synthélabo. (Original work published in 1944).

Méheust, B. (1999). *Somnambulisme et Médiumnité.* [Somnambulism and Mediumship]. Synthélabo.

Melchior, T. (1998). *Créer le Réel.* [Creating the real]. Seuil.

Mesmer, F. A. (2005). *Mémoire sur la Découverte du Magnétisme animal.* [Thesis on the discovery of animal magnetism]. Harmattan. (Original work published in 1779).

Midol, N. (2015). *De la Psychanalyse aux Thérapies Quantiques.* [From Psychoanalysis to Quantum Therapies]. Harmattan.

Morin, E. (2014). *La Méthode IV. Les Idées. Leur habitat, Leur vie, Leurs Moeur, Leur Organisations.* [Method IV. idea. Their habitat, their life, their morals, their organizations]. Points. (Original work published in 1991).

Nathan, T. (2007). *À qui j'appartiens? Écrits Sur la psychothérapie, sur la guerre et sur la paix.* [Who do I belong to? Writings on psychotherapy, on war and on peace]. Synthélabo.

Nathan, T. (2014). *Nous ne sommes pas seuls au monde.* [We are not alone in the world]. Seuil. (Original work published in 2001).

Nathan, T. & Stengers, I. (1999). *Médecins and sorciers.* [Doctors and sorcerers]. Synthélabo.

Neubern, M. (2009). *Psicologia, Hipnose e Subjetividade. Revisitando a História.* [Psychology, Hypnosis and Subjectivity. Revisiting History]. Diamante.

Neubern, M. (2016). Iconicity and complexity in hypnotic communication. *Psicologia: Teoria e Pesquisa, 32*, 1–9. https://doi.org/10.1590/0102-3772e32ne217

Neubern, M. (2018). *Hipnose, dores crônicas e complexidade: Técnicas avançadas.* [Hypnosis, chronic pain and complexity: advanced techniques]. Ed. UnB.

Neubern, M. (2022). When spirits become therapists. Ethnopsychology and hypnotherapy in Brazil. *International Journal of Latin American Religions, 1*, 1–26.

Neubern, M. (2023). Hypnosis, university and democracy: An emancipatory proposal. In M. Neubern & A. Bioy (Eds.), *Hypnosis in academia: Contemporary challenges in research, healthcare and education* (pp. 27–52). Springer.

Neubern, M., & Bioy, A. (Eds.). (2023). *Hypnosis in academia: Contemporary challenges in research, healthcare and education.* Springer.

Neubern, M., & Nogueira, H. (2019). Complex hypnosis contribution to clinical psychology. In C. Antloga, K. Brasil, S. Lordello, M. Neubern, & E. Queiroz (Eds.), *Psicologia Clínica e Cultura 4* (pp. 71–90). Technopolitik.

Nöth, W. (2015). The paradigms of iconicity in language and literature. Em M. Hiraga (org). In *Iconicity: East meets west* (pp. 13–34). John Benjamins.

O'Donohue, W. (2013). *Clinical psychology and the philosophy of science*. Springer.

Peirce, C. (1903). Pragmatism as a principle and method of right thinking. In P. Turrisi (Ed.), *The 1903 Harvard lectures on pragmatism*. (1997). State University of New York Press.

Peirce, C. (1908). A neglected argument for the reality of God. In J. Hoopes (Ed.), *Peirce on signs* (pp. 260–278). The University of North Caroline Press.

Petrilli, S. (2017). *The self as a sign, the world, and the other*. Routledge.

Prigogine, I. (1994). *Les lois du chaos*. [The laws of chaos]. Flammarion.

Prigogine, I. & Stengers, I. (1979). *La nouvelle alliance*. [The new alliance]. Gallimard.

Puységur, A. M.-J. (1784/1785). Mémoire pour Servir à l'Histoire et à l'Établissement du Magnétisme Animal. [Memory to Be Used for the History and Establishment of Animal Magnetism]. In D. Michaux (Ed.), *Aux Sources de l'Hypnose* (pp. 13–132). (2003). Imago.

Reynolds, A. (2002). *Peirce's scientific metaphysics. The philosophy of chance, law, and evolution*. Vanderbilt University Press.

Ribeiro, P. (2023). Hypnosis and academia from an Iberian perspective. In M. Neubern & A. Bioy (Eds.), *Hypnosis in academia: Contemporary challenges in research, healthcare and education* (pp. 125–152). Springer.

Romanyshyn, R. (2021). *The wounded researcher. Research with soul in mind*. Routledge.

Rossi, E., & Ryan, M. (1983). *Life reframing in hypnosis*. Irvington.

Roustang, F. (2015). *Jamais contre, d'abord. La presence d'un corps*. [Never against it, first of all. The presence of a body] Odile Jacob.

Santaella, L. (2022). *Neo-humano. A sétima revolução cognitiva do sapiens*. [Neo-human. The seventh cognitive revolution of sapiens]. Paulus.

Santos, B. (2019). *O fim do império cognitivo. A afirmação das epistemologias do Sul*. [The end of the cognitive empire. The affirmation of Southern epistemologies]. Autêntica.

Seif, F. (2013). Dialogue with Kishtta: A semiotic revelation of the paradox of life and death. *The American Journal of Semiotics, 29*, 101–115. https://doi.org/10.5840/ajs2013291-44

Seif, F. (2018). Wholophilia: De-sign and the metamorphoses of the absolute. In D. Teters & O. Neumaier (Eds.), *Metamorphoses of the absolute*. Cambridge Scholars Publishing.

Seif, F. (2019). *De-sing in transmodern world. Envisioning reality beyond absoluteness*. Peter Lang.

Seif, F. (2020a). The role of pragmatism in De-sign: Persevering through paradoxes of design and semiotics. *Cognition, 21*(1), 112–131.

Seif, F. (2020b). De-sign as a destiny of navigation: The paradox of sustaining boundaries while traversing borders. *The American Journal of Semiotics, 36*(3–4), 179–215.

Sharp, L. (2006). Secular spirituality. Reincarnation and Spiritism in nineteenth-century France. .

Stengers, I. (1995). *L'invention des sciences modernes*. [The invention of modern sciences]. Flammarion.

Stengers, I. (1996). *La volonté de faire science*. [The will to do science]. Seuil.

Stengers, I. (2001). Qu'est-ce que l'hypnose nous oblige à penser ? [What does hypnosis force us to think about?]. *Ethnopsy, 3*, 13–68.

Stengers, I. (2002). *Hypnose: Entre Magie et science*. [Hypnosis: Between magic and science]. Synthélabo.

Zeig, J. (1985). *Experiencing Erickson. An introduction to the man and his work*. Brunner/Mazel.

Chapter 3
Working With

The 18th Camel

Some groups in North Africa tell the story of an important merchant who died and left 17 camels for his sons (Bellet, 1998). The first son would receive ½ a camel, the second 1/6, and the youngest 1/9. These numbers did not allow for an exact division, because each son would receive parts of camels—and camels are only useful if they were alive. The puzzle seemed unsolvable, and the three sons were very frustrated with the impossibility of finding a solution. Nevertheless, somebody told them that a wise man was visiting that area, so they decided to invite him to help them find a solution. The sage accepted the invitation and said he would lend his own camel to favor the new proposal; later, he would retake the same camel as payment. With 18 camels, the oldest son would receive 9, the second 6, and the youngest, 2, totaling 17. The sage man took his camel back and went on his way.

Hypnosis, throughout its history, has been commonly associated with control over the other and technical applications. In this chapter, we claim that such conceptions are insufficient for understanding hypnosis, which is identified through a process of De-sign, creative and semiotic as a human encounter. That innovation, proposed by Milton Erickson (Erickson & Rossi, 1980), implies technique and influence upon the other, yes, but it goes much further: it encourages a deep dive into the aesthetic dimension as a field to be navigated rather than controlled. Dialoguing with sciences and humanities, De-sign (Seif, 2020) enables the inquiry of an essential dimension of hypnosis—human sensitivity—without which technique and effectiveness become not only arid but also lacking in rationality. Therefore, control and technique do not assume dominant status; sensitivity and feeling do, through a relational process, as these are inseparable from the notion of freedom. The perspective of the hypnotic relationship goes from a unilateral vision to that of an important partnership, in which the protagonists are involved not only as individuals but also as signs of different universes (Neubern, 2016).

> *Milton Erickson's therapy and hypnosis are commonly known for their efficacy. However, it is important to highlight that it has diverse elements that bring it closer to different therapeutic proposals* (Neubern, 2016). *Its strong relationship with Firstness approaches it to humanistic and phenomenological therapies, while its highly linked content to Secondness enables a certain confusion with cognitive and behavioral therapies. Even being as an a-theorist, Erickson does not fail to conceive notions close to those of habit in Peirce; he also values the symbolic dimension (Thirdness). In this case, he approaches symbolic therapies, such as Jungian, psychoanalysis, and narratives.*

In this sense, proposing a strong ancestral appeal, Seif (2019) places De-sign as profoundly related to the notion of "intelligence of the heart," as advocated by his Egyptian ancestors. The perspective of "I feel, therefore I am" becomes the point of departure for any inquiry about hypnosis, mainly because it situates love (notably *agape*) as the deepest form of knowing and breaks with the dichotomy between love and knowledge.

The Girl in the Wheelchair

On one occasion (Erickson & Rossi, 1979, pp. 428–442), a young woman in a wheelchair sought out Milton Erickson with the intention of undergoing hypnotherapy. After a tragic automobile accident, she had become paraplegic, incontinent as to feces and urine, and devoid of sensation from the waist down. The accident had caused her to abandon dreams that she had cherished since she was a child: getting married, owning a home, having family and children, cooking, taking care of one's house—ideas inspired by her grandmother. In her new condition, her engagement had fallen apart, and both paralysis and incontinence made her feel quite unwell. In nearly 10 years, she managed to resume her university studies, but she no longer saw a chance for herself in university life, because of the numerous limitations she experienced. Thus, without professional and family prospects, the young woman felt increasingly depressed and developed strong suicidal thoughts. While attending a lecture by Erickson, she understood that hypnotherapy might help her create an intelligent philosophy for life through very deep trance. She further requested that Eriksson be realistic: if he wanted to be kind and compassionate, she would understand that he did not have hopes of a happier future for her. She said she would be back the following Saturday, so he had time to think about that problem.

However, even during that first session, the young woman asked Erickson to hypnotize her and propose post-hypnotic suggestions to prevent her from possible suicidal thoughts. Because of her high motivation, she quickly entered a sleepwalking trance, through which Erickson was able to exercise some of her abilities through phenomena such as depersonalization, time distortion, and hypermnesia, which would be useful in later training. Then Erickson asked her to visualize and listen to an orchestra with a singer: the song referred to the finger bone, as it connected to the foot boner, the leg bone, and so on. Shortly afterwards, another orchestra piece was suggested; she began to visualize and listen, at the same time, to "Doing What Comes Naturally." Erickson asked her if she heard that with one ear and the songs with the other. After gathering more information with someone close to her, Erickson prepared a lengthy induction for the following session.

On Saturday, her therapy session lasted from 1:00 to 5:00 in the afternoon. Erickson began their meeting by producing a careful analysis at the typewriter. She received a copy of the material (to be copied on carbon paper) with some gaps in the sentences; the original was kept in his drawer. Three slightly altered copies were to be kept in different envelopes. She asked him what he planned to do with that material, and he said if that case worked out, he would consider publishing it, but added: "What else?" Still in a waking state, she was told she could come out of trance any time she wanted and that she could analyze carefully everything the therapist told her. He would then give her a series of important information, and the same recommendations would be repeated during trance. After inducing her again into somnambulistic trance, Erickson replayed both orchestras at the same time. A few minutes passed and they were removed, so that the young woman could enjoy, without haste, the information that would be passed to her. However, he said that her condition was really difficult, as not all men might be attracted to her. Then he told her that men were curious beings: they could be attracted to and marry anyone; he told her stories about duckbill women, giraffe-necked women, and Hottentots. He pondered how hard it would be for anyone to tell that Mrs. Hippopotamus would not be attractive to Mr. Hippopotamus. He produced some descriptions about a child who waits for Santa Claus, with all his dreams and expectations. These stories were also mixed with suggestions about body parts: which side was dominant, the connections between them, what she felt first etc., as he tried to verify what she knew about her body, consciously and unconsciously. Erickson also included suggestions about body sensations, highlighting multiple forms of sensations and pleasure one could experience.

Then she added what she could do for herself. That she would go into a house and see a disheveled child, with a dirty face, bruises, a runny nose, but that she would be happy to see it and would very much like to take it in her arms. Later on, she would see another clean, well-dressed child, with combed hair and the air of someone who asked: "who in the world would not like to catch me?". Erickson added that she would not agree with that child and that she would like to find her parents and slap them; she would not want to be received by that child in that way. At the end, Erickson added (Erickson & Rossi, 1979, p. 438): "Man has but one place to have an orgasm – a woman has many." Then he suggested to her that at 5 o'clock he would take her to the car and, with a gesture of a finger in his mouth, instructed the driver to drive quietly. The following Saturday, the session was focused on her professional interests, specifically her postgraduate studies. Nothing therapeutic was requested, and Erickson remained in the process.

Two years after therapy, the young woman had married a doctor who specialized in chemistry and biology of the colon, with whom she had four children. Ten years after therapy, Erickson was supposed to hold a conference at the city where she lived, so she called him and invited him to lunch. She said that after he gave several lectures to her university class, she felt she should invite him to lunch, even though she did not know him personally. Then Erickson presented her with a closed envelope asked her to put it in her bag. He handed her another and asked her to read it and fill in the gaps. She blushed and told him that if another man asked her she would call the police, but as he was someone she cared for, she accepted. He further told her that if she did her homework, he would take a copy and, at another moment, fill in the same gaps. To the young woman's surprise, the answers were virtually identical. Additionally, the sealed envelope had pretty much the same answers. After a long pause, the young woman wondered if she had been his patient at some point and that she remembered that he had given her something very good but that she would not have had time to thank him. She asked him if he would publish anything about her case, to which Erickson replied that he could publish as a general way of working in hypnosis but nothing that focused on her identity.

Iconicity and Love

A traditional reading of this case could highlight the technical precision with which Erickson approached his patient: dissociation involving two songs (as a way of taking her focus off a single idea), the choice of the second song, the use of the typewriter (conveying seriousness about his demands), stories about love choices (which countered her belief of incapacity), the story about the untidy child (something more real and coherent with his desire), references to body parts, pleasure, and her own personality, with the induction of amnesia, as she managed to let go of the moment and process her new constructions more autonomously. Erickson met her demands accurately and effectively; he saved her life not only by preventing her suicide, but also by fostering a context in which she could take the reins of her own life and realize her dreams of getting married and becoming a mother should not be discarded.

However, there is something deeper in this case: the intense relationship between iconicity and love as *agape*. Regarding iconicity, there are several situations created by Erickson that were shown to the patient, carrying strong suggestive power, such as the conditions he posited for her because she was a wheelchair user. The content of the stories told and his work with future memories (which can be considered in the case of that "dirty and untidy" child) are also constituted as significant allegories (Neubern, 2021b), as they involve central themes for the young woman. In general, therapy was constituted as a great dramatic scenario, in which actions were fully imbued with meaning, engaging the patient and promoting an emancipatory context for her. Such an emphasis on iconicity does not seem far from therapies from traditional non-scientific knowledges, as widely shown in ethnopsychology (Nathan,

2001/2014). In that field, the metaphorical content of words and actions have a considerable impact on people's concrete lives.

> *Iconicity is the capacity of icons to convey qualities from objects they represent* (Jappy, 2013; Nöth, 2015). *Since there are no perfect icons (i.e., pure quality), they always have some level of existence—hence the term hypo-icon. One usually works with three types of hypo-icons attached to it—images, diagrams, and metaphors. Images (hieroglyphs, emoticons) transmit characteristics; diagrams portray traits linked to the relations amongst objects. Metaphors are the juxtaposition of two fields to promote new meanings. Allegories are variations of metaphors* (Jappy, 2013). *In metaphors, there is a juxtaposition between two fields that is commonly known. In the expression "Michael Jordan was a monster," basketball is linked to something extraordinary, such as a monster, to highlight the genius of that basketball player. In allegories this relationship is only explicit when the interlocutor has prior knowledge about the fields. This occurs, for example, with certain political protest songs, Masonic signs, religious signs, among others.*

Iconicity, in turn, cannot be detached from love, as it is a constituent of De-sign (Seif, 2019), because technical forms of the case under analysis could not be conceived through simple intellectual exercise or a merely mechanical purpose of producing efficient results. When analyzing the case of the young woman in depth to capture it with such precision, Erickson engaged in a deep dive into himself, evoking for his own self the figures of the artist, the bulldog, and the mathematician. By immersing *himself in himself* and embodying logic to deal with it, Erickson assumed an attitude permeated by *agape*, either by promoting a resumption of greater ideals (life, marriage, children), or by executing in his actions the ideal of the therapist who makes themselves available when caring for the other. *Agape*, therefore, appears first, while the resumption of an ideal, that is so pure and admirable in itself, can hardly be mentioned. At the same time, it constitutes a way of promoting *religare*, in terms of new connections between ego and self—and in a perspective similar to Ludwig Binswanger's (1935/2008): *communicatio* (friendship) and *communio* (love). Through hypnogenesis, her empathy and friendship led her towards deeper connections (love) as the basic condition humans have, to connect to one another.

If we consider Peirce's evolutionary perspective[1] (cited in Ibri, 1992/2017; Raposa, 1989), *agape* also presents explanatory possibilities to the case, because, when associated with iconicity, it becomes possible to first access dimensions of subjective experiences, such as quale-consciousness (CP[2] 6.228) in their fluidity

---

[1] Peirce proposed an evolutionist reading based on love, hence the notion of agapistic (CP 6.306). Based on it, he integrated different notions, such as tychatic (Darwin's chance) and anacatic (Lamark's necessity).
[2] Hartshorne & Weiss (1980) is the reference of CP, which means the Collected Papers of Charles Peirce. I adopted the CP due to the fact that this is the most known reference among semioticians of Peirce's collected papers.

and unity, which do not fail to favor multiplicity. The creative and semiotic aspects of this field of experiences, as it invites De-sign, becomes accessible to the therapist-patient duo by the very context of Firstness created in that hypnotic setting. As a result, once inserted in such a field filled with freshness of the new, changes become possible. It is a field of experiences or perhaps even of new modalities for consciousness (Houser, 1983): habits that organize other processes are malleable, and even situations which had been considered irreversible for the patient can undergo unexpected alterations. Although the young woman had achieved results she had expected for a long time, the ways in which she did so carried the sign of the unexpected, since neither she or anyone in her closest social circle could have predicted that she would be able to marry someone who could accept her, have an active sex life, and become a mother of four children.

At the same time, *agape* constituted itself as a teleological process in her life: the ideal she begins to pursue structures her experience. In other words, the "intelligent philosophy" she sought during deep trance in hypnosis allowed her to reconfigure various parts of her subjectivity, which had been, until then, disfigured and disconnected by the tragedy she had experienced. She lived as if her body parts were disconnected, and she could not feel like a woman, capable of loving and living her sexuality; furthermore, that unpleasant appearance and smell, added to paralysis, disconnected her from her greatest dreams, as previously claimed. However, as she reconnected with her own ideals, these processes were reconfigured into a new condition of body image,[3] and the patient made herself available to her dreams, so they could "come true naturally," according to the music introduced during her first trance induction. The connection with a greater ideal promoted her creative and organizing capacity for *agape*, repairing her disconnected processes which immersed her in deep suffering. In other words, that connection with *agape* promoted a De-signer *status* for her own life.

However, in addition to a reconfiguration her experience following that tragedy, hypnotherapy, founded on *agape*, fostered yet another essential aspect: the incorporation, in her own self, of signs linked to Milton Erickson's self. Not without reason, even under severe amnesia, the patient retained feelings about him—a fondness—that led her to turn to someone she thought was unknown and invite him to lunch. This feeling of fondness, as a sign of an agapistic relationship, maintained the bond between therapist and patient; it was also probably the basis for changes that continued on, as the patient worked to fulfill her dreams. The presence of these signs in her own subjectivity, therefore, seems to have worked in such a way to maintain a minimal bond of consciousness to the therapist through fondness—whose cause was unknown to her. The very intentionality generated there by a "new philosophy of life" was marked by social influences, but it did not exempt it from autonomous action at the same time that it implied a search for new consciousnesses, even if those came from forgotten foundations.

---

[3] Erickson conceived that the knowledge of a patient's body image is the first task of the therapist (Haley, 1985). In general, body image is a complex concept, as people develop images, feelings, meanings, and ideas about themselves (Gallagher & Zahavi, 2008; Gallagher, 2014).

Her recognition of Erickson as her old therapist brought the paradoxical surprise of the new as the old, beloved, and forgotten character. Her recollection of him was that she had attended some of his lectures, not that she had been his patient. That strange man, as he listed details of his sexual life in the envelopes, presented her with signs that carried a strong content of intimacy and privacy, which would not have been known by a stranger. De-sign inquiry, therefore, of this case implies reflection on one's own love, as *agape* and *eros* as well, as most people might not conceive of intimacy with an unknown person or someone long forgotten. The hypnotic context, with *agape* as the basis of their relationship, provided an increase in the porosity of the self (Petrilli, 2017), favoring transmission of sign systems that were quite relevant for the reconfiguration of central themes in their experiences. These signs were fundamental for important processes of semiosis related to her body image, sexuality, and motherhood. The future existed as a teleological perspective, accessible. Nevertheless, most of these processes seem to have occurred, to a large extent, beyond explicit deliberations by the young woman, whose feelings guided her towards an aesthetic ideal (her dreams). All previous history between these protagonists has been preserved as active memory in the creation of semiotic processes that made the difference for her. Thus, it becomes possible to state that what is at the basis of love, in its various forms, is unknown, while what is loved is at once old and new.

Being One and Three at the Same Time

Cases such as the one discussed here lead us to deduce that the therapeutic context created in hypnosis seems to transport its protagonists to a different field of experiences, in which references of time, space, and matter are, at some level, different from everyday ones. It is not only Erickson's considerable precision in his perception and his way of intervening that is striking in terms of De-sign inquiry, but also that partnership jointly established at a different level of consciousness. The notion of *agape* (Peirce, 1893/1998; Seif, 2019) involves them while seeming to transcend them. In navigating this joint field permeated by quali-consciousness, there is a prevalence of possibilities shown in the transit of verbal references taken as absolute from modern human experiences to other more fluid and elusive ones, typical of transmodernity (Seif, 2020). If verbs are also icons (Nöth, 2015), in such a condition, fluidity becomes even greater, since the idea of movement and potentiality are even more stressed in the hypnotic relationship. Therefore, modern psychologists, usually eager for the permanence of diagnosis, intervention, and results, will find it difficult to understand and deal with similar processes, unless they are not willing to review their own notions of reality and understand that modern knowledge, far from a definitive answer about the world, is only a possibility to understand it.

However, mere chance of an elusive field such as hypnosis would not allow for the existence of knowledge, not even of some form of rational intervention. If chance is somehow implicated in new forms of order both in metaphysics (Ibri,

1992/2017) and in science itself (Prigogine, 1994), the clinical relationship does not escape this rule either, because it posits that an elusive field as hypnosis demands alternatives of rationality, not their abandonment. De-sign inquiry requires, therefore, certain attitudes that provide the therapist with the possibility of navigating that field of diaphanous spaces (Gebser, 1949/1985) and polychronic time (Hall, 1969/1983). Considering Carroy's (1991) important statement, that one must be at least two to do psychology, this proposal considers that the therapist is at least three if they are to act as a De-sign inquirer or therapist. In other words, the navigation recommended through De-sign, even if it favors abduction, implies transit between three distinct phenomenological attitudes of great relevance for inquiry in general and for hypnosis in particular.

The First Attitude—To Be With

Several people have been impressed by Erickson's ability to capture the subtlety of aspects of the lives of his students and patients (Zeig, 1985), as discussed here. He can even, following Sebeok's and Umiker-Sebeok's (1979) ideas, be compared to a kind of Sherlock Holmes of hypnosis, given his legendary ability to capture sets of signs that would go unnoticed by most people. Therefore, it is not clear where these abilities might have come from, in addition to his considerable willingness to dedicate himself fully to the people under his care. In the perspective adopted here, that capacity for focus and perception is in itself a hypnotic process since it is characterized by entry into a field of experiences in which common references to reality are changed in a radical way. It is the adoption of a first attitude, that is, a clinical attitude permeated by Firstness, that the therapist uses in moving through processes that share quali-consciousness to a certain extent. That attitude is also characterized by the phenomenological figure of the artist (Peirce, 1903/1997), whose intense discerning capacity is crossed by sensitivity and an aesthetic sense. The chart below is quite illustrative of that attitude.

In Chart 3.1, Firstness is shown as the dominant experience for a clinical attitude toward inquiry, which implies the relevance of feeling, qualities, and potential. The signs that permeate this field of experiences are not necessarily imaginary, though vague and potential, like focal, tactile, and kinesthetic distortions that present themselves indefinitely. In terms of therapeutic relationships, it approaches humanist and existential schools (Ribeiro, 2021), emphasizing the human encounter as present in space (here) and time (now). There is in such a form of relationship the idea of field, initially developed by Kurt Lewin (1951), greatly influenced by contemporary authors (Ferro & Basile, 2015; Ribeiro, 2021). By experiencing, each in their own way, a joint dissociative process, the protagonists of the relationship develop a mutual focus to increase perception and receptivity regarding signs that seem to spring from different points in the field. Usually, these do not proceed from formal or explicit hypnosis, but from an empathic mode of relating; that field provides intense exchange of signs between the protagonists, given that the usual porosity of

Chart 3.1 Terms for Understanding Attitude First or Being With

Phenomenological category	Character	Verbs of reference	Role	Therapist signs, experience, and reflexivity	Signs of autonomy
Firstness; establishment of a relational field; present (time); quality, feeling, and potentiality.	Artist; capacity of discernment; aesthetic sense; return to childhood; abduction.	To be with; to become available; to accept; to feel with; to love.	Building foundations of the relationship based on feelings.	Hypo-icons (images, diagrams, and metaphors); signs of Firstness.	Senses (images, feelings, impressions).

the self (Petrilli, 2017) tends to expand in a hypnogenic interaction. Sometimes that exchange happens in such a subtle way that only the protagonists notice what is happening, according to approximations in some reports on telepathy (Méheust, 1999).

> *The first attitude is fundamental to the clinic of hypnosis, as well as De-sign. It is founded on a relational contract based on feeling and imagining, enabling the therapeutic process. Also linked to abduction, it allows therapist and patient to navigate a shared De-sign inquiry. This is the first step towards the integration between caring (practice) and knowing (thought), that is, between two dimensions dichotomized by the modern paradigm of science* (Morin, 1991/2014).

Nevertheless, merely capturing and collecting signs would not imply a first attitude if there is no predominance of feeling. On the one hand, this refers to the figure of the artist, who is able to maintain impressive technical and discriminative capacities during that deep dive into their own subjectivity, where they connect to imaginary, mnemonic, and sentimental processes. If, in a certain way, imagination precedes intelligence (Colapietro, 1989), the artist's technical capacity and accurate gaze depend on a similar connection with themselves; the same applies to the therapist. The first attitude is predominantly infused by abduction, the central foundation for constructing knowledge (Fann, 2010). The emergence of hypotheses, impressions, fantasies, and images, later on, will feed more complex processes in the therapist's thoughts. There are more than a few references to Erickson (Rosen, 1982) resorting to abduction through self-hypnosis and accessing the wisdom of his own unconscious to deal with more complex issues in his clinic or everyday life. Such a process of reconnection between ego and self is also consistent with De-sign, as a form of rebirth, infused with the freshness of the new, emerges from these new processes of semiosis and demands an infantile attitude, to a certain extent, whose sensitivity enables this new to be recognized and welcomed. The level of detail, immersion, imagination, and creativity that a child can use in a game confirm this idea, although the skills that they potentially present do not always appear in adult life. In short, the therapist-artist brings with themselves a child who, despite small and fragile appearances, can be a great guide during a process of De-sign inquiry.

Still considering Chart 3.1, the question of feeling also refers to the required reflexivity in a hypnotherapeutic process, because perceiving so many sign configurations is not restricted to an organic basis, devoid of experience and culture. Following Merleau-Ponty's (1945/2008) ideas, perception is based on lived systems of the body and permeated by different semiotic processes that generate meaning. Therefore, the therapist connects with these processes so they can not only access an experienced approach to the patient in this relational field, but they also construe a relevant diagram to assist them in how they relate to that other. Most of these signs at this level of relationship arise from perceptual judgments (Peirce, 1903/1997) that emerge from experiences without the inquirer's control, but can constitute precious indexes or diagrams about what happens in a given relational moment. Erickson, for example, soon realized that the young woman would not accept any pity from him, so his lines would need to be logical for her—and she would be very critical in analyzing them. Despite his welcoming attitude, he realized the importance of being frank with her, as she had probably suffered enough through the compassion of other people from her social life.

On the other hand, feeling is also present as a foundation for the hypnotic field, as for the therapeutic relationship itself, and capable of lasting for many years even without the joint physical presence of both. Hypnogenesis plays a central role here, because a therapist without empathic capacity or, in the present perspective, devoid of *agape*, could hardly set themselves as welcoming and available without being betrayed by insincerity. Thus, several biographical references about Erickson (Erickson & Keeney, 2006; Zeig, 1985) highlight the considerable suffering he experienced as a polio victim and wheelchair user in the last 30 years of his life, including severe pain, allergies, and various physical limitations. It would not be an exaggeration to say that his own suffering had deeply mobilized him towards caring for that young woman. The receptive and welcoming characteristic of *agape* does not mean a complete absence of judgment, since perceptual judgments are always present; however, they refer to an intense and loving focus on the person that allows them to get closer through affection, because they feel accepted in the way they present themselves. It is a basic moment of bond formation, as protagonists exercise their *being with*, at the same time they integrate themselves and interpenetrate each other semiotically. The idea of *imagining-with* (Seif, 2019) gains importance here, since this fusional tendency of the selves (Colapietro, 1989), as if they were building a common self, is quite pertinent.

The imaginative and sentimental field formed also has strong connections with the verb *dispose*, which characterizes the movement of potentiality towards creation and transformation. By the very lack of definition that characterizes qualitative processes, there is no way to determine a specific meaning that is available to the other, as psychoanalysts do with listening: the therapist is available as a whole, fully present to this other. There is not yet an interest by the therapist in deliberate knowledge about this other, but in being with them and welcoming them, supporting the statement that one cannot talk about someone, but with someone (Neubern, 2018a). That first basis of the therapeutic contract refers to the Latin etymology for the word "*acordo*"[4] (agreement), which refers to a legitimate consent between the parties. In Latin languages, consent is associated with the heart which, in addition to being the organ culturally related to feelings, carries the same etymological root—*cardio*. In short, the word agreement can be conceived as a contract between hearts, as both agree to contribute to a cause, similarly to the therapeutic contract (Neubern, 2010).

In accepting the young woman's quirks and demands, Erickson also proved himself as attentive and receptive to a range of resources that were present, but inactivated and isolated by suffering. His ability to think logically, as well as his intense desire to pursue one's dreams and step out of the victim condition were initially perceived as ignored signs from her world and, later, through inductive and deductive processes, transformed into stories and attitudes proposed during hypnosis that promoted relevant changes in her life. The processes triggered there—feelings, images, and impressions—became the foundation for a joint navigation in the young woman's subjectivity, allowing for the experience of *co-moving* (Neubern, 2021a), that is, the fusion between shared emotion and subtle movements of navigation applied through the "internalization" of the therapist as a sign, even if physically absent.

In dramatic terms, the phenomenological artist became a philosopher, embodied by the therapist, and never revealed to the young woman because that intelligent philosophy required someone with a wise attitude to suggest possible paths without pitying her miserable situation. Here, the idea of De-sign navigation is present since Erickson assumed this role and acted based on it throughout various themes that were relevant to the young woman. Moreover, an unexplained action establishes a way of introducing, at a level beyond consciousness, the sign of the philosopher who, in addition to conveying interesting knowledge to her, exercised a special form of care towards her, who had until then been isolated in her suffering. On this plane, navigated amongst a profusion of icons, the philosopher was able to exercise his true role as advocated by Socrates—that of a midwife of souls. Because of the stories told, roles and scenes arranged for the patient went far beyond an explanatory function; they formed icons presented to her that, through their suggestive and vague influence, favored new dispositions so that she could place herself in other ways before her own life. Although her somnambulistic trance could suggest clear passivity, this semiotic process occurred at an implicit plane, triggered different levels of agency by the patient, especially those linked to Firstness systems. Erickson's active role and the patient's condition allow us to conceive that the therapeutic relationship between the two was a legitimate partnership.

Regarding the therapist's experience, hypo-icons (Jappy, 2013) were important references for understanding, not only in terms of their abundant presence in such

---

[4] The words *accord* (French) and *acordo* (Portuguese and Spanish) come from the Latin word *accordare* (agreement), as well as the Latin word *cardio*, heart.

processes but also as a logical path for their thinking. If images refer to their objects by mere transmission of qualities, they refer to signs of First-Firstness. In relational terms, these were moments of pure or nearly pure *being with*, as the therapist was available to contemplate the other and live the eternity of the present. As highlighted by humanists (Ribeiro, 2021), it is a fundamental moment for laying the foundations of the relationship of *being with* someone practically without any deliberate thought. It is also the moment to feed the therapist's subjectivity, favoring ego-self reconnections as a creative and imaginative process: profusions of signs can arise from chaotic movements. These signs, permeated by abduction, are not necessarily useful for technical and diagnostic requirements, but are valuable for the therapist so they can perceive possible indices of how, in one's self, they are affected by the patient's presence. Diagrams, on the other hand, refer to Second-Firstness by pointing to relationships between the objects they represent. Slightly deductive, they start off a representation of the other and, though still imprecise, they offer the first lines of relationship with this other: an intuition about how to move in this relational arena, an impression linked to action-consequence; in short, an initial scheme about possible relational games that will arise.

Thus, if images constitute the therapist's first impressions, characterized by what is informally called "feeling", diagrams are rudimentary representations of this relationship, outlining more deliberate actions for later plans and applications. In the therapist's experience, that characterizes a clinical process, such as the one discussed here. There are moments of emergence of images (impressions, sensations, images, feelings) and others that engage with a certain organization of these signs (diagrams), highlighting functionality. With abduction as its central axis, and involving certain reflexivity, the process of De-sign thinking here seems much more related to a connectivity with oneself and with the other, guided by signs in order to privilege the formation of bonds through feeling. There is certainly some deliberation, but its scope is still small, since the integrity of the protagonists, founded by networks of feelings and emotions (Colapietro, 1995), is dominant. Being an experienced therapist, Erickson would never give up such moments, especially in the face of a complex and delicate clinical situation, like his young patient's. Although there are no explicit statements on his part about what De-sign might have been like in terms of diagrams and images, his short stories, wordplay, dissociations, and dramatizations comprised true works of art. In them, in addition to precise similarities between the semiotics of interventions and the patient's demands (Neubern, 2021b), there were also key qualities for that therapeutic process, such as humor, wisdom, ingenuity, simplicity, and beauty itself. Only someone who was deeply familiar with the first attitude would be capable of such constructions.

However, metaphors imply an apex of thinking in the midst of this abductive ocean. As Third-Firstness signs (Jappy, 2013), they represent objects by similarity and convention, involving icons and symbols. By definition (CP 2.227), metaphors juxtapose two distinct fields of knowledge, leading the interlocutor to a conclusion based on similarity. For example, in the expression "love is blind" the fields of human feelings (love) and the field of physical limitations (blindness) are juxtaposed to communicate mistaken gestures by people in love, such as insanity, deviance or lack of perception of obvious things. In the therapist's experience, metaphors can arise spontaneously or from the bricolage through which De-sign operates, connecting images and diagrams that form some symbolic theme. The name of a film, a myth, a work of art, a joke, a book, or a TV series can institute important metaphors for the therapist, who begins to perceive this other through the vague power of an icon—pertinent as a symbol, though. It would not be difficult to find similarities between Erickson's story of the young patient and mythological heroes and heroines in different mythologies around the world (Campbell, 1959; Clément, 2014). These are usually beautiful and virtuous; they go through a tragedy or adventure, come close to death, find help from someone powerful (sages, gods), and return victorious and more aware of reality. Faced with a considerable range of perceptions (composed of images and diagrams) regarding the patient's potential, it is possible that Erickson conceived her as a heroine still affected by tragedy—but who, with his help, would be able to resume her life and fulfill her dreams. It is important to understand that myths are not static, and they can have several versions. They are explanatory potentialities and mix with other myths that engage people much more by example (similarity)than by determination or law.

The experience of the therapist described above, in their relations with the logic of hypo-icons, leads to an understanding of how their interlocutor gains autonomy. On the one hand, the role of feelings can be the basis for a semiotic link between different processes, between systems disconnected by suffering, or by temporality itself. Even without remembering her therapy sessions with Erickson, her feelings took charge and sustained that vague fondness from that meeting, maintaining a bond amid deep dimensions of the self and her everyday actions. Even without remembering her former therapist, she sought him out and invited him to lunch. The therapeutic influence from a hypnotic context promoted her semiotic processes, linked to feeling and imagination, in order to supply her world with basic "raw materials" so she could reactivate her potentialities, generate meaning about important aspects, and seek her dreams.

On the other hand, feelings, impressions, and images seem to serve as Lady Welby's[5] senses (Liszka, 1996), that is, as interpretants linked to Firstness. In the specific case of the young woman, the senses seemed a "remedy", given her deep scars, physical and subjective, from her tragedy. Furthermore, they were also "food" for a thirsty soul, to live her own dreams. The typical navigation of De-sign (Seif, 2019) only became possible to the patient thanks to supplying her world with a profusion of signs linked to the senses, including images and feelings. They served as the basis for new forms of agency and meaning, as she pursued the most important dreams of her existence—it would not be possible to navigate a rocky sea with little water, that is, an internal landscape marked by ruptures and paralysis of almost all existential movements. Thus, autonomy went through a process of world reconstruction, especially through a reconnection (*religare*) with oneself. Even without

---

[5] Victoria Welby was an important collaborator with Pierce's work, with whom she held intense correspondence. In her theory on interpretants, she proposed that senses (images, impressions, feelings), with meanings and significance, act at the level of agency (Liszka, 1996).

awareness of most processes, her actions were successful, in therapeutic terms, because of the deeper integration she began to develop with herself.

The Second Attitude—Dance With

Hypnosis is also usually associated with a technical field, marked by effectiveness and little theoretical depth. Whether due to epistemological and historical controversies associated with it (Stengers, 2002) or due to Erickson's a-theoretical character, academic reflection around the field does not seem to be its greatest appeal among therapists and researchers (Neubern, 2018a). Both are much more interested in technical possibilities, the effectiveness of which has been demonstrated in different fields of application. Nevertheless, the perspective of De-sign allows us to conceive that technique is inserted in an interactive dimension marked by rapport (Melchior, 1998), a discipline of marked mutual responsiveness that induces and maintains trance. Although it also shares dives in quali-consciousness, this field is permeated by Secondness, as a field of experiences in which processes further delimit borders because they exist beyond mere potentialities. A second attitude, therefore, suggests a transition movement between spontaneous reactivity in a relationship to playful and calculated interactions in a game—like dance. Chart 3.2 introduces the main terms for their understanding.

Chart 3.2 above illustrates the second attitude during clinic: as in inquiry, it highlights Secondness as the dominant phenomenological category. Here, there is a prevalence of signs related to different forms of reactions to an event, to the existing individual that has a greater definition in terms of form. Approaching cognitive and behavioral therapies (Beck, 1995), the notion of the field remains (Ribeiro, 2021), but it is slightly modified: there is neither a tendency to absorb the protagonists into themselves nor to merge with one another since Secondness is characterized by the existing. However, the interactive content also refers to trance for the very

Chart 3.2 Terms related to the second attitude—*Dance With*

Phenomenological category	Character	Verbs of reference	Role	Therapist's signs of experience and reflexivity	Signs of autonomy
Secondness; beginning chain of reactions (past, history); reaction; event; existence.	Bulldog; persistence, insistent observation; beginning experimentation; diagnostic, test; ethics, effort; deduction.	To dance with; react to; to interact; follow clues; to touch; mess with.	Construction of rapport; technical application.	Indices and signs of Secondness.	Meanings; teleological and telenomic changes.

responsiveness that constitutes rapport, marked by an intense exchange of signs that, albeit occasionally subliminal, are more delineated than the imaginary and vague signs of Firstness. One may have the sensation of touch that seems to come from outside, because the boundaries of ego, in terms of inside and outside, are more delimited than in the first attitude. In terms of therapist awareness, there is both a reaction of surprise before an unexpected sign, that is, something linked to the involuntary, and a deliberation to interact with it, like dancers do when they react to unknown movements. In such cases, as they observe and perceive the type of dance introduced by their partner, they can accompany it.

Before his patient, Erickson demonstrated capacities of perception and intervention out of the ordinary. The level of detail of the suggestions, their symbolic relevance to important themes for the young woman, the care undertaken (being logical, and not displaying pity in the face of her tragic condition), and the type of role assumed demanded considerable preparation from him. More than that, Erickson demonstrated intense dedication, as which he evaluated and reevaluated, as usual (Zeig, 1985), different hypotheses and paths they should follow to apply interventions. This level of dedication shows that the therapist embodied the phenomenological figure of the bulldog (Peirce, 1903/1997), whose role is linked to commitment to observation and analysis of a given field. For most Americans, bulldogs have become known since the colonization, as extremely persistent dogs, whether when hunting, fighting, dealing with livestock, or defense (Manfield, 2016). Various reports state they only dropped a target (like game) when their objective was reached (i.e. their submission or death), ensuring that animal's reputation of extreme persistence and loyalty. In Erickson's case, reports are common (Zeig, 1985) about how he studied a person's case for hours on end, sometimes for days, reading, thinking about interventions, writing hypnotic suggestions, and planning therapeutic strategies. His bulldog manifested itself, generally, around two highly integrated points: the collection of signs about the other and the selection of hypotheses prepared for application in tandem with his patients. It was an intense process of deduction (Peirce, 1903/1997).

> *The second attitude is linked to the choreography of the relationship, in concrete terms, and to the technical application. However, being permeated by the Secondness, it should not be conceived in isolation, as much research that focuses only on concrete signs do. From the perspective of De-sign (Seif, 2019), it is based on Firstness, the basis of the therapeutic relationship. It is also linked to the Thirdness, either because of the rebellion of the existents ones regarding the generality of habits and laws, or because of the results achieved beyond expectation (desirable outcomes).*

At first, the collection of signs enables the partial elaboration of a diagnosis, not in the classical sense of the term, but as a specific set of arrangements to each person. Still relying heavily on Firstness, especially during creative moments, this collection implies a pivotal moment of understanding the other: how a person thinks, acts, feels, relates to others and the world. More importantly, Erickson (1992) also paid attention to modes of relationship as this person related to their unconscious, with what escaped deliberations, especially in terms of potentialities and hypnotic capacity. That type of diagnosis was developed with focus on the uniqueness of each person, though it did not relinquish its relationship with a generic background (Erickson, 1953). At the same time, the bulldog's attentive gaze focused on minimal cues (Erickson, 1964), that is, on the most subtle and significant indices presented by the person, like their gaze, a tension of musculature of the face, the way their hand might shake, muscle tension, changes in facial expression, among others. Secondly, these signs could be related to regular processes, which tended to be repeated on a daily basis, such as preferences, tastes, habits, among others. In short, transit between minimal cues and more general tendencies of a given person were seen and reviewed by the bulldog, until hypotheses could be created and developed.

In the second attitude, great importance is attached to observation, implying two fundamental aspects. On the one hand, a receptive posture by the therapist perceives movements, words, expressions, gestures, among others, and allows them, little by little, to take shape in broader configurations around their interlocutor. Once they are understood in broad terms, that observation can be repeated several times, either in person or by recollection by the therapist on their records. Some aspects occasionally seem to be missing for a process to become more intelligible, triggering an aspect that oscillates between intuition and rationality. A poorly told story, contradictions between what is said and shown, or involuntary signals of the body in the face of a certain topic often provide that sort of doubt. Hence the importance of indices, as they act as clues during investigation. On the other hand, there is intense reflection on hypotheses formed from the intelligible articulations of the signs emerging in the face of the therapist. They must contemplate the universe of this other (Erickson, 1985) mainly in terms of logic (in their constructions of meanings and agencies) and world references (as modes of reasoning and use of physical senses). Both observation and reflection on hypotheses are based on the sentimental foundation from the first attitude, the first level of therapeutic contract. On this affective soil, created by the first attitude, the technique comes to life, i.e., acquires a teleological dimension and can become an extension of the therapist's self. At the same time, both are also based on an eidetic posture (Ibri, 1992/2017), through which the therapist seeks to be faithful to the ways in which the universe of the other is presented. Even emphasizing the person's potentialities through hypnogenesis, Erickson sought to influence his patients via a set of semiotic systems consistent with those from his world. Understandably, he was critical of imposing therapist theories on the worldviews of their patients (Haley, 1985).

In general, the role of the second attitude relates to the formation of therapeutic rapport (Melchior, 1998), that is, to a mode of relationship characterized by mutual responsiveness between protagonists. The relational field formed through that rapport keeps the therapist conscious and focused on their interlocutor, allowing him to apply techniques masterfully. It is a moment with a certain dissociative content, highly permeated by the phenomenological possibility of movement—instead of the aesthetic contemplation consistent with the first attitude. The therapist, as De-signer, transitions between the first attitude, as they perceive themselves as connected to the feeling that underlies a relationship, and the second attitude, as they establish a game of deliberate influence with the other through interaction and technique. While they dive into themselves and connect to feelings, images, and fantasies, they also connect to the other, with a focus marked by sensitivity and eidetic objectivity. In other words, in the second attitude *Eidos* (Ibri, 1992/2017) prevails over feeling, assuming a role of affective support by the therapist and by the roles it tends to play during the process of clinical treatment. Otherwise, they could easily disconnect from the other, losing sight of one's uniqueness and therapeutic needs. The precision with which the techniques employed by Erickson in the case at hand were thought out and executed would not have been possible had it not been for his strong emphasis on the eidetic character of the second attitude.

The attentive reader may wonder, in the face of such an exhibition, about the role of De-sign (Seif, 2019) regarding the second attitude. Certainly, the rigidity of the therapist linked to that attitude might lead the process towards a restriction to the mechanical application of hypnotic techniques. The risk of an instrumentalist vision turns not only towards a limitation of thought (Psillos & Zorzato, 2021), but also to serious clinical consequences, even capable of risking the patient's integrity. However, De-sign (Seif, 2019) presents an important perspective for understanding in two senses. Firstly, he notes that even the reactive content of signs is not purely mechanical but also formed under a certain influence of chance. Otherwise, there would be no growth (CP 6.37), and individuals would not be able to create and learn. Under the influence of Firstness, De-sign can favor an experience of these reactions, connecting the therapist to the self, so as to adjust the navigation process in tandem. Indices here constitute the signs of the sea that must be considered for the navigation to proceed. In the case discussed here, the young woman is very clear about her conditions for therapy with Erickson: an intelligent philosophy, and no expression of sorrow on his part. It can be inferred that, by capturing these indices, Erickson was even more attentive because he realized that any slip in these categories could generate suffering in the young woman and lead her to abandon therapy. These indices, therefore, can lead to vital levels of reflexivity, especially regarding the need to adjust a therapeutic relationship, as some therapists claim when referring to the importance of a fluid, dynamic relationship (Omer, 1994; Ribeiro, 2021). This also refers to the relational basis of feeling that sustains therapy and constitutes the basic contract for the therapeutic process to advance (Neubern, 2010).

The role of indices in the second attitude is deeply linked to the materiality of the therapeutic relationship, which is even more significant in hypnosis. During trance, patient and therapist comments about feeling touched, pushed, or caressed are not uncommon (Neubern, 2018b), like what can occur in an everyday relationship. Some reports still describe "punches," "blows," "intimate caresses," "trampling," "dressing", among others. People like Erickson's young patient not infrequently express feeling "embraced" by the therapist, given the deep acceptance and respect with which they felt contemplated. Even if these expressions carry metaphorical content, they also imply a range of reactive sensations experienced in one's own body.

Secondly, De-sign (Seif, 2019) opens up the notion of dance as applied to the hypnotic relationship. Out of an interactive agenda, marked by mutual reactions, therapist and patient put themselves under the rhythm of a new interaction, with more refined and modeled movements between them. It would not be an exaggeration to say that such a process has an aesthetic substance, which allows us to consider, metaphorically, that melody and harmony are also components of such an interaction. If Erickson's account of the young woman's care is analyzed, the interlocutors developed a certain harmony through difficult themes that revealed the tragedy of that young woman's life. Nevertheless, they navigated themes with ease, and the story was eventually crossed by moments of humor, poetry, and surprise. This process is consistent with Pierce's idea (1903/1997): a good mathematical logic can produce the same aesthetic effect as a beautiful poem. As an argument (Peirce, 1903/1997), that process implied the construction of important habits, as notes in the third attitude, later discussed in this chapter. It is true that, as noted previously, Erickson proceeded to thorough preparation in constructing suggestions and their respective role. Dance, in this case, was a creative and joint act that, despite preparation, was open to new developments since that became possible—thanks to previous sensitivity by the therapist. In other words, even if they perform an exhaustively rehearsed choreography, the dancer, at the moment of the performance, delivers it as a creative act experienced in a unique way. Otherwise, that action would not be characterized as an artistic process at all.

The second attitude is also related to a particular mode of producing autonomy in the interlocutors. Even involving a reactive dimension and a choreographic dimension of the relationship, it is still relies on the influence of chance and on the creative processes of the first attitude. It is through materiality that hypnogenesis is concretized in order to convey great diversity of signs (mainly symbols), present in the therapist's self. Following the same idea, inspired by Lady Welby's classification (Liszka, 1996), that the signs of autonomy in the interlocutors are linked to two types of meanings: telenomic and teleological (CP 4.551). The idea of a telenomic meaning refers to an ability to express with one's own body language. In the case of the young patient, this relates to a set of suggestions by Erickson on the relationships between parts of her body.

Because of the accident suffered and her paralysis, her body image featured a "broken" or "dysfunctional" woman, unable to exercise her sexuality and motherhood. The sequence of suggestions proposed by Erickson refer to a series of connections between various parts of the body—which would indicate that, despite paralysis, her body's sensation, function, and sexuality were preserved. That telenomic dimension is also symbolic, since it addressed the ways her body worked, that is, habits that were there though inactivated. That process was possible thanks to a favorable symbolic and affective atmosphere that characterized the therapeutic context.

In this dimension, De-sign appears as a form of subtle navigation by the young woman regarding her own self, because, by receiving a series of diagrams and symbols through suggestion and through complex semiosis, her self was able to translate them into a belief that her body could function normally again. Erickson, at this point, seems to have been subtle in reconnecting the patient to her own body, especially in terms of sensitivity. As suggested by Erickson's clinical report, neither his sensitivity nor the functionality linked to these organs would have been affected by the accident. However, the tragedy she experienced led her to produce a series of ideas around incapacitation that, in a way, prohibited her from considering the practice of her own sexuality. Thus, the De-sign that she developed herself did not occur in terms of medical healing for her body but in healing it symbolically. Unable to remember meeting Erickson and in an intentional, more than deliberate, move, the young woman began to connect with herself to restore her symbolic and experience wounds in her body over many years. It was a fundamental process of reconstruction for one's own body image (Haley, 1985) in terms of the organs' very function.

On the other hand, meanings in teleological terms can be shown more by capturing and subsequently expressing some signs that probably appeared in the years after therapy. If the suggestions formed paths to sow new meanings, through her concrete actions, in her everyday life, the young woman was able to reconstruct her own universe: she allowed herself to know and engage with a man who was capable of understanding her—at the same time, both meaning and index meant that deeper changes were taking place within her. It seems that something new might be happening with a young woman who, until that moment, had lived her affective life in isolation, convinced that no man would be interested in her. Nevertheless, even if relevant, these meanings could not bring a more accurate understanding of deeper processes of agency that seemed to be at work there. Only through the third attitude could such processes be made clearer.

Attitude Three—Thinking With

The field of thinking, as already noted, has been historically problematic for hypnosis. The difficulty of approaching content based on a modern perspective has been associated with its troubled historical path and with the significant theoretical fragmentation of the field, characterized by the absence of conceptual consensus (Facco, 2021; Stengers, 2001). At the same time, the strong association of hypnosis with traditional knowledges (Neubern, 2022) and with the imagination identifiable in literature and cinema (Bioy, 2018) have also contributed to that resistance to the practice on the part of researchers. Furthermore, in metaphysical, epistemological, and even theoretical terms, hypnosis exposes several conceptual gaps that prevent or hinder a more comprehensive understanding. De-sign (Seif, 2019) is an important tool for that comprehension, especially as it proposed a frame of concepts that offer intelligibility to diaphanous and elusive processes around hypnosis. Although the task of navigating a person is influenced by chance, it also demands a logic of its own, that is, an immersion on Thirdness. Otherwise, navigation would never be a *métier*, characterized by collective knowledge and endowed with certain rationality. Chart 3.3 introduces the main concepts regarding the third attitude.

Chart 3.3 presents fundamental categories for an understanding, via De-sign (Seif, 2020), on the third attitude, which is predominant in therapies that value the symbolic, such as Jungian, psychoanalytic, and narrative therapies (Neubern, 2016). The emphasis on laws, conventions, and habits is problematic due to the complex

Chart 3.3 Terms for understanding the third attitude, or *Thinking With*

Phenomenological category	Character	Verbs of reference	Role	Therapist signs of experience and reflexivity	Signs of autonomy
Thirdness; law, convention, thoughts, habits. Future (time); symbols, logic, reflection.	Mathematician; abstraction, generalization; logic, meaning; induction.	Thinking with; to think about things and thoughts; to mean; to predict.	Constructing the logic of therapeutic context; accurate reflection on techniques and actions; prediction of future consequences.	Symbols and signs of Thirdness.	Significance (agency).

and fugue nature of the hypnotic field; at the same time, it poses a challenge: if hypnosis is highly governed by Firstness, how would it be possible to think of thirdness in its different manifestations? A first possible answer that question includes the very notion of law in Peirce (Ibri, 1992/2017), which is not characterized by an absolute determination. Even in material nature, there is no total influence of law, as many of natural phenomena escape determinations. The random content of chance, in evolutionary terms (CP 6.74), eventually works as a propellant for expanding the laws that organize it, but do not determine phenomena in an absolute fashion. It follows that, in terms of human subjectivity, law presents an important corollary—habits—that allow the therapist to conceive of a certain organization (Thirdness) in a field marked by feelings, images, and potentialities (Firstness). A direct consequence of habit is a perspective of the future that accompanies therapies in general—and hypnosis in particular. The future, in this case, is not restricted to an expectation for obtaining specific results, though these are also regarded; it extends towards a preparation of the patient so that they can exercise autonomy and creativity. Therefore, in terms of De-sign (Seif, 2019), the therapist reflects on technical choices and context, but does so thinking, above all, of the conditions providing this patient with an autonomous and teleological process regulating the central issues of their life. This may help explain how Erickson devoted himself intensely to preparing his cases, and he demonstrated refined rational skills.

> *In the third attitude there is not, as among modern researchers in science and particularly in hypnosis, the prevalence of the search for the law. De-sign develops a spiral navigation that transitions between phenomenological categories, always based on Firstness. Thus, it recognizes the generalities of Thirdness, especially regarding habits, capturing from them the potentiality of their influence on phenomena. However, it focuses on the navigation of experience that is elusive, polychronic and diaphanous, not being determined by habits, but only influenced by them. The content of the third attitude is much more teleological, mainly because the orientation of intentionality is toward the future.*

In the case discussed here, there is a specific situation that deserves close attention, if we consider the phenomenological figure of the mathematician (Peirce, 1903/1997). Understanding his patient's desire to be a mother, Erickson tells her a story: she would enter an enclosure and find a dirty and disheveled baby. Then, she would want to hug that child, showing all affection possible. Soon after that, she would enter another enclosure and find another child, perfectly combed and clean. Her wish, in the second scenario, would be to find the child's parents and slap them to chastise the absurdity of leaving the baby in such a perfect state. Erickson's insight for thinking as a De-signer occupies two major levels, so we can reflect on the logical or organizational content of hypnotherapy. At the first level, there is an important understanding on the generality of one's own subjectivity during trance. The therapist used a "future memory" (Seif, 2019), that is, an experience that could transcend the linear dimension of time, in terms of present-past-future. Regarding Firstness, a deep experience permeated by feeling and desire is not restricted to past events, but to experiences projected into the future that can guide a person's teleological actions. Moreover, even if being a mother had not happened yet to the patient on the concrete plane, it was part of her desires (*Eros*), long cherished by her. In a rather indirect way –telling stories—Erickson instrumentalized this memory during trance, so that, a few years later, she would make that real in generating her own children.

On a second level, Erickson entered the specific logic governing that patient, in order to contemplate the uniqueness of how she constructed meaning and senses, anticipating contemporary discussions in psychotherapy on the subject (Gonzalez Rey, 2019; White, 2007). In asking for help to acquire an "intelligent philosophy," the young woman demanded help so she could also live life fully, despite various limitations. The figure of the dirty and disheveled child alluded to a frequent and concrete contradiction for many people: despite the child's condition, they could be embraced and loved. At the same time, that idealized child, in terms of cleanliness and tidiness, was nothing more than a farce, a distant condition from the reality of fathers and mothers. This would justify her revolt against that fraud which, in a way, could be associated with the limiting conceptions she had developed about herself. In other words, it would be possible to love someone despite their not being preternaturally beautiful and clean, as she was. The same logic for the possibilities of loving someone outside the standards of beauty was constantly marked in most of the stories told during trance.

In general, the main role of the third attitude lies in establishing logic for the progress of the hypnotherapeutic relationship. The idea of logic, of course, implies verbs and conduct related to rationalization, such as thinking, philosophizing, and reflecting. Nevertheless, it is necessary to highlight two central themes for that logic—that it must be shared and that sharing does not always take place at a deliberate level. In the first theme there is the assumption that the therapist has central importance in establishing that logic, but it must be done together with one's interlocutor. Erickson developed, for the young woman, a professorial role (pedagogue or philosopher) and a series of suggestions that aimed to approach her needs—mainly her way of being and of relating to others. My making himself a sign[6] with characteristics of symbol and icon (CP 2.254–2.263), he began to convey actions and stories that not only held her attention, but also promoted significant processes of semiosis within her subjectivity. Despite her silence during the trance, the processes she developed confirm a considerable level of participation in terms of logic: years later, the results of the therapy could suggest that themselves. This reflection is consistent with Seif's (2019) the idea about thinking together as a form of shared gratitude: "to think is to thank."

The second theme, on the other hand, refers to a level of logic that goes beyond ordinary and deliberate thought. On the part of the therapist, there is considerable dedication to think about the complex and elusive dimension of trance. Surprised remarks are not uncommon from many people who have known Erickson's work, including his ability to think and dialogue with several processes with such familiarity and confidence. Despite various moments of abduction, cases like that patient's suggest a strong connection with induction and Thirdness. On the part of the patient, reflection becomes even more complex, since her amnesia about the encounter refers to a broader view of consciousness, beyond deliberation. If, during her long period of trance, she could receive these stories and, on some level, enjoy them, the amnesia she developed seems to have led her to a distinct process of reflection on important themes in her life. In terms of De-sign, all the influence experienced during her session with Erickson (the stories, his teaching role) were integrated into different semiotic systems that made her the person she was, in order to set off important changes. The semiosis originated from it occurred beyond ordinary consciousness, but it maintained its logic as a third party. As she made her decisions and acted in her daily life; new adjustments between ego and self enabled those changes in the self to "contaminate" other spheres of her thinking, including conscious deliberation. This process of subtle exchange between different modes of consciousness seems to have been greatly aided by amnesia, mainly because of the original content the patient must have conferred to them.

Truly, that the idea of a meta-level of reflection, though not new in psychotherapies (Andersen, 1991; Bateson, 1972), would lead many therapists to make their patients aware of subtle levels of thinking, such as the one mentioned here. However, Erickson was careful in this sense, as he understood the need to preserve one's world logic of each at these levels, especially regarding what he called "unconscious."—hence his tendency not to try to decipher patients any messages from his interventions or their own experience, such as dreams. He did so because he believed the autonomy of the therapeutic process, with all its originality, should not center on the ego, as most therapies seem to suggest, but on a broader and more holistic conception of the self. In terms of navigating De-sign, Erickson's principle could thus be understood: the sea (of the self) would not fit inside the boat (of the ego), but the harmony between the two could characterize a new quality of consciousness.

---

[6] Given that many readers of this work may not be familiar with semiotics, we maintained here only the most common classification of signs, involving icons, indexes, and symbols. However, for further information on the classifications of Peirce's signs, we recommend CP 2.254–2.263 or Liszka's work (1996).

Perhaps the young woman's own suffering was connected to the logic of her boat (ego) and divergent from the logic of her sea (self).

Regarding the reflexivity of the therapist about themselves, the third attitude implies the importance of Thirdness signs, such as symbols, arguments, and habits. In a way, symbols are largely responsible for humans recognizing themselves as semiotic animals (Deely, 2010), as they are aware of dealing with signs; they provide the idea of being two or three (Neubern, 2018a), that is, of taking a double or triple perspective for observing oneself in the imaginary scenarios their own. There are here two possible paths to reflexivity, i.e., to access and understand the processes of Thirdness that occur at levels beyond deliberate consciousness. First, there is the need to connect with these processes for the subsequent construction of pertinent narratives about them. Taking the same precaution to avoid a linear translation, as just mentioned, the therapist connects to experiences that seem to suggest something to them, such as dreams, images, feelings, and intuitions. Because they are predominantly signs of Firstness, these experiences function as a kind of oracle, whose interpretation can be multiple and depends on the consultant or on someone authorized for such a task, as it happens in certain cultures (Nathan, 2011). Thus, based on icons, the therapist can reach a symbolic dimension that has nothing absolute, given the fluidity of experiences beyond deliberation. It is a first moment to access a vast universe, unintelligible in its entirety by law and the therapist.

Specifically on this topic, ethnopsychology can suggest important questions for understanding Thirdness in trance. The deeper dimensions of the self are commonly represented in modern psychology, sometimes as irrational and torment processes, sometimes as mechanical and animalized processes (Ellenberger, 1970/2003). Consciousness would thus be a primacy of the evolution of human beings, an instance for proposing reason and civilization in opposition to animal legacies. Nevertheless, in other societies (Clément, 2011; Nathan, 2011), several cultural technologies conceive the existence of other levels of consciousness and Thirdness, beyond the deliberations of the ordinary consciousness. In other words, such technologies envision and allow access to deeper dimensions of the self that are marked by wisdom and consciousness, with abilities far beyond the consciousness of the ego. As depositories of collective knowledge, these dimensions of the self would be prophecies, spiritual teachings, and paranormal phenomena, such as cures, predictions, exorcisms and apparitions of spiritual beings. In these groups, reading of signs of Firstness leads to a wide universe of Thirdness, revealing knowledge and influent capacities upon the human world. However, although Erickson (1992) has often referred to the unconscious as wise, knowledge on this field still is a great challenge for contemporary psychologies that may not yet have solidified intelligibility categories to understand it.

Secondly, there is the analysis of the habits that the therapist acquires on account of their inquiry. If the interpretant of a good argument creates a habit (Peirce, 1908/1991), a legitimate insertion for an involving field such as a clinic tends to shape the therapist's self, leading them to acquire relevant habits as a professional person and researcher. Inquiry makes itself known by the way it transforms its protagonist (Seif, 2019)—in this case, the therapist. Despite Erickson not having referred to anything about the case in question, his work (Erickson & Rossi, 1980) and his biographers (Erickson & Keeney, 2006; Zeig, 1985) highlight situations that led him to that level of reflection. It would not be an exaggeration to say that his rural *Ethos*, his considerable intelligence and capacity for perception, his weakened health, as well as his great perseverance found in the course of Medicine debate, were decisive in this sense, such as: the fragility and injustices of life, pain and suffering, madness, death, and disease. Therefore, instead of settling on a pessimistic logic, as some therapists have faced with the same themes, Erickson developed a therapy focused on the potentiality of people, on integrating with oneself, respecting human diversity and searching for a happier life. Under a strong pragmatic influence (Short, 2020), his ways of elaborating the artist, the bulldog, and the mathematician contributed to his performance as a De-signer, to the extent that he conflates actions, thoughts, and feelings in the search for an aesthetic ideal of caring for the other.

On patient autonomy, the third attitude has important implications. The case of the young patient is relevant mainly because she is a wheelchair user with a series of physical limitations who, since therapy, began to position herself in a very different way from the way she had since the accident. From a person victimized by tragedy, she began to assume an active position, pursuing her dreams and reaching them. In existential terms (Merleau-Ponty, 1945/2008), she retook a new possibility of moving through life in diaphanous time and polychronic space, though she had not left the wheelchair. However, she went on to develop and exercise her intelligent philosophy and left behind the drama of the accident—she got married and had children. These signs refer to the idea of significance, defended by Lady Welby (cited in Liszka, 1996), that interpreters act at the level of agency of complex semiotic systems. On the one hand, significance involves intentionality in terms of existence, leading a person to think more broadly about life. In these situations, as probably experienced by the young woman, the person can position themselves outside of their own trajectory, as if enjoying a film about their life. This exercise of imagination, typical of De-sign, is intrinsically linked to the way Erickson's hypnotic stories are constructed, as illustrated in this case: because they imply teleological content, they refer to a strong future perspective, connecting them to induction. It is likely that he engaged in this exercise several times to reinforce changes that were already taking place at a deeper level. On the other hand, the intelligent philosophy she sought probably emerged from new contact with her own self, whose processes were submerged under amnesia. At this level, significance implied a change in the agency of systems linked to body image, relationships involving men and women, the possibility of being a mother, and having a different way of facing life. Considering new narratives, though unconscious, originated from changes in the agency of these systems. To the extent that she made herself available to those influences from her own subjectivity, she more capable of exercising her intelligent philosophy, even in the concrete experience of her daily life.

Dialogues, De-sign, and Hypnosis

A clinical case as the one discussed here may not constitute an example of dialogue for many people. Commonly associated with conversation in narrative authors (Anderson & Goolishian, 1988; White, 2007), dialogue is often conceived in terms of an exchange of Thirdness signs, restricted to words as a conventional referent. Therefore, a situation in which a therapist tells stories and utters sentences to a person who seems to sleep and remains silent for most of the time would be very far from an idea of dialogue. There would be no conversation, no narrative evolution, nor a respectful consideration of the symbolic universe of the other, that is, there would be no constitutive elements for dialogue (Anderson & Goolishian, 1988). In other words, Erickson's hypnosis would possibly be restricted, in such perspectives, to a purely technical practice, centered on the therapist's knowledge and the imposition of their ideas on a passive and obedient subject. Nevertheless, from the perspective of De-sign (Seif, 2013), dialogue implies other issues, and hypnosis can be perfectly understood as one of its forms. Roughly speaking, Seif (2019) considers that conversation occurs within references of self, other, space, and time (more or less fixed), just as it focuses more on what exists. Dialogue, on the other hand, implies an imaginative process of interpretation and, by its abductive content, faces what is to come. Consequently, its proximity to trance is surprising mainly because of changes in references to ordinary reality, so dear to conversation, and of the importance of interpretive imagination. The etymology of the terms *Dia* (through) and *Logos* (speaking or writing a word) goes far beyond the restriction to the word itself, as many postmodern authors claim: *Logos* is associated with notions of image, *anima mundi*, and, furthermore, wisdom, rationality, and love (Seif, 2019, p. 274). The kind of semiotic exchange between people, intrinsic to dialogue, is also essential to De-sign.

> *Imaginative interpretation is, for De-sign (Seif, 2019), one of the fundamental characteristics that distinguish dialogue from conversation. It also allows us to consider hypnosis as a mode of dialogue, mainly because of the strong imaginative content that characterizes it. If, in hypnosis, there is a subversion of the references of reality, one goes from the idea in which an ego talks to others to a perspective in which multiple characters and beings enter into interaction. In trance, the person can dialogue with different voices and beings of their self, which is constituted by individual and collective processes. The very notion of otherness is modified in the trance, since the person can interact with beings whom he perceives as others, but they are also part of his self. The capacity of semiosis in such processes is very large, which provides a great therapeutic potential for hypnosis.*

One of the first characteristics of hypnotic dialogue is the polychrony of time (Seif, 2019). Transiting through a dimension of quali-consciousness, the protagonists of the dialogue enter a field permeated by Firstness, that is, a field in which the present seems to integrate with past and future in a circular way (CP 1.498). Thus, the moment of that session in which Erickson told his stories to the young wheelchair user would be integrated into a broader flow of time, which would also feature future processes, as well as past ones. In a way, the hypnotic encounter with Erickson opened a kind of time portal she could always update throughout her life. Thus, the story in which she enters the room and finds a dirty and disheveled child acquires different outlines. During trance it is only a story; at the same time, it involves "future memories," linked to her desire of becoming a mother; it is also an evocation of past memories of her family *Ethos*, through the influence of her grandmother. It is quite plausible that at various times with her children these various temporal facets linked to her desire to be a mother converged upon her, provoking a multitude of emotions, because, thanks to that semiosis promoted by Erickson—who, as a sign, remained present within his patient's self for many years, somehow dialoguing with her.

It is also worth noting that the temporal experience is only dissociable from the spatial one for a didactic purpose, that is, the multiple and diaphanous aspect of space (Gebser, 1949/1985) in trance also accompanied the young woman. Stating with a body that had stopped in time and social life, paralyzed in its functions and incapacitated for life, the young woman began to experience another body, one that could feel the pleasures of seduction, sex, motherhood, and an active and useful life, despite her necessity of a wheelchair. The concrete, opaque, absolute, and immutable content of space and body gave way to diaphanous, light, and multiple processes that provided her with important life changes. Following the same confluence of time experiences, the patient began to live the corporeality of the girl she had once been, the woman she would like to become, and the mother she, in fact, became. It would not be an exaggeration to consider that her deep immersion in the desire of what was to come enabled her to achieve what was most important for her concrete life despite her physical limitations. It is a striking example of the influence of the phantasmagoric world of imagination and desire upon action in the reality of the social world. In this diversity of living spaces, Erickson's voices, images, sensations, speech, and presence remained active in a transformative process of semiosis inside the patient's world.

These considerations refer to another important characteristic of dialogue, as well as trance: the alteration of otherness. In this topic, there are two points of great value for the present discussion. On the one hand, as the trance process unfolds, Erickson becomes a sign within his patient's self, with multiple interpretants. The multiple signs derived from it drive processes of semiosis in central themes of the young woman's life. Certainly, these processes led her to numerous monologues from which she would elaborate elements for the reconstruction of her narrative, ways of perceiving the world and of deciding her interests. Following Peirce's idea (CP 6.338) this monologue served as the basis for new dialogue, providing her with other forms of interaction with people. Under a significant process of body image reconstruction, she no longer presented herself as a "cripple" or as a "victim of life," but as an interesting woman who could attract people's attention with her qualities. On the other hand, this dive oneself also updates her relationships with *Ethos*. If, in the case of the young woman, this resulted in a reunion with her familial *Ethos*, including the influence of her grandmother, in the case of Erickson, it was a reunion with figures and relationships that influenced him to become a person dedicated to the aesthetic ideal of caring for others. His teachers, relatives, friends, and patients, as well as life events, possibly entered the scene to follow his own growth process that, in semiotic terms (Ibri, 1992/2017), changed his own habits and ways of living in the world.

There was, therefore, a meeting of worlds (Neubern, 2016)—which constitutes one of the key points for legitimate dialogue. When the individuals present were subjects of their processes because of the protagonism they exercised, they also represented signs of broader collective belonging. Once those slightly fixed references of reality were altered and the realm of imagination was accessed, there was a profusion of signs typical of metalogue (Bateson, 1972)—not only due to mutual interpenetration, but also to an intense exchange between such universes represented by Erickson and his patient. The meeting between two people was also the meeting between multiple relationships that these people brought within their own selves.

However, the notion of dialogue would be completely mischaracterized if it were not for the solid relational basis promoted by feeling, as emphasized in the first attitude. Without such a basis, respectful consideration of the other, their condition of autonomy, and the reconstructive expansion of narratives (Anderson & Goolishian, 1988), it could be mischaracterized as a simply technical procedure. In the case at hand, through deep consideration of who that young woman was and through appreciating her potentialities, and ways of being, that relational basis became possible—to the point of establishing a legitimate contract. By being present with that young woman, it was possible for them to enter one another's selves because of the typical changes from the first attitude. Both had simply understood that their hearts could walk together, as advocated by the Latin root of the word *acordo* (agreement).

References

Andersen, T. (1991). *The reflexive team*. Noos.
Anderson, H., & Goolishian, H. (1988). Human systems as a linguistic systems: Preliminary and evolving ideas about the implications for clinical theory. *Family Process, 27*, 371–393.
Bateson, G. (1972). *Steps to an ecology of mind*. The University of Chicago Press.
Beck, J. (1995). *Cognitive therapy: Basic and beyond*. Guilford Press.
Bellet, P. (1998). *L'hypnose* [Hypnosis]. Odile Jacob.
Binswanger, L. (2008). Sur la Psychothérapie [On Psychotherapy]. In: L. Binswanger (Ed.), *Introduction à l'analyse existentielle*. Minuit. (original work published in 1935).
Bioy, A. (2018). "O pequeno teatro da hipnose": uma leitura clínica do funcionamento hipnótico [The little theater of hypnosis: A clinical understanding of hypnotic functioning]. In

M. Neubern (Ed.), *Clínicas do transe. Etnopsicologia, hipnose e espiritualidade no Brasil* (pp. 49–68). Juruá.

Campbell, J. (1959). *The masks of God*. The Viking Press.

Carroy, J. (1991). *L'hypnose et suggestion. L'invention du sujet* [Hypnosis and suggestion. The invention of the subject]. Press Universitaire de France.

Clément, C. (2011). *L'Appel de la Transe* [The Call of the Trance]. Stok.

Clément, C. (2014). *Dictionnaire amoreux des dieux et déesses* [Loving dictionary of gods and goddesses]. Plon.

Colapietro, V. (1989). *Peirce's approach to the self*. Suny.

Colapietro, V. (1995). Notes for a sketch of a peircean theory of the unconscious. *Transactions of Charles S. Peirce Society, 31*(3), 482–506.

Deely, J. (2010). *Semiotic animal. A postmodern definition of "human being" transcending patriarchy and feminism*. St Augustine's Press.

Ellenberger, H. (2003). *The discovery of the unconscious*. Basic Books. (original work published in 1970).

Erickson, M. (1953). The therapy of psychosomatic headache. *Journal of Clinical and Experimental Hypnosis, 1*(4), 2–6.

Erickson, M. (1964). The "surprise" and "my friend John" techniques of hypnosis: Minimal cues and natural field of experimentation. *The American Journal of Clinical Hypnosis, 6*, 293–307.

Erickson, M. (1985). *Life reframing in hypnosis*. Irvington.

Erickson, M. (1992). Healing in hypnosis. In E. Rossi, M. Ryan, & F. Sharp (Eds.), *The seminars, workshops, and lectures of Milton Erickson, MD* (Vol. 1). Irvington.

Erickson, B., & Keeney, B. (2006). *Milton H. Erickson. An American healer*. Ringing Rock Press & Leete's Island Books.

Erickson, M., & Rossi, E. (1979). *Hypnotherapy: An exploratory casebook*. Irvington.

Erickson, M., & Rossi, E. (1980). *The collected papers of Milton Erickson, MD*. Irvington.

Facco, E. (2021). Hypnosis and hypnotic ability between old beliefs and new evidences: An epistemological reflection. *American Journal of Clinical Hypnosis, 64*(1), 20–35. https://doi.org/10.1080/00029157.2020.1863181

Fann, K. T. (2010). *Peirce's theory of abduction*. Partidrge.

Ferro, A., & Basile, R. (2015). *Le champ psychanalytique. Un concept clinique* [The psychoanalytical field. A clinical concept]. Ithaque.

Gallagher, S. (2014). *The Oxford handbook of the self*. Ofxord University Press.

Gallagher, S., & Zahavi, D. (2008). *The phenomenological mind. An introduction to philosophy of mind and cognitive sciences*. Routledge.

Gebser, J. (1985). *The ever-present origin*. Ohio University Press. (original work published in 1949).

Gonzalez Rey, F. (2019). Subjectivity in debate: Some reconstructed philosophical premises to advance its debates in psychology. *Journal of Theory and Social Behavior, 49*, 1–23.

Haley, J. (1985). *Conversations with Milton Erickson*. Triangle Press.

Hall, E. (1983). *The dance of life: The other dimension of time*. Doubleday & Company. (original work published in 1969).

Hartshorne, C., & Weiss, P. (1980). *The collected papers of Charles S. Peirce* (CP, 8 vol.). Harvard University Press.

Houser, N. (1983). Peirce's general taxonomy of consciousness. *Transactions of Charles Sanders Peirce Society, 19*(4), 331–339.

Ibri, I. (2017). *Kósmos Noetós: The metaphysical architecture of Charles Peirce*. Springer. (original work published in 1992).

Jappy, T. (2013). *Introduction to Peircean visual semiotics*. Bloomsbury.

Lewin, K. (1951). *Field theory in social sciences*. Harper Torchbooks.

Liszka, J. (1996). *A general introduction to the semeiotic of Charles Sanders Peirce*. Indiana University Press.

Manfield, M. (2016). *American bulldog bible and the American bulldog*. DYM.

Méheust, B. (1999). *Somnambulisme et Médiumnité* [Somnambulism and Mediumship]. Synthélabo.

Melchior, T. (1998). *Créer le Réel* [Creating the Real]. Seuil.
Merleau-Ponty, M. (2008). *Phénoménologie de la pérception* [Phenomenology of perception]. Gallimard. (original work published in 1945).
Morin, E. (2014). *La Méthode IV. Les Idées. Leur Habitat, Leur vie, Leurs Moeur, Leur Organisations* [Method IV. Idea. Their habitat, their life, their morals, their organizations]. Points. (original work published in 1991).
Nathan, T. (2011). *La nouvelle interprétation des rêves* [The new interpretation of the dreams]. Odile Jacob.
Nathan, T. (2014). *Nous ne sommes pas seuls au monde* [We are not alone in the world]. Seuil. (original work published in 2001).
Neubern, M. (2010). O terapeuta e o contrato terapêutico. Em busca de possibilidades [The therapist and the therapeutic contract]. *Estudos e Pesquisas em Psicologia, 3*, 882–897.
Neubern, M. (2016). Iconicity and complexity in hypnotic communication. *Psicologia: Teoria e Pesquisa, 32*, 1–9. https://doi.org/10.1590/0102-3772e32ne217
Neubern, M. (2018a). *Clínicas do transe. Etnopsicologia, hipnose e espiritualidade no Brasil* [Trance clinics. Ethnopsychology, hypnosis and spirituality in Brazil]. Juruá.
Neubern, M. (2018b). *Hipnose, dores crônicas e complexidade: Técnicas avançadas* [Hypnosis, chronic pain and complexity: Advanced techniques]. Ed. UnB.
Neubern, M. (2021a). Epistemologia, pesquisa e subjetividade: Problemas de semiótica, hipnogênese e investigação [Epistemology, research and subjectivity: Problems of semiotics, hypnogenesis and investigation]. In E. Seidl, E. Queiroz, F. Iglesias, & M. Neubern (Eds.), *Estratégias metodológicas de pesquisa em psicologia clínica. Possibilidades e avanços* (pp. 235–258). CRV.
Neubern, M. (2021b). Aspectos alegóricos dos contos de história na hipnose de Milton Erickson [Allegorical aspects of storytelling in Milton Erickson's hypnosis]. *Semeiosis: Semiótica e Transdisciplinaridade em Revista, 9*, 25–36.
Neubern, M. (2022). When spirits become therapists. Ethnopsychology and hypnotherapy in Brazil. *International Journal of Latin American Religions, 1*, 1–26.
Nöth, W. (2015). The paradigms of iconicity in language and literature. In E. M. Hiraga (Ed.), *Iconicity: East meets west* (pp. 13–34).
Omer, H. (1994). *Critical interventions in psychotherapy: From impasse to turning point*. WW. Norton.
Peirce, C. (1893). Evolutionary love. In N. Houser, & C. Kloesel (Eds.). (1998). *The essential Peirce* (Vol. 1., pp. 352–371). Indiana University Press.
Peirce, C. (1903). Pragmatism as a principle and method of right thinking. In P. Turrisi (Ed.). (1997). *The 1903 Harvard lectures on pragmatism*. State University of New York Press.
Peirce, C. (1908). A neglected argument for the reality of god. In: J. Hoopes (Ed.). (1991). *Peirce on signs*. (pp. 260–278). The University of North Caroline Press.
Petrilli, S. (2017). *The self as a sign, the world, and the other*. Routledge.
Prigogine, I. (1994). *Les lois du chaos*. [The laws of chaos]. Flammarion.
Psillos, S., & Zorzato, L. (2021). Against cognitive instrumentalism. *International Studies in the Philosophy of Science, 3*, 247–257. https://doi.org/10.1080/02698595.2021.1961420
Raposa, M. (1989). *Peirce's philosophy of religion*. Indiana University Press.
Ribeiro, J. (2021). *O ciclo do contato* [The contact cycle]. Summus.
Rosen, S. (1982). *My voice will go with you. The teaching tales of Milton Erickson*. Norton & Company.
Sebeok, T., & Umiker-Sebeok, J. (1979). *You know my method*. Gaslight Publications.
Seif, F. (2019). *De-sing in transmodern world. Envisioning reality beyond absoluteness*. Peter Lang.
Seif, F. (2013). Dialogue with Kishtta: A semiotic revelation of the paradox of life and death. *The American Journal of Semiotics, 29*, 101–115. https://doi.org/10.5840/ajs2013291-44
Seif, F. (2020). The role of pragmatism in De-sign: Persevering through paradoxes of design and semiotics. *Cognition, 21*(1), 112–131.
Short, D. (2020). *From William James to Milton Erickson. The Care of Human Consciousness*. Archway Publishing.

Stengers, I. (2001). Qu'est-ce que l'hypnose nous oblige à penser ? [What does hypnosis force us to think about?]. *Ethnopsy, 3*, 13–68.
Stengers, I. (2002). *Hypnose: entre Magie et Science* [Hypnosis: Between magic and science]. Synthélabo.
White, M. (2007). *Maps of narrative practice*. Norton & Company.
Zeig, J. (1985). *Experiencing Erickson. An introduction to the man and his work*. Brunner/Mazel.

Chapter 4
Thinking and Doing: The Challenge of Effectiveness

Traditionally, hypnosis is characterized by a remarkable paradox. On the one hand, it can produce visible results, either in the context of research or in therapy. At present, it would be difficult to find studies that discredit its power to produce results that can be taken as data and serve as public signs to be discussed by experts. There is considerable emphasis on visible (existing) signs usually associated with Secondness, such as results, responses, instruments, and techniques. On the other hand, there is no consensus in sight (Facco, 2021), since researchers and therapists do not have a common conceptual basis around which they can negotiate the meaning of their practices. The ontological gap that characterizes the field of subjectivity (Gonzalez Rey, 2019) constitutes one of the main origins for this problem. As a field permeated by Firstness, hypnosis is too elusive to be approached from a modern and Cartesian perspective. However, the hurdles to explanation—which would place research and theory in a Thirdness field—seem the thorniest for attempts to approach it and make it intelligible in scientific terms (Stengers, 2001). If its effectiveness is evident, why do explanations about hypnosis become so complicated?

A proposal of intelligibility through De-sign is significantly relevant for conceiving hypnosis because it conceives efficacy while also integrated into a broader notion: effectiveness (Seif, 2019). The signs that compose efficient results must, therefore, be understood from the broad perspective of De-sign, which includes a more comprehensive and integrative conception of the self and of hypnosis itself. Thus, responses that function as indices for the efficacy of change in traditional assessments are not always effective. In hypnotherapy, situations can arise in which the desired response is not achieved, but the person achieves some transformative, unexpected, and meaningful experience –desirable outcomes. These can be signs of a new form of integration with oneself, of new ways of facing life, especially for becoming existent.

Effectiveness, therefore, refers to unexpected and teleological experiences, such as desirable outcomes, the integrity of that person with themselves, their autonomy and quality of relationships, constructions of meaning about life, and ways of belonging (*Ethos*). In this chapter, we discuss two case studies and the way effectiveness as a principle of De-sign (Seif, 2019) can contribute to a broader understanding of what can be achieved through hypnosis.

Pains from Life

When Marcia, 38 years-old, phoned me asking for help, she was in despair. After a fall at home and an unsuccessful surgery, she began to feel terrible pain that radiated from the lower part of her spine towards her stomach and her legs. During her seizures, the pain took over various parts of her body, so she could not be touched; it took a long time for her to find a more comfortable position for her body. Being pregnant with her third child, her despair was even greater because she feared for the child; she saw no prospects for the future and seriously contemplated suicide. The medications she could take had no effect, nor did a series of alternative therapies she had sought. Her delivery was scheduled in 3 months, and her relationship with her doctor was not good: both Marcia and her husband considered him cold and arrogant, but he had been the only one willing to give birth with her condition. As a patient diagnosed with depression, severe chronic pain, and a delicate surgery in her history, other obstetricians were not willing to perform her cesarean section.

The first interventions were done in her home, where I visited her, in the company of a team member.[1] In the first two sessions, attempts were made to get her used to trance so that she could see it as a safe experience despite suicidal ideas and severe pain. It was a way of reconnecting with her own body, involving new perspectives of space (mainly in terms of space, safety, and comfort), time (in terms of a desirable future), and otherness (important people in one's life). Results were satisfactory, and Marcia reported significant improvements in pain and depression. There was also an emphasis on recovering her ancestral belonging (*Ethos*), because of her interests in Indigenous and African influences she identified in her family. In the next two sessions, we worked on the strong anxiety she felt about delivery. She had reported insomnia and walking down the street at dawn because of her fears about what might happen. She also claimed to have developed claustrophobia which she feared would be triggered in the operating room. The following sessions emphasized different foci: safe spaces, constructive experiences from her life, and her perception of imaginary points. I helped her visualize an imaginary window in the wall when she would be in an enclosed space, so she could go out and leave her

---

[1] In some cases seen at CHYS, home visits may occur as part of treatment. This is an important moment in the hypnotherapeutic process, mainly because it facilitates the subsequent practice of self-hypnosis. In Márcia's case, because of her difficult schedule, the distance from her home and her physical limitations, only 4 sessions were performed before her delivery.

body safe. The team also sought to emphasize the sense of gustation, given her taste for trying new foods. The intention was to recover the sensation of taste and associate it with a "taste" for things in life, which had been compromised due to depression.

The next few months of Márcia's life brought her very challenging situations. Although she felt well about the birth, she reported that the doctor came to her room in an anxious state, did not allow her husband to be in the room, and treated her badly. Her child, a girl, was born healthy, but Márcia was in terrible pain, and later examinations suggested tissue damage and internal innervation that would need to be accessed during the procedure. In her narrative, she had been a victim of obstetric violence, but it would be difficult to prove what had happened, as other health professionals had warned her. With the rise of the Covid-19 pandemic, her losses of people and the subsequent return to work presented themselves as events of great suffering for her. Pain was still intense, and so was her anxiety, but she refused to continue to work online, imagining she had learned to deal with those situations. From time to time, she reported talking with me in her imagination and receiving flashes from sessions and other crucial moments of her life. She said her life was filled with suffering, as was the case with many others. In addition, it was important for her that she was well because she needed to take care of and raise her children for a worthy life. If she could be okay, maybe a lot of what she went through would not happen to them, or maybe they too would learn to deal with their own obstacles. She stated that her suffering was due to the "pains from life", that is, common events in everyone's lives, and that hypnosis helped her understand and cope. Without realizing it, she fulfilled a request made to me at the beginning of therapy: she needed a new philosophy for life. Contact was maintained via telephone and other means until face-to-face meetings could be resumed.

From Results to Desirable Outcomes

The typically modern idea of result is inspired mainly by the Cartesian perspective, whose worldview is founded on multiple separations (Morin, 2001/2015): the individual is separated from the world; thought, separated from the organicity of the mind; the subject, detached from the object; theory, from practice; reality, fragmented in multiple dimensions that hardly communicate; and result, separated from process and context. That criticism, inspired by De-sign (Seif, 2020a), became a proposal of Religare by re-establishing new ways of relating to these separate notions.

Looking at results in a case like Márcia's could highlight several limitations for her hypnotherapeutic process. It is true that understanding the limitations of a therapeutic procedure is essential, either to alert users and professionals about their scope or to seek improvements when possible. Nevertheless, reflecting on the limits of typically modern and sometimes Cartesian visions underlying the search for results is also of great value. On the one hand, it is based on responses that are constituted as finished units and expressed by the person in the face of a situation (as an instrument for evaluation or an experiment). On the other hand, it is deeply associated with a view of the individualized human mind, closed in on itself, distant from social exchanges, separated from body, nature, and any other form of materiality. Thus, a broader reflection of hypnosis from De-sign (Seif, 2019) requires the inclusion of result in the broader notion of desirable outcomes, while response is taken as a sign (Peirce, 1903/1997). At the same time, the Cartesian mind must be replaced by a broader concept based on the process and complexity of systems and interconnection with itself and the world: the semiotic self (Colapietro, 1989; Petrilli, 2017). In summary, from the perspective of De-sign, the result is a provisional moment that integrates a much broader process in people's ability to imagine and dream, individually and collectively.

Perhaps, if one considers Márcia's care under a rigorous evaluation of her responses to scales, the efficacy of hypnotic interventions would not have been high because a reasonable number of symptoms, like pain and anxiety, persisted despite the adverse context and the improvements reported by her. Moreover, Márcia's self cannot be understood as isolated and closed in itself or even as a hermetic box that produces responses when prompted by its environment. It participates in an intense game of semiotic exchanges with the world and other selves, with which it establishes complex networks and semiotic systems. It is inhabited by complex signs from diverse semiotic exchanges with the world: cultural beings, voices, memories, scenes, images, symbols, and characters internalized from her history. These signs can transform, be forgotten, merge with each other, generate other signs, or simply disappear. In a way, they remain within her imagination and actively participate in the construction of a person's world references.

Understanding response as a sign and the psyche as a self has important implications for inquiry. First, a response is not a purely individual process because it refers to complex webs of semiosis that exist beyond a single self. Even though it carries an authorial character, the sign is also a collective semiotic construction that refers to numerous relationships of the self with itself, with others, and with the world. After her hypnosis sessions, Márcia reported seeing flashes of her meetings with me, in which she found herself talking to him, whether these conversations had occurred or not. Similar scenes with significant people in her history also repeated themselves, especially in moments of crisis, continuing the therapeutic process despite these people's physical absence. From a semiotic perspective, these other beings inhabited Márcia's self, where they had an active role and therapeutic relevance. In short, while the constructions of these beings inhabiting her therapy were authorial, they were also engendered by various semiotic influences present in herself.

At the same time, signs that emerge from a hypnotic relationship are highly polyphonic by the very nature of that relationship. The relational field created between both (Ribeiro, 2021) not only mobilizes vast social influences that cross them but also seems to amplify and mobilize them for therapeutic work. The very condition of quale consciousness, typical of trance, acts to amplify inhibited processes and generates a random infinity of signs with considerable therapeutic potential. What appears as a possible index of efficacy lies in the chain of broader semiotic processes generated by similar activity in amplifying the relational field integrated into the trance. Therefore, the concreteness of response is linked to a fluid and elusive network of signs merging the potential of Firstness with the existent related to Secondness. As an objective response, the sign is linked to a complex, fluid, and polyphonic encounter of social worlds (Neubern, 2016), as different influences are accessed and mobilized.

Responses do not occur as mere reactions of an automaton, even if they arise outside the person's deliberations. They are signs that refer to active constructions of the self involving involuntary levels of agency in the body and even the subject's reflective and conscious processes. This point raises central questions related to the construction of signs in the hypnotic experience. They must refer to the condition of the protagonists, as the therapist and subject are inserted as subjects (Morin, 1991/1996). A relationship that situates them as mere automata is highly questionable, whether the therapist is limited to applying techniques or the patient is restricted to providing answers—either in technical or ethical terms (Erickson & Rossi, 1979). This is because subject protagonism is associated with creation, intentionality, and a certain freedom of construction in choices (Morin, 1991/1996), all characteristics that are totally or partially inhibited when people limit themselves to reproductive and mechanical actions. The qualitative aspect, therefore, permeates a response and should be considered as basic condition for research or therapy. Otherwise, the inquiry can lose its legitimacy.

Secondly, signs do not constitute themselves as something completed but refer to a process in continuous motion: semiosis. Thus, signs always refer to other, new signs, suggesting that responses allow only for a transient view of that specific moment of hypnosis. As signs, responses do not sprout magically from the self, as if emerged from a simple act when facing a situation. They refer both to new signs, with which they can connect, as well as to broader semiotic systems, with their own agencies that impose a certain logic (or meaning) for the systems of the self. A simple score obtained via scale or questionnaire by a patient like Márcia would hardly reveal the procedural content of that sign, nor would it display how it was inserted in other semiotic systems. The relevance of a sign should be conceived in terms of the systems in which it is inserted, especially if they are rigid or not set in the habits that govern them. Roughly speaking, rigid systems tend to block or inhibit their possibilities of semiosis, while systems that promote modifications tend to promote them.

Another critical aspect of semiosis during a hypnotic process is temporality itself. De-sign inquiry breaks with the absolute notion of reality and, in doing so, creates diaphanous space for the *polychrony* of hypnotic time (Seif, 2019). Response, as well as result, have nothing of absolute and constitute themselves as transient signs in the flow of elusive phenomena during hypnosis. Repeated imaginary conversations with me could be thought of via the verb "to be" in the present, with the consequence of reducing pain and anxiety. This is one of the temporal dimensions sought by research from the perspective of the modern sciences, associated with Peirce's deduction (Atkins, 2016). The same response, if one conceived the potentiality with which it could be intertwined, would present a range of possibilities not yet concrete, leading both therapist and patient to conceive the situation "as if" linked to abduction. In Márcia's case, potentiality could lead both to a review of the past, as is common in hypnosis (Erickson & Kubie, 1941), and to an evaluation she developed about her future prospects. Another essential facet of response temporality related to what "must be" is very associated with intentionality towards the future and with induction. Commonly, as it happened with Márcia, this mode of rationality is associated with the reconnection to a person's *Ethos*, from where they extract significance about who they are and what they can do to accomplish in the world. This rationality includes the creation of existential meanings about great themes in life.

> *Peirce considered that there were basically three modes of inference or construction of reasoning during inquiry* (Atkins, 2016; Fann, 2010). *Abduction, linked to a creative experience of constructing hypotheses and highly permeated by Firstness; deduction, which involves the logical refinement of hypotheses and is linked to Secondness; and induction, focused on the verification of hypotheses and Thirdness since such verification would seek a general rule or law. The branch of semiotics in which these forms of inference are studied is named Peirce's Critical Logic.*

Thirdly, signs have materiality and do not constitute abstract entities, disconnected from the reality experienced in hypnosis. By comprising logical concepts for thinking about the world (CP[2] 2.227), signs have some dimension as existent since, otherwise, they would be excessively vague and impossible to think and analyze in a philosophical reflection or in the inquiry of a clinical case. It follows that responses expressed by a person like Márcia should be understood as signs within the various semiotic systems of her daily life in micro- and macro-social terms. A given score of 3 or 4 for a person would imply different meanings. Márcia was originally from a poor family, and she lived through many kinds of deprivation. Her African and Indigenous heritages were expressed by that appearance, which probably brought her more obstacles in terms of access to universal values (health, social welfare, and education) and social ascent. She carried, within herself, the fear of failing as a mother and leading her children to poverty. The fall at home, the unsuccessful surgery, and her problems with health services confirmed the premise that she would have no way out of a life of poverty and deprivation. It should be noted that the environment of poverty in Brazil, in its diversity of objects, can produce true semiotic scars on a person's self and in their own corporeality (Neubern, 2018a). For someone marked by social vulnerability as Márcia, a response considered of little effect could have much more value than for a person from another condition.

---

[2] CP means the Collected Papers of Charles Sanders Peirce (Hartshorne & Weiss, 1980), being the first number, the volume, and the last before the point, the paragraph. Despite its difference concerning the other citations, CP will be preserved in the present work because of its familiarity with the semioticians for whom this book is also intended. Another Peircean acronym is MS, which means the Annotated Catalogue of Papers of Charles S. Peirce (Robin, 1967).

On the other hand, the materiality of signs is also present in the hypnotherapeutic process that is developed, especially on the semiotic systems that are activated to promote change. The particular emphasis on a person's uniqueness (Erickson & Rossi, 1979) is fundamental for the therapist to understand the logic of that person's particular universe, including its potentiality. In Márcia's case, I adopted some essential strategies that privileged her potential for focus: experiences with central people (including children), since I realized the powerful meanings that those relationships carried for her; her ancestry, including her resumption of *Ethos*; accentuated perceptual cores on targets that escaped negativism of depression and opened her to suggestions that favored therapy. Materiality in hypnosis is strongly related to sensations of Firstness, either because of the potentiality they imply for change or because of a proliferation of sensations and experiences that they can promote. It also relates to the reactivity of Secondness, which involves the self in a more concrete way, including corporeality. With Marcia, these processes led her towards new ways of dealing with pain and reducing depressive and anxious symptoms, although they remained somewhat. The focus on specific modes of sensation, stimulating sensations as alternatives and changes in forms of reaction were fundamental so that progress could occur.

In other words, the materiality of the response as a sign is an essential reference for the work of the therapist as a De-signer, because, below the concreteness of the response as an existing sign (an index, for example), there is a dimension of fundamental potentiality for the therapeutic process, marked by Firstness. Trance, given its proximity to quale-consciousness (CP 6.228), is, *par excellence*, a potential experience in which the rigid references of reality for the person can be reviewed or even reconfigured. At the same time, a response must also be positioned in terms of Thirdness, where symbols, agencies, and laws are located, as well as future prospects. Therefore, when Márcia imagined an important figure in her life, such as a son, this carried something concrete, an existent, when reporting the episode; because it was an imaginary dimension, that sign had great potential for therapeutic intervention in trance in order to favor new possible paths. The same image could also favor, as in fact, it did, her adherence to new symbolic perspectives of the future, especially in terms of existential meanings on life. Signs need to be thought regarding their insertions and their modes of agency within semiotic systems and their consequent symbolic productions. An index, for example, lasts over time as an efficacy response and should be thought of in terms of symbolic changes, as in the case of habit changes. It is possible to verify that Márcia learned to access, at some level, processes from her corporeality regarding pain in order to reduce its intensity during a crisis. She was also able to establish new ways of dealing with anxiety and depression, mainly because of her ability to focus on other types of experience.

Nevertheless, one of the points that drew the most attention was the way she redefined her complex moment of life, permeated by many difficult situations: "the pains from life." As a symbol, the power of this simple phrase covers distinctive topics simultaneously: it situates suffering as a human condition and not as a kind of particular persecution of life against Márcia, as she previously conceived. This was not a victim of suffered circumstances from a history of poverty but a person who, like others, was subjected to illness, disappointment, death, pain, and loss. At the same time, by situating it in a common condition of human suffering, the phrase promoted a crucial temporal dimension since life could show situations of suffering but moments with other types of experiences, as well. It would be up to her to be available for these other moments when life provides them. Therefore, results are not found in a simple phrase repeated by a patient but in the effective semiosis that such a phrase can promote in the universe of their experiences with themselves and with others.

This same phrase, "the pains from life," in turn, can be conceived beyond the limits of results. Neither I nor the patient expected that such a metaphor would be forged, which is constituted as an ingenious creative process. At the same time, it does not seem difficult to conceive that Marcia had considerable baggage and reasons for a solution of this level: there were no prospects of cure for her injuries and pain, but she needed something that would help her raise her children and guide them in life. Moreover, in my understanding, this idea was not a mere wish for survival since Márcia always wished to live a pleasant life. In this way, to the extent that a metaphor took her from a posture of victimization and situated her in the common condition of other people, she was able to regain her desire for good things in life despite the limitations imposed by pain. The metaphor that qualified so many sufferings as "the pains from life" is not a mere result but as a legitimate desirable outcome (Seif, 2019). Its creative content, unexpected and linked to a desirable future, not only guaranteed her such a condition but also provided her with a remarkable shift in life in the face of the situation with so many adversities.

Therefore, from the perspective of De-sign, in addition to results, hypnosis must favor the emergence of desirable outcomes. It is not the expression of response that suggests deeper changes but the reconciliation of the person with themselves (Binswanger, 1935/2008). In the same way, they are not transformations from unconscious to conscious, as Freud would say (1917/1996), which would guarantee such a process, but the person's access to a self that is reinvented and enriched from the hypnotherapeutic relationship. Access to oneself can become more common and frequent, bringing the possibility of that person becoming re-enchanted by the process of self-discovery. By one's own imagination, coupled with subtle trance processes, one can travel through time, space, to find one's world and desire distinct paths for oneself. However, immersion in such potentialities should produce something in the concrete plan because, otherwise, it might become useless (Ibri, 1992/2017). It needs to be materialized in the world, not in the coldness of finished responses and results, but through signs that announce its transformation. The etymology of the word sign linked to *signature* is valuable here since it refers to legitimate something. In this way, signature is closely linked to authorship, being a form of self-legitimation. Desirable outcomes are signs or signatures for new versions of oneself.

Effectiveness

> *Charles Peirce* (1903–1997) *stated that experience is our great master. It was necessary for the researcher or scientist to start from their own experience rather than from an artificial doubt, as suggested by Descartes, on the search for truth. Doing a critique of William James's ideas of pragmatism, Peirce (CP 5.3; 5.429) asserted that a final action should not be the final purpose of a concept. To verify the relevance of philosophical theories, the search should be for general ideas or even for rational purposes. If an intellectual conception results from practical consequences, these should not be thought of as concrete and existing events but as meanings attached to them (CP 5.9). Somewhat anticipating the discussion between revelation (realism) and construction (constructivism) of reality* (Hacking, 2000), *Peirce's pragmatism proposes a continuity between the existing concrete of Secondness and meanings already linked to Thirdness. The results of a hypnotherapeutic process would be linked to its practical implications or meanings. People's conduct, in their configurations of visible and invisible signs, are signs that refer to their beliefs, known to them if only partially. Regarding the patient, this relationship is linked to a reflective attitude that implies self-interpretation, self-criticism, and self-control* (Colapietro, 1989). *As for the therapist or researcher, in addition to this reflexivity, there is the perspective that the final result produces significant changes (habits) in one's ability to think about their field of study. In both cases, it is the experience that is transformed from the inquiry process, which cannot be boiled down to a set of answers.*

Even though it has some aspects in common with the artist, the De-signer should be different from them (Seif, 2019). While the artist wants to express their subjectivity, the De-signer is committed to meeting another's needs. The De-signer also cannot be compared to the technician, as the latter remains linked to commitment and result. As mentioned, the De-signer has a relationship with the other, and from that, desirable outcomes emerge that can meet a necessity but also refer to a creative process originating from joint participation in which both are protagonists. If, roughly speaking, the artist has a commitment to beauty in itself and the technician is focused on efficacy, the De-signer is deeply committed to effectiveness (Seif, 2019). Effectiveness, therefore, can be understood as the way in which the therapist, as De-signer, integrates the aesthetic sense of the artist and the efficacy of the technician, an essential issue for Ericksonian hypnosis (Havens, 1992). The question of how hypnosis works begins to gain new contours by integrating the result of efficacy with the desirable outcomes of effectiveness. In a certain way, during a hypnotherapeutic process, both therapist and patient act as De-signers, contributing to a new living design (configuration) of the experience. To that end, effectiveness implies key notions, such as new ways of integrating with oneself (ego/self), the rise of intentionality, alternatives for autonomy and relationship and reintegration into the *Ethos*.

In the context of this book, these notions will be developed based on case studies of hypnotherapy, as their relevance to confer intelligibility to effectiveness is highlighted. Therefore, the question of how hypnosis works passes through a broader inquiry of the person's experience, as the aesthetic and the technical aspects are integrated and produce something new that transcends them. Before that, there will be a brief discussion on the debate between Freud and Erickson regarding the resolution of the symptom. This debate is important because it introduces relevant points around key notions related to effectiveness.

Asthma Letters

On one occasion, a 35-year-old married woman went to Erickson (Erickson & Rossi, 1979, pp. 237–240) to verify if her asthma was organic or psychogenic, as her doctors claimed. Mrs. G. initially showed a certain irony, as she stated she was almost sure that her problem was organic, but she would like to be sure about it. The interesting point was that her crises occurred all year round, except for the summer when her father did not write her unpleasant letters claiming the inheritance that G.'s mother had left her after passing away. Mrs. G. showed a great facility for trance, which led Erickson to promote the necessary preparation via trance for therapy. Then he took a provocative stance, telling her that, in 20 min, she would go into an asthma attack from a signal (three pencil strokes on the table) and that the attack would cease when she received another signal (a lighter placed in the ashtray). Until then, they could talk about anything. Her response to provocation was: "You must make a high idea about yourself, huh?" However, at the appointed time, Erickson (p. 237) knocked his pencil three times on the table and told her:

> The day is hot. It's July 8. It's summer. There is no smoke, dust, or cold. You do not have any lung infections. And now you have a severe asthma attack. 20 minutes ago, I told you what would happen, and if it were psychogenic, you would respond like this. And the attack will stop when I make it stop. It is psychogenic. Do you see this lighter? That's right. It's not medicine; it's not magic. When I do something with it, your attack will cease. Look closely. Make sure now that your asthma is psychogenic. Just look.

G., in a trance, triggered a strong asthmatic reaction; soon afterwards, Erickson inserted the lighter into the ashtray, and the crisis ceased. He also told her that she could go deeper into a trance in a comfortable and protected way and remember everything that was important. G. recalled some hard times experienced with her mother before she died, already paralyzed from heart issues. Her father, however, remained silent about her mother, offering her no attention or care. G.'s first asthma attack occurred after receiving an unpleasant letter from her father claiming the entire inheritance (a farm). He was already united with a promiscuous woman of dubious character. Over the years, her father kept sending her aggressive letters regarding her mother and asking for full ownership of the farm despite having received a part. These were letters written at different times of the year, with the exception of summer, when both were on vacation. G. always thought of answering them, but eventually gave up and was in great pain. Erickson asked her what she should do about all this, and G. replied that she would bring her father to justice through a lawyer. Her father could help her on the farm and do whatever he wanted for his part, but never, without her authorization, regarding the farm and her other assets of G.. This was fully supported by Justicein's trial, and G. became much calmer on this matter. For 5 years, she continued meeting Erickson in sporadic encounters. She never had an asthma attack again.

The Symptom in the Erickson vs. Freud Debate

The above case poses an old clinical discussion: to what extent is symptom resolution a sign of therapy effectiveness? Freud and Erickson differ considerably on this point. The former considers that the symptom is only the tip of an iceberg, and that clinical resolution should come along with underlying causes. For this reason, he considered hypnosis a kind of cosmetic for treating only symptoms, while his proposal—psychoanalysis—was a kind of surgery for treating the causes and guaranteeing more convincing and lasting cures (Freud, 1905/1996, 1917/1996). Milton Erickson, on the other hand, made a different proposal: his therapy focused on reorganizing the symptom along with a series of systems within the self in which it was inserted. In a surprising similarity with Charles Peirce (Neubern, 2016), his proposal involved notions such as sign configuration, agency, and reintegration of the self. Although he did not name such processes and systems, his own technical approach allows us to infer that Erickson had a very precise level of understanding about them.

For him, hypnosis occupied a special place in this process, given its ease in promoting changes at different levels and facilitating the person's autonomy in dealing with the issues of his life (Erickson, 1992). Nevertheless, cases such as G.'s may suggest mistaken interpretations of Erickson's hypnotic approach, starting with his approach to classical hypnosis. For the hastier reader, what he would have done with his asthmatic patient would be to provoke memories of repressed processes and, once she became aware of them, her symptoms would be healed. For a psychoanalyst, such a solution would probably be palliative since, in his report, there is no mention of elaborating repressed feelings about G.'s parents. The psychoanalyst would also consider that solution fragile for not reaching its possible Oedipal causes, favoring the return of the symptom or its replacement by another.

Such conceptions, however, also have many limitations. On the one hand, reading classical hypnosis brings with it a Cartesian idea that is still quite present in theories and research on Medicine and Psychology: the sign is detached from semiotic networks. G.'s asthma, therefore, as a symptom, would be detached both from her history and from her daily meaning. Even with a history of its origin from trance, the absence of a sign (Peirce, 1903/1991) would not allow for a conception of the materiality of semiotic networks. How would asthma be inserted in such systems? What is its specificity as a sign; what meanings would it have for them, and what relationships would it have with modes of agency? These are questions that are not contemplated in this reading. Psychoanalytic criticism makes sense here, since the historical insertion of asthma is empty as a constituent of the self. Another noteworthy point is that the report is not clear on whether G.'s memories of her asthma were repressed in the sense that they may have been inserted as systems in the unconscious. What seems more plausible is that the theme in question was difficult for her to reflect upon and that she had not yet found the appropriate context to deal with it. Critical theories about repressed memories could significantly relevant at this point (Loftus & Ketcham, 1994).

On the other hand, the psychoanalytic understanding also presents its problems, mainly because it displays the symptom as the result of a conflict between unconscious desires and cultural interdiction. First, the idea of a cause underlying the symptom maintains a linear and causal relationship with the self's modes of agency, which is problematic in semiotic terms because while there may be some linearity, the organization of the self refers to networks of semiosis in complex modes of agency. Relationships between a visible sign, such as the symptom and its networks of semiosis, sometimes visible, sometimes invisible, refer much more to recursive and systemic processes. Hence the difficulty in theorizing subjectivity and hypnosis is so often denounced by Erickson (1992).

Secondly, the universalism in psychoanalytic writings does not enable the consideration of the singular content from semiotic constructions involving the person. The references to G.'s parents in the case do not contain an Oedipal undertone, given that probable feelings of hatred, resentment, hurt, guilt, and gratitude can assume multiple configurations, influenced by different social processes throughout one's life. Such ideas could, through hypnogenesis, be imposed upon G. as narratives, which possibly underwent to their original meanings around father figures. At the same time, most narrative reconstructions do not imply elaboration in the sense of making the unconscious conscious, as proposed in the psychoanalytic method (Freud, 1917/1996). By allowing herself to reflect upon her memories, G. was able to assume a different role concerning her father and interrupt the abusive relationship and injustices on his part. This probably led her to change several networks of meanings about him, but there is no indication that such a process took place during elaboration. Most signs linked in a network to that theme do not fit with an individualized and universal notion of the unconscious.

Thirdly, doubts about the effectiveness of G.'s therapy are unfounded. Roughly speaking, 5 years of absence of symptoms would in itself be a good indicator that the therapeutic process was effective. Cases such as G.'s can imply effective and lasting processes, mainly because they trigger new modes of organization in terms of the different agencies involved. The universalist perspective that healing would only take place under a single path—that of the psychoanalytic method—falls apart in the face of the diversity of possible processes, as noted in hypnosis (Erickson & Rossi, 1979), as well as in other therapeutic methods (Beck, 1995; Nathan, 2001/2014).

Key Notions

The idea of desirable outcomes (Seif, 2019) can be summarized as follows. On the one hand, it implies a reconciliation of the persons with themselves (integrity), especially in terms of the relations between ego and self. On the other hand, it refers to the idea of fulfillment (Neubern, 2022a), that is, something that is achieved via intentionality (teleological sense). Thus, the navigation that characterizes the path of a desirable outcome starts from reintegration with the self, including terms of the imaginary and *Ethos* (belonging), so they can be inserted in the existential plane in another way, previously unimaginable. Such ideas, far from being devoid of practicality, are coherent with Peirce's pragmatic proposal (1903/1997), mainly by situating meanings conveyed as actions in the form of practical results.

The common point that runs through all these topics is the future perspective that characterizes intentionality (Deely, 2009) and constitutes the apex of discussion on desirable outcomes. There is, at this point, an important aspect linked to temporality, which is marked by circularity in lived experience (CP 1.498). Because of the primacy of Firstness, the De-signer plunges into the present, where they can find the past and, above all, dispose of themselves to the future. There is a reconciliation with oneself, especially in terms of integration and *Ethos*, while they are open to the future in terms of intentionality. Their autonomy emerges not as a rupture over determinations but as a way of integrating them to new paths in terms of existence. It is a way of resizing the existential place, integrated with the *Ethos* and one's ability to choose new modes of relating to others and to the world. This process is characterized by the ability to reflect on oneself, linked to what Colapietro (1989, p. 87) considered self-interpretation, self-criticism, and self-control. More than that, it can refer to the surrender of the ego to a greater ideal that may come to inhabit it. This ideal, admirable in itself (aesthetic), implies a constant effort by the ego to reach it (Ethics), requiring logical rationality (semiotics). De-sign inquiry takes place in a hypnotic process and approaches the pragmatic proposal of seeking coherence between belief and conduct (Seif, 2020a).

Integration, Imagination, and Intentionality

A first point linked to integration that hypnosis can promote is the very imaginary life of the self. It is possible to consider that hypnosis commonly provides a more exuberant and accessible imaginary life to people, from which important changes can emerge, in therapeutic terms, full of achievements in terms of meaning. Imagination has been successfully used even in severe situations of psychopathologies, as demonstrated by the great work by Nise da Silveira in Brazil (2015). By giving shape to their feelings and experiences through paintings and sculptures, Silveira's patients left critical situations, in psychopathological terms, for an integrative process that was more consistent with themselves and others. This demanded an internal movement of imagination, whose therapeutic possibilities are diverse, as

Sartre himself (1940/2005) suggests: an image would be able to bring with it symbolic elements, feelings, and the person's own corporeality. Then, imaginary processes have considerable clinical importance because, while they have a flexible and malleable content, they also have an important influence on changes and habit formation (CP 6.136).

> *Nise Magalhaes da Silveira (1905–1999) was one of the most important psychiatrists in Brazil. Her work preceded the psychiatric reform for the humanitarian treatment bestowed on mental health patients. Greatly influenced by Carl Jung, she employed the arts to assist in the integration processes for seriously ill patients, with excellent results. She was also a pioneer in highlighting the role of animals in helping such patients. Currently, in Rio de Janeiro, her legacy can be seen in the Museum of the Unconscious, located at a psychiatric hospital that still adheres to Silveira's therapeutic proposal.*

The integration promoted in hypnosis finds one of its most important themes in terms of relations with pragmatism and De-sign (Seif, 2020a). If pragmatism advocates coherence between belief and conduct, working with images provided during trance is of great significance since it promotes influences on beliefs from the imagination and other qualitative experiences. Thus, when Seif (2020b), for example, refers to a desirable future, he presupposes the imaginary life enriched and cultivated by De-sign to achieve it because the experience of desiring is strongly traversed by imagination, as well as by Love, in its Eros form. In a certain way, imagination permeates and readjusts the paths between belief and conduct, rendering that a common path for pragmatism and De-sign. It becomes one of the main vehicles for people to seek ideals and desirable futures (Seif, 2019), around which they can guide their daily behavior.

The enrichment of the imaginary promoted by hypnosis is deeply associated with the emergence of intentionality. It is true, as Peirce acknowledges (6.220), that processes of Firstness that go nowhere become useless. However, this "place reached," far from the limited idea of visible and isolated responses, is here conceived as a purpose or meaning for life. In other words, the imaginary is fundamental for life as a great process of De-sign so it can have a purpose. Even if a person does not present the answers expected by a researcher or therapist, they are deeply engaged in pursuing this purpose, surrendering to a higher ideal (MS 1.339). By developing the habit of going into a trance, the boundaries between the ego and self become more fluid, intensifying semiotic networks between them. Imaginary processes act strongly in this transit and, due to the icons' vague character, offer ample construction alternatives for the person. The ego, in its fleeting and illusory condition (CP 7.571), surrenders more easily to that process, making itself available to pursue this ideal. Thus, the wealth of semiotic processes that images provide allows the meanings sought to reach, in the psychic and/or concrete life of the person, some level of realization, that is, that they become existing with meaning.

The imaginary life promoted by hypnosis, therefore, cannot be conceived as something without practical value since its processes become fundamental in the organization of the self. If, on the one hand, the phenomenological base of experience is a quality, on the other, it provides the emergence of intentionality. This precedes other achievements that a person builds during their trajectory. If, as a process of quale consciousness, it is fluid and influential on forming habits, imagination is also something prior to deliberation. That is why, before deliberate wanting, there is desire and intentionality; that is, processes give desirable outcomes and unexpected content. Without that, the construction of meanings in life (Frankl, 1959/1984) would be an impossible task, mainly because it would move people around the world by presenting themselves as phenomena marked by Firstness. Desire, feeling, quality, ecstasy, and a possible collection of new narratives that can spring from it when people least expect it are some of the experiences that permeate desirable outcomes.

In both cases discussed here (Márcia and G.), there are significant processes of integration. In G.'s case, the relationship with her abusive father came out of a marginalized condition and became a central topic in her therapy. From the moment she allowed herself to visualize and face various episodes that pointed to an abusive relationship, she was able to reintegrate with herself. The hypnotic experience helped her do so, at first, via her condition as the daughter of an abusive father. G. did not seek to break with her father but to be a daughter treated with dignity. This became possible by recognizing, via trance, the suffering that her father imposed on her through his demands of inheritance and attacks on her mother. The trance provided G. with a valuable experience regarding the transparent visualization of the lived space (Gebser, 1949/1985), as when she clearly remembered her father's destructive behaviors, her mother's delicate health, followed by her death and the abusive letters sent by her father. For some fear or trepidation not explicit in the account, these scenes did not seem repressed but clouded by suffering. Moreover, trance allowed her to have a more transparent view, and she could see what action she should take. It also provided a circular experience of time, as it showed her the past and opened herself to a different future via intentionality. As this suffering was integrated by reflexivity, it ceased to express itself via symptoms to receive the due treatment at the social level—with measures to stop the abuse. There is, in this process, an integration between body (mainly the symptom) and social life (mind), between her and her father, as well as between the past and the present. The very memory of her deceased mother was restored to the extent that, in her world, her mother began to be respected and protected.

In Márcia's case, even if her pain remained and generated insecurity in life, the prospect of being a good mother to her children gave her new configurations about herself, with the construction of new narratives. The suffering caused by so many difficult situations had a role in her existence, and this would strengthen her so she could be a good mother and better raise her own children. In her therapy, she sought to work on the transcendence of an attitude of survival towards an attitude of knowing experience. While in the first, Márcia would live and meet her basic needs, as well as those of her children, in the second, despite a series of traumatic events, it would be possible to extract meaning from the difficulties of living a life with purpose.

In short, integrating the person with themselves is one of the main topics that help to understand desirable outcomes in hypnotic processes. The flexibility of imagination and feelings, combined with the organizing power of symbols and habits, enables lived experiences as separate from a person, such as the symptom so that it can be integrated into their self under new perspectives of meaning. More importantly, they provide considerable subjective enrichment, which is fundamental for new modes of agency as well as new ways of existing in the world. Intentionality, linked to a desirable future (Seif, 2019), can be understood both through a person's ability to generate meanings about their existence and their capacity to dream new ways of life. The dream here refers not only to the phenomenon of the dream that occurs during sleep (Nathan, 2011) but also to its figurative sense of wishing via imagination (Seif, 2019). Here is the condition of a stronger and more intense transit between ego and self that occurs mainly through imaginary pathways, as children commonly do. However, unlike them, in the integration discussed here, this transit is made with the social and concrete conditions of reality also integrated into the self. It is about a new position before the world since the person goes through a process of reconciliation with oneself (Binswanger, 1935/2008).

> *Body image reconfiguration necessarily permeates integrative processes promoted by hypnosis. If therapy, in general, is conceived as a form of self-reconciliation, it requires new modes of relating to one's body image, as it is one of the most central self-subjective systems* (Gallagher & Zahavi, 2008). *Although Erickson did not elaborate much about body image, he stated it was the first field to be known by the therapist, especially in brief therapy* (Haley, 1985).

As the person rediscovers and reconnects, they are also facing their problems, conflicts, suffering, and limitations that have so often provided an experience of paralysis in life. Then, as they "wear" their own self and body (Neubern, 2018a), they make themselves available to the flow of existence, creating powerful meanings for life and the future. Thus, the ability to imagine a desirable future occurs both despite these limitations and thanks to them since they are integrated into new senses of the complex ecology of the self. The idea of rebirth, reported by many people who underwent hypnotherapy, does not refer to the emergence of an alien self without a relationship to that person's own history and context; instead, it is a self that integrates different facets, remains capable of creating and, in a certain way, of living in today's imagination—the desirable future in the project of a new life.

Autonomy and Relationships

Desirable outcomes can be present in different dimensions of changes that come from a hypnotic process—autonomy in particular. Many clinicians report that people commonly seek therapeutic help when they feel their autonomy is compromised or paralyzed in some sectors of their lives (Haley, 1985; Minuchin & Nichols, 1995). In a way, autonomy can be thought of on two major fronts. On the one hand, there is a series of determinisms influencing the self from different fields, such as biology, environment, sociology, anthropology, gender, economics, spirituality, religion, ethnicity, and history, among others. On the other hand, some are the most immediate social influences, embodied in the ways people relate with each other. Thus, while in the first way of conceiving autonomy, there is a diversity of influences on a person's life, in the second, the question of the other takes center stage in semiotic (CP. 5.313) and existential terms (Binswanger, 1935/2008). As Edgar Morin (1990) would say, autonomy and dependence shape a paradox when thinking about living beings, particularly human beings. Relationships developed by a person and their multiple determinations become essential to conceive desirable outcomes linked to autonomy.

Based on Peirce's notion of the self (Colapietro, 1989; Petrilli, 2017), three aspects can be highlighted regarding desirable outcomes from hypnosis and their relations with autonomy. First, if the self interpenetrates with other selves and the world (CP 5.313), the hypnotic process should analyze and work on ways for such semiotic exchanges to take place. In different modes of violent or toxic relationships (such as harassment, sexual abuse, kidnapping, and assault), victims report feeling the abuser seems to have fixated on them. From a semiotic point of view, these reports are significant, as they refer to intense semiotic processes that are established from similar relationships. Thus, the repetition of the scene, the image, and the lines of the aggressor come to life in that person's universe, causing intense suffering. Through hypnosis, they can reconfigure these processes and interrupt their abuser's ability to paralyze them. More importantly, the person begins to have as a reference of the world other types of desires and experiences with which to connect, disengaging from suffering. These are changes that occur in terms of agency, conceiving transformations in logical constructions (meaning) of the self regarding specific themes of life. Later, the feeling of paralysis dissolves, and the person assumes different attitudes toward their relationships and life in general.

In G.'s case, her recollection of various abusive scenes with her father led her to have different attitudes. Although Erickson did not describe further details about changes made in terms of her imagination, with its senses and emotions, G.'s active attitude refers to changes in beliefs on a deeper level. By recalling in trance various abusive scenes with her father and her mother's suffering, G. was able to assume a distinct role in her relationship with her father. From an abuser-victim relationship with the father, possibly configured at a deeper symbolic level of herself, she began to maintain a distinct relationship as she left the condition of the victim, defended herself and her mother, and asserted her rights as daughter and heir. Erickson's question about what she would like to do with it all seemed to be more of an index for her to allow herself to take on a new role. It is as if she had been expelled from herself through the belief that she should accept her father as an abuser in her own world. Some children commonly submit to that type of relationship with their parents because they believe if anybody questions them, they will be disrespectful or aggressive toward their parents. Moreover, when imagining a desirable future (Seif, 2019), an abusive figure will be removed from the scenario of the self and deprived of its influential power. In the same way, this desirable future can also undo false paradoxes, like being accepted as a child—as long as they accept to be abused by their parents.

In Márcia's case, the abusive sign was much more fate itself, especially because of various negative events in her life. As with many people, drastic and unfortunate events often make them believe that fate is working against them and that they do not deserve to be successful and happy in their lives. Therefore, one of the axes of therapy was to recognize the suffering generated by such events while promoting alternatives of significance for them. From a person who felt like a victim of her circumstances, Márcia began to see herself as someone who survived many difficult moments—but someone who could also achieve, in her experiences and concrete life, desires linked to her meaning of life. Such an action of intentionality, born from hypnosis, was relevant in terms of her frequent access to trance, especially during moments of crisis. Whether through the formal search for self-hypnosis or through spontaneous moments of reverie, Márcia placed herself in reflective processes in which she could find alternatives for dealing with issues and situations she experienced. The resumption of access to traditional knowledge, as discussed later, was fundamental for both.

Secondly, the self is a complex semiotic process (CP 5.313). Significantly linked to the previous topic, hypnosis must contemplate the flows through which signs are translated into others. In many clinical situations, people refer to their suffering through words such as "gloomy," "gray," "sticky," "bitter," "heavy," and "paralyzing" (Ellenberger, 1958/2004; Neubern, 2018a). These signs contaminate fields of experience, hindering or preventing alternatives altogether. This way, suicide and other self-destructive behaviors can become the path since the experience of their worlds does not allow them to glimpse any hope. These cases suggest that the semiosis in these people's selves remains linked to a negative logic, which implies how agency in the systems of the self have worked. Again, there is the condition in which certain premises (beliefs) come to govern behaviors, but they do so from a perspective of destruction. It is a system of signs that blocks possibilities for one of the most essential characteristics of semiosis: growth (CP 5.3; 5.433). It would not be an exaggeration to say that the negative trait of these semiotic processes, typical of depression, tends to block the development of other networks, putting the self, as a whole, at risk. If the self is a system of signs (CP 5.225) prevented from fulfilling its role in terms of growth, its psychic illness becomes a practically obligatory path.

Hypnosis is commonly used in such circumstances on two fronts. At first, the focus is on expressed signs, as if they were considered in isolation. They are situated in experiences with distinct sensations and meanings to reconfigure the type of experience they represent. Hypnotic inductions marked by contact with water (bathing in rivers, seas, and showers) are common, because, in addition to the pleasure intrinsic to it, it also suggests cleaning undesirable substances, that is, signs of negative semiosis (Neubern, 2018a). In G.'s case, the symptom of asthma was the initial sign: a symptom about which doubts hung. Her doctors saw its psychic origin, while she attributed it to organic origins. This controversy resembled indices of her difficulty in entering the complex theme involving her father's abuse more closely. More specifically, in Márcia's case, I sought to emphasize an association between gustation and several other experiences in her story. In opposition to the dominance of signs linked to pain and lack of taste for life, I appropriated her pleasure in trying different foods to associate them with moments with her children and husband, caring for plants, expecting a new child, doing her work, and cooking, among others. During trance, experiences referring to different logics focused and activated semiotic networks that had, until then, been blocked by suffering. Thus, trance enabled a qualitative experience of sensation (taste) to spread and spread to other fields of experience that had been compromised by depression. It is, in summary, a sign of Firstness leading to processes of Thirdness, because of the generalization it seemed to acquire. Done through different axes and themes, this procedure can disturb dominant hostile networks and promote alternative networks with the self.

This same way of proceeding is maintained on the second front, whose emphasis relies on the agency. The therapist tends to oppose dominant negative logic through other technical resources, such as metaphors and stories, and above all, dramatic action. The therapist embodies a role of new logic to the other (Neubern, 2016). Thus, Erickson took on the role of a provocative man (like G.'s father), who would tap the table with a pencil and provoke asthma attacks; however, unlike the patient's father, he was willing to take care of her. This mode of communication, rooted in iconicity, is configured as the clinic of showing (Neubern, 2016) and has a great capacity to influence modes of agency. When Erickson stated that, with one gesture, she would go into an asthma attack, he merely presented her with a situation without explaining it to her: the pencil tapping on the table was a way of addressing the painful impacts of her father's letters. At the same time, when he signaled to her that the crisis would end with the lighter in the ashtray, he showed her the message (without explaining it) that what made her suffer so much could be over. After this gesture, she had no more asthma attacks. Erickson seemed, therefore, to have become a symbolic icon for someone who knew her situation and could effectively help her. From there, it was possible for her to enter a challenging field of experiences (negative memories) and decide what to do with them.

Similarly, I allowed my role to be perceived as a "Professor" by Márcia, since she reported needing a philosophy of life that would allow her to understand a journey marked by so much suffering. Although Erickson does not discuss her treatment in detail, her case was also marked by novelty content, typical of desirable outcomes, which may include signs linked to different phenomenological categories. With Márcia, in turn, the surprise of the news came both from the emphasis on sensory experience associated with pleasure and from the expression coined by herself as "pains from life," as mentioned above. From the point of view of a De-sign inquiry (Seif, 2020a), this novelty can be understood as an index of reactivation or creation for new semiotic networks.

Thirdly, autonomy also refers to relationships with the unconscious. In clinical terms, most situations of suffering are paralyzing precisely because they escape a person's known attempts to deal with them, where Peirce's self-control can be located (CP 1.406). Nevertheless, there are two classic questions regarding autonomy that oppose hypnosis. The first is that the ego, by itself, is unable to deal with these problems, given its limited capacity for action in the psychic world. This limitation becomes even more remarkable when the ego is closed as an individualized instance, and bears control, constituting, for Peirce, a practical joke or a disappointing illusion (CP 4.69). The ego, in itself, plays the role of negotiator with multiple determinations that affect it more than that of a "Superman" who might be capable of controlling it. Secondly, hypnosis as a procedure is associated with external control by an authority, the researcher or the therapist, over a person (Méheust, 1999). Even today, the idea that hypnosis is a procedure that does not provide autonomy to people remains present among researchers and healthcare professionals despite recent research and clinical studies (Neubern & Bioy, 2023). In addition to these two problems, a hypnotic process would not be able to provide autonomy because of the limited character of the individualized ego and the authoritarian content of that therapeutic procedure.

Part of these objections has already been answered in the chapter "Working with", in which it is highlighted that the hypnotic relationship should be based on a partnership between therapist and subject instead of being based on the authority-submission binomial. The principles of utilization and indirect communication (Erickson & Rossi, 1979), from the perspective of De-sign (Seif, 2019), show how hypnosis can be constituted as a partnership in which the autonomy of the protagonists is fundamental. However, the limits of the ego or the individual for promoting broader changes in terms of experience deserve further discussion.

The first point to be highlighted as a response to such objections is the notion of self as a sign (CP 5.225). If the self is a sign or system of signs, it is made of multiple semiotic processes while it engages in them. It follows that semiosis is potentially infinite, which places the self far beyond diffuse limits. Therefore, even if a person's self has a singular and unrepeatable character, it does not affect notions that forge the Modern individual's body, mind, or brain (Dumont, 1983). The separation between people cannot be conceived in a radical way, since each person always brings with them others with whom they relate, who are also signs in turn and who, during trance, can become more explicit than they usually act for that person. In G.'s case, there was a clear emergence, during her session with Erickson, of signs linked to her father, his current wife, and her mother. Not only did these characters appear, but a whole symbolic plot rose and engaged with their idea. From this internal, imaginary, but inhabited world, G. actively placed herself in the actions of the concrete world, making important decisions for her own integrity. In short, change is not centered on individual action by isolated and closed persons themselves but on collective interactions that transit between the imaginary stage of a self and complex social plots from the concrete world.

Therefore, even transcending the polarities between individual vs. social or internal vs. external, there would be a question as to whether these semiotic networks might create something different or repeat what they received. At first, the notion of sign (CP 5.484) implies the lack of a complete relationship with both its object and its interpretant, conveying only some characteristics from the first to the second. In a complex situation like a hypnotic trance, the same sign can be implicated with an object in different ways at different times. There is, therefore, recursivity (Santaella, 2004) on the triad that composes the sign, which raises the possibility of a new one. Furthermore, the multiplicity that characterizes reality (Ibri, 1992/2017) reminds us of a creative dimension of reality itself. Absolute and deterministic laws prevented the growth of signs—inconceivable in semiotic and metaphysical terms.

The self becomes, for Peirce, a specific form of mind primarily on account of its ability to think or develop inferences (CP 6.101). This conscious ability to use, play, think, manipulate, and produce a genuine bricolage with signs is what, in a way, would differentiate humans from animals (Deely, 2002). Thus, consciousness would be coupled with a reflective capacity in which the self could self-control, self-criticize, and self-interpret (Colapietro, 1989). This would allow ego and self to produce autonomy amid various determinations that constitute and influence them throughout life. While signs, ego, and self receive strong determinations from the world (biology, genetics, economy, politics, religion, environment, society, culture), at the same time they manage to exercise their capacity for self-creation. Hypnosis, through the lenses of De-sign (Seif, 2019), adds some important points about the relationships between determination and autonomy. The first of these links refers to imaginary enrichment brought by hypnosis and plays a central role in changing relationships between ego and self. The plunge into a qualitative state of consciousness enables greater transit between these instances, characterized by a more vivid and intense flow in signs of Firstness. Regarding the self, a series of unconscious processes can be reactivated and become explicit in their influences. Imaginary enrichment brings innumerable semiotic processes that, by implicating such systems, already provide them with some kind of reconfiguration. Although the individual self (ego) is "illusory" or a "practical joke" (CP 4.69), it plays a role in these exchanges, as it greatly reduces one's sense of control over body and mind. Admittedly, in general, this role of disinflation[3] is explicitly allowed by the person who, with the therapist's help, allows themselves to navigate a fluid experience. Even in cases of total amnesia, the ego remains active and holds its senses of preservation and criticism against eventual danger and/or abuse.

> *Even going through this disinflation, the subject does not lose control of what happens during trance. The hypothesis of loss of control, since the time of Mesmer and Puységur, was one of the reasons for ostracism and resistance to hypnosis. However, contemporary therapists are practically unanimous in considering that this hypothesis does not hold. What seems possible are processes of collective manipulation present in sects* (Nathan & Swertvaegher, 2003) *and extremist movements* (Dimsdale, 2021) *that make people deliberately consider socially reprehensible or even criminal attitudes. Despite their technical similarity, such cases do not refer to hypnosis.*

In G.'s case, for example, negative memories were not repressed or inaccessible in the unconscious. Her doctors' statements about the psychic origin of her asthma should have pointed out many elements already known to her. The question seems to have passed much more through a fear of dealing with these questions, as she may have felt powerless. In Márcia's case, on the other hand, the resumption of other experiences in the hypnotic narrative evoked memories and images that had been forgotten due to her attention on themes from her own life. They would not, therefore, be forgotten because they were morally reprehensible or difficult to deal with but because they did not seem relevant in the face of the narratives she began to adopt about herself. In general, dominant narratives and settings that people adopt eventually cause a hypnotic effect on them in that they help patients focus intensely on particular themes and experiences to the detriment of others.

The key point of this process is: as the ego allows itself this disinflation, it becomes coherent with its role as a medium between the world of the self and the real world, with its physical and social constraints. In conditions promoted by hypnosis, it takes the role of a sign and behaves as representative and creator at once. Admittedly, they represent a series of collective influences, as mentioned, and carry the baggage that characterizes it as belonging, in some way, to these niches (*Ethos*). Márcia, for example, allowed herself to face her complex situation as she felt reconnected with her family and ancestral origins. Possibly, G. was also able to improve her changes as she connected with feelings linked to her parents and her own sense of dignity. Signs that inhabited her, through their multiple relationships with the world, acquired new meanings that were decisive for her attitude towards her father and life itself.

Moreover, the ego also has the role of creator, which makes it capable of transforming, through its own rationality, the various influences it receives. In its condition as a creative sign (MS 318) that it develops in dialogue with the world, it provides growth as well as ideas. This is one of the most critical topics in desirable outcomes (Seif, 2019) since all conscious activity in the person's rationality leads to networks of unexpected signs that surprise them, and on which they can build narratives but cannot develop absolute control. Desirable outcomes have a certain autonomy as they are also signs and, at the same time, influence that person, given their teleological content. They can even be said to have a somewhat hypnotic influence on people because they promote important alternatives to life. This is how Márcia understood her mission of being a good mother to her children, not only as survival but because she should be able to adopt constructive attitudes and make good choices in life despite her suffering. It is very likely that something similar developed in G., especially because future prospects were an essential principle for Erickson's therapy (1992).

The relationships between ego and self play an essential role in the autonomy-dependence paradox. If, from a metaphysical and semiotic point of view, the ego is a practical joke, it is nevertheless relevant in clinical terms. As a medium, it learns to deflate itself through hypnosis in order to become available to multiple influences of the self. If, as in some psychopathology cases, the ego can be trapped and become a mere repeater of these influences, in other situations, it can exercise its freedom through creation. Nevertheless, that freedom should not be only conceived in terms of "despite determinations", although this makes sense for many people, like Márcia. It also creates because of such determinations, as they offer limits. As Raposa (2020) would say, if the ego is comparable to a surfer under the sea of the self, it is thanks to gravity, the movement of the waves, and other determining factors that the surfer manages to be creative and develop the most daring maneuvers. In terms of De-sign (Seif, 2019), this creation is specially related to limits because, as they understand them, that person can transcend them. Márcia and G. managed to develop and build critical change because, among other reasons, they understood the determinations imposed by the suffering they experienced. They served as beacons that signaled where they could jump in terms of their new life.

Finally, reflexivity, a person's ability to think about himself, constitutes one of the most critical topics in terms of autonomy. Seeing it as consciousness, Peirce (Colapietro, 1989) described it in terms of self-control, self-criticism, and self-interpretation, in which inferences and the growth of signs themselves would be developed. Although the ego has a vital role in such processes, it would not be coherent to consider their exclusive focus as a kind of box from which ideas sprout and develop. The question goes much further through bonds of Love (*Agape*), characterized by an intense semiotic network present in thinking processes (Seif, 2019). As the ego learns, through trance, to deflate itself, this powerful imaginary flow runs through it more efficiently, and some crucial processes can reset. The person might allow themselves, for example, more prolonged and pertinent moments of reverie, letting this flow permeate themes of their life, from where they can extract important ideas and reflections, as it happened with Márcia. They can also see themselves at the same time in the audience and on the stage of this imaginary theater; from there, they can extract valuable ideas for therapeutic needs, as it occurred with G. In short, by learning to act deliberately as a sign or a medium, the ego favors multiple, individual, and collective potentialities so they can help transform that person's life, especially in terms of new ideas.

At this point, the knowledgeable reader of Erickson's work could easily make a connection with his notion of wise and therapeutic unconscious—so it can be appropriately activated for therapy. This topic really deserves numerous and profound studies; theories that recognize internal wisdom in helping a person to reconfigure and even transcend their difficulties are not common in Psychology and related sciences. Ethnopsychological studies (Nathan, 2021; Neubern & Nogueira, 2019) can be paramount for that since they highlight collective influences and wisdom manifested in people's selves, in cultural technologies such as trance, oracles, and in dream interpretations. However, Peirce (MS 1.399) names an essential alternative to inquiry: only by submitting the self to an admirable ideal a whole level of reflexivity be obtained. It is as if the very connection with something that is collective and intersects the self can lead a person to a fuller awareness of themselves and their own life. An idea could be transformed into signs in such a way that agents fulfill their roles as signs, that is, in making inefficient relationships efficient (CP 8.332). The idea might be realized through signs linked to those behaviors and meanings experienced by the person.

It would be difficult to sustain that such a process was totally concretized for both clinical cases described here. Social ideals (which do not always coincide with Peircean ideals) are often a source of suffering due to the oppression they breed among people. Moreover, De-sign provides a hint: the notions of *Eros* and *Agape* as teleology (Seif, 2019). In G.'s case, her own compassion for her sick and wronged mother served as drive to oppose her father's oppressions. Being true to her mother's desire, being well with herself, and preserving her image as a mother formed likely ideals for her changes. As for Márcia, on the other hand, her own suffering led her to dialogue with life, questioning its sense of justice. Something seemed to support her so that she would not be crushed by various difficult situations she had been in. Her own body, aching and incapacitated, seemed vehemently opposed to so many setbacks. Therefore, Eros could provide something of that ideal (of preserving oneself and pursuing a life with pleasure). More importantly, her love for her children gave her a more pronounced search for a new way of life, as they needed her example and a healthy mother's presence. Even if these ideals did not provide these two women with the fullness of rationality, according to Peirce (Colapietro, 1989), they served, to some extent, as organizers of their integrity and autonomy, they even provided a way to assimilate pain, the grotesque, the morally reprehensible, and injustice into a new logic for their own lives.

Ethos

The idea of desirable outcomes implies a new insertion between the matrices of belonging or *Ethos* that precede people's lives. *Ethos*, in its Greek etymology, is a word that refers both to habits (hence its connection with Ethics as a philosophical discipline), and to habitat or dwelling, to the idea of belonging (Figueiredo, 1992). In the conception adopted here (Neubern, 2018b), *Ethos* could not be associated with the idea of individualized self as devised by the Modern paradigm because it requires a complex view of self, as proposed by semiotics (Colapietro, 1989; Petrilli, 2017). The self is a sign or, more appropriately, a sign system: it needs its roots to be understood.

The self that constitutes a person has individuality and identity, but it is in constant interpenetration with the world on different levels. In a way, the determinations that precede it, especially at the level of collective agency, also serve as its object in semiotic terms. Reconciliation with oneself, as promoted in hypnotherapy, causes the sign to revisit its object in recursive terms and to modify itself in the process. A return to the origins is, therefore, one way of favoring new modes of growth in semiotic terms, enriching the self based on that type of reunion. Even if it is a return to foundations—its objects—that experience has a character of novelty, which promotes new paths of semiosis. Like an existential gaze (Binswanger, 1935/2008), this movement of returning to oneself attributes them to a new place in the world, with new possibilities of moving and feeling comfortable. This place, for the person, includes a sense of familiarity even if it is new; to that, they feel belonging and a sense of possession. The place in question is formed by a matrix of semiotic relationships, deeply marked by affection, bonds with people, places, elements from nature (rivers, seas, forests, animals, skies), rites, objects, beings, and a whole cosmology (Nathan, 2021) that is fundamental for this common ground where these diverse signs can meet.

For understanding this place, ethnopsychology can be a beneficial influence because the *Ethos* lived by people, as signs, does not always coincide with materialistic logic that organizes macrosocial influences on individual selves. Nathan (2015) brings a significant example when referring to the biblical figure of Abraham. Under the voice of an unknown God, he leaves his family in Ur to seek a new land and have offspring "as numerous as the stars of heaven". This experience, at first, incorporates all elements of delirium, hallucination, or failure because Abraham and his wife Sarah were already advanced in age, and it was difficult for them to breed such numerous offspring. Moreover, God did not allow his image to be represented by idols made by men; that was an opposite sign to his family's original craft—the manufacture of idols. God himself was not represented by the great traditions of his people, and his contact with Abraham constituted a heretical experience for his physical *Ethos*. Nevertheless, Abraham follows this voice and becomes the patriarch of three of the world's major religions—Judaism, Christianity, and Islam.

In the perspective adopted here, it is not correct to consider Abraham's relationship with God as a successful hallucination, as it became socially shared. It only refers to a relationship that is neither direct nor linear between visible, public signs and the broader semiotic processes of Thirdness that compose great social organizations. If we think in terms of a semiosphere (Lotman, 2001), a large portion of social and biological processes are orchestrated at broader levels by large invisible *machineries* that do not always express themselves clearly to humans. Thus, Abraham, as an active and creative sign, became the representative of a new *machinery* linked to the idea of a unique, creator and invisible God, who already existed amongst his people but remained marginalized. As he founded a new community, new semiotic processes were embodied and brought to life in social practices. This may explain why some people live and experience situations differently from those already institutionalized, so they introduce new trends to their fields (Satprem, 1970/2019). As signs, these individuals manage to embody the influence of agency and *machinery* formed on the margins of the dominant, giving them life in everyday social exchanges.

Abraham's example is relevant for assimilating the notion of *Ethos*: linked to a person, it will not always correspond to previous theoretical notions held by a psychologist or researcher. Even if one's blood-related family, for example, is an important group, reconciliation with the *Ethos* will not necessarily go through it. Under an ethnopsychological reading (Neubern, 2022b), *Ethos* can refer to the a person's relationship, as a sign, with broader agencies and *machinery* as they reconnect through intentionality. In this reconnection, there is, on the one hand, an experience of diaphanous spaces (Gebser, 1949/1985), breaking with the absolute content of material reality and demanding a vision of transparency. At the same time, insertion into *Ethos* involves a multiple dimension of time that comes from the fatalistic linearity of Modernity (Hall, 1969/1983) and opens a broader and more circular encounter between present, past and future. Thus, someone can establish new modes of negotiation with various signs that make up their *Ethos*, promoting significant reformulations of meaning about their history and new possibilities of destiny. Trance constitutes a critical cultural technology in different groups as a way of promoting reconciliation with the *Ethos* (Neubern, 2018b).

Among the cases discussed here, Márcia's is much more helpful in terms of *Ethos*. During her trance sessions, ego decentering and disinflation were fundamental for her to access this world of ancestry, providing her with important reconstructions of meaning. At that point, there was a valuable change in significance for her situation. Her ethnic condition of African and Indigenous origins was linked to poverty and marginality in Brazil (Souza, 2019). Due to the nature of vulnerability, people like Márcia often feel inferior and victimized in everyday events that commonly confirm social constructions around that perceived inferiority. The instance of obstetric violence she suffered during her delivery demonstrates these mechanisms of social exclusion and violence. In tandem with her accident, it became a nucleus that made her relive social situations that confirmed her "inferior" social condition and, as a consequence, led to a life without hope. Suicide seemed, therefore, a possible solution to end suffering.

However, after reconnecting with her *Ethos* in trance, she accessed two relevant factors that contributed to that change. First, her African and Indigenous origins, socially excluded in Brazil, were also a source of wisdom, joy, and beauty. Through them, Márcia managed to resume her cultural activities (capoeira, folklore, traditional music) and see herself in a privileged identity: despite exclusion through numerous cases of historical violence, her ethnic condition made her feel privileged because of the cultural and symbolic richness of her *Ethos*. This resumption was fundamental for her to build the idea that her pains were pains of life, that is, a beautiful sign of a desirable outcome. Secondly, this kind of experience removes a person from a condition of loneliness. She is no longer alone in the face of such obstacles; instead, she has the presence and wisdom of Gods and ancestors who inhabit her *Ethos*. Even though her pains had persisted, and she still faced many difficult situations, she could retake a life of meaning from this encounter and from her concern for her children. Access to her Ethos has become for her a possible legacy to be transmitted to her children.

Effectiveness and the Therapist

As discussed, De-sign implies a dialogical relationship (Seif, 2019), intensely involving protagonists as De-signers. It was also pointed out that hypnosis, due to hypnogenesis and to the porosity of the self, favors the intensity of that relationship in contrast to an ordinary conversation. The therapist does not come out unscathed from such a mode of relating since their own being is integrated into it; as a result, their subjectivity is a central parameter for the conception of effectiveness.

Effectiveness can be thought of on different fronts for the legitimacy of research. The constructions that explain and highlight desirable outcomes require logical coherence, as some authors of qualitative tendencies would say (Gonzalez Rey & Mitjans, 2017); otherwise, one does not have a research perspective, only the personal expression of an experience. This logical coherence can even favor an idea of resisting constructs, as Modern researchers would say—a resistance in which desirable outcomes, as logical constructions, would be able to maintain themselves even under the criticism of competent researchers. Another essential way of conceiving legitimacy refers to the very role of the subject and the collectivity they represent as a sign. Desirable outcomes emerge because of the subject's condition and given their protagonist content—not to mention acknowledgment by those who represent the collective *Ethos* represented within that subject.

Nevertheless, it is in the therapist's own experience that desirable outcomes can have remarkable consequences in terms of legitimation. If, as Peirce (musement) would say, the consequence of a good argument is a habit, the therapist is also transformed by what they help create because, from the perspective of De-sign, hypnosis is not an individualistic process but a shared experience that profoundly influences both parties, therapist and patient. Thus, the dialogue with oneself, temporal and circular reflections upon one's own trajectory, and an attitude of openness to desirable futures stem from their meditative moments, in which trance may seem more subtle or clear. If they help someone else connect with their own *Ethos*, they can also provide that encounter with themselves, especially in terms of aesthetic ideals. Hypnotherapy transcends the question of technical application and professional exercise to be situated as a path of self-transformation.

References

Atkins, R. (2016). *Peirce and the conduct of life. Sentiment and instinct in ethics and religion*. Cambridge University Press.
Beck, J. (1995). *Cognitive therapy: Basic and beyond*. Guilford Press.
Binswanger, L. (2008). Sur la Psychothérapie [On psychotherapy]. In L. Binswanger (Ed.), *Introduction à l'analyse existentielle*. Minuit. (original work published in 1935).
Colapietro, V. (1989). *Peirce's approach to the self*. Suny.
Deely, J. (2002). *What distinguishes human understanding?* St Augustine's Press.
Deely, J. (2009). *Intentionality and semiotics. A story of mutual fecundation*. University of Scranton Press.
Dimsdale, J. (2021). *Dark persuasion. A history of brainwashing from pavlov to social media*. Yale University Press.
Dumont, L. (1983). *Essais sur l'Individualisme. Une perspective anthropologique sur l'idéologie moderne* [Essays on individualism. An anthropological perspective on modern ideology]. Seuil.
Ellenberger, H. (2004). A clinical introduction to psychiatric phenomenology and existential analysis. In R. May, P. Angel, & H. Ellenberger (Eds.), *Existence* (pp. 92–126). Jason Aronson Book. (original work published in 1958).
Erickson, M. (1992). Healing in hypnosis. In E. Rossi, M. Ryan, & F. Sharp (Eds.), *The seminars, workshops, and lectures of Milton Erickson, MD* (Vol. 1). Irvington.
Erickson, M., & Kubie, L. (1941). The sucessful treatment of a case of acute hysterical depression by a return under hypnosis to a critical phase of childhood. *Psychoanalytic Quarterly, 10*(4), 122–142.

Erickson, M., & Rossi, E. (1979). *Hypnotherapy: An exploratory casebook*. Irvington.
Facco, E. (2021). Hypnosis and hypnotic ability between old beliefs and new evidences: An epistemological reflection. *American Journal of Clinical Hypnosis, 64*(1), 20–35. https://doi.org/1 0.1080/00029157.2020.1863181
Fann, K. T. (2010). *Peirce's theory of abduction*. Partidrge.
Figueiredo, L. (1992). *Revisitando as psicologias. Da epistemologia à ética das práticas e discursos psicológicos* [Revisiting psychology. From epistemology to the ethics of psychological practices and discourses]. Vozes.
Frankl, V. (1984). *Man's search for meaning*. Pocket Books. (original work published in 1959).
Freud, S. (1905). Sobre a psicoterapia [On psychotherapy]. In: J. Salomão (1996). (Ed.), *Obras Completas de Sigumund Freud* (Vol. VII, pp. 239–252). Imago.
Freud, S. (1917). Terapia analítica [Analytic therapy]. In: J. Salomão (1996). (Ed.), *Obras Completas de Sigumund Freud* (Vol. XVI, pp. 523–540). Imago.
Gallagher, S., & Zahavi, D. (2008). *The phenomenological mind. An introduction to philosophy of mind and cognitive sciences*. Routledge.
Gebser, J. (1985). *The ever-present origin*. Ohio University Press. (original work published in 1949).
Gonzalez Rey, F. (2019). Subjectivity in debate: Some reconstructed philosophical premises to advance its debates in psychology. *Journal of Theory and Social Behavior, 49*, 1–23.
Gonzalez Rey, F. & Mitjans, A. (2017). *Subjetividade: teoria, epistemologia e método* [Subjectivity: Theory, epistemology, and method]. Alínea.
Hacking, I. (2000). *The social construction of what?* Harvard University Press.
Haley, J. (1985). *Conversations with Milton Erickson*. Triangle Press.
Hall, E. (1983). *The dance of life: The other dimension of time*. Doubleday & Company. (original work published in 1969).
Hartshorne, C. & Weiss, P. (1980). *The collected papers of Charles S. Peirce* (CP, 8 vol.). Harvard University Press.
Havens, R. (1992). *The wisdom of Milton H. Erickson*. Irvington.
Ibri, I. (2017). *Kósmos Noetós: The metaphysical architecture of Charles Peirce*. Springer. (original work published in 1992).
Loftus, E., & Ketcham, K. (1994). *The myth of repressed memories. False memories and allegations of sexual abuse*. St Martin's Griffin.
Lotman, Y. (2001). *Universe of the mind. A semiotic theory of the culture*. Indiana University Press.
Méheust, B. (1999). *Somnambulisme et Médiumnité* [Somnambulism and Mediumship]. Synthélabo.
Minuchin, S., & Nichols, M. (1995). *Family healing. Strategies for hope and understanding*. Norton.
Morin, E. (1990). *Science avec conscience* [Science with consciousness]. Seuil.
Morin, E. (1996). A noção de sujeito [The notion of subject]. In D. Fried Schnitman (Ed.), *Novos paradigmas, cultura e subjetividade* (pp. 45–58) Artes Médicas.
Morin, E. (2015). *La méthode V. L'humanité de l'humanité. L'identité humaine* [The method V. The humanity of humanity. Human identity]. Points. (original work published in 2001).
Nathan, T. (2011). *La nouvelle interprétation des rêves* [The new interpretation of the dreams]. Odile Jacob.
Nathan, T. (2014). *Nous ne sommes pas seuls au monde* [We are not alone in the world]. Seuil. (original work published in 2001).
Nathan, T. (2015). *Quand les dieux sont en guerre*. [When the gods are at war]. Synthélabo.
Nathan, T. (2021). *Secrets de thérapeute* [Therapist secrets]. L'Iconoclaste.
Nathan, T. & Swertvaegher, J. (2003). *Sortir d'une secte* [Leaving a sect]. Seuil/Synthelabo.
Neubern, M. (2016). Iconicity and complexity in hypnotic communication. *Psicologia: Teoria e Pesquisa, 32*, 1–9. https://doi.org/10.1590/0102-3772e32ne217

References

Neubern, M. (2018a). *Hipnose, dores crônicas e complexidade: Técnicas avançadas* [Hypnosis, chronic pain and complexity: Advanced techniques]. Ed. UnB.

Neubern, M. (2018b). *Clínicas do transe. Etnopsicologia, hipnose e espiritualidade no Brasil* [Trance clinics. Ethnopsychology, hypnosis and spirituality in Brazil]. Juruá.

Neubern, M. (2022a). The role of De-sign and intentionality in understanding hypnosis. In F. Seif (Ed.), *Intentionality and semiotic labyrinths* (pp. 113–126). SSA/ Philosophy Documentation Center.

Neubern, M. (2022b). When spirits become therapists. Ethnopsychology and hypnotherapy in Brazil. *International Journal of Latin American Religions, 1*, 1–26.

Neubern, M., & Bioy, A. (Eds.). (2023). *Hypnosis in academia: Contemporary challenges in research, healthcare and education.* Springer.

Neubern, M., & Nogueira, H. (2019). Complex hypnosis contribution to clinical psychology. In C. Antloga, K. Brasil, S. Lordello, M. Neubern, & E. Queiroz (Eds.), *Psicologia Clínica e Cultura 4* (pp. 71–90). Technopolitik.

Peirce, C. (1903). Pragmatism as a principle and method of right thinking. In P. Turrisi (Ed.). (1997). *The 1903 Harvard lectures on pragmatism.* State University of New York Press.

Petrilli, S. (2017). *The self as a sign, the world, and the other.* Routledge.

Raposa, M. (2020). *Theosemiotics. Religion, reading, and the gift of meaning.* Fordham University Press.

Ribeiro, J. (2021). *O ciclo do contato* [The contact cycle]. Summus.

Robin, R. (1967). *Annotated catalogue of the papers of Charles S. Peirce.* University of Massachusetts Press. (MS Peirce).

Santaella, L. (2004). *O método anti-cartesiano de Charles S. Peirce* [The anti-cartesian method of Charles S. Peirce]. Ed. Unesp.

Sartre, J. P. (2005). *L'immaginaire.* Gallimard. (original work published in 1940).

Satprem. (2019). *Sri Aurobindo and the adventure of consciousness.* Lotus Press. (original work published in 1970).

Seif, F. (2019). *De-sing in transmodern world. Envisioning reality beyond absoluteness.* Peter Lang.

Seif, F. (2020a). The role of pragmatism in De-sign: Persevering through paradoxes of design and semiotics. *Cognition, 21*(1), 112–131.

Seif, F. (2020b). De-sign as a destiny of navigation: The paradox of sustaining boundaries while traversing borders. *The American Journal of Semiotics, 36*(3–4), 179–215.

Silveira, N. (2015). *Imagens do Inconsciente* [Images of the unconscious]. Vozes.

Souza, J. (2019). *A elite do atraso. Da escravidão a Bolsonaro* [The elite of backwardness. From slavery to Bolsonaro]. Estação Brasil.

Stengers, I. (2001). Qu'est-ce que l'hypnose nous oblige à penser ? [What does hypnosis force us to think about?]. *Ethnopsy, 3*, 13–68.

Chapter 5
Hypnosis, De-sign & Paradoxes

De-sign, Hypnosis, and Paradoxes

De-sign is a way of thinking centered around paradoxes (Seif, 2020a); they are not a problem to be solved but a constitutive process of human life. Whenever they relate to absolute conceptions about reality, paradoxes become insurmountable problems, producing impossible alternatives in the plan of thoughts and, in the plan of human experience, many possibilities for suffering, as highlighted by some authors. Gregory Bateson (1972) states that, when a society understands the relation between disease and health as an exclusive paradigm of choice (A or B), the more it produces medicine and health technologies, the more it will produce disease. Perhaps the antinomic understanding of this problem that denies an ecological comprehension of paradoxes nourishes the biological persistence of many pathological agents (such as viruses and bacteria) in the face of many people's neurotic search for the perfect health. In his turn, the French philosopher Edgar Morin (1980) proposes that, if death is conceived as opposed to life, life will probably become much more difficult, because people would not establish a deep and meaningful understanding of death, an inevitable phenomenon. Not without reason, the fear of old age and death (considered the opposite of youth and life) are frequent causes of suffering in contemporary societies (Han, 2015).

However, when Seif (2019) proposes the idea of transmodernity, in which reality is permeated by polychronic time and diaphanous spaces, paradoxes are integrated into human life mainly because polarization between their categories becomes meaningful. Therefore, in Bateson's example, the De-signer will conceive of health and disease in their multiple interactions (oppositions, complementarities, convergences, conflicts, recursiveness) and observe modes of continuity amongst them (synechism). There is no perfect health or absence of disease, since human systems always integrate functioning forms that include both health and disease, quarrelling, complementing, and nourishing each other. In Morin's problem, the De-signer will understand that a human being lives as much by dying (considering the numerable cellular deaths during their life), and dyes as much by living (considering the long duration of their organism). In a word, as a form of promoting mental health, reflections about death are good strategies to cultivate life. Both cases are permeated by Seif's idea of perseverating through paradoxes (Seif, 2020b): they are not problems to be solved but experiences that provoke, stimulate, and promote the De-signer's teleology. The de-signer's intentionality emerges precisely from these tensions through a process of thought construction in which one can perceive continuity beyond these polarities.

The De-sign and its view of paradoxes is essential in hypnosis inquiry for many reasons. Hypnosis is strongly permeated by Firstness (CP[1] 6.228), implicating a field of experience that is not encompassed by the Cartesian conception of reality (Peirce, 1903/1997). Nevertheless, as a challenge towards absolute notions of reality, hypnosis is deeply implicated with the paradox of fabrication *vs.* revelation. That is perhaps one of the main reasons for historical polemics around that topic (Stengers, 2001, 2002). Hypnosis is also linked to the paradox of determinism *vs.* freedom, because somebody who is under the direct influence of a therapist (control) can develop essential strategies and choices during their life (Erickson, 1992). The word "hypnosis", in its Greek roots ("that which is similar to sleep") is another form of paradox derived from the above, because people in a trance (sleep) can become more conscious about their quotidian situations (Tanembaun, 2021). Another form of paradox related to hypnosis involves the dichotomy madness *vs.* sanity, especially because hypnosis transits between experiences that seem arbitrary and scientific proposals of rationality. Hypnosis navigates border experiences with magic, madness, dreams, and mysticism, which often conflicts with science but, on the other hand, can be favorable for therapeutic procedures (Bioy, 2018). Many therapists report that clients commonly search for hypnosis because they believe that only this "magic technique" can help them deal with their problems (Neubern, 2018).

Concerning these paradoxes, De-sign is essential to produce intelligibility. Historically, they have been a contradictory challenge for scientists and therapists, who tried to settle them through experiments and therapeutic methods that were unable (at least in their majority) to treat them as paradoxes. Even the old polarity state *versus* non-state seems to follow the same logic (Neubern, 2023), mainly because researchers preferentially try to solve that opposition through the more refined context of experiments. Despite the relevance of these efforts, paradoxes cannot be conceived as a problem to be solved, since that is not their nature (Quine, 1976); consequently, research experiments and therapeutic techniques form endless attempts. Suppose they do not need new insight into the most precise instrument of statistics, the context of a laboratory or of therapeutic interventions. In that case, paradoxes must be thought of on a metatheoretical and logical level, as proposed by

---

[1] Hartshorne & Weiss (1980) is the reference of CP, which means the Collected Papers of Charles Peirce. I adopted the CP due to the fact that this is the most known reference among semioticians of Peirce's collected papers.

De-sign (Seif, 2020b), over a simple principle: paradoxes must be tolerated, and the De-signer must persevere through them to establish a teleological process. This is the main foundation for transforming contradictions into paradoxes, as illustrated in the next session.

From Contradictions to Paradoxes

Dialogue is one of the most critical principles in De-sign inquiry (Seif, 2013). More complex than conversation, as discussed in Chap. 3, dialogue is also an imaginary process that implicates broader consideration between interlocutors and simultaneously shapes an integrative process within themselves—the idea of *Ethos* (Neubern, 2022). Therefore, dialogue is either a monologue, because a person will interact and negotiate with many sign systems of their own self, through deep interaction with their interlocutor, who is also a complex system or simply a semiotic world. As discussed in hypnosis, dialogue is a meeting of worlds (Neubern, 2016), since the human self is a semiotic world inhabited by sign systems originating from different kinds of relationships with others, sociocultural life, and the environment. Since trance an elusive experience, the De-sign idea of navigation is pertinent for dialogue during hypnosis, because interlocutors are implicated in refined and fragile forms of internal and external interactions, with particular semiotic modes that are, nevertheless, extremely important for creating habits and new semiotic systems in human experiences.

In terms of metaknowledge, dialogue is crucial to transform contradictions into paradoxes. Intending to furnish alternatives to an understanding of hypnosis, De-sign will not offer techniques or instruments to search for efficacy, but instead conceptual tools derived from the notion of dialogue. The first metaknowledge contradiction was born between wisdom and scientific knowledge, mainly concerning specialized disciplines. The more a discipline advances in a specific field, the more it creates obstacles for thinking about context, socio-political exchanges, economic conditions, financial determinations, cultural influences, and communities (Morin, 1991/2014). Consequently, scientists can develop a deep understanding of their objects of study, ignorant regarding the context that favors their study and the consequences of their discoveries. Likewise, modern sciences display a solid accuracy for "seeing" the world while being simultaneously "blind" to watching themselves. Modern sciences can easily be implicated with different contemporary tragedies: national and international social inequalities—the richest 1% of people pocket twice as much wealth as the other 99% (Oxfam, 2023); wars with mass assassination methods—threatening a new war with worldwide proportions (Chomsky & Polychroniou, 2023); and severe ecological threats that risk future generations on the planet (Wallace-Wells, 2020; Weiszsäcker & von Wijkman, 2018). Of course, establishing relationships between science and these contemporary tragedies can be considered unjust, because science is implicated in solving many human problems daily as well, and many scientists were recognized by their active and humanistic attitudes. Albert Einstein, David Bohm, Marie Curie, Nise da Silveira, Eugène Minkowski, Léon Chertok, and Milton Erickson are some relevant examples of that.

Nevertheless, the question is not about individuals and their ethical values, but about how robust power mechanisms in contemporary societies can quickly appropriate modern science as collective knowledge (Santos, 2019; Stengers, 2023). Once modern science turns to explaining and controlling reality (i.e., logic), it disengages from the commitment about how it should be, i.e., ethical principles (Gergen, 1996). For modern science, the three central modern values (Lyotard, 1979)—truth, beauty, and justice—are separated; only truth remains the central reference for its goals and procedures. Therefore, that strong emphasis on results, to the detriment of ecological consequences, refers to the separation between objectivity and subjectivity, or object and subject, which are opposed as irreconcilable notions. Although many philosophers (Bachelard, 1938/1996; Kunh, 1962/2012; Lakatos, 1980; Popper, 1959/2014) have developed relevant comprehensions of objectivity and subjectivity in epistemology, the great majority of scientists reveal forms of thinking that confirm these separative trends. Consequently, it is challenging for them to practice an epistemological reflection and a recursive discussion on the numerous dimensions of socio-cultural conditions that precede their activities. In some way, the contradiction that the more scientific knowledge advances the more wisdom seems to be absent becomes plausible, among scientists and people in general.

De-sign inquiry principles (Seif, 2019) are crucial to help science transform this contradiction into a paradox. Two of them, among many others—teleology and dialogue—can be applied towards this end. However, as contradiction is thought through teleology and dialogue, many other oppositions also become paradoxes. On the one hand, teleology places the scientist on an aesthetic plane, an essential foundation of wisdom. Following a transmodern perspective (Seif, 2019), searching for truth is not an absolute process; reality is polychronic and diaphanous. Truth is highly implicated in aesthetics because it serves a collective ideal, whose goals promote communitarian experiences. As a result, scientific discovery is not only a result but a social process of collective integration into a broad sense of self-experience, as proposed by Peirce (cited in Colapietro, 1989), shaping a communitarian self. Beyond the practicality of a result, scientific discovery should propose different forms of integration between personal necessities and collective values, seen as goodness and beauty for the community. This form of thought conducted in De-sign inquiry (Seif, 2020b) integrates Peircean normative sciences (aesthetics, ethics, and logic) as it includes teleology in a broad sense: a result must be conceived within an integrative perspective. It is also a form of overcoming the contradiction of subjectivity *vs.* objectivity, because it establishes a subjective condition—teleology—as a form of achieving legitimate objectivity. This line of reflection could be prolonged through concepts such as synechism and semiosis, in which the subject is semiotically present in the object of study and vice-versa. Briefly put, wisdom does not dissolve scientific practicality but instead inserts it into an integrative and collective perspective, as communitarian aesthetic and ethical values must be seriously considered. Facing the object of inquiry, the subject will always be implicated with these values and simultaneously will believe themselves responsible for this object, since they are also semiotically present.

On the other hand, dialogue places the scientist as a community member rather than an isolated entity (Seif, 2013). The Peircean idea of scientific community (CP 5.311) is here amplified, because scientific procedures, data, and results develop into semiotic nets and systems of meaning through different social processes. Therefore, dialogue is a generative process in which other social actors, affected directly or indirectly by the actions of science, can establish the conditions of the scientist's work. Tensions, conflicts, negotiations, and agreements are not restricted to relations between governments, corporations (the two institutions that generally finance scientific research), and scientists, including varied entities, persons, and representatives of several groups interested or affected by scientific affairs (Stengers, 2023). Then, from a passive attitude of suffering the consequences of scientific processes, other social agents must be actively inserted into a dialogic attitude towards science. Even if this idea seems idealistic for many people, wisdom emerges from collective processes, as numerous social groups participate in dialogical meetings about their wishes for their own lives. Science is not absolute but fallible in many aspects (CP 1.141), opening the possibility (and the necessity) for wisdom through dialogue.

Through De-sign the contradiction between scientific knowledge and wisdom can be transformed into a paradox: the more the former advances, the more it relies on human wisdom, because its powerful consequences require rationality in terms of ethics and aesthetics. Teleology and dialogue, among other De-sign principles, allow the inquirer to investigate apparent oppositions from different perspectives, promoting a flexible and systemic understanding of various possibilities for connection between them.

The transition from contradictions to paradoxes is extremely relevant for hypnosis, especially regarding intelligibility. Reality *vs.* fiction permeates the history of hypnosis, as well as of its practice and research. If modern paradigms do not recognize Firstness (Peirce, 1903/1997) as an ontological dimension, then many vital processes of hypnosis and human experience are understood as false or as opposite to reality. De-sign is a significant way of thinking to demonstrate that imagination, feelings, desire, and lies are also constitutive of reality and inseparable from it. Another frequent contradiction in hypnosis is the opposition between determinism and freedom, as hypnosis is frequently associated with manipulation and control (Bailly, 1784/2004). Nonetheless, De-sign inquiry (Seif, 2013) is closely associated with abduction, and its imaginative work is essential to demonstrate that hypnotic experiences can display high levels of creativity and lead people to an emancipatory attitude towards life. Without dropping deterministic references, hypnotherapy can effectively help people make relevant choices in their lives. Madness *vs.* sanity has been another contradiction related to hypnosis since its beginning, when Charcot (Cited in Chertok & Stengers, 1989) associated it with hysteria. As elusive cultural dimensions penetrate the trance experience, they threat the pretense of rationality for many professionals and researchers. Not without reason, hypnosis is often associated with risk of disorder or with a technique that triggers pathological processes

(Neubern, 2018). In the next sessions, De-sign principles will be employed in inquiry, demonstrating how these contradictions can become paradoxes.

Reality vs. Fiction

Erickson (1954) was invited to work with a man who had had his arm paralyzed. He was a factory worker, who seemed to have a diminished cognitive capacity and received little formal education. The factory physicians diagnosed him with hysterical paralysis, – essentially claiming that is problem was not real, but psychological. Consequently, he received a week for treatment only; and if he were not healed, he would be fired. He was anxious about that prospect, because he was set to retire the following year, but his "psychological" problem might lead him to lose his job. Erickson arranged with two colleagues to begin the intervention indirectly, discussing his case medically in his presence. Sitting on his bed, he seemed shy during the doctors' discussion about his situation. They stated that the main hypothesis was that the patient had a real problem called "inertia syndrome" with a good prognosis: the problem would be solved within a week. They said that, during the next few days, his arm would show progressive improvement, characterized by a gradual fade of paralysis. Then, by the end of a week, the man probably would feel only a vague sensation of numbness in his wrist. Nevertheless, they needed to confirm this hypothesis during hypnosis. Erickson induced him into trance, and the same promise was made again, with a few differences. They confirmed the diagnosis and the same prognosis; the patient experienced these predictions during the week. He was able to return to work and 1 year later he retired.

This case study has many elements to be considered through De-sign principles (Seif, 2019, 2020a). It suggests that institutional oppression can be transformed into a joke. When the factory doctors stated that the worker did not have a real problem, they imposed a type of violence against him, disqualifying his experience as a falsehood or as a moral issue. In their turn, Erickson and his colleagues answered the problem with a joke or a lie, since "inertia syndrome" is a fabricated diagnosis. By De-signing his new context, they transformed the message from "you do not have a real problem" (with the subliminal message of false experience and/or moral accusation) into "yes, you have a real problem" (by fabricating a problem, but respecting his experience). This false diagnosis was a form to validate the worker's experience and to protect him against the company's oppression so that he could retire as planned. The falsehood of "inertia syndrome" which was also a truth for the patient, was De-signed by Erickson's dramatic performance, along with his colleagues. The performance worked as suggestion and proposed a new relational context. The worker was indirectly implicated in it, perhaps without realizing he was under a hypnotic treatment that would work perfectly during that week.

However, this form of intervention can highlight many discussion points about paradoxes. Reality and fiction permeate hypnotic practice, frequently associated with falsehood, lies, deception, and their opposition to truth, security, and confidence, commonly defended by the Modern Sciences (Stengers, 2001). Many therapists could argue that therapeutic successes will not last when fabricated and without deliberate subject participation. For them, hypnosis can implicate serious problems about truth and human experience, with theoretical and ethical consequences. Nevertheless, hypnosis can furnish a paradox in which fictional processes can achieve actual results, or false ideas can lead people to live authentic experiences. On the one hand, falsehood can contain partial truths, which is an issue for clinical practice, not only in hypnosis but in other practices such as psychotherapy and medicine. Surely, the pseudo-diagnosis "inertia syndrome" had many ethical implications, because the patient believed he had received a real diagnosis which could let him prove his negative experiences with other professionals to Erickson and his colleagues in eventual lawsuits. However, despite the false diagnosis, it encompassed true messages for that specific context. Firstly, it was a form of answering the company's doctor disqualification of his symptoms; had had been accused of producing a false problem, which was, in fact, a *real* psychological problem (hysterical paralysis). As a result, a lie was used to confront another to promote a context of acceptance for the patient, protecting him from oppressive interventions. Secondly, despite the false diagnosis, the subjects saw it as true, because it was implicated with a future form of functioning recognized by himself. "Inertia syndrome" was linked to a predictable form of development during a certain period, after which the symptom would disappear almost completely. A lie was used to promote true development in the patient's self, read by his systems of agency as a true mode of communication.

Many therapists could argue that, despite therapeutic results, false ideas are always problematic because they do not offer reliable references for procedures. Some contemporary examples sustain this criticism, mainly because they illustrate how narratives used by people of authority can lead others to tragic situations. The problem of false memories induced many patients to think they were abused by their parents, which caused patients to take legal action against them (Hacking, 2000). Extremist movements were able to recruit young people without previous dangerous conduct and turn them into terrorists, capable of operating bomb attacks and other violent events (Berger, 2018). Even the criticism of narrative impositions can be inserted into this discussion as a form of violence (McNamme & Gergen, 1995) because, despite the absence of tragic consequences like the previous examples, it denounces how therapists frequently impose their theories on clients' experiences in complete disregard of their particular senses, necessities, and ways of being. Subsequently, false ideas and narratives can produce effects and simultaneously contain ethical problems and forms of violence. Frequently, they mobilize people from their vulnerabilities or personal needs toward actions whose consequences can vary from disregarding their own constructions to drastic events. Nevertheless, to contradict this argument, one might propose that Erickson's intervention was linked to the false term "inertia syndrome," but it was true in reference to the patient's experience: it implicates a progressive development. For that, Erickson considered the patient's subjectivity, his ways of communication, his modes of agency, and especially his need for acceptance (he had a real problem, not a false one) and retirement. These topics comprised the patient's personal truth and were also the foundation for a successful result. Consequently, despite similarities between Erickson's intervention and the abovementioned examples, the former contemplated the patient's truths and allowed him to pursue his life freely, that is, into an autonomous condition. These subtle differences may appear fragile, but they are essential to think about the transmission of ideas in various social practices.

> *Peirce's metaphysics* (Ibri, 1992/2017) *doesn't consider the dualistic idea of mind and spirit because it should be discarded by Okham's razor. Materialism, in turn, could not be entirely refuted, but it suggested a mechanic universe since it didn't contemplate feelings and creation. Then, Peirce chose an idealistic perspective, in which all things would be derived from the mind (a Superior Mind). Nevertheless, laws and habits are not human conceptions but are components of the real universe, which is real (objective) and idealist. Then, objective idealism implies that: (a) the universe's laws are not human creations but real phenomena; (b) the universe is idealist because it is mediated by laws and habits; (c) it implicates synechism since there is a continuity between mind and matter; (d) there is a common constitution of human mind and the universe which allow the former to knowing the later.*

On the other hand, some experiences that are not necessarily false, such as imagination and feelings, can also be opposed to reality. As discussed in Chap. 2, imagination includes a historical paradox about hypnosis, described as a form of unreal process to disqualify Mesmer's ideas (Chertok & Stengers, 1989). For the Cartesian paradigm, Firstness processes are a source of error, a risk for scientific inquiry in its search for reality (Peirce, 1903/1997). However, these experiences, in which Firstness is predominant, are essential for constituting one's reality. Objective idealism, one of Pierce's most critical contributions to understanding reality (Ibri, 1992/2017; Raposa, 1989; Reynolds, 2002), is a fundamental principle to comprehend how Firstness participates in the construction of reality. This doctrine emphasizes that mind and matter are not dual dimensions of the universe, refusing a dualistic perspective (CP 6.24). For Peirce (CP 6.277), matter is a limited case of mind or, in other words, it is a mind frozen by habits, whose regularity is neither absolute nor perfect. His work *Law of Mind* (Peirce, 1892/1998) is crucial in this relationship: feelings are the stuff of the mind, and ideas are nothing more than *continua* of living feelings (CP 6.138; 6.150). As signs, ideas tend to grow and spread, continuously connected to one another. Nevertheless, if intrinsic qualities from feelings remain unchangeable, their intensity diminishes and, consequently, the attainment of generality is accompanied by loss of vitality. Whenever a general idea attracts many other ideas in the mind (habit formation), it loses its original intensity and liveliness (CP 6.136).

These ideas are central to thinking about the paradox of fiction *vs.* reality in hypnosis. The main question here is to persevere through the paradox's oppositions to promote teleological processes. First, elusive hypnotic processes can hardly be approached by scientific methods; for many authors, especially modern ones (Stengers, 2002), they cannot even be recognized as reality. Therefore, hypnotic processes such as in the abovementioned case were inhabited by Firstness experiences, such as sensations, feelings, and imagination. These demonstrated an essential role in concrete change. The way techniques like storytelling before and during trance can promote concrete change is a question whose explanations are not consensus among researchers, but unanimous in terms of results. Hypnosis works, but the scientific community does not know how. Nevertheless, following Peirce's objective idealism (CP 6.24), the inclusion of Firstness processes is indispensable to understanding that paradox, because Firstness is responsible for offering intelligibility, spontaneity, and creativity in nature as well as in the human mind. Otherwise, understanding would be materialistic, whose law imposes almost absolute determination on phenomena and little space for creation and the new. If the materialistic hypothesis were correct, Erickson's patient probably would not be able to change, and his hypnosis, a quale-consciousness experience (CP 6.228), would not exist. Through this reflection on De-sign, the paradox acquires another version, in which reality cannot exist without unreality.

Secondly, the non-real processes of hypnosis feature something of reality. If Erickson's intervention is again compared with extremist movements and narrative impositions, some ingredients are essential for differentiating the former: Erickson read the patient's subjectivity as a whole, obeyed its own forms of functioning and communicating, respected his autonomy, and met his needs. Many authors could argue that extremist leaders are also skillful in reading a person's subjectivity, as notable amongst terrorists (Berger, 2018) and religious sects (Nathan & Swervagher, 2003). However, their interventions commonly produce social and individual suffering, mostly because they emphasize individual vulnerabilities and needs but fail to consider a holistic understanding of subjectivity, autonomy, and other necessities. For them, ethics and aesthetics are separated from logic; they are only interested in some groups or categories that will be used for their goals. Erickson's work, in turn, exhibited a broad comprehension of the human self, including notions of agency, systems, communication, and a deep respect for each person's way of being. Despite his focal intervention, his form of hypnotherapy seemed to ally aesthetics primarily through teleology and ethics, including notions of acceptance and naturalistic hypnosis, with logic for precision and effectiveness. His intervention could be local and simultaneously ecologic, respecting self-organization on individual and social levels. To sustain the idea of the patient's truth, Erickson's hypnotherapy implicated a kind of reality with many facets, in which elusiveness, quality, potentiality, beauty, and goodness were necessary to obtain and overcome results. The notion of reality becomes meaningless.

Determinism vs. Freedom

Years ago, I received Sonia, a 55-year-old woman, for hypnotherapy. She was in a deep, anxious crisis, contemplating suicide, with solid difficulties in leaving her home. Sonia worked at the university and she felt paralyzed in her departmental activities and her life in general because she had many phobia attacks. Her first explanation described the episode in which she was a victim of a tentative sexual assault on the university campus, when she threw the attacker to the ground with a Judo blow and hit him several times on the head with her bag. Despite her successful self-defense, she was traumatized; according to herself, this episode triggered the anxious crisis. Nevertheless, during her first interview, she did not make many references to the sexual assault, focusing much more on her current suffering at home, her hindrance to work, her suicidal ideas, and her desperate fear of being alone. She developed extreme dependency on her domestic worker, who was commonly abusive and belittling toward Sonia. "I need her because I can't be there alone … and she knows this … so I'll tolerate her abuse because I have no options now." At that time, she was almost 10 kg overweight and ate compulsively before a crisis. The doctors told her that she should lose some weight, but she felt it an impossible task at that point. Her psychiatrist was described by her as a very special and intelligent man, and he would always be right about her treatment. Sonia also demonstrated a strong sense of obedience toward her parents, making decisions only when authorized by them: to buy an apartment, to do something important with her money, or even to begin a love engagement with a man should necessarily approved by her father and mother. As a religious woman (she was a member of a Pentecostal church), she understood that she should be obedient to God and her parents, and a rebellious attitude would go against the church's spiritual teachings.

I adopted an authoritative attitude during Sonia's hypnotherapy when he noticed that she needed somebody to guide and direct her actions. She always called him 'Professor' or 'Doctor,' stating that she would also like to learn Psychology, that it could be pleasant and helpful for her condition. Therefore, through this authoritative attitude, I worked on three different therapeutic axes. First, the conversations would be developed in a constructive way, avoiding the negativism that seemed to dominate her mind. Of course, she could speak about suffering, but as an insertion into her quotidian life, she could find many experiences that were not dominated by anxiety and negativism. More importantly, she was gradually induced to find pleasant and constructive experiences with which she could establish new connections. Second, she would perform some tasks related to these constructive experiences, aiming to concretize them in her daily life, especially at home. Despite it being September, she decorated her home with Christmas objects (lights, Santa Klaus figurines, trees) because this scenario made her very happy. After 2 months, she invited some colleagues to dinner and watched TV—her home had become an agreeable place to receive friends. This second axis was developed during a 1-h weekly session.

From Contradictions to Paradoxes 123

Therefore, the third axis was the most significant to demonstrate the general logic of her hypnotherapy approach. This axis was applied during sessions of two or three weekly hours, characterized by deep trance and total amnesia. I heard during her long trance sessions stories about human development from early childhood to adult daily life, emphasizing that there were always some determinants on the human self (body, mind, social world) that were remade in some way through an organisms' choices. Then,

> a baby is in the crib and feels hungry ... *spontaneously she cries and as soon as possible an adult comes to feed her ... then, the baby learns how to call adults and get them to meet her needs ... and she doesn't speak or think as an adult ... but she has a kind of intelligence which allows her to make adults meet her needs ...* if she is hungry, cold, unsatisfied, she learns how to call adults ....

These stories emphasized systems of sensation, especially connecting her with vital forms of experience that had been blocked, in some way, by anxiety. During trance sessions, I commonly focused on a short period of development, working for two or three sessions on a specific experience from a period, such as childhood. In 6 months, she went from early childhood to adulthood as if she were reliving themes of her personal trajectory. Despite intensive amnesia, she always presented themes approached during trance in conversations, as illustrated in this excerpt when adolescence and sexual interest usually become central for people.

> S – *"Doctor, are you married?"*
> T – *"Yes, I am."*
> S – *"Oh, thanks. It is only curiosity."*

In the next session, the dialogue continues:

> S – *"Do you know, Doctor? I'm very interested in a boy from my church..."*
> T – *"A boy? Who is he?"*
> S – *"He is not exactly a boy... he is 57 years old... and I'll introduce him to my father, who wants to know his intentions about me..."*
> T – *"Oh, that is a respectful idea, Sonia. And if your father disagrees with your relationship, what do you want to do?"*
> S – *"I'll be very sad... but I must obey my father... our family is honorable and loyal to God."*

I conceived that hypnotherapy was permeated by her deliberate will to obey and to accept social determinations and personal needs that were frequently repressed by social and moral values. If she were able to connect to herself otherwise, feeling and experiencing legitimate processes commonly out of her focus, she could learn a precious value: disobedience. Sonia needed to be inserted into a context in which she could disobey without the expectation of punishment, especially in a religious sense. After 6 months of therapy, she had no more anxious symptoms and displayed an autonomous attitude toward routine situations, such as taking the bus to work and being alone at home. She fired her domestic worker and decided to live for a few months without that kind of service, experiencing the pleasant solitude of her home. I tried to assign tasks that would be difficult for her (such as some changes in her treatment), but she refused. He insisted and said that he was the Doctor, and she should obey him, but Sonia replied, *"I'm really grateful to you, Doc, but I will not accept these changes. So, I think that I don't need therapy for many months. I'll stop it. If I need it, may I search for you again, Doc?"*, followed by a positive answer. A year later, I met her casually at the university: and Sonia had lost 10 kg, she seemed to feel well about her body and her appearance. She said she had no more symptoms and was very happy with her life. Her last statement was: *"I'm studying a discipline on child psychology just now… and I don't know why I love it so much."*

When Sonia searched for hypnotherapy, she was paralyzed by many contradictions, which produced intense experiences of suffering, such as anxiety and suicidal thoughts. The first way of understanding these contradictions is her extreme obedience and dependence on her parents and on the church's tenets. Obedience, on the one hand, was a condition for her to be accepted by her family and consequently to take the role of a good "girl," that is, somebody with a good family and religious values. Possibly, the violent episode when she was attacked triggered and developed the radicality of obedience, making her still more dependent on her parents and her values worked as inflexible references for life. On the other hand, her strong deliverance to the social world, as she intended to belong to it, also produced a radical negation of many aspects of her personal world, in which necessities, desires, and phantasies were disregarded or even repressed. Then, to belong to the social world, she should deny her own self, making it impossible to reconcile with her own *Ethos*.

A second form of understanding, the semiotic perspective, poses that this arrangement of belonging without belonging produced a block upon vital processes to impeach the signs that would through semiosis. Seeing social laws as extremely rigid and determinist, Sonia was not able to follow her own development, which forced her into a dual solution: she should deny creative processes (especially in terms of sexuality and autonomy) and assume a childish attitude regarding the world and her parents. Although she was 55 years old, she was determined to obey her parents about essential subjects, such as financial investments and long engagements, even if her parent's decisions opposed her desires. Suicidal thoughts arose in her because an adult woman could not survive in that context, since autonomy would cause direct conflict with rigid social laws and values. Then, the processes linked to sexuality, creativity, development, and self-autonomy, while semiotic processes, could not accomplish their finality of becoming efficient (CP 8.332). This deterministic form of Thirdness strongly repressed them. Suffering and her symptoms were contradictory signs of health, referring to a self-system blocked in its vitality and cycle; it also served as a morbid experience. Symbolically, between life and death, Sonia suffered because many parts of herself were disregarded and inaccessible (which made her search for help) and promoted her own degeneration through rigid obedience to the social environment.

Sonia's hypnotherapy process can be conceived as a form of transforming contradictions in paradox, especially through Seif's (2020a) idea of persevering through paradoxes. The oppositions in her experience could and should not be eliminated but only tolerated in a new relational and experiential context. The term "toleration" here must be clarified considering De-sign: it is often used as a form of conformation to disagreeable or dissatisfied reality. Nevertheless, *tolerance* means a wise attitude: some determinations must be respected, opening new possibilities to deal with them. When they are recognized in their own logic and meanings, people can begin significant and qualitative changes to create possibilities for negotiation and transformation. In other words, through Seif's idea of dialogue (Seif, 2013), the De-signer must find people "where they are," and not in a condition they expect, which could transform dialogue into a form of violence. Otherwise, De-sign and hypnotherapy (Erickson & Rossi, 1979) degenerate into their essential principles and become mere forms of manipulation and oppression. In Sonia's condition, I could not expect from her a level of emancipation and autonomy commonly sought by many persons in contemporary societies (Han, 2015), in which individual rights and freedom are dominant values and must not be submitted to other social instances, such as family and church. This contemporary form of individuality in Western societies is commonly associated with emotional and financial autonomy, as well as with success in the professional world.

Sonia, in her turn, was born and raised in a particular social context in which social values of obedience and submission were vital. I quickly perceived that many contemporary ideas were incompatible with her *Ethos*, and the most important task for him would be to "meet her where she was," especially through understanding the meaning of obedience in her social world. He noticed that Sonia came from a conservative social world in which family was one of the most important social references with whom one should not be in disaccord, at least in essential themes. A single woman should be a virgin to be respected, and her parents should approve any emotional engagement. As mentioned above, the Pentecostal church had a central role in her social world, attributing a sacred meaning to virginity, family obedience, and the purity of the soul. For many people in this social universe, the church's narratives were present in varied contexts and social practices of daily life, such as work, sex, modesties, family, neighborhood, body, marriage, money, and politics, offering some perspective on meaning and belonging. However, this same social context was also deeply inspired by fear, and rebels could be marginalized and expelled from their groups; for Sonia, this would be the worst thing that could happen to a person. To be in conflict with her father or with God was an inconceivable situation for her.

This scenario meant that Sonia was a different person in the university context, and her world's references and needs clashed with those of many women in that same institution. For her, the relationship with her social world could implicate many forms of repression, but they were essential in offering perspectives for meaning, social bonds, and belonging. It was through these tools that she was admitted at work, made some friends and felt accepted by family and church members. More importantly, all her victories were blessed by a sacred entity, which was also an essential condition for life. Facing the semiotic complexity of her social world, I suddenly comprehended that he could not attack its values and practices, since they were essential references in Sonia's life. They crisscrossed Sonia's self, creating semiotic systems with many contradictions that must be integrated into other systems of logic and intentionality. Her conservative values were not oppressive tools of the social world (at least consciously) and should be respected in hypnotic processes to maintain her engaged in a therapeutic perspective.

Therefore, the first strategy adopted by me was an authoritarian attitude, in which he would work with Sonia, apparently, into a unidirectional form of communication. He was the "Professor" who would order her some tasks and explain things in life to her. As she asked for life guidance, the Professor would take this charge, especially through scientific knowledge. However, I expected that, at some moment, she rebel against him, essentially because the hypnotic context would trigger feelings, desires, and needs repressed within herself. Apparently, this rebellion would be confronted by me through signs of reprobation but would be accepted at a communicative metalevel. As a De-signer (Seif, 2020b), I would become a sign system mirroring Sonia's self by integrating repressive values and repressed experiences into a new perspective: these two dimensions could create new forms of articulation. These measures would promote within Sonia's self the way in which her contradictions became paradoxes or a way in which determinism would be reconciled with freedom.

On the one hand, the orders to focus on constructive notions intended to connect Sonia with repressed experiences, permeated by desire, feelings, and phantasies. In Seif's perspective (2018), the main idea of these orders was to help Sonia connect with Eros, an erotic form of love, strongly necessary for her therapeutic process. The Generator of Desire, or G.O.D., was essential for her; all repressive systems created after an anxious crisis would direct Sonia towards a morbid experience of life, in which everything linked to pleasure, creation, feelings, and desire should be denied. Nevertheless, I noticed that no allusion to sexuality could be made because Sonia's values. Any immersion in the repressive mindset would translate into pornography, which would risk abandonment of therapy. When she transformed her home using Christmas decorations in September, she was reconnecting with something pleasurable that was also socially accepted. The conversations during therapeutic sessions on these commands were permeated by interspersal techniques, emphasizing body experience in terms of feeling, pleasure, and good sensations. The choice for each ornament, the music, the disposition of objects, dinner with friends were all pleasurable experiences that promoted constructive experiences in Sonia's self and could not be chided by their social world. In some way, Sonia was able access these dimensions; even without conscious deliberation about them, she began to promote new kinds of semiotic configurations.

On the other hand, she developed a complex storytelling process that subliminally emphasizes the paradoxes between determinism and choice, such as in the following excerpt.

> So, when a little baby is hungry, they can't avoid this organic necessity, which is a biological determination, but they learn to *attract adults to take care of them, and they also learn when and how to attract adults.* More than that: *the baby can choose to call for adults even when they are not hungry... Because they can choose how and when to do it...*

This kind of suggestion was applied during trance for many months and covered all development phases. Therefore, seemingly simple storytelling conceals semiotic details and intentions that must be comprehended, especially regarding their iconicity (Neubern, 2016). First, they were announced as lessons on human development, a proposal that Sonia joyfully received. As I assumed the role of "Professor," his job should be demonstrated through these lessons, in which Sonia apparently assumed a passive attitude. Surely, both knew it was not a regular university lesson but a therapeutic context, so they accepted this dramatic relationship as a possible form of the therapeutic connection that met Sonia's needs and desires. Secondly, this context was perfused by icons relating to the role of these protagonists in different forms of suggestions (Neubern, 2016). When I took on the role of "Professor," he did not explain it to Sonia, but only behaved according to it. It was a form of drama: whatever he did, spoke, and acted became a form of showing, without explanation, something to his interlocutor (Shapiro, 1999). Frequently the "Professor" was an iconic system that allowed a navigation process (Seif, 2019) through which he could move around Sonia's experience, present in herself as a respectful agent for change. Within the trance experience, the "Professor" might surely have his goals, but he was specially engaged in a navigation process, inviting Sonia's systems to dialogue and leading them to promote therapeutic change. He addressed her desires, pleasures, phantasies, ideas, and feelings, commonly repressed by her social values. While the "Professor" inside Sonia's experience incorporated the scholar's authority throughout these lessons, he would also offer some alternatives for questioning, reacting, and opposing her marginal experiences during conversations and trance immersions. She introduced essential marginal themes from her experiences in conversation. When the lessons approached typical themes of adolescence, especially sexuality, she began to ask about my love engagement and, a week later, she mentioned her interest in a man from church.

Thirdly, the communication present in this therapeutic context was perfused by iconicity. Storytelling is commonly structured as diagram systems, making them powerful modes of subliminal communication. In some way, Sonia understood the stories as if she were in a university classroom, like she claimed herself. Nevertheless, these stories were composed of many blocks of daily descriptions on human development, permeated by different forms of icons. In a grammatical sense, adjectives, verbs, and adverbs are icons (Nöth, 2015), as well as tools for describing an event (Neubern, 2016). Interspersed techniques (Erickson, 1966), characterized by different emphases on sentence fragments (voice tone, rhythm, pauses, elasticity of words), are also iconic processes used in hypnosis (in this induction, interspersed phrases are displayed in italic). In short, these constructions are essential to induce trance states (quale-consciousness), especially because they provoke experiences of Firstness. Therefore, they have a special role in constructing trance: feelings, memories, and scenes can be easily potentialized to promote change, as it happened with Sonia.

The story she heard featured a baby who felt sensations or necessities, which means determination, and described how the baby naturally learned to deal with them (autonomy), especially how to attract adults. The baby is an icon in this sense, implying somebody who is still natural and pure. The baby was a message for Sonia about how autonomy is naturally and biologically present in human beings. The infant was also described deliberately as a boy to create an apparent distance from her in forbidden themes, such as sexuality. However, the baby's purity was a message: nature transcends differences between males and females; their learnings are essentially the same. Sex, for example, was a natural and important phenomenon in human development and could not be mistaken for pornography. During storytelling, autonomy was closely associated with icons (in grammar and interspersed forms) to evoke repressed experiences with which Sonia could establish new forms of connection and integration. At the same time, determinations were also considered a natural phenomenon, that is, they were not bad things, and she could find forms of negotiation in them, as the baby did. It was a form of respecting her social and conservative values and introducing new possibilities for dealing with them from her necessities.

Sonia's hypnotherapy was, then, a typical process in which intentionality emerges almost independently from deliberation. In some way, her deliberations sought to maintain obedience to social values, persons, and institutions, despite her wishes to find some form of satisfying her needs. Through trance, she was able to access many forms of experience from which intentionality emerged and subtly dominated many dimensions of herself. She was implicated not only with her obedience to social values but also with a new form of life philosophy of welfare, as repressed experiences became accepted and cherished. Sonia was, then, committed to feeling good as well as to be continuously accepted by her family and her church. Nevertheless, the semiotic roots of this paradox were not accessible in her deliberative mind, as Sonia was frequently unaware of their dynamics. During trance, for example, the polychronic experience allowed her to be a child, an adolescent, and an adult woman, even if she deliberately saw herself as an adult and often behaved like a frightened child. Curiously, the possibility to review (and relive) these phases promoted an integrative experience, allowing her to exercise autonomy. Eventually, she could behave like a child, still a dominant mechanism in her mind, but she could also evoke the woman in some moments, especially when she needed to confront authorities whose actions opposed her wishes.

The last meeting with her, 1 year after therapy, was illustrative of how this dynamic was installed in her mind. She was still searching for coherent activities in relation to her wishes, but she was not entirely conscious of what motivated these searches. After therapy, agency systems implicated with her teleological processes of welfare worked intensively in her without being known by her deliberate mind. Sonia lost weight, claimed she was happy and fine, and affirmed that she loved Child Psychology. However, she did not know how and why these things were so important.

Madness vs. Sanity

Madness and sanity compose one of the most striking contradictions in contemporary societies. Especially in the Modern era, as discussed by Michel Foucault (1963/2015), people who were previously conceived as possessed by demons were seen by the Catholic Church's theology as "mad," that is, an object of the medical domain. In short, they were no longer productive in capitalistic terms, isolated from the social world and cast into insane asylums. The main criteria to consider somebody mad in those societies included an insufficiency of productivity and functionality. Normal were those whose minds could meet the capitalistic criteria of work and production. However, works such as Freud's (1916/1996) demonstrated that many people who were functional and productive could fall into madness, which questioned the contradiction between functionality and dysfunctionality.

Madness is also understood through the idea of the norm or, more precisely, as a distant condition from the norm (Canguilhem, 1952/1999). The statistical psychiatric tradition of the DSM (APA, 2022) series is perhaps the most illustrative example of how madness is defined through measurable symptoms and classified into numerous forms of mental disorders. Despite their practicality, these criteria do not solve that contradiction, because they maintain that distance between normalcy and madness through statistical support. Symptoms are taken as symbols, even though they are indices originally; consequently, human experience is conceived through a boring regularity that makes sense perhaps for the psychiatrist, but remains quite distant from the subject's world. The psychiatrist and many psychotherapists inhabited by statistical models generally understand people's experiences as external object, to be controlled through techniques in which the goal is efficacy. Since Charles Blondel (1914), the criticism against this model is common because it situates normal and abnormal as defined and separate entities, establishing an insurmountable separation between the subject's world (internal) and the psychiatrist's inquiry (external).

Nevertheless, some humanistic psychotherapy perspectives can direct the readers towards clues on how to transform the contradiction between madness and sanity into a paradox (Erickson, 1964; Ellenberger, 1958/2004). The main idea they share is continuity and mutual dependence between these two dimensions, both important to human comprehension. In other words, human beings can be understood deeply through neither of these notions nor through their opposition. As mentioned by classic authors, such as Blondel (1914) and Canguilhem (1952/1999), the continuity between madness and sanity must be comprehended from the subject's perspective, positioning teleology as an essential point. Therefore, as a paradox, the polarity between madness and sanity transcends openness toward the future and multiple meanings for life generated by this process. When a therapist prescribes an alcoholic subject something apparently absurd, such as zig-zag driving through streets to avoid bars (Haley, 1993), they introduce the patient to an aesthetic experience, commonly therapeutic for people who are devoted to changing. In these cases, the pathological experience is recognized and integrated into a broad self-system not defined by it but still shaping a teleological movement. Aesthetics is a crucial dimension because it affects the emergence of meaning and also relates to a certain cultural proximity to madness. Artists and mystics in Modern societies are commonly associated with madness because they frequently challenge the criteria for normalcy in terms of moral values as well as references to reality.

From the same perspective, when Nise da Silveira (2015) introduced severe psychiatric patients to painting, poetry, and sculpture, she also evoked aesthetics as a therapeutic experience. Through aesthetics, "mad" patients would recognize their humanity beyond "normality" and "craziness;" despite their differences on social criteria for normalcy, they could recognize and reconcile their own experiences at the individual and social levels. In other words, aesthetics became a way to lead them back from madness to a wholesome form of life, in which their singularities could be respected and recognized. It is important to remark that Silveira's work remains an important reference for therapeutic efficacy and effectiveness nowadays.

Nevertheless, through De-sign thinking (Seif, 2019) the notion of aesthetics by itself is not enough to understand how the contradiction between madness and sanity becomes a paradox. Humanity may be recognized as a desirable outcome for this teleological movement, transcending the paradox madness vs. sanity. Semiotic animals (Deely, 2010) as a concept is pertinent because the human condition favors different forms of play with signs. The therapeutic trajectory, then, especially promoted by trance, shapes the double and multiple routes between feelings (Firstness signs) and forms (Thirdness signs), as discussed by some authors (Atkins, 2016; Langer, 1977). Without the idea of deterministic control, hypnotherapy can promote symbolic systems that offer a certain frame of reference for icons, preserving their potential for creation and innovation. In these processes, despite deliberate limits of the ego, the self remains creative as a semiotic system and, in some way, is free to deal and play with signs as children, mystics, and artists commonly do. The freedom and beauty of the aesthetic experience are then stated by a kind of reason that is typical of De-sign inquiry. The following case studies illustrate this idea.

John and Barney

Jeffrey Zeig (1985) described one of Milton Erickson's most curious clinical cases, when he accepted to work with John, a man with severe schizophrenia. Initially, Erickson noticed that John's family would not collaborate with the treatment, but they agreed to give him a monthly sum of money so that he could rent an apartment and afford his keep. Erickson also asked John to adopt a dog from a public shelter, and as his apartment was small, the beagle should be raised in Erickson's house, with John responsible for going there every day and caring for the dog (whose name was Barney). Erickson created Barney as a character through which he could write letters to establish a specific form of communication with John. Frequently these letters contained curious stories, through which Barney reported a strange relationship with Erickson's family. Erickson was the Old Codger; his wife, Elisabeth, the Lady of the House; and his sons were commonly described in kind terms. In the dynamics of that story, Barney was generally doing something interesting and pleasurable, like playing in his room, especially, with some of Erickson's children. Then, the Old Codger arrived suddenly and blew a scary horn, leading Barney to experience something as scary as dying. After that, the Lady of the House appeared to pet him, which made him feel comfortable again in that house. Through time, Barney developed a pattern concerning Old Codger; in the beginning, he could not understand this perverse man and how the Lady of the House, who was especially kind, could be married to him. However, years ago, Barney had confessed to John that, if he gave the Old Codger some juicy bones, maybe he would become a good man. For many years, John went to Erickson's house three times a day, where he spent time with Erickson's family, being Barney one of his most important references for communication. A few days after Erickson's death, Barney died; John and Ms. Erickson went to the public shelter to adopt two other dogs, beagles like Barney. For many years, John visited Erickson's family, especially because he had made a commitment to take care of Ms. Erickson and his new dogs.

Despite the richness of this case study, the conversion of contradiction between madness and sanity into a paradox through De-sign thinking (Seif, 2019) can be understood in two basic ways. Firstly, that communication developed by Erickson, his family, the dog, and John evolved into a very specific kind of dialogue, in which icons and symbols worked therapeutically. Erickson established a nomination on psychotic processes (Ellenberger, 1958/2004) through different persons implicated with John's therapy. Barney was the psychotic patient (John), always suffering the cruel expectations of something overwhelming and destructive; Erickson, the Old Codger, was the bad side of the psychotic self, who produced the possibilities and sentiments of total chaos, which is experienced as death. Ms. Erickson, the Lady of the House, was the good side of the self, who was friendly to Barney, promoting good experiences for him. That feeling of strangeness demonstrated by Barney about the marriage between the Old Codger and the Lady of the House was a form of representing deep and almost irreconcilable breakages within his psychotic self. Barney's essays of social contact with Erickson's sons represent psychotic desire and his difficulty to create and maintain social bonds that were often disturbed by crises, symbolized there by the scary horn triggered by the Old Codger. These stories, then, denoted a gradual process of integration, as the psychotic scenario remained in John's self, but gained new possibilities of integration, for example, between the Old Codger and the Lady of the House, as well as Barney and Erickson's sons.

However, Erickson's storytelling still had other important characteristics. Erickson created a performative context in which storytelling happened according to theater logic—"as if" (Schechner, 2013), introducing the subject to dramatic play. John surely knew that Barney was not able to write letters, but he accepted the role of receiver. Following the principle of indirect communication (Erickson & Rossi, 1979), Erickson never explained to his patients occult meanings into the narratives he used in therapeutic contexts. Neither was his technique announced, or the content explained to them; in John's case, for example, he was not told that Erickson was the Old Codger or that the scary horn was a psychotic crisis. The story was not shown as technique, but as casual conversation. Nevertheless, although there was casual and informal content, storytelling was a powerful form of subliminal hypnosis. The signs presented in the story were icons, only visible to the subjects (Neubern, 2016). However, their effects as interpretants were symbolic (arguments), especially because, as icons, they not only mirrored the subject's psychological demands, but as symbols, they promoted essential changes directed at therapeutic ends, favoring changes at agency levels. This process was an intriguing form of dialogue: many semiotic actions reached beyond the ego's deliberation, charged by intentionality and producing new meanings for John. Many of his everyday practices and actions were also iconic symbols, composing a general therapeutic context. When John rescued Barney from the public shelter, he created a sign about himself, considering psychotic subjects often live the logic of salvation from death. In short, the general logic behind his therapy, daily practices, and storytelling meant John's salvation happened through care and affect. Seeing Barney a sign system for John's psychotic condition, the prescription to take care of that dog stood for that kind of care.

Secondly, following the same perspective, De-sign thinking helps understand the integrative process in this case. In therapeutic processes, symbols are important because they favor the creation of sign systems that frame (or re-frame) the experience of the self (Neubern, 2023), which has been consensually accepted by different forms of therapy (Erickson, 1992; Silveira, 2015; White, 2007). Therefore, in a Peircean perspective (Nöth, 2015), symbols are not only words, that is, consensual constructions of human language and culture, but also habits, regularity, and laws from animal life and nature in general. The imaginary processes likely present in John's therapy were permeated by crucial symbols to reorganizing his self-experience. They worked as a form of bonding between different parts of John's experiences that were contradictory or even irreconcilable. Analogically, symbols work as the glue that reconnects the broken parts of an object, like the Old Codger and John's ego.

Thinking on the other facet of this problem, the contradiction madness-sanity is closely linked to the dichotomy ego-self that, in psychotic cases, assumes a more radical level. John could not recognize that his extreme distress, accompanied by fear of destruction, was an experience generated within his own self. It implicates breakage with the person's sense of belonging, or *Ethos*, which leads them, in Modern societies, to an anomic condition commonly associated with diagnosis (Nathan, 2001/2014). Favored by their emotional and vital insulation concerning the social and cultural world, people like John are stripped of their different senses of belonging and socially recognized as objects of mental disorder. They have a classification instead of a name; they are permeated by symptoms, not social and affective bonds; they have problematic functions, not desires, phantasies, or life plans; there are no other persons in their subjective and social world, remaining only meaningless objects. In short, they are cast out of their own humanity, ratifying that separation between madness and sanity.

Nevertheless, the integration between ego and self implicates a new existential place in the world. The insulated ego is recognized and inserted into a multiple self (a semiotic one) in which relationships are alive and active through meaningful constructions. John is no longer limited to his madness; instead, he is a man with significant bonds and life goals. Through therapy, he unblocked his vital flow towards the future, something commonly seen in psychotic subjects (Minkowsky, 1933/2005). However, if his schizophrenia is not entirely healed and John remains subject to his intense suffering, somebody could ask how these changes affected his life at the individual and social levels. Although visible progress was obtained through that uncommon form of therapy, John remained socially recognized through his schizophrenia, and his crises, albeit less frequent, were still present.

Some comments should be made, especially considering that John's schizophrenia was severe and his possibilities for social and individual integration were limited. As a De-signer, Erickson promoted in John's self a teleological movement: life was now inhabited by an essential proposal—to care for someone. It became an ideal for him evolving from the dog to Ms. Erickson after his therapist's death. Following a Peircean perspective, Erickson's therapy promoted an evolutive process in which the future was partially unblocked. Evolution, according to Peirce (1893/1998), is based on love, crucial for teleology and for the construction of meaning. It favored not only personal integration but also social insertion, one that perhaps could be conceived as a new form of belonging. However, the remaining limitations hindered further evolution as well as social exchanges, which suggested regression or unsuccessful treatment. John was still a schizophrenic; many symptoms remained; his self-integration remained fragile to a certain extent, and his affect exchanges found frequent obstacles. For those reasons, the desirable outcome was precisely understanding that these oscillations were an important moment in his processes and should be seen as a broad cycle of life. After a crisis, he was no longer desperate and hopeless, since it had merely been a bad moment in the cycle, as "Barney" taught him. Then, his life projection toward the future was resumed, because good experiences could follow bad events.

Ramakrishna

Ramakrishna Paramahamsa (1836–1886) leads us to think about the many words associated with his biography (Saradananda, 1952/2018). *Trance*, whose Latin etymology is "to cross" or "to pass by," is pertinent for seeing his trajectory as permeated by spiritual experiences and by *transit* between many paradoxes. Ramakrishna's trance perseveres and transcends paradoxes (Seif, 2020a), such as spiritual and profane worlds. One of his tantric experiences was described by him as a young man, who erotically touched with his tongue many parts of his body and their respective chakras (Clément & Kakar, 1993). *Eccentric*, whose etymology means "what is out of the center," is another sign in his life, especially because he was commonly out of the dominant logic in social life. For many people, he was a crazy man. He was married, but he remained celibate; on many occasions, he enjoyed dressing like women and behaving like them without being discovered by people. The word *ecstasy* is also meaningful here, as its Greek root *ékstasis* means "to take someone out of their own mind" or simply "someone who is out of themselves," introducing paradoxes of rationality *versus* irrationality, or sleeping *versus* waking. Ramakrishna lived in many trance states in which he seemed to lose consciousness while his body fell asleep abruptly. He was inserted into a cosmic dimension permeated by a luminous ocean of waves that embraced him; he was not dissolved into this ocean, but delivered to its wisdom. He was simultaneously asleep and awake.

> *Ramakrishna (1836–1886) was born in a Brahmana family that lived in very poor conditions* (Rolland, 1928/2018). *Born Gadhadhar Chattopadhyay, his childhood was marked by difficult conditions, such as poverty and the loss of family members. Mystical experiences permeated by spiritual visions with fainting and trance. Despite his talent for the arts, he could not maintain his studies, receiving little formal education. When he was around twenty years old, his brother instructed him to assume, as a priest, a Khali temple near Calcutta. His feverous dedication to the temple's activities contrasted with his intensive suffering related to the obsessive idea of obtaining a Goddess' vision. Despite the accomplishment of this desire, he manifested many psychiatric symptoms but recovered his mental health through Indian practices and Yoga. After a few years, he became one of the most prominent Indian gurus in the XIX century.*

Nonetheless, his experiences produced relevant meanings for himself and especially for those who were interested in his teachings (Clément & Kakar, 1993). Once he was in trance when he visualized an old Muslim man who gave him something to eat. Then, he noticed that this man was feeding many other people, and Ramakrishna listened to a voice telling him that God was unique. It is important to remark that there were many conflicts between religions in India at that same era; the voice guided him towards a conciliatory position. On another occasion, he visualized a scenario with food but also urine and excrement; then he heard a voice suggesting that all things were divine and he could eat everything. As a guru he should recognize, but especially live his teachings, according to which God is everywhere. However, in another circumstance, he saw beautiful women, refined treats, and money; and the voice asked him if he could take advantage of one of these elements, which was followed by an assertive "No" from Ramakrishna. When he fixed his eyes on these women, the voice suggested to him that inside them there was only shit and urine. He was a renouncing and celibate man despite his view that God was everywhere. In synthesis, the expression "the Madman of God" was a sign expressed by some persons (Vivekananda, 1962) that integrated paradoxes intertwined with his trajectory, such as divinity and profane, animality and humanity, and especially madness and sanity.

Therefore, trance experiences were crucial in his life as integrative processes, facing the risk of madness (Clément & Kakar, 1993). When he was in charge of a temple devoted to Khali, near Calcutta, as a priest, Ramakrishna was obsessed with obtaining a vision of the Divine Mother. He often went naked and alone to the forest during the night, looking for the Goddess, demonstrating strong tormented reactions with his unsuccessful expeditions. Insomnia, anxiety, lack of appetite, loss of weight, and sudden seizures with intense crying were some of his symptoms. Once, when he decided to commit suicide if he were again unsuccessful, he finally visualized the Goddess, which triggered an intense trance experience (Rolland,

1928/2018). He fell unconsciously, lost contact with the exterior world and felt a flow of happiness never known by him despite his several mystic experiences. All external limits and references disappeared, leaving only a vast and luminous conscious ocean with numerous waves that involved him, giving him the sensation of being inserted into the depths of infinity. The sensation of Divine presence accompanied him, who felt constant happiness.

Although he was rendered euphoric with this vision, his family and his close social circle were worried about him (Clément & Kakar, 1993). Sometimes, he was seen conversing with the statue of the goddess, trying to insert food into her mouth; he claimed the statue was moving her face and breathing; if he perceived the Divine presence abandoning him, he would fall to the ground and cry desperately. After unsuccessful Western medical treatments, his mother led him to an *Ojh*, an Indian kind of exorcism, and to an *Ayurved*, a typically Indian form of medicine, which benefited him gradually. Intending to solve his mental health issues for once, his family arranged a marriage for him, essential in Indian culture, despite Ramakrishna's firm idea to remain celibate. Nonetheless, his new form of dealing with intense spiritual experiences remained through esoteric tantra methods and mentored by a guru named Brahmani Bairavi (Saradananda, 1952/2018). Progressively, Ramakrishna recovered his mental sanity without losing his eccentricity, which made him famous in the yogi world. He became well known because he attained the highest degrees in mystical experiences by different yogic and spiritual discipline, something uncommon even among yogis. His teachings, wisdom, and ability to introduce people to mystical experiences made him one of the most important Indian references in Yoga, as the guru of many yogis and international fame.

Despite its complexity, the integrative processes of Ramakrishna can be conceived through two basic axes. On the one hand, he assumed new modes of agency in different processes integrated into his experiences, especially during trance. Following Vaishnavite tradition (Clément & Kakar, 1993), his discipline promoted an organization for the *Bhavas*, translated by mood or state of mind in which somebody is invaded by an emotion. There are many *bhavas* describing feelings toward God, such as *Shanta* (the wife's devotion toward her husband); *Dasya* (the fervent faith of a servant); *Shakya* (friendship); *Vatsalya* (the mother's feelings for her baby); and *Madhurya* (the passionate woman's emotions concerning her beloved). Ramakrishna was inserted into this tradition, but he practiced the *Bhavas* not only through meditation but also in an uncommon way. When he practiced *Madhurya Bhava* (Radha's love toward Krishna), he was dressed and behaved as a young woman for 6 months; in *Dasya Bhava*, he wore artificial tail in allusion to Hanuman, the Monkey God that symbolizes friendship; and when he practiced the *Vatsalya Bhava* (in allusion to Yasoda's feelings toward her baby, Krishna), he dressed as a woman. One of his disciples would lie on his lap like Ramakrishna was breastfeeding him while he spoke with the other disciples.

This creative form of psychodrama allows us to think that the integrative and therapeutic processes by Ramakrishna were not a form of control but a De-sign mode of dialogue (Seif, 2013, 2019). Surely, he could perform a kind of show of emotions that previously seemed out of control. Nevertheless, this cultural technology established a particular connection that promoted different forms of semiotic exchange between his ego, different self-systems, and the social world. Therefore, he prolonged his contact with spiritual cosmology and everyday life, favoring many opportunities to insert sign systems of gods in his concrete social life—with its contradictions and vicissitudes. Gods, as signs, were embodied through him, and could exchange words, impressions, feelings, and meanings with people. As a good therapist, in that sheltered context, he could bring out the strange, the ridiculous, the grotesque, and the immoral to deal with and help his disciples learn these teachings by experiencing them. Dialogue is demonstrated here not only through the word *exchanges* but particularly by different kinds of semiotic exchanges amongst the components of a complex system composed of his ego, self, and social circle. These exchanges fostered experiences that has been previously threatening and disorganizing. They became *familiar* and then *available* to new forms of negotiation. Surely, his ego was integrated and stronger than before; he could influence those experiences with some level of control. However, that control was obtained through other sources from the self and the social world, which seemed integrated into a new form of inner contract: new forms of intentionality. Ramakrishna's teleological processes were characterized by new characters in meaning construction, with a new quality of emerging feelings. In synthesis, a large contingence formed by new Firstness qualities and Thirdness signs seemed more relevant than the ego's brute force of control, typical of Secondness and commonly conceived as essential by many therapists.

On the other hand, Ramakrishna is an example of reconciliation with his own *Ethos* (Neubern, 2023). Many psychiatrists could argue that, through cultural techniques, the symptoms of a potential psychopathology were integrated as new modes of agency and self-organization, turning into socially accepted behavior (Nathan, 2001/2014). Nevertheless, without entering the debate on sociocultural and biological causes of madness (Laplantine, 1993), an ethnopsychological perspective (Neubern & Nogueira, 2019) is coherent with De-sign principles (Seif, 2019) for understanding his processes. Based on Ramakrishna's particular *Ethos*, he should be somebody in charge of a great spiritual mission (Saradananda, 1952/2018), diffusing Yogi and Hindu spiritual traditions as a guru. The obstacles he met during his life could be seen as tests, preparing him for this spiritual mission, as with many mystics and saints (Clément & Kakar, 1993). So, his experience of poverty, psychiatric symptoms, and crises could be understood as a stage when he was not conscious of his mission yet; he was also being tested, prepared for it. Paradoxically, the goddess' vision introduced him to a new mode of consciousness and simultaneously triggered many intense symptoms. His first step towards a new social role was transitioning from a patient's condition (in terms of *Ojh* and *Ayurveda*) to a Bairavi disciple. In both situations, social roles were culturally understood from a spiritual perspective: they communicated a deity's intentions, spells, and spiritual missions that should prepare them for a new form of social insertion concerning future perspectives.

Ramakrishna became, therefore, a central name in Indian communities and within their spiritual machinery (Nathan, 2001/2014). As a guru, he was a sign of access to the spiritual world through which gods could transmit their teachings to the social world in the physical plane; he could also guide other persons in their spiritual voyage. He was a sign of intersecting between the spiritual and the physical planes, between gods and human beings, taking a relevant role in Indian communities. Despite his eccentric behavior, he was recognized as an illuminated man, attracting many people who wished to receive spiritual teachings. His name became increasingly known in different parts of India, and many young men searched for him to become his disciples (Saradananda, 1952/2018). After his death, he was remembered by other yogis as one of the most important gurus in the XIX century, and his disciples, such as Vivekananda, as well the Ramakrishna Order, circulated his legacy around the world.

Nonetheless, his integration with *Ethos* was a typical De-sign process that could be understood through two key notions: renewal and rebirth (Seif, 2019). When he left Gadhadhar to become Ramakrishna was not the point when he became responsible for the Khali temple, but the first stage of a process that began with the Goddess' vision and his integration through Bairavi's teachings. Renewal means that old experiences were renovated as they happened, such as desirable outcomes. He could not consciously know his destiny, but he moved through a new intentional impulse towards the future—he behaved like a De-sign navigator. However, from a polychronic perspective (Hall, 1969/1983), the past was still present in his experiences, and new constructions could emerge from it, not following a linear logic but under a circular time perspective, in which the past can inhabit the future. As stated by Aílton Krenak (2022, p. 11), a Brazilian Indigenous philosopher:

> The rivers, these beings who always inhabited the world in different ways, suggested to me that if we could conceive a future, it would be an ancestor future, because this ancestor was still here.

His interaction with the gods, his extreme sensitivity, and trance experiences remained in his life, but were now permeated by a new flow of feelings, vitality, and symbolic constructions. However, they took many semiotic shapes, highly motivated by a constant Divine presence in his own self—which was a sign of illumination for him, a sign that posed a limit between common men and those who could see God (Vivekananda, 1962). If he could see God and feel him constantly in his self, old experiences would be understood through God's eyes, as proposed by Jacob Moreno (1980), the creator of psychodrama. Freshness of feelings and meanings impregnated these experiences, placed toward an unknown but comfortable and desirable future. Following Vaishnavite tradition, he was inhabited by God and, consequently, he could not see the world (internal or external) through human eyes. In semiotic terms (Raposa, 2020), under the influence of his ideal (the Divine experience), connections with his self systems would be extremely different compared to when he has been simply an eccentric man.

Rebirth, in turn, was marked by radical change, especially concerning the relationships between self and ego. In semiotic terms and, more specifically, in symbolic terms, human beings experience death rebirth during their life cycle experiences. The idea of palingenesis (Seif, 2019) is also coherent with this: after a symbolic death, such as a university diploma or a divorce lawsuit, a person can be reborn, re-introducing themselves to the social world through new roles, appearance, attitude, and habits. Nonetheless, a spiritual rebirth has other essential features, as illustrated in Ramakrishna's trajectory (Saradananda, 1952/2018). James's idea of conversion (James, 1902/1987) is pertinent to understand it, though Ramakrishna's process did not involve a change of religion. His rebirth can be comprehended through two basic moments: firstly, his life before the Goddess's vision, when his ego would search for spiritual illumination and was frequently disorganized by spiritual processes manifested through his self. At that stage, there was no reconciliation with himself, even though he was a boy inserted and accepted in his native culture and social circles. Strangely, despite his relatives' suffering, the young Gadhadhar did not seem to express his unusual behaviors, such as visions and fainting, as a conflict. They were granted some degree of naturality. However, thinking through his native traditions (Vivekananda, 1962), his trajectory was still incomplete, because his huge potential was unavailable, and he had not yet accomplished his mission. From an ethnopsychology perspective (Neubern & Nogueira, 2019), he seemed to be *de-placed* from his own self and, consequently, he could not be integrated with his *Ethos*. Following *Bhava's* allegories, he could be compared to the lady who desperately waited for her beloved (*Vatsalya*) or to the anxious mother before childbirth (*Madhurya*).

> *Iatrogenic situations are possible in all forms of therapy, from Medicine to other Cultural Technologies. In a psychotherapy perspective* (Neubern, 2018), *some conditions can favor iatrogenic events: (a) when the ego is fragilized due a psychopathologic element and/or an intense stress experience; (b) when the therapist or the therapeutic agent is not competent to apply techniques; (c) when the therapist or the therapeutic agent does not understand subjects' singularity, including their meanings, motivations, and feelings; (d) when there is no protective therapeutic context, especially when destructive values and affects inhabit their relationship. Hypnosis, particularly, has a strong therapeutic potential due to its condition of quale-consciousness, which can catalogue it into the Egyptian idea of* Pharmakon (Stengers, 1997): *a substance can be either medicine or poison, depending on its application. Nonetheless, Erickson's legacy demonstrates how hypnosis can be used safely, especially by creating a protected relational context.*

After the Goddess' vision, there was a second moment: he was submitted to a process of conversion. Before his work with guru Bairavi, he was deeply affected by the impact of this vision, which could possibly implicate risk of psychiatric disorganization, occasionally present in mystical trance experiences. Therefore, submitted to yogi discipline, Ramakrishna became more and more integrated; his ego occupied a new position, facing the self and his cultural machinery. As a guru, he became a servant of God, renouncing profane desires and working to accomplish spiritual intentions in the social world. Surely, his ego was still strong and creative, and his personal characteristics remained, so his old relatives could recognize him. Nevertheless, the changing his name was a sign of a new role in the social and the spiritual worlds, like in the baptism sacrament of many religions. He developed an intimacy with the Divine: he could communicate and negotiate with it. The Divine inhabited him; as Ramakrishna, he should work to serve Them. The actions of the ego—efforts, works, feelings, thoughts, and discourse—should serve this aesthetic ideal (Colapietro, 1989) to accomplish his spiritual mission among other human beings. Ramakrishna became a complex sign-system whose objects were the Divine, and his interpretants would be placed into the human soul.

Beyond Paradoxes

In Bram Stoker's book (1897/2023), Dracula was almost immortal. Stronger than twenty men, humans would eventually defeat him after a great deal of hardship. Victim of a curse, he was to become a time traveler, feeding on blood and watching entire generations rise and fall. He was a unique witness to many historical events, though he could not become part of history; he should remain anonymous. As the Living-Dead, he obtained what men commonly desired: money, influence, power, women, and immortality. When he met Mina, his beloved, he decided to kidnap her and take her to his castle. His hypnotic power influenced her, and she could not resist his orders. She drank his blood, which would in time transform her into a vampire. The only way to avoid her tragic fate would be Dracula's death. A heroic expedition, composed of her fiancé, Jonathan Harker, Van Helsing, the monster hunter, and other men, would rescue Mina, find Dracula, and kill him. She became free because she was mortal again.

This curious romance entails many relevant paradoxes. Dracula, the Living-Dead, needs to feed on blood (the life substance), to stay alive. He lived for many centuries cultivating power, brute force, and wealth, but he remained alone, since his extraordinary condition could not accommodate company. When he met Mina, he tried to control her, but his death was a form of liberation. Not only was Mina was, but especially him. Dracula, perhaps, is a symbolic icon of the slavery created by human beings when they try to solve paradoxes. He was condemned to an eternal life, without any death experiences, which caused the impossibility of innovation and rebirth. More importantly, he could not experience love, because it cannot exist without freedom; it requires paradoxes. As a teleological and evolutive process (Seif, 2018), love is inseparable from paradoxes—continuity and finitude, freedom and determination, passion and rationality, life and death. Dracula lived a double tragedy: he tried to enslave Mina, which would kill his love, and found death as a form of salvation for both. In other words, only death could transform this romance into a love story.

Dracula is also a sign frequently associated with hypnosis (Bioy, 2018), not only because of his hypnotic powers. Both are related to darkness, Dracula being a literary sign linked to witches and demons. Meanwhile, hypnosis is a practice related to exorcism and sister to other marginal movements, such as mesmerism and metapsychism. As discussed above, hypnosis, a scientific practice associated with the subjective world (Neubern, 2016), becomes essentially paradoxical in De-sign inquiry (Seif, 2020b). It can provide objective data, that is, objective signs of reality, through diaphanous, imaginative, and elusive experiences. It can propose numerous forms of control, but the desirable outcomes are legitimized only through the subject's autonomy. It can construct uncommon contexts to handle madness and produce integrative processes, the consequences of which favor mental health. Its quale-consciousness conditions further its game with extremes, such as internal *versus* external, spiritual *versus* profane, and conscious *versus* unconscious.

Nevertheless, De-sign thinking (Seif, 2019) recognizes hypnotic paradoxes without holding the inquirer fixed on them. Beyond reality and fiction, there is a continuity of knowledge, with new discoveries, ideas, and utopias, without which science loses its most important meaning. Hypnosis is, then, a constant challenge for absolute notions for the limits of reality, demonstrating these are not fixed, and knowledge is always unfinished. Beyond determinism and freedom, there is a flow of existence translated into wisdom, because a person learns what they should accept, what they should change, and the difference between these. Hypnosis is, therefore, a privileged form for obtaining consciousness, especially in ethical terms. Beyond madness and sanity, there is the human condition, with its unlimited capacity for acceptance and compassion of human diversity. Hypnosis is, again, a form of celebrating our human condition: we can recognize our madness in others. De-sign is a kind of trance through the etymological root of "to cross" or "pass by" toward an aesthetical ideal named love. Utopias, unfinished knowledge, wisdom, consciousness, and compassion are, then, teleological movements of love emerged from paradoxes.

References

APA. (2022). *Diagnostic and statistical manual of mental disorders* (5 TR). APA.
Atkins, R. (2016). *Peirce and the conduct of life. Sentiment and instinct in ethics and religion.* Cambridge University Press.
Bachelard, G. (1996). *La formation de l'esprit scientifique*. Puf. (Original work published in 1938).
Bailly, J.-S. (1784/2004). Rapport des comissaires chargés par le Roy de l'examen du magnétisme animal [Report of the commissioners entrusted by the King with the examination of animal magnetism]. In A. Bertrand (Ed.), *Du magnétisme animal en France* (pp. 70–117). (Original work published in 1824).
Bateson, G. (1972). *Steps to an ecology of mind*. The University of Chicago Press.
Berger, J. M. (2018). *Extremism*. The MIT Press.
Bioy, A. (2018). O "pequeno teatro da hipnose": uma leitura clínica do funcionamento hipnótico [The little theater of hypnosis: A clinical understanding of hypnotic functioning]. In M. Neubern (Ed.), *Clínicas do transe. Etnopsicologia, hipnose e espiritualidade no Brasil* (pp. 49–68). Juruá.

Blondel, C. (1914). *La conscience morbide. Essai de psychopathologie générale* [The morbid conscience. General psychopathology essay]. Félix Alcan.
Canguilhem, G. (1999). *Le normal et le pathologique* [The normal and the pathological]. Puf. (Original work published in 1952).
Chertok, L., & Stengers, I. (1989). *Le Coeur et la raison. L'hypnose en question de Lavoisier à Lacan* [The Heart and the reason. The hypnosis in question from Lavoisier to Lacan]. Payot.
Chomsky, N., & Polychroniou, C. (2023). *The illegitimate authority. Facing the challenges of our time*. Haymarket Books.
Clément, C., & Kakar, S. (1993). *La folle et le saint* [The madwoman and the Saint]. Seuil.
Colapietro, V. (1989). *Peirce's Approach to the Self*. Suny.
Deely, J. (2010). *Semiotic animal. A postmodern definition of "human being" transcending patriarchy and feminism*. St Augustine's Press.
Ellenberger, H. (2004). A clinical introduction to psychiatric phenomenology and existential analysis. In R. May, P. Angel, & H. Ellenberger (Eds.), *Existence* (pp. 92–126). Jason Aronson Book. (Original work published in 1958).
Erickson, M. (1954). Special techniques of brief hypnotherapy. *Journal of Clinical and Experimental Hypnosis, 2*, 109–129.
Erickson, M. (1964). The "surprise" and "my friend John" techniques of hypnosis: minimal cues and natural field of experimentation. *The American Journal of Clinical Hypnosis, 6*, 293–307.
Erickson, M. (1966). Interpersal hypnotic technique for symptom correction and pain control. *The American Journal of Clinical Hypnosis, 8*, 198–209.
Erickson, M. (1992). Healing in hypnosis. In E. Rossi, M. Ryan, & F. Sharp (Eds.), *The seminars, workshops, and lectures of Milton Erickson, MD* (Vol. 1). Irvington.
Erickson, M., & Rossi, E. (1979). *Hypnotherapy: An exploratory casebook*. Irvington.
Foucault, M. (2015). *La naissance de la clinique* [The birth of the clinic]. Puf. (Original work published in 1963).
Freud, S. (1916/1996). Fixação em traumas. O inconsciente [Fixation on traumas. The unconscious]. In J. Salomão (Ed.), *Obras Completas de Sigumund Freud* (Vol. XVI, pp. 323–335). Imago.
Gergen, K. (1996). *Realities and relationships*. Harvard University Press.
Hacking, I. (2000). *The social construction of what?* Harvard University Press.
Haley, J. (1993). *Uncommon therapy. The psychiatric techniques of Milton Erickson, MD*. Norton.
Hall, E. (1983). *The dance of life: the other dimension of time*. Doubleday & Company. (Original work published in 1969).
Han, B. (2015). *The burnout society*. Standford Briefs.
Hartshorne, C., & Weiss, P. (1980). *The collected papers of Charles S. Peirce (CP, 8 vol.)*. Harvard University Press.
Ibri, I. (2017). *Kósmos Noetós: the Metaphysical Architecture of Charles Peirce*. Springer. (Original work published in 1992).
James, W. (1987). *The varieties of religious experience*. The Library of America. (Original work published in 1902).
Krenak, A. (2022). *Futuro ancestral* [Ancestor future]. Companhia das Letras.
Kuhn, T. (2012). *The structure of scientific revolution*. University of Chicago Press. (Original work published in 1962).
Lakatos, I. (1980). *Methodology of scientific research programs* (Vol. 1). Cambridge University Press.
Langer, S. (1977). *Feeling and form*. Charles Scribner's Sons.
Laplantine, F. (1993). *Anthropologie de la maladie*. Payot.
Lyotard, J.-F. (1979). *La condition postmodern* [The postmodern condition]. Minuit.
McNamme, S., & Gergen, K. (1995). *Therapy as social construction*. Sage Publications.
Minkowsky, E. (2005). *Le temps vécu* [The time lived]. Gallimard. (Original work published in 1933).
Moreno, J. (1980). *Psicodrama* [Psychodrama]. Cultrix.
Morin, E. (1980). *L'homme et la mort* [Man and death]. Seuil.

Morin, E. (2014). *La Méthode IV. Les Idées. Leur Habitat, Leur vie, Leurs Moeur, Leur Organisations* [Method IV. idea. Their habitat, their life, their morals, their organizations]. Points. (Original work published in 1991).
Nathan, T. (2014). *Nous ne sommes pas seuls au monde* [We are not alone in the world]. Seuil. (Original work published in 2001).
Nathan, T., & Swertvaegher, J. (2003). *Sortir d'une secte* [Leaving a sect]. Seuil/Synthelabo.
Neubern, M. (2016). Iconicity and complexity in hypnotic communication. *Psicologia: Teoria e Pesquisa, 32*, 1–9. https://doi.org/10.1590/0102-3772e32ne217
Neubern, M. (2018). *Hipnose, dores crônicas e complexidade: Técnicas avançadas* [Hypnosis, chronic pain and complexity: Advanced techniques]. Ed. UnB.
Neubern, M. (2022). The role of De-sign and intentionality in understanding hypnosis. In F. Seif (Ed.), *Intentionality and semiotic labyrinths* (pp. 113–126). SSA/Philosophy Documentation Center.
Neubern, M. (2023). Hypnosis, university and democracy: An emancipatory proposal. In M. Neubern & A. Bioy (Eds.), *Hypnosis in Academia: Contemporary challenges in Research, Healthcare and Education* (pp. 27–52). Springer.
Neubern, M., & Nogueira, H. (2019). Complex hypnosis contribution to clinical psychology. In C. Antloga, K. Brasil, S. Lordello, M. Neubern, & E. Queiroz (Eds.), *Psicologia Clínica e Cultura 4* (pp. 71–90). Technopolitik.
Nöth, W. (2015). The paradigms of iconicity in language and literature. In M. Em & Hiraga (Eds.), *Iconicity: East meets west* (pp. 13–34).
Oxfam. (2023). https://www.oxfam.org/en/tags/inequality
Peirce, C. (1892/1998). The law of mind. In N. Houser & C. Kloesel (Eds.), *The essential Peirce* (Vol. 1, pp. 312–333). Indiana University Press.
Peirce, C. (1893/1998). Evolutionary love. In N. Houser & C. Kloesel (Eds.), *The essential Peirce* (Vol. 1, pp. 352–371). Indiana University Press.
Peirce, C. (1903/1997). Pragmatism as a principle and method of right thinking. In P. Turrisi (Ed.), *The 1903 Harvard lectures on pragmatism*. State University of New York Press.
Popper, K. (2014). *The logic of scientific discovery*. Martino Fine Books. (Original work published in 1959).
Quine, W. (1976). *The ways of paradoxes and other essays*. Harvard University Press.
Raposa, M. (1989). *Peirce's philosophy of religion*. Indiana University Press.
Raposa, M. (2020). *Theosemiotics. Religion, reading, and the gift of meaning*. Fordham University Press.
Reynolds, A. (2002). *Peirce's scientific metaphysics. The philosophy of chance, law, and evolution*. Vanderbilt University Press.
Rolland, R. (2018). *The life of Ramakrishna*. Prabhat Prakashan. (Original work published in 1928).
Santos, B. (2019). *O fim do império cognitivo. A afirmação das epistemologias do Sul* [The end of the cognitive Empire. The affirmation of Southern epistemologies]. Autêntica.
Saradananda, S. (2018). *Sri Ramakrishna and his divine play*. Vedanta Society of St. Louis. (Original work published in 1952).
Schechner, R. (2013). *Performance studies*. Routledge.
Seif, F. (2013). Dialogue with Kishtta: A semiotic revelation of the paradox of life and death. *The American Journal of Semiotics, 29*, 101–115. https://doi.org/10.5840/ajs2013291-44
Seif, F. (2018). Wholophilia: De-sign and the metamorphoses of the absolute. In D. Teters & O. Neumaier (Eds.), *Metamorphoses of the absolute*. Cambridge Scholars Publishing.
Seif, F. (2019). *De-sing in transmodern world*. Peter Lang.
Seif, F. (2020a). De-sign as a destiny of navigation: The paradox of sustaining boundaries while traversing borders. *The American Journal of Semiotics, 36*(3–4), 179–215.
Seif, F. (2020b). The role of pragmatism in De-Sign: Persevering through paradoxes of design and semiotics. *Cognition, 21*(1), 112–131.
Shapiro, B. (1999). *Reinventing drama. Acting, iconicity, performance*. Greenwood Press.
Silveira, N. (2015). *Imagens do Inconsciente* [Images of the Unconscious]. Vozes.

References

Stengers, I. (1997). *La malediction de la tolerance. Cosmopolitiques* 7 [The Curse of tolerance. Cosmopolitics]. Synthélabo.

Stengers, I. (2001). Qu'est-ce que l'hypnose nous oblige à penser ? [What does hypnosis force us to think about?]. *Ethnopsy, 3*, 13–68.

Stengers, I. (2002). *Hypnose: entre Magie et Science* [Hypnosis: Between magic and science]. Synthélabo.

Stengers, I. (2023). *Apprendre à bien parler des sciences. La vierge et le neutrino* [Learn to talk about science well. The Virgin and the neutrino]. Synthélabo.

Stoker, B. (2023). *Dracula*. Global Publisher. (Original work published in 1897).

Tanembaun, S. (2021). *L'hypnose ericksonienne: un sommeil qui éveille* [Ericksonian hypnosis: The sleep that awake]. InterEditions.

Vivekananda, S. (1962). *What religion is*. Julian Press.

Wallace-Wells, D. (2020). The uninhabitable earth. Life after warming. .

Weiszsäcker, E. U., & von Wijkman, A. (2018). *Come on! Capitalism, short-termism, population, and the destruction of the planet*. Springer.

White, M. (2007). *Maps of narrative practice*. Norton & Company.

Zeig, J. (1985). *Experiencing Erickson. An introduction to the man and his work*. Brunner/Mazel.

Chapter 6
The Multiple Faces of Love

> *Love is a fire that burns unseen, a wound that aches yet isn't felt, an always discontent contentment, a pain that rages without hurting,*
> *A longing for nothing but to long, a loneliness in the midst of people, a never feeling pleased when pleased, a passion that gains when lost in thought.*
> *It's being enslaved of your own free will; it's counting your defeat a victory; it's staying loyal to your killer.*
> *But if it's so self-contradictory, how can Love, when Love chooses, bring human hearts into sympathy? (Amor é fogo que arde sem se ver, é ferida que dói, e não se sente; é um contentamento descontente, é dor que desatina sem doer. É um não querer mais que bem querer; é um andar solitário entre a gente; é nunca contentar-se de contente; é um cuidar que ganha em se perder. É querer estar preso por vontade; é servir a quem vence, o vencedor; é ter com quem nos mata, lealdade. Mas como causar pode seu favor nos corações humanos amizade, se tão contrário a si é o mesmo Amor?)*
>
> —Luís Vaz de Camões

Vagueness and Surrender

Few words are as vague and complex as love. Love can mean an experience with no sense and simultaneously evoke numerous meanings, words, images, memories, and feelings, conferring those who live it an experience of the infinite. It is not without reason that poets and mystics will be essential to help me write his chapter. In the poem above, Luís Vaz de Camões (1524–1580), an exceptional Portuguese poet, presents a beautiful reflection on love, which is well aligned with De-sign thinking. First, the multiplicity of experiences, many of them paradoxical, situate love as Eros, which creates all other forms of love (Seif, 2018). Eros, also known as "the Generator-of-Desire" (Seif, 2018, 2019), or God, is well represented by this poem since it embodies both unity and multiplicity, with qualities that are simultaneously contradictory and complementary, as illustrated by the curious, yet surprising expressions "discontent contentment", "a pain that rages without hurting", "it's being enslaved of your own free will". While an aesthetical experience and ideal (Peirce, 1903), Eros is essentially vague and incessantly creates a diversity of experiences whose power of attraction is irresistible. Then, Eros is the trigger of the De-sign process and also a hypnotic one, because it exerts a powerful *seduction* on the subjects, which causes them to lose many of their references to reality, such as the blurred boundaries between oneself and their beloved selves. During love experiences, the porosity of the self (Petrilli, 2017) is intensively amplified, and the beloveds frequently have the experience of semiotic interpenetration. Semiotic interpenetration is demonstrated through the confusion between lovers regarding the originality of their feelings, ideas, thoughts, desires, stories, memories, and imaginative processes. In these cases, Eros, the creative generator, produces a form of mutual fecundation that produce multiple processes of semiosis.

> *Love is a multiple and complex phenomenon that keeps many similarities with De-sign (Seif, 2018). It is vague, paradoxical, and can't be achieved entirely by words. It manifests primarily as Eros, which can generate other sons/daughters: Agape, Divine love; Amour, whose binds the beloveds; and Philos. Its degeneration commonly leads people to pornography, in which the partner becomes a mere pleasure object. Nevertheless, it can lead people to the sublime, implicating them in an aesthetic of Beauty and the grotesque, whose aesthetic is remarked by darkness. Love is frequently a challenger for the realities' limits, as illustrated by everyday reports to the great literacy works. Then, it is constantly implicated with trance in numerous forms of experience. They are together during tragedies when people seem to lose their reason and become near madness. They are partners in the daily daydream moments when people are perceived as if they were not present. In short, they are closely related in Sacred moments when somebody is immersed in a Numinous experience.*

As incomplete and fragile beings, human seeks integrated into the cosmic whole. Seif (2018) introduces the concept of *Wholophilia*, encapsulating such profound longing. The different forms of love originated from Eros are the way to attain this ideal, which offers humans a paradoxical unique, but multiple roads. *Agape*, the Divine love, is perhaps the highest experience of cosmic integration and the highest form of reasonability (Otto, 2017). *Philos*, manifested in social causes and friendships, constitute one of the most essential human experiences. It introduces persons to alterity, engaging them in valuable lessons on ethical conditions and affective exchanges with their neighbors. In some way, *Philos* is a basis of the communitarian foundation (Binswanger, 2008), being a crucial reference for *Ethos*. From an ethnopsychological perspective (Neubern, 2022b), the binds of the individual belongings promoted by *Philos* are not limited to persons, including ancestors, spirits, saints, demons, and gods that integrate persons into nature and the cosmos. *Agape* and *Philos* share many common characteristics, being integrated into human experience, especially in trance practices in which they are concretely represented, such as in philosophical meditation or in a mystical experience. In turn, *Amour* implicates passion and perhaps sexual desire, as illustrated by the Shakespeare tragedy of *Romeo* and *Julieta*. Closely linked to *Libido*, an instinctual form of love (Seif, 2018), *Amour* is socially related to sexual practices, commonly implicating some level of commitment between the lovers, such as marriage, dating, and engagement.

Nevertheless, post-modernity has assisted radical changes in sexual practices concerning a broad range of possibilities, from the inclusion of different forms of gender construction (Butler, 2006) to practices that exercise sexual pleasure, without emotional engagement (Baumann, 2003). *Amour* is also historically associated with hypnotic practices, whether in the context of affective relationships (Carroy, 1991), or concerning the potential for abuse (Chertok & Stengers, 1989). In this sense, this form of love is commonly associated with seduction, and permeated by elements of hypnotic communication (Carroy, 1991). From the Design perspective (Seif, 2019), seduction is related to service, a relational condition that fosters autonomy and self-growth for all involved parties. The conventional understanding of 'service' is often associated with:

1. the notion of help, entailing unilateral engagement - undermining autonomy -, or
2. the notion of manipulation, which involves deceit.

Seduction, however, pertains to notions of respect and empowerment.

As discussed by Seif (2019), *Eros* creates all kinds of love in which *Eros* is always present. Eros's creative processes can move from quotidian to sublime experiences and sometimes turn to grotesque experiences and tragic events. While aesthetic ideal (Otto, 2017), the *Divine* experience or Numinous is conceived as *Agape*, which maintains its vagueness (Raposa, 1989) that exerts an irresistible attraction on people. It is reasonable to consider that *Eros* underpins the Creator (Alpha), while the End (Omega) is interspersed by *Agape*, as an endless process of search and meaning production. In some way, certain mystical figures embody the mutual fecundation of *Eros* and *Agape*. Examples include Ramakrishna and Saint Teresa de Avila, who treated Jesus as her beloved, especially during her writings and trance experiences (Avila, 1988). Nonetheless, there are many situations where Eros degenerates into pornography, disconnecting people from *Agape* and leading them to many forms of tragedy, as happened with many Catholic priests (Ballano, 2019) and with the famous Brazilian healing medium João de Deus (Felitti, 2020). In these cases, seduction becomes manipulation, especially because people are deceived and engaged in practices that undermine their integrity (Nathan & Swertvaegher, 2003).

Philos shares some aspects with *Agape*, especially concerning their aesthetic attraction and consequent vagueness. *Philos* is also another form of love created and highly permeated by Eros (Seif, 2019) because the former engagement with something or someone needs the desire forged in Eros. In the book *Grande Sertão Veredas*, Guimarães Rosa, one of the most influential Brazilian writers, presents the story about a strong friendship between two *jagunços*[1] or gunslingers, Riobaldo and Diadorin, the handsome blue-eyed man. Both men were courageous and brave, which led them to be respected and admired by their colleagues. Nonetheless, during many passages, Riobaldo has an internal crisis, grappling with unfamiliar feelings towards Diadorin. At that time, homosexuality was socially unacceptable, and Riobaldo was immersed into an intense conflict, struggling to recognize that he really loved Diadorin since his friend was a man. In few words, for that simple man, created into a social environment of violence and poverty, *Philos* could not be mixed with *Eros* and *Amour*. However, the story is finished with a twist, when Diadorin was killed during a gun conflict: Diadorin was a woman who assumed a masculine personality, intending to survive and to revenge her family.

In many ways, this story is an excellent work to be analyzed through *Eros'* notion developed by De-sign (Seif, 2018, 2019). First, it demonstrates that, through *Eros*, *Philos* was inhabited by *Amour*, Riobaldo's rejection and repressive efforts, and Diadorin's efforts to maintain a secret about her real identity. If Riobaldo could not recognize *Amour* towards Diadorin and struggled to reject this feeling, she probably corresponded to his feelings, but she was conscious of her social situation and true intentions. Otherwise, she could not fulfill her mission of revenge. In short, despite rejection, conflicts, ignorance on the subject, and the deliberated dissimulation, *Amour* inhabited *Philos* in a very curious design configuration. Second, Diadorin, moved by the strong desire for revenge, created a character that seemed to transform her profoundly and fool others. In this sense, she could not be compared to Jeanne D'Arc, since this historical character was broadly recognized as a woman. Jeanne D'Arc, for instance, performed a warrior role, and such role was recognized and accepted as a woman leading an army. Unlike Jeanne, Diadorin adopted a male identity to achieve an existential goal –revenge –, modulating herself in many ways in order to fulfill her objective. At the same time, she was a De-signer, and the desirable outcomes of her journey, because of many of the consequences of her appearance and the affective relationship with Riobaldo, were unexpected. Her courage and bravery became an almost perfect disguise for her angelic woman traits.

Third, Riobaldo experienced a moral dilemma: he could not come to terms with the possibility of having homosexual desire toward his best friend, contrasting with the societal morals and expectations of that time. De-sign thinking (Seif, 2019) conceives that Riobaldo's dilemma implicated the conflict between social values, assimilated by ego, and the deep experiences that inhabited the self. During almost all the story, he could not conceive that his feelings were not a moral problem, but an aesthetic and imaginative experience. In some way, it is possible to conceive that Riobaldo could perceive in a subliminal level Diadorin's beauty that could attract him intensively and, simultaneously, be rejected by his moral values commonly promoted by his ego and social entourage. Riobaldo's conflict was not of a moral

---

[1] In Brazil, *Jagunço* is regional a term that indicates man who is contracted for killing or defending farms. Typically, they are hired in groups by wealthy land-lords who own large. *Grande Sertão Veredas* is a fiction that integrates many elements of Brazilian rural life of the first half of the twenty century.

domain, but of an integrative one; *Amour*, in himself, could recognize Diadorin independently of moral and social filters but through the irresistible beauty that, in imaginative level, dragged him against his deliberate will. As a tragic story, the truth, perhaps as a desirable outcome, emerged only through Diadorin's death, offering for Riobaldo the opportunity to solve his dilemma. In other words, only after his beloved death - a social event that revealed the truth - could he recognize and accept his feelings of love in order to reconcile his (ego's) moral values and his deep process from the self. It is possible to conceive that the homosexual conflict was a superficial branch of something deeper concerning a subliminal perception and desire of someone who could not show oneself without a disguise.

Amour, also derived from Eros, is commonly associated with the transcendence of social limits. In some religions, the sexual relationship linked to *Amour* is conceived as a sacred meeting between gods, such as the case of Krishna and his consorts (Bishop, 1997) or between Jesus and humanity (Avila, 1988). In this sense, it is somewhat close to *Agape*. The *Amour's* extreme pleasure and bliss that emerge from these meetings are closely associated with fertility, which can take the form of different practices or events, such as spiritual rebirth through baptism, devotee faith, prosperity, birth children, and abundance in agriculture, hunting, fishing, and livestock. Thus, divine or spiritual creation is a very pleasurable event that takes place through *Amour*, having its original sources in *Eros*. In Modernity, *Amour* is detached from its divine aspects, being idealized as one of the most important goals of human existence, which is related to heterosexual relationships and is also well represented in many Hollywood movies. Nevertheless, beyond movies and books, Tobie Nathan (2013) reports many situations in which *Amour* is responsible for transcending social obstacles, such as the Swedish princess who fell in love and married a young African and commoner despite many threats from their entourage. Some years ago, in Brazil, there was reported in social media stories about middle-class white girls involved with black boys from the *favela*[2] who were engaged with drug traffic. In both situations, *Amour* seems to transcendence many kinds of obstacles, such as economic, social class, cultural and sometimes law, implicating lovers in different kinds of risks.

In these cases, *Amour* works as a form of trance, making lovers ignore or disregard certain risks, regardless of the moral options or the tragedies of such individuals when crossing social boundaries. In some way, these stories are well represented by the popular saying in which "love is blind", meaning the loss of reason that many people express when they are experiencing *Amour* (Neubern, 2016). As a Peircean metaphor, this popular saying juxtaposes two different fields of experience (love as a feeling and aesthetic experience, and human blindness) in order to illustrate how somebody can lose their reason and social reality references when falling in love. Not without reason, *Amour's* experiences are frequently described in forms that

---

[2] *Favela* is a Brazilian term used to design poor communities that commonly are around the big cities. This link is interesting to show many examples of woman and girls who were implicated with drug traffic, as cited above: https://www.terra.com.br/noticias/brasil/policia/musas-do-crime/

implicate De-sign principles (paradoxes, uncommon senses, sublime and grotesques moments, changes in materiality, time, and space) and trance reports that are well familiar to researchers and writers (Carroy, 1993). While son or daughter of *Eros*, *Amour* can have an important role in human development because it implicates the sense of otherness, the possibility of loss, devotion to somebody, and a strong pleasure in life, in short, experiences that commonly exert changes, integration and new quality of life. It promotes deep connections with the self, especially to favor the contact with quale-consciousness processes and their creative potential.

As a diaphanous experience, *Amour* can be persuasive in exerting seduction on humans. Love described as *"a fire that burns unseen"*, tends to evoke confusion as individuals find themselves immersed in an endless net of paradoxes. This complexity can shape beliefs and behaviours as if their emotions are guiding forces. *Amour*, characterized as *"staying loyal to your killer,"* is a form of voluntary surrender to the beloved, something not conceivable in conventional circumstances. Despite its vagueness, *Amour*, as the other *Eros* sons, exerts a strong attraction over people, justifying its proximity with blindness or slavery, despite their targets being conscious and free in their actions. In this sense, not only can 'faith can move mountains', as the Christian parable suggests, but Amour is often depicted as the catalyst of the most amazing and irrational actions (Nathan, 2013).

Nonetheless, *Amour* can be degenerated in two ways, the consequences of which can be harmful for those engaged in these modes of experience. On one hand, *Amour* becomes pornography, in which physical pleasure is privileged over anything else, and seduction is a kind of manipulation. As commonly occurs in Western societies, inspired by Modernity (Seif, 2019), in pornography, there is no consideration toward the other as a person, who is only an object to be used for pleasure. In some way, when pornography, *Amour* becomes blind in such a fashion that the beloved can't see and consider his partner as a person, breaking with the sense of alterity, which is associated with many kinds of sexual problems, such as impotence, anorgasmia, and praecox ejaculation, and psychopathology conditions. On the other hand, *Amour* is closely associated with madness, mainly because of its inherent breaking with realities references. Martins (2005) highlights that the Greek word *Pathos*, the root of the word psychopathology, is a common root to designate passion and madness, an association frequent in popular day-life thinking that conceives *Amour* as a loss of reason. Murders, suicides, some forms of sexual crimes and depression, obsessive jealousy, long periods of grief, and other forms of psychopathology are frequently associated, in Western societies, with the tragic degeneration of *Amour* in madness.

Eros and Hypnosis

In the following sections, through De-sign principles (Seif, 2018, 2019), I will analyze how the complex relationships between *Eros* and other forms of love can occur linked to trance experiences. Nevertheless, the following reflections will answer the question of whether *Eros* is a creative potency and why it can be related to destructive processes in human life. The first section will treat an Erickson case study (Erickson & Kubie, 1941) about a young woman who was depressed and tried suicide many times, especially because she lived an intense sexual conflict. *Amour*, in this sense, will be the main reference to thinking about this case study, even because this form of love was degenerated by her education and social milieu and established through hypnotherapy. The second section, in turn, will compare two famous Brazilian mediums—Chico Xavier and João de Deus—in their different spiritual trajectories, with the former recognized as a kind of contemporary saint (Souto Maior, 2003) and the latter by his remarkable spiritual healings (Rocha, 2017) and numerous sexual crimes (Felitti, 2020). *Agape* will be the central reference in this comparison, being conceived as a sublime sacred experience for Chico Xavier and a degenerative experience translated into pornography and violence for João de Deus.

The Girl Who Could Not Love

Love, Death, and Hypnosis

Many years ago, Erickson was asked by his colleague, the psychoanalyst and psychiatrist Lawrence Kubie (1896–1973), if he could help him in the treatment of a young woman, 19 years old, who was very depressed and tried suicide five times. Analysis was not working, and Dr. Kubie was worried about the girl's integrity. Kubie called for Erickson's help using hypnosis (Erickson & Kubie, 1941). During the clinical story, the girl reported that his mother was a puritan who tried to teach her family religious values. When she was 7 years old, her mother told her to avoid becoming too close to boys because they could do "nasty things" with girls, making a subtle allusion to sexual content. At 13 years old, she had her first menstruation and, almost at the same time, her mother died. After this tragedy, she became emotionally attached to a neighbor's family, especially to a girl the same age as her best friend. The friends were always together, sharing secrets, such as their interest in boys. When they were around 17, they fell in love with the same boy, but Erickson's patient decided not to reveal her interest, protecting and respecting her friend, who married him. Erickson's patient became despondent, but she chose to sacrifice her own feelings to protect her friend's happiness. Nonetheless, a few months after the marriage, her friend suddenly died, and Erickson's patient felt again an intense grief concerning the loss of somebody essential in her life.

Moreover, her situation became more complicated since her friend's husband demonstrated interest in her. He spent some months in another city, but when he was back, he searched again for Erickson's patient, who felt contradictory feelings concerning him because she was also interested in a possible engagement, but that man could mean a betrayal toward her beloved friend. She felt depressed and, after suicidal attempts, she became a patient at a psychiatric hospital. After these events, she accepted her family's suggestion to search for therapeutic help, but, as mentioned above, the psychoanalysis was not working positively. When invited by Doctor Kubie, Erickson knew that the patient would not accept receiving hypnotic treatment, which led the therapists to arrange a form to introduce her to hypnosis in a positive way. Erickson invited her roommate to a hypnotic session, and this girl asked the patient to accompany her during the procedure. When Erickson, the roommate, and the patient were in the room, he induced them into a deep and comfortable trance state; apparently, he was more interested in the roommate, but he used many indirect suggestions toward the patient. In a trance, he asked her if she agreed to follow some sessions of hypnotherapy, and she answered affirmatively. After the trance, the same question was asked, and the patient confirmed her agreement. The roommate was then discharged.

During the first session, he promoted many focus deviations, causing her some confusion about reality references. Slowly, he oriented her into a regressive trance in which she was invited to tell her mother's teachings about life. Speaking as a child of 7 years old, she said that her mother said that she should keep her distance from boys, who could do "nasty things" with girls, which was understood as sexual practices. Erickson told her that her mother was attentive and protective to her daughter, and these teachings were appropriate for a 7-year-old girl. Then, he induced her to amnesia and let her go home. The next session was a similar procedure, but in age regression, he inserted an important statement in which her mother was appropriate to educate a little girl. However, as your mother had died, she did not have the opportunity to say something to educate an adolescent or a woman. Again, she was induced to amnesia and sent home. In another session, after a similar procedure, he took the place to teach her about human development since he was a PhD Psychiatrist who could give her many scholarly lessons on the subject. In a trance, she was told much information on human development, from childhood to adulthood, as a natural and biological process, especially concerning body and psychological changes, sexual attraction, and sexual relationships. At some moment, she tried to leave the room abruptly, but Erickson did not allow it, inviting her to continue in a trance in the armchair. Thus, he suggested to her that things should occur naturally and that personal values should be respected. After that session, she acknowledged Erickson because he protected her from taking an abrupt decision with which she intended to find her beloved in to have intercourse. As virginity was an essential value for her, a sexual relationship at that moment could be tragic. Nevertheless, she was engaged and continued her therapy with Doctor Kubie, who reported to Erickson some months later that she had many improvements, without depressive symptoms or suicidal ideas. After some months, the patient and her boyfriend were married and had a child.

Conspiration and Seduction

The abovementioned case study is illustrative of the dissociation between *Amour* and sex, producing intensive suffering in the young woman. Even if Erickson did not mention any pornographic practice of his patient, at the imaginary level, she created a strong opposition between *Amour* and pornography, reducing the former to the latter. In a repressive social context, her mother taught her to avoid sex, which was conceived as a destructive and nasty practice. Possibly, it was a standard value at that age, especially concerning children's education, but nobody could predict that the attribution of sex and love to depreciative values could be at the center of her conflict. In this sense, the intersection of the ego with social values and practices produced a disconnection with the dynamics of the self, which, while a semiotic system, would grow in different ways. At this point, death had an essential role because its intensive emotional impact reinforced the close association between *Amour* and depreciative values. Her mother's death possibly created a strong sense of fidelity. The patient were to remain a good daughter, as she had been expected to be since her childhood. From a similar perspective, her friend's death probably promoted also a decisive deed of fidelity because this friend was critical in her life after her mother's death. If death is an event that sacralizes people who die, the patient's two losses intensified her repressive mechanisms against whatever kind of feeling related to *Amour*. Through her rigid moral attitude of fidelity to dead and beloved persons, suicide seemed to be the best option facing her natural *Amour* life desires, of which the dynamic should probably be unconscious. Although the young woman acceptation to submit to psychotherapy, at that moment she was not able to find a solution different from death.

In this sense, the beginning of Erickson's intervention can be conceived as a typical form of seduction and conspiracy following a De-sign thinking (Seif, 2019). Seduction because his interventions could not be understood as manipulation since he contemplated her needs and asked for her consent during and after the trance. From a similar perspective, conspiracy is conceived in this case in its original meaning of "breathing together". Due to her delicate risk situation and resistance against hypnosis, Erickson chose to introduce her to the trance experience, leading the young woman to a level of processes about herself that common ego thoughts could not achieve. In other words, instead of approaching her at an ordinary level of consciousness, which would lead her to reject hypnosis, he chose to lead her first to experience and, only after that, to obtain her permission for treatment. Erickson did not ask her directly if she would accept hypnosis, but he led her to know it through her own experiences, feelings, and thoughts.

This procedure is what I call "the clinic of showing" (Neubern, 2016), which is also a form of establishing relationships through iconicity, that is, thought signs that are presented and not necessarily explained. It is also a form of seduction in which many icons are utilized, promoting vagueness and subliminal messages that go toward the subject's inner world and engage him in that relationship. When a man sends flowers to his beloved woman, he will not explain to her what those flowers mean in order to offer her many possibilities of imagination and desire concerning *Amour*. If she had some resonance with this gesture, he might become a sign system in herself, which can promote other possibilities of semiosis. She can think about him, create imaginative scenes with him, and establish imaginative dialogues with the signs whose object is that man as a semiotic system. Again, these dialogues are also monologues (CP[3] 6.338), possessing the seeds of desirable futures and desirable outcomes. In turn, the case study was slightly different because Erickson was moved by Eros, who was transformed into *Philos* but not in *Amour*. In this sense, it is possible to conceive *Philos* closely related to *Asclepius* or *Quiron*, the mythologies gods related to healing that exerts their influences and powers from their empathy with human suffering. In this sense, being an old man and a Ph.D. Psychiatrist Erickson might become a positive and respectful sign to go inside her world and promote therapeutic changes. In a word, despite his masculine condition, he would not seem a threat concerning her sexual conflicts.

In turn, the conspiracy must be understood through a broad meaning from the arrangement among Erickson, Kubie, and the roommate, intending to implicate the patient in hypnosis, to the intimacy established between Erickson and the patient. In some way, the arrangement obeyed the same idea of seduction, in which they tried to consider her risks and necessities. Firstly, she should experience hypnosis before accepting or rejecting it as a treatment. That arrangement was a kind of theatre incorporating De-sign principles (Seif, 2020a) that involved seduction, trickery, and deception, especially because she could trigger an adverse reaction against them if she discovered that agreement and their intentions concerning hypnosis. However, being the protagonist of her own decision, she was again engaged in a new perspective of healing, which was a very positive achievement for her treatment. Analogous to the theatre, as the leading actress, she not necessarily was aware of all the arrangements that prepared her performance and her central participation in the spectacle. However, if the actress knew about some agreement that did not respect her autonomy, she could decide to abandon the team. In short, this case study's line of healing and trickery is subtle, and the risks of adverse consequences must not be neglected.

Nevertheless, conspiracy can also be conceived in Erickson's statements during the patient's trance. During age regression, Erickson and the young woman established an intimate conversation concerning the teachings made by her mother when

---

[3] Hartshorne & Weiss (1980) is the reference of CP, which means the Collected Papers of Charles Peirce. I adopted the CP due to the fact that this is the most known reference among semioticians of Peirce's collected papers.

the patient was a child. They were speaking on delicate subjects configured into the core of her sexual conflicts, that is a conversation that could not be made in a public context. During Erickson's scholarly lessons, despite the technical appearance of his statements, he touched on crucial subjects of the patient's sexual meanings and feelings. Being an indirect form of suggestion (Erickson & Rossi, 1979), those lessons appear to be a technical explanation at a conscious level, but they implicated, in a subliminal form, the subjective systems of experience. Erickson's empathy and acceptance toward her were essential to producing an intimate context as a private space symbolically similar to a private room, accessible only for specific persons. In that space, the therapist and patient could indeed brief together or *conspire*, as of Farouk Seif's idea (2019). However, as a trance process, that relationship was still more complex because of the typical trance semiotic interpenetration. In this context, Erickson became a sign system. The symbolic and experiential room of conspiracy was, then, inside each of the protagonists and simultaneously between them, as a form of Kurt Lewin's field theory (Lewin, 1951) discussed in Chap. 3. In synthesis, conspiracy is linked with this context as sharing a quale-consciousness process where therapist and patient could model, as in a craft workshop, the conflictual contexts of the patient's self.

Amour Meets Eros Again

Erickson's interventions in this case study are illustrative examples of De-sign inquiry (Seif, 2020b), which can be understood through two primary forms. On one hand, he reframed her mother's role in the patient's educative process, as an appropriate form of protection for a child. Her mother's death was reframed in a way that it does not allow her to give appropriate lessons to a young woman. From many perspectives, her mother could be understood as a repressive woman whose teachings had a special role in her daughter's conflicts. However, when Erickson's statement contemplated the adequacy of her lessons, the risks of precocious sexual practices, the patient's age, and the mother's death (that impeached her to continue her educational role with her daughter), he inserted many truisms (obvious sentences) into a new frame of reference, changing essential meanings concerning the mother's role in her life. Therefore, that intervention was crucial to protect her mother and, as a consequence, reduce the intensity of the patient's repressions. In this way, Erickson promoted a palingenesis process in the patient self since her mother's death was related to the intensive repression, but after the intervention, she could be associated with an attentive and adequate mother, meaning that the patient could remain a good and obedient daughter who would not need much repression. In short, her mother could continue living in the patient's self as a living sign associated with protection and education, not repression. In other therapeutic approaches, the archeology searching for an internal truth could have led her to confront her mother as a repressive figure, which could have promoted obstacles to understanding her mother otherwise being iatrogenic for the patient.

On the other hand, his suggestions worked to promote changes concerning her general meaning of sexuality. For that patient, sexuality was linked to pornography and betrayal, the first concept related to her mother's lessons (the *"nasty* things"), triggering feelings of *betrayal* to her deceased mother and friend. From her semiotic configurations, she lived in a dilemma because she was a normal woman who felt sexual desire, but she also maintained the idea of fidelity towards these two significant figures. Sexual desire or engagement could mean betrayal concerning her mother's lessons and her friend's marriage. However, Erickson adopted a scientific approach to confer naturalness to her feelings and sexual desires, framing them as a natural human condition instead rather than a sin or moral deviation. Within such lens, sexual desire lies beyond the dichotomic paradigm nature versus culture (Deely, 2010) but as something that follows its course independently of human values or judgments. In this sense, Erickson's lessons promoted the continuity of sign growth, leading them to follow their natural condition of making inefficient relationships efficient (CP 8.332). Erickson's indirect suggestions, through the idea of *naturality*, worked to reduce the repressive power created by the patient's personal trajectory, intending to block her sexuality. In some way, it is possible to conceive that the patient's ego accepted his suggestions well because they were scientific and coherent. Nonetheless, through a subliminal influence (Erickson & Rossi, 1979; Neubern, 2016), the idea of naturality was very coherent for her at an unconscious level since it was a form of recognize her desire, conferring to the patient the permission to follow her own growth movement. Thus, the sign systems of Nature and Science authorized her to accept and manifest her sexual desires, allowing her to concretize her old dream of marriage.

Through these two ways, *Amour* was reconstructed, disengaged from pornography, and reconnected to *Eros* (Seif, 2018). To promote this reconnection, Erickson invited his patient to make an uncommon navigation through her personal universe, especially in a polychronic experience. During trance, she could be and interact with herself as a child, comprehending herself as an adult and projecting her future memories about sexual life, marriage, and family. Perhaps for her, the experience of sexuality in an imaginary way was one of the most important desirable outcomes achieved through that navigation. At the same time, she persevered through her own paradoxes (Seif, 2020b). This way, the patient realized she could live her own sexuality and continue to honor the memory of her mother and friend. After that imaginary journey, she could reconcile with her past, preserve her deceased loved ones within herself, and foster the emergence of teleology about a desirable future. In some way, *Eros* was back to herself, and it could exert its creative power again in her quotidian life.

Mediumship, Angels, and Demons

Chico Xavier and Agape as Charity

> *Historically, mediumship was a term forged in European countries during the XIX century (Monroe, 2007). It refers to a human natural ability to communicate with spirits, which can be expressed through many forms. However, mediumship does not necessarily have a connection with the Sacred because it does not necessarily implicate the mediums in a Divine experience, nor obligate them to engage in spiritual mission. In this sense, many examples of mediumship can be classified into a profane or a Sacred type, which is more common among religiousg (Nuñez, 2008/2012). Chico Xavier was perhaps the most prominent Brazilian representative of the latter who promoted a close association of Kardec's legacy with Christian principles. As a sign, he became a representative (medium) of this Christian Spiritism whose proposal was to diffuse principles such as the existence of spirits, mediumship, reincarnation, and cause-effect law (karma) allied to love, forgiveness, and charity. In his devotion to love as an Agapistic ideal, Chico Xavier's mediumship is not limited to formal charity or mediumistic activities, being extended to everyday attitudes in the social world, where the medium should demonstrate his coherence (integration) with Agape.*

Francisco Cândido Xavier (1910–2002) was perhaps the most important spiritist medium in Brazil's XX century. Popularly known as Chico Xavier, he is considered the essential name for adapting Allan Kardec's[4] legacy to Brazilian culture, transforming Spiritism became a particular form of Brazilian religion (Stoll, 2003). On one hand, it was always respectful towards Kardec's principles of rationality, constructed through the marriage between faith and reason. Chico Xavier positioned himself as a server/follower, with Kardec, the French master, and all spiritists aware that if he presented something opposing Kardec's ideas, people should follow the latter. On the other hand, Chico Xavier personal closeness to Christian principles, particularly those of Catholicism, led him to become a symbol of the Christian sacred within Spiritism (Neubern, 2022a). As discussed by the theologian Rudolf Otto (2017), the Sacred or *Numinous* can't be achieved through human efforts but

---

[4] Allan Kardec was a pseudonym adopted by the French educator Héppolyte Léon Denizard Rivail (1804–1969), a disciple of Pestalozzi. When he was 50 years old, he began to study the mediumistic phenomena, being convinced of the veracity of the spiritual world after some years of study. He created the term Spiritism to designate the teachings made by the spirits through the medium abilities of many individuals. He insisted that his role was only to organize the information obtained through contact with the mediums, being himself the "*Codificator*" and not the creator of Spiritism. In its French origin, Spiritism was a philosophical doctrine that had important interfaces with Science and Religion.

only through superior Grace, which can be understood only through experience. No words can describe the Sacred, but we can have some references about it through the emergent meanings obtained from Chico Xavier experience. Thus, despite his explicit fidelity to Allan Kardec's ideas, for whom, in some way, everything can be known, Chico's medium works, and everyday attitudes open a diaphanous place for the Sacred, whose seeds were still in Kardec's books but not entirely recognized. Chico Xavier's teachings, which are attributed to Christian tradition as Sacred, are commonly linked to terms such as moral and something that is not yet accessible to human words and knowledge (Neubern, 2022a).

In this sense, Chico Xavier's legacy tries to conciliate Spiritism's reasoning, inspired by the French Enlightenment, with the Christian tradition, which incorporates the unique blend of Brazilian miscegenation including African, Indigenous, and Eastern influences (Carvalho, 1994). Hence, he meticulously elucidated his ideas in numerous books, texts, and interviews, ensuring the continuity of French Spiritism. He believed that clear explanations about the spiritual world and its interaction with the physical plane were essential for human understanding. Nonetheless, frequently in Chico Xavier's poetry, writing, chronicles, interviews, and storytelling crafted by himself or recounted by his followers—a language rich in metaphors, diagrams, and analogies prevails, reflecting his cultural and religious *Ethos*. These effective forms of communication allow us to highlight at least two main elements of Chico Xavier's *Ethos*. First, the sign systems point to the subtle universe of experience beyond human rational reach, that is, the field of the Sacred that presents a different logical functioning. Like the Catholic Saints and the Yogi Gurus, Chico's experience sometimes seemed to obey an aesthetical logic permeated by love, poetry, scenes, and stories that communicated their messages intending to touch feelings and offer many meanings and possibilities. The realm of the spirits, constantly visited by him, was governed by laws and orders quite distinct from those in the human world; the materiality, time, space, cause, and even moral and beauty values were not always coherent with the human world, mainly because the former was eternal and pre-existent concerning the latter.

Spirits live many lives through reincarnation, can transform their bodies and matter through their thoughts, and predict future events in the human world. Several boundaries between standard references adopted in social reality are blurred, leading modern human beings to believe that they are not only alone, as proposed by Tobie Nathan (2014), but also that their logic of certitude is insufficient. In this spiritual world revealed by Chico Xavier, matter vs. spirit is a confused opposition because what is subtle for humans can be material for spiritual beings; male vs. female is also a problematic reference since spirits can rebirth as men and women. A desperate cancer situation for a man can be conceived as a kind of emancipation, interpreted as the payment of past karmic deeds. In such a diaphanous and uncertain universe, De-sign principles (Seif, 2020b) and iconicity (Neubern, 2016, 2022b) play a special role in communication. This is because the elusive spaces, paradoxes, meaning multiplicity, feelings, and polychronic time are more coherent with this world. This concepts contrast with the absolute and unique notion of reality conceived by modern science, which inspired Allan Kardec. The European metapsychic research in the XIX century (Blum, 2004) aimed to understand the mediumistic phenomena as any other natural phenomena, through empiricism. The spiritual world presented by Chico Xavier, however, was inhabited by aesthetical ideals, especially *Agape*, that should implicate human beings into an ethical form of life permeated by love and charity. In this sense, Chico Xavier should be closer to Francis of Assisi or Ramakrishna, than Eusapia Paladino or Daniel Dunglas Home, two important mediums studied by metapsychists (Blum, 2004).

> *From an ethnopsychology perspective* (Nathan, 2014), *spirits are beings produced by the spiritism machinery devices (the mediumistic meeting), as electrons are beings produced by physics through its devices, the laboratory. Then, I don't intend to discuss in this book if spirits are real for two main reasons. First, they commonly don't answer to scientific devices, although the parapsychological effort* (Maraldi, 2021). *Similarly, electrons don't answer to mediumistic meetings because they constitute a different form of reality that must be accessed through scientific laboratories. Second, ethnopsychology tries to access and understand people's experiences through their knowledge references, implying that the researcher must not attribute significance to a person's spiritual manifestations. If a medium reports a spiritual apparition, the researcher can't interpret it as a delirium or imagination but following the original meaning of this apparition into his machinery cosmology. Nonetheless, through De-sign inquiry, it is possible to comprehend spirits as signs of collective machinery with its specific semiosis process* (Neubern, 2023).

Chico Xavier's work is a typical form of communication permeated by metaphors and other icons. This form of communication was more coherent with the Brazilian culture, in which emotional expression is commonly more stimulated than in European cultures. This cultural value for emotions was closely related to Chico Xavier's personality, who was in the center of social representation of spiritism (Lewgoy, 2004). He was a humble man of poor, mixed, and rural origins, and he was known in his entourage as somebody who always intended to serve other people (Souto Maior, 2003). His powerful medium skills were undissociated from a primary goal—the service for the benefit of others—such as the letters written from dead people to be sent to their families (Barbosa, 1978). In addition to all these mediumistic activities, he was always implicated in helping desperate people who had lost somebody important, the orphans, the poor without food and clothes, prisoners, the sick, and the elderly abandoned. Unlike French Spiritism, which intended to prove the existence of the soul through scientific methods (Sharp, 2006; Monroe, 2007), Brazilian Spiritism, led by Chico Xavier, aimed to alleviate people's suffering in all possible forms. In some way, it is possible to affirm that while French spiritism tried to be coherent with science, Brazilian Spiritism intended to communicate with ordinary people's suffering in order to eliminate or alleviate it. This successful strategy was crucial to constructing a cohesive community around his name, which integrated Kardec's rationality with Christian sanctity values, such as love, humility, discipline, service, and charity (Nuñez, 2008/2012). Chico Xavier was, in this way, the object of a large network of signs, the scope of which covered different sectors of the Brazilian society, including poor people from various cities and TV celebrities, politicians, liberal professionals, businessmen, artists, and government authorities. This extensive network included not only spiritists but also many people from other religions and spiritual backgrounds. It is no surprise that, according to opinion research (Souto Maior, 2003), he was declared the most prominent Brazilian personality, surpassing notable figures such as Santos Dumont, the father of aviation; Juscelino Kubitschek, a famous president; and Pelé, the legendary soccer player. This extraordinary network included books, radio, magazines, documentaries, soap operas, and films, being frequently linked to the creation and the help of many charity institutions.

Furthermore, Chico Xavier's legacy was also crucial to popularizing a mediumistic culture in which many people could develop their communication abilities with the spiritual world (Stoll, 2003). In different spiritist centers in Brazil, people could submit to courses to study mediumship and initiate the mediumistic training that could vary following each person's abilities. Psychography (the writing influenced by spirits), psychophony (the speaking), vision (the capacity to see the spiritual world), audition (to listen to it), healing, and clairvoyance (to perceiving beyond the physical limits of time and space), among others were part of the enormous group of mediumship abilities found in Spiritism practice. However, these practitioners were always stimulated to adopt charity as a main practice because it educates the mediums in good virtues. If mediumship would allow communication with spirits, charity would promote the quality of these exchanges since good feelings, attitudes, and thoughts were essential to a medium spiritual health. Charity, in its essence, was more an attitude or a guiding life principle than a concrete practice. As defined by the spirits to Kardec (2021), it encompassed benevolence toward all, indulgence toward the imperfections of others, and forgiveness of offenses. In this sense, the mediumship practice could be conceived as charity because it was commonly related to a major social goal. Nevertheless, in accordance with Christian principle, neighbors should be recognized everywhere, especially among those enduring profound forms of suffering related to problems such as the loss of a loved one, social vulnerability, poverty, and mental and physical illnesses. Mediums could place themselves in others' places to obtain an idea about their situations and alleviate them. The Christian principle of treating others as one would like to be treated is strongly reinforced by the concept of reincarnation. Through multiple physical existences, the medium or their closest connections may find themselves in the same situations of suffering as those they currently helped.

In some way, these affective communities were quite similar to Puységur's communities in French XVIII century (Puységur, 1784). But, although Puységur believed in the spiritual world, he promoted only the idea of somnambulistic states in which one could access cosmic wisdom, and influenced by the pure desire of service, helping people. Chico's legacy, in turn, extended this affectivity to the spiritual world, which was always interacting with the world of the living, inspiring women and men to act in different forms. Many of his psychography books presented particularities of spiritual life that Allan Kardec had not introduced yet, such as cities, organized social life, institutions, technology, vehicles, medical procedures, education, and events, which were common elements with human social life that produced an intensive identification and the idea of multiple universes in many people (Nathan & Stengers, 1999). Chico Xavier's psychographies highlighted that human beings were not alone, but always in exchange with the spiritual world. More than that, people could establish emotional binds with spirits, who could be defined precisely as human beings without physical bodies and whose frequently spiritual trajectory (reincarnation) could be closely related to the medium's missions. In short, through Chico's detailed presentation of the spiritual world, love, friendship, charity, and forgiveness should be extended to both human beings in the physical realm and to spirits.

Therefore, it is possible to conceive that Chico Xavier's work promoted the construction of a social community similar to Peirce's idea of community. Different persons were integrated through emotional bonds, the *commens* (CP 3.621), in order to create a network of mutual help, inspired by values such as charity, faith, and hope. From an ethnopsychological perspective (Neubern, 2018a), this network was crucial in offering various forms of belonging, either in the social or the spiritual realms. Nevertheless, as a religious community, people were engaged in the search for the truth, giving continuity to Kardec's legacy, but with a broad perspective in which the spiritual world would be much more detailed and the relationships with Christian ideals, especially concerning the Sacred (Neubern, 2022b), were more explicit. These communities were heterogeneous in many aspects, but they had in common the emotional relationships and some criteria to explore and accept (or reject) the information concerning spiritual revelations. If many spiritist institutions and federations were sometimes accused of being excessively conservative, they had, in turn, an essential role in proposing criteria to avoid ethical abuses and distortions of spiritual truths. On some occasions, even Chico Xavier was under questioning because, despite his importance to spiritism in Brazil, he was only a man, and consequently, he could also fail in his ethical attitudes and revelations concerning the spiritual world.

The social scenario described above is essential to understanding Chico Xavier as a Christian sign, which is very similar to Catholic Saints. *Agape* became more and more central in his life, being the ideal through which Chico could fulfill his spiritual mission and promote the formation of a cohesive collective around his work. His personal trajectory was predominantly inspired by an alchemical transformation (Jung, 2023) in which his ego's aspirations were renounced or converted into a sacrifice considering *Agape*. As a De-signer (Seif, 2019), Chico Xavier should serve people and humanity, but even his personal desire should serve the Christian ideals of love, devotion, humility, and charity, which could be verified in narratives concerning different parts of his life (Souto Maior, 2003). He was born in difficult conditions, with his family being very poor, leading to situations of deprivation and maltreatment. He lost his mother when he was 5 years old, aggravating his family situation. Chico was of mixed-race origin and studied only for 4 years when he was obligated to work with the intention of helping his family. Being a man of feminine attitudes, rarely was he seen in confrontation against others since he would prefer dialogue and cordiality. From a traditional perspective, this social scenario did not seem to offer the necessary conditions to creating a spiritist leadership, mainly because Brazilian society is still currently very patriarchal and patrimonial, being influenced mainly by slavery's legacy (Souza, 2019). In this sense, Chico Xavier was quite different from other spiritist leaders from the Brazilian XIX and XX centuries, who commonly were men, white, had university diplomas, and were very good at debate confrontations. For instance, Bittencourt Sampaio was a journalist and lawyer; Francisco Dias da Cruz and Adolfo Bezerra de Meneses were doctors; Eurípedes Barsanulfo and Divaldo Franco were educators. In short, the spiritist leaders came from Brazilian society's dominant sectors, while Chico was a poor boy from the rural zone, from a mixed-race origin, and without a high level of formal education, despite his incredible intelligence. Hardly a person with these origins could become a leader of the Brazilian spiritism movement, which was formed mainly by middle-class people and required some level of familiarity with scholarly life.

Nevertheless, despite the numerous obstacles, Chico Xavier became the leader of that movement, contradicting the Brazilian socio-cultural determinations described above. It is possible to conceive that this leadership was possible in two ways, closely related to *Agape*. First, he was an exceptional medium, being able to manifest the most different kinds of spiritual phenomena. He wrote more than 400 books throughout psychography, including novels, poetries, self-help messages, history, and "technical" books related to spiritist principles, such as mediumship, reincarnation, and spiritual evolution. Many of his letters from dead persons sent to families contained amazing information concerning the intimacy, peculiarities, and details known only by specific individuals not previously known by Chico (Barbosa, 1978). Commonly, the signatures of these letters were quite similar to those of the same persons when they were alive. But, beyond the books and writings, Chico presented abilities to predict future events, healing, and different forms of physical phenomena in which spiritual influences can have a perceptible effect on the physical realm. He could see spirits with the same naturality he saw others, which led him to be understood as an inter-existent being (UEM, 1993), a man who can participate and interact consciously and simultaneously with the spiritual and the physical realms. Numerous narratives confirm Chico's diverse and powerful abilities. For instance, a mother verified details and the signature of her beloved son who had died tragically (Barbosa, 1978). Chico would relay information about someone who died far away without any prior communication (Gama, 1998). He was known to facilitate spectacular healings, contradicting medical predictions (Vilela, 1994), and produce tangible apparitions of spirits or spiritual objects, such as flowers and perfumes (UEM, 1993). Despite never studying them, he displayed knowledge in sciences like Medicine, Astronomy, History, and Physics (Souto Maior, 2003). In summary, his biographies are filled with numerous reports of incredible mediumistic phenomena, similar to those associated with saints, prophets, and mystics from various spiritual traditions where the Sacred is sought as an agapistic ideal.

Agape, in turn, was also cultivated in everyday attitudes, in which his ideal was, in some way, translated into concrete actions with firm ethical values. His vast book production could have allowed Chico a comfortable life due to the millions of dollars that his work produced, but he never accepted money for his psychographies (Souto Maior, 2003). He affirmed that he was not the real author of these books and that all the money they generated was destined for charity institutions. Chico never accepted money or other forms of award for his works, being inflexible in this subject (UEM, 1993). His life was always modest, and he lived on a small salary as a public agent from the government, through which he supported his brothers, sisters, nephews, nieces, and, after them, his adopted sons. He had never been married, affirming that his family should be the books and the suffering humanity. Although he was not a typical masculine man, on some occasions, he was approached by women who were firmly rejected. Frequently, he renounced important things (such as jobs, awards, money, and comfort) because he was instructed by the spirits that he should be coherent with Christian ideals. Facing offenses, attacks, betrayals, and calumnies, especially from close people, he kept silent and was never seen speaking or planning forms of revenge. As commonly reported in the stories, Emmanuel, his spiritual guide, continuously asked him to maintain devotion to his mission, which could be the best medicine for suffering and the best advocate against attacks (Gama, 1998). During many years of his life, Chico slept only 3 hours per day because he had to be at his job from 8 AM to 6 PM. At home, he should help his numerous family members, and at 9 PM, he should begin to work with psychographies until 3 AM. His weekend was devoted to helping people through spiritual and material assistance, in which he frequently organized donations of clothes, food, and medicines for poor families. His fragile health was another point commonly cited in stories since Chico Xavier frequently sought surgeries or other medical procedures (Souto Maior, 2003). Especially his heart and eyes were cited as the source of many health problems, and for many of his followers, he arrived at 90 years old only due to spiritual intervention, who comprehended that he deserved more years of life to fulfill his mission.

Regarding the storytelling about Chico Xavier, it is noteworthy that many accounts emphasize his spontaneous reactions in surprising situations. Once, as reported by Gama (1998), he was belated to take a bus that would lead him to a job interview. That event was quite important for him since the salary was better than his current salary, and he was his family's unique source of money. While trying to run toward the bus, he heard a child's voice claiming for him insistently. He turned back and saw a little boy who said he needed to speak with him, leading Chico to hesitate between running toward the bus and the boy's claim. Thus, he decided to stay and listen to the boy who gave him a little flower and said: "I wanted to give this flower to you, Uncle Chico!" On one hand, the medium was confused and apprehensive because he lost an important job opportunity, but suddenly he felt something sublime possessing him, an intensive feeling of love for that boy and a spiritual lesson that should be organized by his guides, as a form of learning test. The essential in life was not the ego's conception of job or survival but the attention, welcome, and tenderness present in simple moments such as the little boy's. Through these moments, the superior spirits could communicate with human beings, which would be the most sublime form of mediumship. Thinking from De-sign principles (Seif, 2020a), if the job interview were a form of result, the feeling he would have when he decided to be with the boy would have been a beautiful and blissful form of a desirable outcome. In a word, this moment was permeated by *Agape* and became a crucial lesson for Chico Xavier and many of his followers.

Through these two axes of thought, the mediumistic powers and the love attitudes, we can conceive how Chico Xavier was devoted to *Agape* and consequently became a sign capable of creating and forming communities around it. In other words, he was not only a powerful medium constantly in contact with the spiritual world, but he was also a man who incarnated Christian love in such a way that his ego was progressively surrendered to this ideal. The messages originated from his work, and his character intensively impacted the social world because they integrated exceptional mediumistic skills with touching examples of love, humility, and devotion. More than that, it is possible to conceive that the impressive impact of these messages received their strength from Chico's own self-integration. In this sense, he had many common points with Saints and Yogis because his personal trajectory implicated the movement of integration between him as a human being and the collective ideals present in the self. As a testament to his selflessness, Chico Xavier dedicated himself more to serving humanity than to pursuing personal aspirations. He often became a symbol of the Sacred, inspiring and uplifting souls to share in this same ideal. In synthesis, Chico's mediumistic power was secondary compared to the strength (Seif, 2019) he cultivated through extensive work, devotion, acts of charity, disciplines of self-perfection, and practicing love.

Eros, then, was converted into *Agape*, in which the aesthetic ideal is diffused and brings many people to integrate communities. On the one hand, following the contradictory idea of love, as in Camões poetry, Chico's personal desire was to be a kind of slave since he strove to become an unconditional server of *Agape*. It is possible to conceive that his ego's aspirations and desires were sacrificed to serve the Christian love through Kardec's spiritism. In some way, he seemed well protected against vanity, egoism, pride, and other human feelings considered real threats to medium missions. On the other hand, the communities that surrounded him protected him from skeptics questioned his reputation. The magazine "*O Cruzeiro*" suggested he was only a creative man who made much fiction in an altered state of consciousness; Umberto de Campos' family sued him, alleging the copyrights concerning psychographies made by this illustrious man. A few members of Chico's family were accused of bribes to accessing the medium. However, since the accusations were never substantiated with proof or evidence, they remained merely allegations without any follow-up in either the justice system or within the spiritism movement. They never shook the medium reputation, which is still under high social consideration (Neubern, 2022b).

John of God: From Eros to Pornography

> In Spiritism and other spiritual knowledge, mediumship is closely associated with sexuality. They view sexuality as a creative energy inherent in the human soul, the source of different forms of creation in art, science, philosophy, sports, and everyday activities. This perspective aligns with the principle of Eros as G-O-D, emphasizing Eros's creative role in the human experience. Therefore, mediumship is seen as a creative act that requires adequate training and some forms of discipline. In essence, sexuality must be directed toward non-sexual ends (sublimation), aiming a balanced form of life. When lack these two pre-conditions, training and discipline, they easily become entangled in sexual issues, making them susceptible to negative tendencies and malevolent spiritual influences that distort Eros into pornography. That was the case of John of god.

On December seventh, 2018, Brazilian society was surprised by a massive scandal. Some women were interviewed by Pedro Bial, a famous journalist, concerning sexual abuses made by John of God, an internationally famous healing medium.[5] Bial's TV program had a national reach. Bial's interviews brought a different perspective of John of God, now being presented as a criminal instead of a healer who attracted people from across. The globe. The interviewees didn't know each other and described, with detail, the same procedure of violence adopted by the medium: the invitation, the private meeting in the office, the words, the explanation, and the forms of abuse. Two women were interviewed using disguised methods to obscure their faces and distort their voices, ensuring their identities remained anonymous. However, two foreigners agreed to reveal their identities. The former was a Netherland actress who was abused by him after being introduced to work in his group as an initiated medium, while the latter was a North American tourist guide who resisted the sexual abuse and was threatened by John of God. The women agreed to giving this interview with the intention of denouncing him, aiming to prevent further violence against women. After this interview, the Public Ministry of Goiás and São Paulo, two Brazilian states, created a task force and received more than 300 similar reports from women in Brazil and abroad. John of God was also implicated in illegal gang possession and uranium trafficking. He tried to escape, but after some days of police persecution, he decided to surrender, being put in a

---

[5] https://www.youtube.com/watch?v=8AkKEeQKboQ . We need to highlight that, before the scandal, there was some scholars researches (Machado, 2016; Rocha, 2017) on John of God's healing works. However, after the scandal, most of the available material was on YouTube or in video documentation, such as Netflix (2021). Felitti (2020), a journalist book documentation, was one of the few written works in this way.

preventive prison. Currently, he is in domiciliary prison (because of his fragile health and advanced age), having a sentence of 189 years.

Before the interview, John of God was only known by many incredible remarks. He was born in 1942 in a small city, *Cachoeira da Fumaça*, to a poor family. His official name was João Teixeira de Faria, having his childhood in a rural zone. He had only 2 years of formal school and lived many years as a *garrafeiro*, that is, a native healer who introduced herbs into a bottle intending to use this instrument as a medicine. Nevertheless, when he was 16 years old, he had a spiritual vision, and Saint Rita de Cassia told him that he should search for a spiritist center in a neighboring city. When he arrived at this center, he was attended by King Salomon, a healer spirit, who performed numerous procedures through John, beginning his spiritual mission.

The poor boy from the rural zone began his healing mission, which was accompanied by many forms of persecution, especially from the Catholic Church and the Medical Associations. He met Chico Xavier on a few occasions, who told him his mission should be made in Abadiânia, a 19.000 inhabitants small city of Goiás, a center state of Brazil. At Abadiânia city, he created the "*Casa de Santo Inácio*" (Saint Ignatius House), a spiritual center that used the name of his spiritual guide. Although he was still a victim of some persecution, João gradually obtained the sympathy of politicians and rich people, which allowed him notoriety and fame. From the 70 s, when he began his work, to 2018 when the scandal arose, Abadiânia was inserted into an international map of spiritual movements (Rocha, 2017), attracting people from different parts of Brazil and other countries. Many hotels, tourist agencies, transport, and commerce centers were inserted in Abadiânia, and foreign money, such as dollars and euros, became frequent in this city. English, French, Spanish, and German were foreign idioms commonly used in Abadiânia, everyday commercial life, or the spiritual works coordinated by John of God and his team. In turn, John of God was invited to travel to many countries, such as the USA, Canada, Germany, Switzerland, Peru, Australia, and New Zealand (Rocha & Vasquez, 2016; Rocha, 2017), where he promoted his work.

Nevertheless, the sexual scandals highlighted by the interview had massive consequences for many reasons.[6] First, John of God was inserted into a spiritual healing tradition (Nuñez, 2008/2012) closely linked to spiritism and permeated by Christian values, such as charity, humility, and love. Sexual abuse was not reported among these healers until the case of John of God, which starkly contradicted the collective values of the spiritist community. Although John of God never adhered to any organized movement or institution (Rocha, 2017), he can still be associated with this tradition, where mediumship is intertwined with concepts such as reincarnation and

---

[6] After the scandal revelation, four women which were patients in our group research (CHYS), reported they or somebody from their family were harassed by John of God. Two of them were spiritists, one umbandist, and one esoteric. I also decided to interview some mediums, trying to understand what had happened with this medium from an ethnopsychological perspective. The interviews with these specialists and our patients obtained a lot of information that I used in writing this section.

healing practices through spiritual possession. Thus, the scandals, at least potentially, inserted suspicious and harmful meaning in this healing tradition since sexual abuse is in irreconcilable opposition with spiritism tradition's main values.

Second, John of God was a kind of celebrity whose healing work attracted influential politicians, TV, cinema, and government authorities (Machado, 2016). His public image in TV, documentaries, and magazines was commonly related to a powerful man who, through mediumship, had healed many people from severe illnesses. Despite his poor origin, he became rich, having farms, houses, lands, and a business society with miners. He was also known for many marriages, having sons and daughters with different women. However, if his richness and numerous marriages were not common among other spiritist healers, these facts did not make him suspicious of illegal conduct. The medium created an intensive social network involving businessmen, politicians, artists, doctors, jurists, policemen, and many people who worked for him (Felitti, 2020). National celebrities, such as the singer Roberto Carlos, the humorist Chico Anysio, and the actress Xuxa Meneghel, went to Abadiânia to meet him. Likewise, famous international names, such as Shirley Maclaine, Oprah Winfrey, Bill Clinton, and Hugo Chavez also made the journey to see him. On one hand, this social network of celebrities and influential individuals allowed John of God to become very influential since he could easily obtain favors (such as private flights) from prominent figures. It is likely that many attempts to report this medium were blocked by his influential allies, who had direct economic and political interests in protecting him. On the other hand, these networks formed by national and international groups that frequently visited Abadiânia, implicating tourist agencies, hotels, transport, and local commerce. Among these groups, there were people who searched for spiritual or physical healing, tourists, adepts who tried to extend John of God's practices to other places (Rocha, 2017), and a tourist net that mobilized hotels, flight companies, transport, taxis, and hotels, among others. Thus, the sexual scandals would put severe questions concerning the medium's relationships, economic interests, and the political protection he should receive during many years of criminal conduct.

Third, the inquiry concerning his crimes concludes that he committed sexual abuse for many years before 2018, when he was reported. Some reports highlighted that in 1980, there was a denouncement from a 16 years-old-girl who accused him of sexual abuse. This law process did not advance probably because her family was threatened by his agents, who worked as personal security but frequently intimidated his enemies. However, during the criminal investigations, women of different ages reported stories with numerous and cohesive similar facts, which led the authorities to conclude that his sexual abuses were numerous and had been occurring for some decades. It also suggested that John of God was highly protected by his network, which implicated the "spiritual narratives" that supposed unusual forms of treatment and coercive measures adopted by his immediate assistants, policemen, hotel owners, and commerce people (Felitti, 2020). Some victims reported that the medium affirmed that if they did not accept that form of treatment, their familiar members' health who was seeking spiritual healing would deteriorate. These victims feared being the target of spiritual attacks if they refused John of

God's abuse. Therefore, when spiritual narratives did not work, his agents would act through threatening physical attacks, something that police authorities would not consider. It was a common fact among people from Abadiânia that John of God was protected by armed men who frequently intimidated individuals in opposition to the medium's interests. As confirmed during the Bial TV program, the victims reported cases of abused women who tried to report the medium but were convinced to abandon their intentions through "spiritual explanations", where the medium tried to heal them by utilizing bizarre methods or through explicit threats such as violence and death. In synthesis, he had many instruments of protection, including "spiritual explanations," the social pressure of adepts and immediate collaborators, explicit threats, and the alliance with influential people and government authorities.

> *John of God's treatment was commonly based on spiritual direct intervention through his mediumship, which could implicate cuts on the body made by an inappropriate knife and without asepsis. People were also invited to integrate a collective meditation, where they were supposed to be permeated by a benefic energy flow. Magnetic passes through hand impositions were another form of therapeutic tool commonly used as well as medicine prescriptions based on passiflora, a phytotherapeutic product made by passion fruit. They considered that these medicines would receive adequate fluidic energy for each person* (Rocha, 2017).

These circumstances were crucial to situating John of God as a controversial character because he was related simultaneously to spiritual values and an enormous list of crimes. In some way, his trajectory was remarked by numerous healings reported by people from different places who were hopeless and searched for him in Abadiânia as the ultimate hope for treatment (Rocha, 2017). Many of these individuals were diagnosed with cancer, multiple sclerosis, depression, psychiatric disorders, chronic pain, and neurologic problems, among others, and they reported finding in John of God's treatment healing or at least significative improvement. The medium used uncommon methods for spiritual treatment, which were conducted by the spirits that possessed his body, known as "incorporation." Some of these spirits were well-known by the Kardecists, such as Bezerra de Menezes, Oswaldo Cruz, and Dr. Fritz, who were doctors during their last physical life, but some others were linked to other collective practices, such as King Salomon, Dom Ignacio de Loyola, and other entities from the East. Such a rich and mixed spiritual pantheon suggests at least two main consequences concerning the medium's followers' movement. First, these spirits could be conceived as symbols of the Sacred (Otto, 2017), as they were commonly understood in their original *Ethos*. In fact, many persons reported living experiences during the treatment that were permeated by sacred elements that could hardly be described through words, such as being possessed by overflowing feelings of love and peace, independently of their illnesses (Machado, 2016). Thus, the efficacy of many spiritual interventions was not limited to physical effects since they became meaningful for many who understood that treatment healed their souls. In this sense, John of God was at the center of a cohesive community that shared values and practices closely linked to *Agape*, such as love, fraternity, charity, and forgiveness, which would be essential for soul healing. The services of helping poor people maintained by a Casa and the help support that commonly received desperate people from many countries were practices closely related to *Agape's* ideals cultivated among these community members.

Second, John of God was also a symbol of innovation because his ideas and practices were not affiliated with an official religion, such as Spiritism, and mixed many collective knowledge, such as Spiritism, Catholicism, Umbanda, and Esoterisms. In this sense, Cristina Rocha (2017) highlights that these characteristics were very similar to the New Age spiritual movements around the world in which there was a tendency to refuse official religious affiliations, to adopt mixed ideas and practices, mainly from the East, and to search for an inner integration with the spiritual self. Therefore, the practice of spiritual current, widespread among spiritists and urbanists, was inserted by elements of Eastern meditation and reiki, Buddhist and yogic teachings, among others, which was appreciated mainly by the adepts. These mixed practices crossed the Brazilian frontiers, making communities related to John of God's name in countries such as Australia and New Zealand. These numerous social nets had not only economic implications for Abadiânia and other cities around the world; they were closely linked, at least as a cause, to Agape, placing the Brazilian medium as a Sacred symbol that could touch and attract individuals from different cultures. His reputation was bolstered by numerous reports from people claiming to have benefited from his help, the endorsement of various celebrities who became his patients, and the tributes from notable figures and institutions, such as the Dalai Lama (Savaris, 2015).

Nevertheless, his numerous crimes were undeniable and suggested a parallel life that was quite different from *Agape's* ideals, remaining distant from public criticism for many years. Perhaps the first implication emergent from the criminal investigations was that his criminal attitudes became habitual forms to obtain his goals, being also based on the certainty that his actions would go unpunished. At the center of a prominent power structure, John of God acted as a tyrant, selecting and persecuting women at will, obtaining money through illegal forms, and mobilizing a powerful network to protect his actions. Regarding women, many reports emerged after the TV program, alleging that only 'beautiful' young women were often found crying during the treatments. These women were frequently approached by assistants and adepts who attempted to silence them with spiritual explanations. Frequently, those women were chosen to integrate his closer assistance, being approached by him through the justification that they had a mediumistic gift that should be trained by himself, that they were special, and that they had a shared past life. They were invited to share lunch with him and his collaborators, accompanying them to the table reserved for "special" people. Some of these "special" women reported him during the police investigations and mentioned that after the sexual abuses, they were approached by the abovementioned mechanism of intimidation. In synthesis, the police investigation confirmed that, beyond the victims and their families, numerous individuals knew what happened to these women, including many Casa assistants, hotel proprietaries, tourist guides, and taxi drivers, but they did not support these abuses being reported because they were afraid of possible threats and economic loss.

In this parallel life, John of God seemed to be an authoritarian man, who frequently imposed his desires upon others. Some reports (Netflix, 2021) affirmed that he was the most important authority in Abadiânia and that everybody had to accept his orders. During elections, he was explicit in supporting the political candidates of his interests (Rocha, 2017), who probably would win the disputes due to the large influence he had among followers and commercial owners. Among spiritists and other religions, the support for candidates and political parties, like those practiced by John of God, is controversial since this support can bring negative consequences for religious institutions. However, even in the Casa, some announcements could be found during elections, and people would not feel comfortable discussing politics if their point of view was in opposition to the medium's. In general, affairs, when he had an intention, his personal assistants would do anything to address it, even if they had to contact an authority or an influential businessperson to facilitate the process or proceed illegally. If anybody decided to move to Abadiânia and follow him, John of God would decide their professional role in the city, their place of residence, and if they should work directly for the medium. Nobody could begin a business in Abadiânia without the medium permission, and the investigations detected that hotels, taxi drivers, and commerce directly linked to tourism should pay a regular fee for the medium. If someone among these traders refused to pay him, his armed personnel would approach them directly, obligating them to choose between the payment and life in another city. In this sense, he obtained money from other illegal or ethically inadequate sources. The Casa offered its services apparently free because, commonly, people should pay for some elements sold at higher prices, such as crystals and *passiflora*, a popular phytotherapy medicine based on passion fruits. Some reports also suggested that he had illegal business with miners and uranium and obtained significant income during a number of his international travels (Netflix, 2021).

Mediumship and Eros: Between Agape and Pornography

Chico Xavier and John of God were both inscribed into an incredible Brazilian tradition of healing mediumship. The former died in 2002, many years before the publicity of John of God's scandals. They knew each other, and Chico was decisive in revealing John of God's mediumistic healing mission in Abadiânia (Rocha, 2017). Although John of God refused to integrate a defined movement opposing Chico concerning Kardecism, they shared many practices, such as mediumship and charity, and ideas, such as spirit survivance after death, interventions, reincarnation, and a sizeable collective fame. Nonetheless, while Chico was considered by many people a kind of contemporary saint (Stoll, 2003) who devoted his life to helping people, John of God committed many crimes, which condemned him to many years in jail. Both men shared Sacred experiences that touched thousands of people, but their destinies differed remarkably. While Chico had all his trajectory related to *Agape* as an aesthetic and Sacred ideal, John of God presented many signs that he was also inserted into a parallel life clearly opposed to the Sacred. If the former tried to cultivate love in its purity, the latter was taken by pornography, which dominated many of his actions during his life.

For many people, this tragic difference is impressive, being hardly intelligible, because the sublime doesn't share many aspects with the grotesque (Seif, 2019). In contemporary Western societies, where Christian values seem to be dominant, somebody who works on behalf of the Sacred can't be implicated with the darkness since these two dimensions are held in tension. However, through De-sign thinking (Seif, 2020a, b), it is possible to conceive this apparently irreconcilable opposition into paradoxes from which somebody can achieve meaningful experiences. If a man is comparable to an angel, such as Chico Xavier, the De-sign inquiry can ask how he dealt with his own darkness, especially concerning sex and power to achieve such a sublime experience which persisted throughout critical life moments and his mediumistic practices. On the other hand, if a man is comparable to a demon, such as John of God, by many victims and investigators, De-sign inquiry can investigate how he dealt with the sublime experiences related to individual and collective processes and the possible reasons that led him to maintain his strong connections with human darkness.

In the following pages, I'll try to navigate this complex field of healing mediumship using De-sign categories (Seif, 2019, 2020b). In some moments, I emphasize the integrative movements between ego and self, and in other moments, I highlight the relationship between these two individuals and their respective communities. It is important to remark that the current analysis is still preliminary because many elements need to be better understood in order to address a more cohesive inquiry. Both mediums were not deeply studied by academic research (Neubern, 2022a; Rocha, 2017), and John of God, particularly, was not still the object of academic work after the scandals. However, the lines sketched here are pertinent as a starting point from a very complex field of study.

Communities

The communitarian aspect is essential to understanding these two mediums' trajectories since it provides significant information about the context, sociocultural influences, modes of leadership, and relationships among community members. From a Peircean perspective (Apel, 1995; Liszka, 1996), a community is formed around an idea to search for the truth that would be achieved in the long run. Of course, Peirce referred to a scientific community, which was not the case for the communities analyzed here. Nonetheless, Peirce's analysis was also based on Catholic communities (Raposa, 1989) that could support the scientific communities and also the communitarian networks organized through both mediums, in which truth and love were ideally associated (Stoll, 2003; Rocha, 2017).

> *Spirituality is an individual and collective experience, and consequently, if the inquirer seeks understanding, he needs to conceive the profound articulation between these two dimensions* (Raposa, 1989). *As mentioned before, during trance, many collective semiotic processes can be manifested, but they also implicate individual subjective constructions such as meanings, images, and feelings. Being trance a quale consciousness state, De-sign inquiry is coherent in conceiving this double aspect of spirituality, especially through principles such as paradoxes, desirable outcomes, integration, and navigation. Similarly, the different forms of love are closely associated with trance and also transit between individual and collective dimensions.*

Thus, as mentioned above, the spiritist community created around Chico Xavier's work and character was deeply motivated by the emotional appeal of his meaningful work. In some way, many of his psychographies developed Kardec's idea, giving continuity to the French Spiritism codification, especially concerning the term "moral," which could mean not only ethical behavior but also something from the feeling and spiritual domain (Neubern, 2022b). Nevertheless, many other facets of his legacy should implicate people emotionally because his mission was devoted to support those in suffering. Chico Xavier obtained national notoriety through his work named "Wiping Away Tears," in which he wrote his psychographies in front of a live audience. Some attendants would receive letters purportedly from their deceased loved ones (Barbosa, 1978). Commonly, mothers, fathers, and other family members were deeply touched by these letters, bringing news about their beloved with surprising details and, sometimes with similar signatures. Of course, such details were sometimes contested, such as the integrity of the signatures, but the emotional content of that practice should dominate social attention, attributing to Chico a considerable social value. Two other factors still reinforced his reputation. First, all his effort was devoted to charity, even if this virtue was conceived as a concrete practice or even if it was a benevolent attitude toward especially those who distracted or attacked him. Love, forgiveness, and humility were signs constantly associated with Chico (Souto Maior, 2003). Second, he was a typical renunciant because he never accepted any award, lived in a very modest condition during his life, was celibate, and even his private life seemed to be devoted to his mission.

Even during his life, Chico Xavier was recognized as the most important Brazilian spiritist medium, which he emphatically denied (Souto Maior, 2003). He was explicitly affiliated with Kardecism, but he was not politically involved with the Brazilian Spiritist Federation (Federação Espírita Brasileira, FEB), with which he maintained a respectful relationship and autonomy. During the first edition of his mediumistic book "Liberation" (*Libertação*), Emmanuel, his spiritual guide, wrote a critical note against FEB's refusal of the book's first version. Then, even if some people, such as John of God, considered him a kind of Kardecist Pope (Rocha, 2017), he seemed to remain loyal to his spiritual mission, attentively coordinated by Emmanuel. Then, sharing the same Kardecist principles, his work was under some form of institutional control, but he maintained his autonomy (which implicated the submission to the spiritual world), and he became one of the most influential Brazilian spiritual leaders in the XX century. His charisma was intensively permeated by his devotion and humility concerning spiritual instructions and by his loving and welcoming way of treating people. As a sign of the Sacred (Neubern, 2022a), he became the focal point of numerous networks of Spiritist ideas, fostering the development, to some extent, of communal identities in the Peircean sense. (Petrilli, 2017; Seif, 2019). With intelligence, he exerted a kind of soft power, where people felt respected and considered seriously his instructions concerning different everyday life themes. Through affective relationships and meaningful practices, people felt themselves free to serve or follow him.

In this sense, Chico Xavier was a skillful De-signer since his approaches toward others were based on service (Seif, 2019), leading people to feel respected, comprehended, and frequently available to become also servers of the Kardecist's ideals. Furthermore, it is plausible to consider that as a special sign, he inhabited the networks of that spiritual and collective self, promoting the continuity of his *Agapistic* ideas, which is a form of dialogue that transcends the ordinary limits of time and space (Seif, 2013). In a word, Chico Xavier was a De-signer who, through his voluntary submission to Agape, especially through service, attracted many individuals who would also freely serve the same ideal. Many people who had never had a direct contact with him was also inspired by his works, interviews and, especially, by the stories told about him, that highlighted his devotion, humility, and charity. During his life trajectory, he had only voluntary collaborators to help him in mediumistic and charity works, never adopting bodyguards or professional secretaries. For many people, collaborating with him was an honor, a meaningful activity based on the voluntary desire to search and serve *Agape*.

Chico Xavier was also a De-signer concerning the forms in which he dealt with social belonging paradoxes (Seif, 2020b). From a sociological point of view (Lewgoy, 2004), Chico Xavier symbolically occupied a curious space in this community. On one hand, he concentrated many marginalized belongings in Brazilian society, such as his poor and mixed origins, a rural zone, few formal instructions, and feminine attitudes (Gama, 1998), that is, features almost entirely opposed to the typical Kardecist leaders (Neubern, 2022b). It is possible to conceive that these *Ethos* influences were closely associated with Christian values of humility and devotion, which led people to attribute him quite different qualities than the other leaders. On the other hand, he was also conservative in many values, which was extremely attractive for Brazilians who, historically, are religious people (Carvalho, 1994) and belonged to a patriarchal and patrimonialist society (Souza, 2019). Chico Xavier was embedded in a symbolic system that integrated some level of marginalized *Ethos* and conservative social values, leading him to transit among different social sectors, including persons from different religions. This double belonging and his coherence concerning his spiritual and charity work led even his critics to respect him despite the intellectual discordances. Perhaps his teleology and spiritual mission were related to the integration of different individuals around Agape, going beyond the limits of a unique religion. Following De-sign thinking (Seif, 2020a), it is possible to conceive that he worked within his religious limits (Kardecism), especially by introducing the Christian Sacred experiences (Neubern, 2022a), transcending its limits, in order to attract and touch people from different social and religious belongings.

In this sense, the community constructed around Chico Xavier's name had interesting forms of control, especially against attacks. Perhaps the unique occasion on which he was asked to a formal defense was the legal case moved by Umberto de Campos' family, who claimed the copyrights of some psychographic books attributed to the famous writer. Some spiritist lawyers defended Chico, who was claimed innocent by the Brazilian justice (Souto Maior, 2003). The journalistic attacks that considered him an impostor and the denouncing by friends and close collaborators that accused him of receiving some form of compensation had never received an answer from Chico Xavier's part and quickly were discredited by the media and the population. Even his explicit support of the military and authoritarian government did not seem to affect his social image (Lewgoy, 2004). Facing multiple criticism and attacks, the medium preferred to remain silent and devote himself to his works (Gama, 1998). In synthesis, the reports against him did not have continuity, probably because they were never evidenced, and, in consequence, they were forgotten or transformed into calumnies promoted by those who intended to harm him. Perhaps one of the most crucial defense factors against the attacks was that Chico Xavier seemed to remain coherent with his values, which were confirmed both publicly and in his private life.

John of God, in turn, symbolized different kinds of community. On one hand, he was a spiritual leader who could heal people with many forms of diseases (Pellegrino-Estrich, 2001). During his long trajectory in Abadiânia, John of God became known as a powerful healer who used uncommon methods and healed people for whom the traditional Medicine and medical treatment could not help (Cumming & Leffler, 2008). Despite the controversies concerning the efficacy of his treatments (Machado, 2016), his reputation as a healer traversed national frontiers and obtained followers from different countries. In this sense, his work was coherent with two contemporary spiritual trends: Brazilian syncretism and the transnational New Age movement (Rocha, 2017). The former included elements from different religions and spiritual practices, such as Catholicism, Kardecism, Umbanda, and Esoterism. The latter was simultaneously a mixed movement, including Western and Eastern elements, and a criticism against the traditional Western institutions, such as the official religions and the Medicine. John of God and his followers were not affiliated with a religion, declaring themselves as spiritualists. For them, more important than religious affiliation was the inner connection with the self, our true spiritual essence. Thus, the aesthetic ideal for this community was intensively inspired by the impressive healing demonstrations and was characterized by this internal and collective search for the spiritual truth through the connection with the self. Welcoming and solidarity were two of the most important characteristics highlighted by those who arrived in

Abadiânia searching for treatment or spiritual meaning (Rocha, 2017), which was still stimulated by using foreign languages, such as English, French, German, and Spanish.

Many people reported they experienced Sacred feelings (Otto, 2017) during the healing treatments, especially when they implicated love and peace toward everybody (Machado, 2016; Rocha & Vasquez, 2016). These feelings could arise when facing John of God's presence or during the collective meditations, which were considered an essential form of treatment continuity. An influential spiritual leader, and that collective practice seemed to be crucial for creating and maintaining a spiritual community to which persons could feel they belong (Ethos). Therefore, from the adepts' perspectives, these two elements promoted an intensive connection with the spiritual world, the development of mediumistic abilities, and the main goal, access to the inner self (Rocha, 2017). New Age ideas inhabited all this social universe, and people could feel free to act and choose without the imposition of religious rules, which were much more implicated with human creation than with the spiritual experience. Consequently, many adepts were enthusiastic in promoting John of God's works through books, marketing, personal testimony, and different forms of active work, intending to attract more people. Some of them moved to Abadiânia, intending to improve the treatment or even to search for a meaningful life (Cumming & Leffler, 2008).

As mentioned above, this community allowed the creation of many forms of commerce, including little hotels, transport, flights, and tourism agencies. Abadiânia experienced massive foreign investment through foreign money and business that were uncommon for his inhabitants until John of God's international fame (Rocha & Vasquez, 2016). Possibly, John of God was interested in obtaining partnerships with foreign people as a form of avoiding persecution from the Catholic Church and Medical Associations, which accused him of the illegal practice of Medicine. He was conscious of the past persecutions against another famous Brazilian medium, Zé Arigó, who was sent to jail and suffered a lot since he healed many people through unusual forms of spiritual surgeries (Fuller & Puharich, 1974). John of God travels to many countries and the foundation of international communities inspired by his work, in fact, gave him more respectability concerning his adversaries. Furthermore, the Casa expanded its structure, obtaining much more financial resources after the arrival of foreigners who commonly became patients and sometimes turned into collaborators. After the scandal, some people related to him reported that he lost utter control of his attitudes, especially concerning money, when he perceived the large quantities of dollars and euros were available in Abadiânia (Felitti, 2020).

On the other hand, he created a parallel community of people who helped him exert different immoral or illegal conduct. The report of the victims and other witnesses sustained that many people related to John of God knew what happened concerning his abusive behaviors and also his illicit business, but they preferred to avoid problems for economic reasons or even fear (Felitti, 2020). Thus, this entourage was frequently effective in order to insert facts into narratives that valorized him as a seductive man and a successful businessman. When his attraction to a beautiful woman was evident, many people described him as a flirtatious man able to seduce women, which was highly valorized in a patriarchal society. His proprieties and good relationships with influential people were conceived as a success, mainly because he was of poor origin and competent enough to rise socially and economically, another feature valorized in Brazilian society (Souza, 2019). As mentioned before, this active narrative fabrication also included his close collaborators in spiritual treatments who frequently explained to the victims still in crisis that what happened was not an abusive act but an unusual form of spiritual intervention, and they should be proud to receive that honor. Furthermore, if the victims were resistant to that explanation, they could propose a veiled threat in which they or their family members would not be healed if they didn't collaborate or still that they should suffer spiritual persecution or attack for the same reason (Netflix, 2021). The threats could still be explicit through the medium's armed men, who could attack and kill people who wanted to report the medium. It is not without reason that he was frequently accompanied by armed bodyguards, probably because he envisioned the possibility of any form of revenge from the victims' family members.

As a leader, John of God was quite different from other Brazilian mediums (Nuñez, 2008/2012). During his work in the Casa, he commonly sat in a big armchair, which was very similar to a throne. Many people passed before him with a reverent attitude, and some tried to kiss his hands as a form of recognizing his unique role in that place. This particular special configuration and these attitudes were not well considered by many spiritists, for whom it created a form of idolatry.

Differently from Chico Xavier, John of God was a symbolic system that represented and reproduced the dominant values of Brazilian society, such as patriarchy, *machismo*, and patrimonialism (Souza, 2019). Despite his poor origins (Machado, 2016), he was a white man who became rich, had many women, and used to be oppressive toward people who were below his position. His political preferences confirmed the socially dominant influence in his subjectivity and social world, being affiliated for some years with a conservative political party that did not express preferences for progressive causes. Therefore, he was socially much closer to the big businessman and farmer owner than the typical image of the Saint, Devotee, or Guru, who should incorporate ethical values such as humility, love, and renouncement, which commonly would promote an intensive aesthetic appreciation among other people (Raposa, 2020). Although these characteristics were not an insurmountable barrier to assuming his spiritual mission, they would implicate some obstacles to doing so because frequently, they could bring interests, values, and social relationships opposed to the Sacred. Furthermore, from the point of view of the Brazilian's *machinery* related to his missions (Carvalho, 1994), these belongings would implicate him with negative spiritual experiences that could become a strong influence capable of removing him from his spiritual mission. In a spiritual language (Avila, 1988), it is possible to conceive that his soul would be devoured by the temptations (or demons) of power, sex, richness, and vanity promoted by these social belongings.

In this sense, it is possible to consider that his interpersonal approaches were not based on De-sign principles such as dialogue and service (Seif, 2019). Perhaps for many individuals who found a meaningful perspective through his work, it is possible to consider something of service since they became active John of God's collaborators in Brazil and other countries (Rocha & Vasquez, 2016). However, his main forms of approach were centered on an authoritarian perspective that commonly did not offer autonomy and was quite oppressive, as the example of many collaborators and victims. Consequently, for some people, his healing works seemed to be a form of help because he was the center of the process, despite his constant affirmations that God was the real healer in his mediumistic activities (Rocha & Vasquez, 2016; Rocha, 2017). Moreover, the scandal exposed a form of relationship in which *Eros'* desires were converted into pornography (Seif, 2018) through sexual violence. His spiritual authority as a medium healer contrasted with the women's vulnerability, many of them desperate by illnesses of complex treatment or other problematic situations. Being transformed into sexual objects, the women were utilized and manipulated by him despite their appeals and resistances that were ignored by the medium, intending to obtain pleasure. These forms of relationships were not based on partnership but in imposition through which the women were ignored as human beings, and John of God's sexual pleasure was the unique goal to be attained. If we consider these women's semiosis processes, which originated from this violence, sign systems related to fear, culpability, depression, insomnia, social isolation, and suicidal ideas would be easily found.

All of these social scenarios were favorable to conceiving that John of God maintained a double life in which the two sides were absolutely incompatible. Nevertheless, it is possible to consider that he created a different form of conciliation in which the spiritual side related to his social image as a medium healer was submitted to his authoritarian and criminal social role. Many victims related that they were first invited to meet John of God alone when he was "incorporated" by a spiritual guide (Felitti, 2020), which is opposed by all spiritual knowledge available in his Ethos. From the spiritual perspective of Umbanda (Scorsolini-Comin, 2023) or Kardecism (Neubern, 2022b), for example, if he were under a spiritual influence, a good spirit never would invite a woman to be abused, mainly because they would know his intentions. But from the same perspective, being a medium, he would attract negative spirits who would be able to inspire criminal attitudes, such as sexual abuse. Nonetheless, independently of the form of inspiration, these reports were one among many signs of utilizing spiritual ideals for personal interest and criminal ends, as if *Agape* was under the service of pornography. It was a possible form of integration of the two sides of his life, where the spiritual ideals were degenerated, and the grotesque aspect of human darkness became dominant.

Furthermore, the TV scandal and the consequent police investigations revealed not only that he had a double life but mainly that the criminal side of his life became hegemonic (Felitti, 2020). Perhaps the fact that, during his trajectory, he opposed submitting to any form of control by institutions or social relationships was decisive for succumbing to the dark side. John of God became the ultimate authority in his town as well as in his spiritual work, and without any form of opposition, he was vulnerable to his own individual and social influences. Nevertheless, due to the courage of some victims, this criminal system was revealed, and John of God was punished by the Justice. In a De-sign perspective (Seif, 2020a), the fragile and vulnerable women become the start of a great revolution, in which individual suffering experiences were converted into a collective concern. They seemed to be inspired by the Greek notion of tragedy (Campbell, 1959). In this notion, suffering leads the collective to a deep learning about life and destiny. "No woman should be again submitted to those forms of violence," they said, revealing a deep empathy toward other women, girls, mothers, daughters, and family members. The victims didn't know they had transcended the limits of individuality, time, and space. Not only the victims were impacted, but many others also had their beliefs destroyed or hurt by the scandal since they searched for an alternative and meaningful form of life. Perhaps it was the collective beginning of escaping from the different forms of pornography in that scenario to return to Agape's way, and if we can't predict the future, we can at least create what should be desirable for us (Seif, 2020a).

Sacred and Darkness

The ordinary idea of comparing Chico Xavier to a contemporary saint (Ranieri, 1970) was based on numerous stories presented by his followers. These reports highlight not only his exceptional mediumship abilities but also a man almost entirely devoted to love, humility, and charity. He presented almost all mediumistic skills well developed that commonly surprised his varied audience, composed of persons from different religions, authorities, curious and desperate individuals, spiritists, and followers who were impressed the phenomena produced through these abilities. As a medium, he should make a considerable effort to exert the role of a mediator between the spiritual and the physical worlds in order to accomplish the mission of diffusion of the Kardecists' ideas, such as the existence of the soul, its communication with the human beings, and reincarnation. Nevertheless, by integrating Kardec's doctrine and Christianism (Stoll, 2003), all of these ideas should be transmitted through love and devotion, primarily through his everyday life attitudes. Then, on one hand, he could promote impressive phenomena, such as the numerous confirmative information brought by spirits, healings, tangible spiritual manifestations, revelations, premonitions, and knowledge inaccessible to him; he was, on the other hand, a man almost entirely without a private life, since all his available time beyond work and family obligations were devoted to helping people or to mediumship. Despite his fragile health and few economic resources, his everyday life was intensively remarked by his dedication to his spiritual mission until his last days (Souto Maior, 2003).

> *The idea of Sacred is associated with the Numinous experience* (Otto, 2017), *which is not accessible to human knowledge but implicates meaningful productions in the human soul. Being Divine totally other as the Creator, human beings can't know Him but can envisage his presence through his impact in their own experiences. The Sacred is individual as experience, but due to the typical interpenetration between the self and the world, it is also permeated by collective knowledge and practices. It is possible to consider that the worship, including the Sacred, is a form of ethical effort toward the ideal, Agape. In turn, Darkness is a term taken from* Carl G. Jung (2023), *but with some modifications. Originally, it referred to individual experiences remarked by feelings such as passion, sexual desire, jealousy, revenge, dominance, and fear, among others. Nevertheless, from a De-sign perspective, these feelings are signs of collective narratives and practices present in society, being also permeated by semiospheric actions.*

Through a De-sign perspective (Seif, 2019), many aspects of Chico Xavier's legacy can be analyzed, and the following storytelling is a good case study for it. Elias Barbosa (1978) reported a touching story of a family that received a psychographic letter from his daughter, Yolanda Giglio Vilela, 27 years old, who had died in a crash accident. The Catholic family was desperate because, in the crash circumstances, they suspected Yolanda had been the cause of the accident or had searched for it deliberately. In this work, "Wiping Away Tears," many people arrived to hear the letter dictated by the spirits and sometimes families could only give the spirit's name from whom they wanted to receive communication. However, many situations were out of control for many reasons. Sometimes, a person would receive a message without providing any information to Chico's collaborators. Commonly, however, people would provide only a few pieces of information, and Chico's collaborators would solely provide the spirit name to the medium. However, it was a frequent fact that the messages brought a lot of information known only by a few family members. Moreover, during the preparation and the psychographies, Chico was immersed in a trance state and not aware of the movement around him. In Yolanda's case, the letter asserted that she did not cause the accident and that his mother could be sure that she never thought about suicide since she would never betray her faith. She reported that some days before the accident, she felt a kind of "expansion" in her head and arms, which was commented on by her brother. She made references to meeting Uncle Orlando, Priest Antônio, Aunt Geni, and Grandma Carolina, who were dead people member's family or close to the family. She also referred to the spiritist group *"Calvário do Céu,"* which she and his brother began to go to, and signed the letter with her nickname, *Landa*.

Yolanda's letter is a good example of Chico's legacy. The surprising levels of details and coincidences triggered the feelings of many people. The Sacred experience (Otto, 2017) was commonly reported during these moments, especially in feelings of surprise, peace, worship, deep emotions, and consolation, which was the main goal of that spiritual work. Moreover, many mediums that watched a session of "Wiping Away Tears," made reference to numerous invisible Sacred signs commonly present in Christianity (Csordas, 1997) and other spiritualist traditions (Corbin, 2015): intensive, colorful, and beautiful light-flowing on the audience; superior creatures like angels flying to assist the work, and sometimes, help individuals in the audience. Mediums also reported seeing a spiritual landscape that is quite different in time and space in comparison with the immediate physic environment, portals that open in the sky and allow the passage of lights and spiritual beings, and the presence of dead people. However, what seems to be significantly concerning in this context is not the presence of these sign systems, but the desirable outcome (Seif, 2020a) attained through them and the deep appreciation of several individuals. In this sense, the Sacred can be conceived as a paradoxical form of the desirable outcome because it makes itself present in that community, and simultaneously, it is unattainable. The vagueness of these feelings (Raposa, 2020), the sensation of something beyond human knowledge and control, something that is powerful and deeply permeated by Love constitute a form of aesthetic ideal (*Agape*) that is always present but beyond human reach. Perhaps it is through navigating De-sign (Seif, 2019) that the evolutionary Peircean principle is conceived in multiple forms of time experience. In such experience, the Sacred is lived intensively in the present and also open to what is still not apparent.

In this sense, a man such as Chico Xavier can also incarnate the Divine (possible perfectibility not yet achieved) while remaining a human being. Moreover, from an ethnopsychology point-of-view (Neubern, 2018a), the idea of past reincarnation cultivated among spiritists implicated more elements in its polychronic understanding since Chico had had many lives with special missions, and during his current life, he would oversee diffusing and developing Kardec's ideas in Brazil (Costa, 2008). In a ethnopsychology perspective, Chico had two specific forms of experience concerning his spiritual mission. First, he would often perceive the spiritual world, which was sometimes arduous because he sensed people's intentions, feelings, and thoughts through this perception. His everyday mental functioning would be in a constant form of trance (Neubern, 2022a). Chico was aware of ego/world references and the changes promoted by spiritual influences. Spiritual scenes, appearances, voices, premonitions, and revelations seemed to be frequent, but many of these manifestations should not have been told without Emmanuel's permission. Second, Chico Xavier had not only the past as a poor boy, influenced by poverty, rural entourage, mistreatment, and affective solid bonds; after some years, he also became conscious of many of his past lives and, as a consequence, what his current spiritual and collective mission in Brazil should be. These two points made him constantly integrated into the missionary's role, even during his rare leisure moments with his most intimate friends (Costa, 2008; Gama, 1998). Thus, while a semiotic system, Chico Xavier became a sign of the Sacred on some level, being representative of its concerns among human communities through a constant ethical dedication to *Agape* as an aesthetical ideal. His ego seemed to gradually submit to this ideal, making him seem coherent in facing the social world, which was a potent form of attracting people from different belongings and social sectors (Lewgoy, 2004).

Furthermore, Chico Xavier's mission gradually became known as a collective one, which should have led him to be conceived as a high-level spiritual man. His spiritual guide's name, Emmanuel, was an abbreviation of Manoel da Nóbrega (1517–1570), a prominent priest who was one of the most important political figures during Brazil's colonial age. Emmanuel's first introduction to Chico Xavier was quite a curious moment (Gama, 1998). Chico was near a waterfall and had a spiritual vision of a big and luminous cross was on fire. From that cross emerged a man dressed in sacerdotal clothes, asking him if he, Chico, was prepared to work for Jesus Christ and the spiritism. The 17-year-old medium answered he was prepared as long as the high spirits supported him. Emanuel replied that he would always help, but his mission would require three main principles. Chico asked about first, and the response was discipline. The medium asked about the second, and the response was discipline. Finally, Chico asked about the third, and discipline was again the response. This scene, highly permeated by iconicity (Neubern, 2022a), can also be understood as a desirable outcome (Seif, 2019) since, at that time, Chico was hardly preparing himself for a mediumistic work he didn't know exactly what it should be. It is possible to envisage that this desirable outcome would lead Chico and his followers in different and perhaps unexpected ways, such as the medium's collective mission in Brazil (Albuquerque, 2015). During the scene, nobody knew who that priest was, who remained silent concerning his spiritual identity for some years. However, gradually Chico and his colleagues understood who Emmanuel was, and consequently, which should be the extent of Chico Xavier's mission. A second consequence of this complex semiosis process was that the medium should take discipline advice seriously since his mission should not allow for errors. Perhaps this charge was the reason of Chico's submission to disciplinary rules that seemed to be cruel to many people (Souto Maior, 2003).

To remain at this level of Sacred experience, it is possible to conceive that Chico was implicated in three ethical working axes. Initially, he cultivated spiritual experiences and searches through prayer and mediumistic activities, which were closely associated with Christian cosmology. Many of his spiritual scenes were permeated by numinous characters and revelations that frequently produced intense experiences that could not be translated into words, remaining inaccessible to human understanding. Despite his reticence to reveal direct contact with beings such as Saint Mary, Francis of Assisi, or Jesus Christ, these elevated spiritual beings were frequently associated with his experiences (Costa, 2008). In many reports (UEM, 1993), these trance experiences could provide intensive emotional experiences in Chico's intimal audience, which was accompanied by beautiful and impacting revelations (through voice or writing communication) and physical phenomena, such as lights, perfumes, or flower petals falling in the room. To obtain the possibility of accessing this level of experience, he adopted a renounced lifestyle in which he didn't use alcohol or smoke, avoided excessive and inappropriate food, and was celibatarian. But the main principle he practiced was cultivating good feelings, words, and thoughts in order to avoid negative ones. He was known to be severe with himself, making the possibility of offending or harming someone a devastating idea. This same discipline was also applied to his charity activities, which were the second axe of his effort. He frequently visited poor communities, hospitals, prisons, and orphanages to help these people, being always kind and interested in attending to their needs. However, these rigorous and beloved attitudes should also be present in his informal moments because everyday situations would also require a charity attitude. Then, public and intimate spaces outside of his formal activities frequently featured multiple stories about his *Agape's* attitudes toward his neighbors (Gama, 1998).

His *Agape's* attitude was frequently comprehended as a form of dealing with different modes of darkness. As a De-signer (Seif, 2019), Chico Xavier seemed to integrate evil, temptations, attacks, resentments, and betrayal into a broad experience in which Love embraced all these dark experiences (Peirce, 1893). Many reports describe his visions about the spiritual world with demoniac figures tried to scare and threaten him. In other reports, he was tempted by spirits related to sexuality, money, and power, intending to divert him from his missions (Gama, 1998). Chico's entourage also reported many situations of attack from different individuals, sometimes among his close collaborators, journalists, and even those he helped. His life trajectory was remarked by accusations of charlatanism, accepting money and other benefits for his spiritual works, accusations that were neither proven nor seemed to be consistent (Souto Maior, 2003). Nevertheless, Chico seemed to remain focused on his mission, and perhaps, in some way, he ignored these accusations. Frequently, he declared that all attacks, even those promoted by people, had a spiritual motivation, and these events should be conceived as tests promoted by the Divine as well as opportunities for exerting love (UEM, 1993). During his spiritual trajectory, he seemed to become more and more integrated with his missions, leading him to an integrative experience between his ego (the server) and his *Agapistic* ideal (the Lord). Then, for him, ethics and morality were not promoted as external values originated from social institutions, but this integrative process (Seif, 2019) provided him with the most essential spiritual values that served as a reference for everyday challenges, always permeated by spiritual intentionality. Darkness, manifested through negative spirits or human attacks, could compose his cosmology as a transitory condition of many spirits and human beings and a necessary test for his mission and spiritual evolution. In a word, the negative influence was part of that universe, but they should never divert him from his spiritual mission.

Therefore, this mixture of charity, spirituality, and discipline was perhaps the main subject in the stories told about Chico Xavier, that had a unique role in creating and cultivating many communities around his name (Neubern, 2022a). These story tales had a different format in comparison with Kardec's legacy, which was commonly argumentative texts, intending to debate some ideas and convince the reader. However, they were forms of anecdotes, being also diagrams describing Chico Xavier's attitudes concerning the most different spiritual and everyday situations. As diagrams (Jappy, 2013), many of these stories were not so explicit concerning their moral messages, leading people to construct more-or-less freely their parts and achieve their own conclusions. During many spiritists practices, these tales were associated with Kardec's teachings, but they also implies that spiritists should speak about their own subjectivity. It is crucial to highlight that these forms of communication have an intensive impact on constructing and reinforcing social relationships in a community (Neubern, 2022a). Being diagrams, it is powerful to implicate people through feelings, mainly because it is a form of the icon, which also has the possibility of dissolving the ordinary barriers between them and the different protagonists across different stories. The encounter of emotional needs, desperate situations, identification with the story's subjects, and the search for meaning and ideals of life, among others, are some of the psychological processes promoted by this diagrammatic form of communication. Moreover, they seemed to be much more accessible than the argumentative thinking in Kardec's texts, which required some level of scientific and philosophical understanding. Anybody could work around tales, and they would still be associated with a casual perspective, humor, drama, and common sense.

Tales also had an essential feature in Chico's context. They were constructed from spontaneous reactions to face unexpected situations (Neubern, 2022a). Chico Xavier was frequently observed by his entourage, even during informal moments of his social life. Almost constant vigilance on Chico's behavior seemed to be intensively tiring, but, on the other hand, it should also be a form of discipline training for him. Therefore, many examples can be highlighted in this sense, such as the child's approach with an apparent unimportant demand, an absurd commentary concerning his personal life, a calumny, an accusation of receiving improper benefits, injuries, and threats, which would commonly be followed by an apparent fragile human reaction of humility, no violence attitude, fear, ignorance, and respect, which should empower him still more as a humble and Christian man. Commonly converted into humor tales, these stories are signs of three intensive forms of control under which Chico Xavier was also submitted. First, there was immediate social control, and he was judged by people from all backgrounds, from a family member or a person assisted by Chico to an eminent spiritist who was in contact with him. As Chico commonly refused to behave as a judge, he was constantly surveilled, in a constant search for any contradiction. This complex form of surveillance, which could easily furnish information for the media, was democratic in some way because the leader (role constantly refused by him) was constantly evaluated by his followers. Second, as mentioned above, Chico was affiliated with Kardecism, considering Kardec's ideas as the superior revelation that all spiritists, including himself, should follow. Then, despite his innovative role in Brazilian's lecture on Kardec's legacy (Stoll, 2003), he was commonly obedient concerning many rules established by spiritist institutions.

Third, Chico Xavier developed an extreme submission to the spiritist machinery (Neubern, 2022a), whose control instruments, such as his spiritual guides, were commonly invisible to other people. His close spiritual guide, Emmanuel, was known to be severe with him, intending to help him remain focused on his mission, which was extended to the most different everyday life moments and his formal activities. Emmanuel's imposition worked as a form of avoiding many personal desires or human weaknesses as well as highlighting the duty concerning a Divine commitment. In a curious story (Souto Maior, 2003), Chico is on a turbulent flight among many desperate people thinking they were going to die. Emmanuel, with a stern facial expression, appeared and asked him the reasons for such desperate manifestations, and his pupil answered that everybody in the plane was going to die. The spiritual guide answered that death was not a problem since it was the destiny of all human beings, and Chico should, at least, die with diginity. In synthesis, the spiritual relationship between Chico Xavier and Emmanuel cultivated Chico's role as a renunciant encouraging him to renounce all ego-driven desire or temptation to fully dedicate himself to his spiritual mission. In a way, it was a form of private control where Chico, without any witness, accessed the invisible beings and machinery devices that could regulate his subjectivity. It was, perhaps, the most critical and valued form of control for the medium.

These characteristics made Chico somebody extremely seductive (Seif, 2019), especially for women. As a De-signer, he was seductive not only because he was considered a highly spiritual leader but also because of his feminine attitude, which was not a form of threat. Women searched him not only because of his mediumship but mainly because he was trustworthy and capable of offering a lot of affection. His mediumistic abilities were notorious, but he was not known as a powerful man since his seductive influence was much more related to his coherence concerning Agape's ideal. In this sense, his strength was much more attractive than his powers (Seif, 2019) because he displayed a sign that represented the incarnation of *Agape* into a human body, which could influence and attract intensively many people. The idea of seduction was manifested through a respectful attitude in which women felt protected, loved, and considered in their needs. From an ethnopsychological perspective (Neubern, 2018a), in his spiritual mission, he should renounce conceiving women for sexual partners because his role should be dedicated to love all human beings through *Agape*. Thus, *Eros* became *Agape* without a place for *Amour* or pornography, leading him to treat women as daughters, followers, and sisters. On many occasions, he could be among them as a partner with whom they could confess secrets and share confidential ideas. Even prostitutes are always reported to be supported by him (UEM, 1993). When he was young, his father led him to a brothel because he thought that after a sexual exchange, Chico would become a normal boy. However, some minutes after being introduced to the women, he listened to a collective prayer coming from the social room. Mr. Xavier was shocked and revolted when he realized his son *seduced* all women into a collective prayer instead of being engaged in a sexual relationship. In other stories, prostitutes revealed they decided to abandon their profession, searching for a decent life inspired by their contact with Chico Xavier (Gama, 1998). In a word, his seduction concerning women was not based on using them but on an emancipatory relationship in which they might follow their lives from their own needs and desires.

John of God, in turn, was never compared with a saint, being conceived socially as an ordinary man who could work serving the Sacred (Rocha & Vasquez, 2016; Rocha, 2017). Before the scandal revelations, his attractiveness was more related to the marriage between the spiritual powers and humankind who could be imperfect but also devoted to a good cause. From a general perspective, his interest in women, money, and political influence was not commonly contested by followers or public opinion, and perhaps, the persecution he suffered from the Catholic Church and Medical Associations provided him with sympathy from many people. In social understandings, he could be considered as Zé Arigó's heir, a famous healing medium who suffered a lot with the same kind of persecution and had a tragic death in a car crash (Fuller & Puharich, 1974). Then, if powerful Brazilian institutions persecuted him, he was also in a social role able to receive collective sympathy from a society for whom Spiritism is extremely familiar (Carvalho, 1994). The impact of his amazing treatments and cures was intensive, and quickly, he was considered as a sign of the Sacred.

Cristina Rocha (2017, pp. 91–95) presented the case of an Australian woman, Ana, whose death from lung cancer was imminent, as predicted by doctors. With her husband and son, they went to Abadiânia and felt welcome by the social network related to the *Casa*, which provided emotional and logistic support for people, especially because they were foreigners. She began the direct treatment with John of God and his spiritual entities and was also frequently sent to the collective meditation composed of many patients and followers. Suddenly, her symptoms seemed to present an intensive regression, and her doctors shared feeling of shame and surprise. They could not believe in her health evolution, and some of them seemed to feel guilty since they did not offer her any reason for hope. Ana became a healer, returned to Australia, and exerted this profession as a new way of life, much more meaningful than before. Although she died from the same cancer 7 years after her travel to Abadiânia, her story was astonishing basically for two reasons. First, she and her family had the opportunity to live with quality for 7 years more than the medical prediction, which was really significant for them. From an ethnopsychological point of view (Neubern, 2022b), her death was not a sign of failed treatment because the spiritual world is in charge of deciding if and when someone will die. Ana's temporary improvement was a sign of Divine Mercy, which is above human science and understanding. Second, her treatment was also understood as a spiritual healing in which not only the body should be treated but especially the soul. Her new way of life was quite significant for her and her family, also considered the main reason of her physical improvement.

As Chico Xavier, John of God also received an astonish revelation near the waterfall, when he was swimming (Machado, 2016). Saint Rita de Cassia, a Catholic Saint, appeared to him through his mediumistic vision, revealing that he should go to a spiritist center to pursue his healing mission. This passage indicates that he also was blessed by the Sacred, since a Catholic saint composes part of a great Brazilian machinery of spiritual healing (Nuñez, 2008/2012). Such an event revealed to John of God a significant spiritual mission, which was accepted by the medium. Nonetheless, if John of God was blessed by the Sacred to fulfill his work, which were, then, the reasons that led him to become the protagonist of many crimes? How could he display a Sacred sign and simultaneously an evil sign, incarnating darkness intentions toward vulnerable people? How could he transit between *Agape*, promoting spiritual healing, and pornography, abusing violently of many women? I think that each of these questions should require, at least, a PhD investigation to obtaining some answers, due their complexity which implicates sociological, anthropological, psychological, economical, and mainly ethnopsychological topics that are implicated and require intensive and varied forms of inquiry. However, through De-sign thinking (Seif, 2019, 2020a) and ethnopsychology (Neubern, 2022a, 2022b), it is possible to envisage some alternative ways of intelligibility.

Perhaps, the main point of possible explaining on these contradictions is that John of God did not pursue, through ethical effort, *Agape's* ideal (Seif, 2019). In other words, he failed to come up with an integrative experience between ego and self, becoming extremely instable and working sometimes as a representative of the Sacred, and sometimes as a darkness instrument. He was not known as a man worried about surveilling his thoughts, words, and feelings, being frequently exalted for his strong temperament which were sometimes incoherent with his spiritual proposals. Thus, his apparent normality seemed to be a disguise of a deep subjective and spiritual process where he was increasingly devoured by his own darkness (Csordas, 1997). Differently from Chico Xavier, in which darkness would compose a part of his cosmology without dominating him, John of God became submitted to his darkness experiences, especially concerning sex, money, power, and vanity. Even his intensive mediumistic abilities were manipulated intending to obtain his goals, without considering if these goals could implicate suffering or harm to someone. In some way, he obtained a kind of integration but not based on *Agape's* devoted search, since his deepest and even darkest purposes should be the main reference.

Key consequences derived from this problematic form of integration. First, his deliberated absence of ethical effort led him to be converted into an ally of evil spirits, such as reported in some spiritualistic traditions he seemed to belong (Neubern, 2022a; Scorsolini-Comin, 2023). In these perspectives, mediums are frequently tempted by negative spirits who intend to lead them to errors and to deviate them from their spiritual missions. Being imbued with a collective mission, John of God would receive many forms of temptations because if he failed as a medium, the negative impacts would also be collective. In spiritists cosmologies, there is a constant battle between good and evil spirituality, who dispute the access and the influence on individual and collective thoughts. Mediums are at the center of these disputes because they have a special role in communicating with the spiritual world, obtaining a considerable range of social influence. Thus, following an ethnopsychology thought (Neubern, 2018a), it is possible to consider that his personal failure as a medium was closely associated with the negative spiritual dominance of Abadiânia, which became the scenario of many forms of crimes (Felitti, 2020). However, it was not only the concrete crime that mattered for spirits, but the diffusion of harmful forms of thinking. Through negative values and thoughts, evil spirits can influence and perhaps dominate many people's minds. In short, John of God's failure was considered by many people[7] as a reason to disbelieve in spirituality and spiritual practices in general.

---

[7] This information was obtained through the report of some mediums interviewed by myself, as explained in the beginning of this section.

The communitarian dimension was also impacted by John of God's contradictions. On one hand, many people seemed to search Agape's ideals through dedication to healing practices under a Sacred perspective and meaningful way of life (Rocha, 2017). Commonly, who arrived in Abadiânia reported a welcoming social net of support that led them to believe they were inserted into a brotherhood community. Then, among this Agapistic community, some persons arrived in Abadiânia, submitted to spiritual treatment in the *Casa*, and did not perceive any kind of immoral or illegal conduct. Prominent researchers such as Rocha and Machado constantly mentioned here did not mention suspicions concerning these conducts, which obtained considerable social visibility after the scandals. On the other hand, there was another form of community organized around economic interests, many of them based on illegality (Felitti, 2020). As mentioned above, these criminal holdings exerted parallel control in town, using intimidation, armed threats, and political influence. Since economic extortions to sexual abuse were frequent practices in that community. Both communities exerted their practices, intending to produce their results in many aspects irreconcilable to one another. Both communities had John of God as a leader, a spiritual leader for the former, and consequently a Sacred sign, and a criminal boss for the other; that is a sign of the negative dimensions of the Brazilian society. The victims' reports highlighted that the medium mixed both roles during his spiritual practices, which was an intensive form of violence since they were there searching for spiritual treatment. The abundance of numerous reports in this way led people to argue that he was a charlatan because a criminal man could not serve as a Sacred instrument (Felitti, 2020).

From an ethnopsychological perspective, this astonishing contradiction can be explained through some principles. First, following the collective Brazilian traditions, such as Umbanda, Kardecism, and Esoterism (Carvalho, 1994), mediumship doesn't have a direct relationship with moral conduct, as can be illustrated by many historical examples, such as Eusapia Paladino, Rasputin, and Rajneesh. For these groups, psychic powers commonly are conceived as karma, granted by higher spirituality as a way to pay off karmic debts from past lives. Rarely is a medium recognized as a missionary as Chico Xavier, who would be an elevated spirit with a collective mission. Thus, John of God could have a power frequently used by good spirits intending to heal people despite his numerous immoral conducts. Among some spiritists and mediums I interviewed, he was conceived as a man who received a spiritual mission, which presupposes that he had good personal qualities. Before establishing Abadiânia, Chico Xavier confirmed he had a spiritual healing mission in that town (Rocha, 2017). Nevertheless, as he failed in discipline, he deviated from the Sacred goals, becoming an ally of evil spirits. Second, as explained by my interviewees, the Sacred experiences reported by people were probably caused by well-intentioned people who sincerely tried to obtain or promote benefits. Therefore, many healing reports did not happen due to John of God's individual merits but based on the faith and good intentions of people implicated in spiritual healing practices. In short, despite his failure, the spiritual community could still mobilize healing devices.

Still in the communitarian dimension, John of God lived an intensive paradox concerning control and freedom (Seif, 2020b). John of God did not submit to a long mediumistic preparatory training as Chico Xavier did. John of God practiced his healing abilities without constant mentorship and systematic study. He did not affiliate with an institution, such as Brazilian Spiritist Federation (FEB), which could help his trajectory through some forms of regulations. If he was explicitly adept at syncretism among different spiritual traditions, he was, above all, an adept of freedom, a term adopted by him through an absolute perspective. Without social control from his partners or even the social authorities, he became in control of everything: the spiritual works and activities in the Casa, the life in Abadiânia, and the personal lives of his followers. Differently from the stories about Chico Xavier, he was not described as a man constantly under spiritual surveillance, which intended to lead him to avoid temptations. Furthermore, he was the control, and nothing in his social network seemed to be capable of opposing against him. As a consequence, John of God became increasingly authoritarian and tyrannical. However, this massive control exerted on the external world disguised an internal conflict where his ego became increasingly dominated by darkness. His greed for more money and power seemed to have unrecognized limits since numerous of his actions were practiced and known by many people in the city. As he did not cultivate self-perfection through spiritual discipline, he could no longer access the Sacred through his own efforts, making room to several negative influences that permeated his self and his trajectory. His intense sexual appetite frequently searched constantly for more victims for many years, which could range from at least 300 women! Undoubtedly, the victim's reports described that he feared to be revealed and reported, indicating he had a good sense of reality. As he did not believe he could be punished, in his imaginary world, he conceived himself as a God who should be above human laws and social conventions.

At this point, John of God's tragedy is perhaps a contemporary version of the original sin (Seif, 2019). By conceiving himself the ultimate potency concerning the spiritual world and human laws, he established a relationship of contempt for spirituality in order to ignore its knowledge, advice, and rules. Without submission and obedience to something higher than himself, he thought he could occupy God's place concerning his life and others'. In doing so, he was deluded into thinking that he would be free to act in whatever way he wanted without any consideration of possible consequences. Nevertheless, this massive delusion made him believe he was alone when, in fact, his self was inhabited by many semiotic systems related to the negative side of his social belongings, such as *machismo*, patriarchy, and patrimonialism. Despite his firm belief that he could control the world around him, he was subtly and constantly influenced by these systems, which, after several years, seemed to control the majority of his deliberate decisions. In synthesis, he was devoured by his own dark tendencies, mainly because he did not recognize anything above him in the spiritual and human world. It is possible to conceive that his constant trance practices favor this peculiar system of inner domination due to the trance's capacity to potentialize experiences. It is not without reason that in spiritists' and scholars' knowledge (Nathan, 2011), imaginary production and sexuality are closely associated.

As a leader, John of God became a dubious sign, mainly for those who perceived his double insertion in quite different communities. Although many attributions of an elevated spirituality (Machado, 2016), he was much more known because of his mediumistic powers, which promoted spectacular interventions and healing processes. John of God was not a source of attraction through strength, as Chico Xavier was. He did not fulfill a broad and intensive integration among his ego, a sign commonly related to everyday and profane life and the self, in which one can find the most profound spiritual experiences. He was a powerful medium, somebody who could produce results and obtain efficacy, but his personal character was not capable of touching people on behalf of the Sacred. Despite many followers' reports of this way, the collective knowledge that permeated his belongings confirmed that he should not be understood as a Sacred sign. Thus, as reported by many victims and people close to him, the expectation of a confident and protected meeting was suddenly converted into a desperate experience provoked by sexual harassment, in which the supposed Sacred symbol was transformed into an evil representative. In some way, it is possible to conceive that pornography used *Agape's* mask until John of God was alone with a woman, whom he did not perceive as a human being but a sexual object. She should not deserve any form of respect or empathy, being used as an object intending to satisfy his sexual desires, even if she cried, protested, or opposed his approaches.

Through De-sign thinking (Seif, 2020a), it is possible to conceive that these forms of relationships promoted by John of God led women to massive forms of suffering. These women were emotionally available since he was a spiritual authority imbued with power to help them. Furthermore, they were already vulnerable dealing with personal and familiar suffering, which implicated complex forms of illnesses and their multiple consequences in terms of economic loss, depression, social isolation, medical impotence, and work problems, among others. These two elements, their availability and vulnerability, favored either a form of relationship characterized by a massive receptivity on their part or the almost complete lack of defense Thus, as any therapist, John of God could be conceived as a sign whose interpretants are developed inside their selves (Neubern, 2016) but remarked by a significant difference, because he introduced suffering and violence in his victims selves. However, his entrances into these women subjective worlds were extremely violent, not only during the sexual acts but mainly in their long duration throughout the victims' lives. It was a pornographic relationship (Seif, 2018) that remained many years after the event, creating a kind of navigation that infiltrated destructive signs in different parts of their selves, which could paralyze and make them feel dominated.

In this sense, John of God was a destructive sign that directly affected their imaginary experiences, which are essential for the semiotic productions of the self. Probably, as a sign, John of God produced numerous imaginative repetitions of sexual violence capable of affecting deep levels of agency and meaning production, especially concerning the victims' self-image (Neubern, 2018b). As a sign, the morbid scenes of violence became imaginary processes that could be easily reactivated in everyday life in order to make them live again the original violence, sometimes with many details. Many victims felt invaded by this traumatic event, paralyzed in the present, and blocked concerning the future. The violence created persistent semiotic nuclei that remained for many years and occupied large spaces in subjective experience, establishing the continuity of John of God's empire upon them. Depression, suicidal ideas, social isolation, insomnia, anxiety, nightmares, and destructive conduct were examples of the symptoms reported by the victims.

These experiences, as suffering trances, promoted the continuity of the violent relationship capable of leading the victims to feel themselves slaves of John of God. As a sect mechanism (Nathan & Swertvaegher, 2003), the remaining medium's inner presence inside the victims' selves could promote the sensation of being frequently surveilled or the presence of signs (voices, images, scenes, spirits) that accused them of being guilty or traitors. Nonetheless, their courage to report him was a significant act of change, being the first step in stopping his criminal practices through law limits. It was a therapeutic measure for many women who kept themselves silent, were discredited by their social networks, and suffered constant sexual abuse consequences. Some of them searched for professional help but remained hopeless concerning justice because of John of God's political power and ignorance of the extension of his crimes. But beyond professional help and individual experiences, the reports against him imposed the necessary limits on John of God to understand that he was not a God but just a man who should obey human conventions and answer for his actions. More than that, it promoted collective attention concerning human tragedies, abusive leaders, and what we should expect concerning spiritual movements.

Love and Absoluteness

Luis de Camões's poem concerning love is a sage form of expressing and understanding this sublime human experience. The verses used to open this chapter highlight the numerous paradoxes related to love experiences that commonly lead people to extreme feelings transiting between the sublime and madness. Wholophilia (Seif, 2018) is a relevant principle to establish a dialogue with love in its multiple faces because this principle sustains that human incompleteness moves people to search for completeness through love. If the partner is God (*Agape*), a beloved (*Amour*), or a friend (Philos), human beings will try to fulfill their imperfect and incomplete condition through a kind of fusion with this interlocutor, which is blissful, ecstatic, orgasmic, and even tragic, by possessing the risk of slavery or self-dissolution. Love, in this sense, is simultaneously a trance experience and a De-sign navigation since it plays with limits of the ordinary consciousness, but also a risk that is not far from death, a frequent destiny of many love stories, such as the drama included Rioboldo and Diadorin (Guimarães Rosa, 2015). Similarly, Erickson's patient (Erickson & Kubie, 1941) tried suicide many times because the love she felt in her subjectivity could not be understood in social life, and the hypnotic work became a safe manner to respect her family values in order to allow a concrete experience of love with her beloved. Probably, her absolute love feeling would lead her to death without therapeutic intervention.

John of God, in turn, is an illustrative example of *Eros'* degeneration into pornography (Seif, 2019). His tragic story reveals how love can also be related to darkness, which is commonly rejected by many people for whom love should be considered only through good values. As an insatiable beast, darkness devoured almost all his subjective world through pornography, vanity, and greed, which promoted destructive experiences for many people, especially women, and discredited spiritualistic ideas and movements, at least in some level. The absoluteness in his case was so ferocious that darkness devoured almost all the rest of signs of *Eros*, *Agape*, and *Philos*. From a De-sign perspective (Seif, 2019), he was the sign representing many sociocultural and semiospheric oppressive dimensions, which worked intensively intending to diffuse negative influences among human beings. Nonetheless, through the massive reports against him, human justice imposed essential limits on his absoluteness, leading him to face the ordinary reality that he was just a man. This degenerate form of love—pornography—met conventional barriers that stopped an uncontrollable desire whose consequences were already tragic for many people.

But Chico Xavier seemed to navigate through *Eros's* waters as a legit De-signer since he exerted love intensively without abandoning different forms of control that didn't allow him to be lost in absolute experiences. On one hand, he seemed to understand Camões's wisdom as somebody who loves deliberately chooses to be a slave. Chico was not only tolerant concerning social surveillance, even if it was unfair to him, but he was also highly obedient toward Emmanuel's instructions. Many stories about him reported that he frequently searched his guidance, and, more than that, he seemed to internalize the interdictions of his personal desires. In other words, he was conscious about his role in the spiritual and human worlds and, especially, concerning his spiritual mission. On the other hand, his relationship with *Agape* kept, at least ideally, the absolute desire for fusion. Paradoxically, by maintaining some forms of control, he could furnish in some level moments that envisaged a *Wholophilic* experience in which people felt themselves overflowing with love and transcending the ordinary limits of reality. His own mediumistic practices seemed to promote many *Agapistic* moments that became possible despite and thanks to the limits he accepted.

References

Albuquerque, T. (2015). Chico Xavier e a construção simbólica do Brasil como "coração mundo" e "Pátria do Evangelho". [Chico Xavier and the symbolic construction of Brazil as "heart of the world" and "homeland of the Gospel"]. *Caicó, 16*(36), 129–148.

Apel, K. (1995). *From pragmatism to pragmaticism*. Humanity Books.

Avila, S. T. (1988). *The life of St Teresa by Avila herself*. Penguin Classics. (Original work published in 1567).
Ballano, V. (2019). *Sociological perspective in clerical sexual abuse in the Catholic hierarchy*. Springer.
Barbosa, E. (1978). *Enxugando lágrimas*. [Wiping away tears]. Ide.
Baumann, Z. (2003). *Liquid love: On the frailty of human bonds*. Polity.
Blum, D. (2004). *Ghost hunters. William James and the search for scientific proof of life after death*. Penguin Books.
Binswanger, L. (2008). Sur la Psychothérapie. [On Psychotherapy]. In L. Binswanger (Ed.), *Introduction à l'analyse existentielle*. Minuit. (original work published in 1935).
Bishop, C. (1997). *Sex and spirit*. Duncan Baird Publishers.
Butler, J. (2006). *Gender troubles. Feminism and the subversion of identity*. Routledge.
Campbell, J. (1959). *The masks of God*. The Viking Press.
Carroy, J. (1991). *L'hypnose et suggestion. L'invention du sujet*. [Hypnosis and suggestion. The invention of the subject]. Press Universitaire de France.
Carroy, J. (1993). Magnétisme, hypnose et philosophie. [Magnetism, hypnosis and philosophy]. In I. Stengers (Ed.), *Importance de l'Hypnose*. Synthélabo.
Carvalho, J. (1994). O encontro de novas e velhas religiões: Esboço de uma teoria dos estilos de espiritualidade. [The meeting of new and old religions: Outline of a theory of styles of spirituality]. In E. A. Moreira & R. Zicnan (Orgs.), *Misticismo e novas religiões* (pp. 67–98). Vozes.
Chertok, L., & Stengers, I. (1989). *Le Coeur et la raison. L'hypnose en question de Lavoisier à Lacan*. [The Heart and the reason. The hypnosis in question from Lavoisier to Lacan]. Payot.
Corbin, H. (2015). *Temple et contemplation*. [Temple and contemplation]. Entre Lacs. (original work published in 1958).
Costa, C. (2008). *Chico, diálogos e recordações …*. [Chico, dialogues and recollections]. UEM.
Csordas, T. (1997). *The sacred self. A cultural phenomenology of charismatic healing*. University of California Press.
Cumming, H., & Leffler, K. (2008). *João de Deus. O médium de cura brasileiro que transformou a vida de milhões*. [John of God. The Brazilian healing medium who transformed the lives of millions]. Ed. Pensamento.
Deely, J. (2010). *Semiotic animal. A postmodern definition of "human being" transcending patriarchy and feminism*. St Augustine's Press.
Erickson, M., & Kubie, L. (1941). The sucessful treatment of a case of acute hysterical depression by a return under hypnosis to a critical phase of childhood. *Psychoanalytic Quarterly, 10*(4), 122–142.
Erickson, M., & Rossi, E. (1979). *Hypnotherapy: An exploratory casebook*. Irvington.
Felitti, C. (2020). *A casa. A história da seita de João de Deus*. [Home. The history of the sect of John of God]. Todavia.
Fuller, J., & Puharich, H. (1974). *Arigo—Surgeon of the rusty knife*. Thomas Y Crowell Company.
Gama, R. (1998). *Lindos casos de Chico Xavier*. [Cute cases of Chico Xavier]. Lake.
Guimarães Rosa, J. (2015). *Grande sertão veredas*. Nova Fronteira. (Original work published in 1956).
Hartshorne, C., & Weiss, P. (1980). *The collected papers of Charles S. Peirce (CP, 8 vol.)*. Harvard University Press.
Jappy, T. (2013). *Introduction to peircean visual semiotics*. Bloomsbury.
Jung, C. (2023). *The man and his symbols*. Bantman. (original work published in 1964).
Kardec, A. (2021). *The spirits book*. Independently Publisher. (Original work published in 1857).
Lewgoy, B. (2004). *Chico Xavier, o grande mediador. Chico Xavier e a cultura brasileira*. [Chico Xavier, the great mediator. Chico Xavier and Brazilian culture]. Edusc.
Lewin, K. (1951). *Field theory in social sciences*. Harper Torchbooks.
Liszka, J. (1996). *A general introduction to the semeiotic of Charles Sanders Peirce*. Indiana University Press.

Machado, M. H. (2016). *João de Deus. Um médium no coração do Brasil*. [John of God. A medium in the heart of Brazil]. Fontanar.
Maraldi, E. (2021). *Parapsychology and religion*. Brill.
Martins, F. (2005). *Psicopatologia I*. [Psychopathology I]. Puc Minas.
Monroe, J. W. (2007). *Laboratories of faith. Mesmerism, spiritism, and occultism in modern France*. Cornel University Press.
Nathan, T. (2014). *Nous ne sommes pas seuls au monde*. [We are not alone in the world]. Seuil. (original work published in 2001).
Nathan, T. (2011). *La nouvelle interprétation des rêves*. [The new interpretation of the dreams]. Odile Jacob.
Nathan, T. (2013). *Le filtres de l'amour*. [The filters of love]. Odile Jacob.
Nathan, T., & Stengers, I. (1999). *Médecins and sorciers*. [Doctors and sorcerers]. Synthélabo.
Nathan, T., & Swertvaegher, J. (2003). *Sortir d'une secte*. [Leaving a sect]. Seuil/Synthelabo.
Netflix. (2021). *João de Deus: Cura e Crime*. [John of God: Healing and crime]. TV program.
Neubern, M. (2016). Iconicity and complexity in hypnotic communication. *Psicologia: Teoria e Pesquisa, 32*, 1–9. https://doi.org/10.1590/0102-3772e32ne217
Neubern, M. (2018a). *Clínicas do transe. Etnopsicologia, hipnose e espiritualidade no Brasil*. [Trance clinics. Ethnopsychology, hypnosis and spirituality in Brazil]. Juruá.
Neubern, M. (2018b). *Hipnose, dores crônicas e complexidade: Técnicas avançadas*. [Hypnosis, chronic pain and complexity: Advanced techniques]. Ed. UnB.
Neubern, M. (2022a). When spirits become therapists. Ethnopsychology and hypnotherapy in Brazil. *International Journal of Latin American Religions, 1*, 1–26.
Neubern, M. (2022b). Chico Xavier and the sacred experience: A semiotic and ethnopsychological perspective. *International Journal of Latin American Religions, 2*, 1–24.
Neubern, M. (2023). Hypnosis, university and democracy: An emancipatory proposal. In M. Neubern & A. Bioy (Eds.), *Hypnosis in academia: Contemporary challenges in research, healthcare and education* (pp. 27–52). Springer.
Nuñez, S. (2012). *A Pátria dos curadores. Uma história da medicina e da cura espiritual no Brasil*. [The homeland of healers. A history of Medicine and spiritual healing in Brazil]. Ed. Pensamento. (original work published in 2008).
Otto, R. (2017). *The idea of the Holy*. Pantianos Classics. (original work published in 1917).
Peirce, C. (1893). Evolutionary love. In N. Houser & C. Kloesel (Eds.), *The essential Peirce* (Vol. 1, pp. 352–371). Indiana University Press.
Peirce, C. (1903). Pragmatism as a principle and method of right thinking. In P. Turrisi (Ed.), *The 1903 Harvard lectures on pragmatism*. State University of New York Press.
Pellegrino-Estrich, R. (2001). *The miracle man. The life story of John of God*. Terra.
Petrilli, S. (2017). *The self as a sign, the world, and the other*. Routledge.
Puységur, A. M.-J. (1784/1785). Mémoire pour Servir à l'Histoire et à l'Établissement du Magnétisme Animal. [Memory to be used for the history and establishment of animal magnetism]. In D. Michaux (Ed.), (2003). *Aux Sources de l'Hypnose* (pp. 13–132). Imago.
Ranieri, R. (1970). *Chico Xavier: o santo de nossos dias*. [Chico Xavier: The saint of our days]. Editora Eco.
Raposa, M. (1989). *Peirce's philosophy of religion*. Indiana University Press.
Raposa, M. (2020). *Theosemiotics. Religion, reading, and the gift of meaning*. Fordham University Press.
Rocha, C. & Vásquez, M. (Org.). (2016). *A diáspora das religiões brasileiras*. [The diaspora of Brazilian religions]. Ideias e Letras.
Rocha, C. (2017). *John of God. The globalization of Brazilian faith healing*. Oxford.
Savaris, A. (2015). *The mentalist. John of God and spiritual healing*. Horizonte.
Scorsolini-Comin, F. (2023). *O divã de alfazema. Ensaio clínico sobre a clínica ethopsicológica*. [The lavender couch. Clinical essay on the ethopsychological clinic]. Ambigrama.
Seif, F. (2013). Dialogue with Kishtta: A semiotic revelation of the paradox of life and death. *The American Journal of Semiotics, 29*, 101–115. https://doi.org/10.5840/ajs2013291-44

Seif, F. (2018). Wholophilia: De-sign and the metamorphoses of the absolute. In D. Teters & O. Neumaier (Eds.), *Metamorphoses of the absolute*. Cambridge Scholars Publishing.

Seif, F. (2019). *De-sing in transmodern world. Envisioning reality beyond absoluteness*. Peter Lang.

Seif, F. (2020a). De-sign as a destiny of navigation: The paradox of sustaining boundaries while traversing borders. *The American Journal of Semiotics, 36*(3–4), 179–215.

Seif, F. (2020b). The role of pragmatism in De-sign: Persevering through paradoxes of design and semiotics. *Cognition, 21*(1), 112–131.

Sharp, L. (2006). *Secular spirituality. Reincarnation and Spiritism in nineteenth-century France*. Lexington Books.

Souto Maior, M. (2003). *As vidas de Chico Xavier*. [The lives of Chico Xavier], Planeta.

Souza, J. (2019). *A elite do atraso. Da escravidão a Bolsonaro*. [The elite of backwardness. From slavery to Bolsonaro]. Estação Brasil.

Stoll, S. (2003). *Espiritismo à brasileira*. [Spiritism in Brazilian way]. EdUsp.

UEM (Ed.). (1993). *Mandato de Amor*. [Mandate of love]. Ed. UEM.

Vilela, J. (1994). *O gigante deitado*. [The lying giant]. O Clarim.

Chapter 7
Hypnosis and Trance-Modernity

Caetano Veloso, a famous Brazilian singer, composed a song-music named "An Indian.[1]" Being a hero compared to Mohamed Ali and Bruce Lee, the Indian would come from the stars through the highest technology vehicle would land in the heart of the southern hemisphere, in America, after the destruction of nature and the extermination of Native peoples. But what he would say, as a teaching to humanity, would be nothing more than the obvious ... this beautiful song is chosen to introduce our last chapter concerning Trance-Modernity, which will be suggested, but no entirely explained, in the next pages.

Trance-Modernity is a way of thinking and living derived from Transmodernity (Seif, 2019). It presupposes trance as a central reference for personal integration and social ideals. Because trance is a process of quale consciousness (CP[2] 6.228), in Trance-Modernity firstness processes are understood through their ontological *status*, which can have some crucial implications for this topic. Following De-sign principles (Seif, 2019; a), this chapter describes a complex perspective for human beings, simultaneously unique and multiple, individual and collective, practical and aesthetical, in transit and in fluid conceptions of reality. This human being is permeated by practices of trance, natural or produced as *dispositifs*; consequently, one learns to deal with their own multiplicity, and, simultaneously, with the collectivities in which one is inserted. The following arguments try to answer two main questions for Trance-Modernity. If reality is not absolute and rigidly stable, instead, it is a navigational process through diaphanous and polychronic (Seif, 2019), how can we deal with such a complex process, always in transformation? The axis to answer

---

[1] https://www.youtube.com/watch?v=rb_gaaibOHw "An Indian", by Caetano Veloso.
[2] CP means the Collected Papers of Charles Sanders Peirce (Hartshorne & Weiss, 1980), being the first number, the volume, and the last before the point, the paragraph. Despite its difference concerning the other citations, CP will be preserved in the present work because of its familiarity with the semioticians for whom this book is also intended. Another Peircean acronym is MS, which means the Annotated Catalogue of Papers of Charles S. Peirce (Robin, 1967).

this question lies in *Rebirth and Ethos*, through which multiple senses of belonging from our lives compose a contemplative attitude towards reality, which is prominent for control and results. This axis is inspired mainly by Krenak's (2022) idea that life is not useful, but a cosmic dance. The second question is: if we are permeated by the world and simultaneously act as transformative agents in the world, which attitudes should we adopt towards it? Many answers are proposed, but their common principle is a notion of reality that is mainly inhabited by firstness, implicating an ontological dimension highlighted by traditional knowledge, the integrity of the self, and the relationship between service and collectiveness. A case study I conducted myself serves as basis for the arguments, highlighting necessary topics for a broad idea of Trance-Modernity.

"We Can't Allow Little Claudia to Die"

A few years ago, Claudia, 55 years old, a public servant, contacted me again, seeking hypnotherapy (Neubern, in press). However, peculiarly, she carried significant changes considering our first therapeutic process, almost 10 years prior. Claudia had broken away from Spiritism and medium practices, which had been the most important principles in her life. She had witnessed many incorrect behaviors by some spiritist leaders as well as by her close friends. For her, Spiritism seemed corrupted by political conflict, vanity, ambition, and violence; as a woman, she was frequently harassed by colleagues and prominent figures. She reported that many colleagues were abusive towards her because they believed that, as an important medium, she should always be available to attend to their needs. On some occasions, she was approached sexually by men. She was also deceived by central spiritist leaders, with whom she had severed contact because they were not dedicated to their spiritual teachings in everyday life. Many of them were interested in money, power, and fame, commonly arrogant and aggressive with people like her, whose intentions were to be coherent with Jesus's teachings when they tried to collaborate with spiritist institutions.

Nevertheless, Claudia's suffering was further increased by the political polarization in Brazil, as extremist movements and politicians suddenly became a strong representation in national political institutions. She experienced many moments of desperation, asking herself or her close friends how to reconcile Jesus with people like Bolsonaro and his collaborators. *"If Jesus's teachings were love, forgiveness, compassion, and charity"* she wondered, *"how could these ideas be reconciled with people who defend violence, weapons, racism, and who attack women's and gays' rights, the destruction of forests, among other absurdities?"* She was devasted when she realized many spiritists were sympathetic to these extremist ideas and supported them in political movements. More importantly, some people transformed spiritist institutions into places of political conflict, kindling disharmony and suffering in spiritual practices—for example, describing mediumistic revelations that supported extremist politicians. Claudia and many other members did not support this situation and abandoned the movement, declaring themselves as people without religion.

Nonetheless, Claudia's experience was perhaps more complex because she questioned many of her own beliefs and her mediumistic experiences. She could not believe in God anymore, since the world was unfair and unequal, and innocent people were frequently massacred by hunger and wars, like in Ukraine and Gaza. Her mediumistic experiences were also in doubt; for her, they were probably imaginative creations to be appreciated by her colleagues. If that were the case, there was no need to continue engaging in them.

When she arrived at hypnotherapy, she was depressed and inhabited by negative ideas. She declared that she did not intend to commit suicide, but she could understand and be empathic towards people who did it. Claudia remained affected by complex and severe self-immune diseases, but her main issue was her rupture with Spiritism, including its practices, institutions, beliefs, and people. She believed that she was correct in her choice, but she felt an enormous solitude, strange pains across her body, and a lack of something essential for her life.

Inspired by De-sign (Seif, 2019) and by Erickson (Erickson & Rossi, 1980), I surmised that Claudia needed to be acknowledged in her decisions and ruptures. Spiritism has always been essential in her life, and breaking with its ideas, people, and institutions were crucial to her life. Indeed, I envisaged that she still had many doubts because her spiritual experiences and practices in Spiritism were meaningful and personal and could not be determined by other people's actions or institutions. She did not want to be judged, but frequently used a language based on judgement, which I applied to my statements as a form of confirmation. Then, I told her that she was very coherent in evaluating numerous incompatibilities in people who claimed to follow Jesus's teachings and still engaged with extremist movements; that she was quite correct to deny any forms of abuse to herself, especially because she was a woman; that she was right to deny mediumistic messages that supported wrong values and leaders; that she was also coherent in feeling desperate concerning international news about war and inequality since they were *a part of the truth*, and the next years would be hard for many people worldwide. However, I also told her that it *was only a part of the truth* and that she could not change the world, but she could change her own world. If she was so clever as to highlight suffering and problems, *she would also be clever enough to emphasize significant things to change her world of experiences*. She could not only avoid some of the news (which was very pessimistic) but *focus on the small experiences in her own world*, such as the moments in her garden or while playing with her three grandchildren. If she was correct to deny many things in Spiritism, it would be *hard for her to deny her own spiritual experiences*—present in her life since she was a little girl. *She had attested to her own experiences many times during her life*, evaluating them as positive, constructive, emotional, and coherent with Jesus's ideas, and, consequently, *they could not be undermined by human immoral behaviors*.

She observed me attentively and shook her head, subtly confirming my statements. I had three main goals with these suggestions, being the first to lead her towards a feeling of confirmation that her attitudes and ideas were logical and coherent with her own integrity and values. It was a form of confirming acceptance for fragile points, often attacked by their social circle. Secondly, I wanted to change her focus from an external and pessimistic evaluation to an internal and constructive experience that she was able and legitimate. Claudia was extremely focused on the external world and on the media's narrative, based on experts' negative statements. Thirdly, I intended to prepare her for a trance experience in which these three points should be approached. Trance experience must be constructive; due to its quale-consciousness nature, it can promote many significant changes in human experiences, especially in narrative and creating new meanings.

During trance, Claudia displayed many emotional expressions; she especially cried profusely. She reported that her spiritual guide, a Hindu man, smiled at her and said he and the other guides were also around her, but she refused to perceive them. Next, a handsome and strong guide, an Indigenous (White Feather) man, appeared, leading other spirits related to her ancestral ties, such as her Indigenous and enslaved roots, her grandfather and grandmother. She remembered that her grandparents were *"mateiros"*, people who knew how to live in the forests, obtaining food, shelter, and medicine (they were specialists in herbal treatments). "Old Slaves", spirits from Umbanda of former enslaved people, were also frequent presences in her life, especially in difficult moments, when they helped her. White Feather was also related to her interest in herbs and even in her current life, when she walked through forests or woods. He told her that the butterflies that followed her during her walks were a sign of his presence, guiding and protecting her. Then, White Feather conducted a ritual: all spirits were in a circle, and Claudia was also there, but as a child. He proclaimed that "we can't allow little Claudia to die," followed by significant memories that appeared as scenes for her. She remembered that once, when she was six, she put her hands on a "crazy" woman, who seemed possessed by evil spirits and suddenly seemed healed. She described many scenes with her grandparents walking into forests and teaching her about herbs, but in her strongest memory she was on a farm, and people told her mother about a woman who seemed to behave like a wolf. Some people believed that woman had transformed into a werewolf during the moonlight, but she constantly walked on all fours, as an animal. Claudia listened to these reports and told her mother she would meet the "wolf-woman" in the forest and nobody should go after them. She would be protected, and there was no reason to worry. She found the woman and put her hand on her head and, 1 h after she left for the forest, she came back followed by the "wolf-woman" who seemed normal.

After this trance experience, Claudia presented significant and therapeutic changes. She was still pessimistic about many subjects, especially the international context, but she was much more focused on her own world, which included her house and garden, her close relationships, and her inner experiences. She quickly incorporated the idea that she could not change earth on a macropolitical level, but she could change something in her small world. She was a beautiful woman who deserved good partners in love and friendship, and she would no longer tolerate abusive relationships. Good practices around ecology, friendship, and education, would be included in her background. She believed that Brazil and the world would face difficult times during the next decades, but she was more concerned about what kind of learning she could promote for her sons and grandchildren. Nonetheless, even though she has not yet found a conceptual system to process her mediumistic experiences, she recognizes that she belongs to this world, and this world belongs to her. Thus, she needed to acknowledge this world and be reconciled with it again.

Her sons and grandchildren deserved their best future, and she wanted to leave them a meaningful legacy.

Rebirth and Ethos

Claudia's experience can illustrate many aspects of conceiving Trance-Modernity. Through trance, she reconnected with her ancestors and received the important message of rebirth: her inner child should not die. While a child, she seemed completely integrated with her spiritual mission, with many demonstrations. As a woman, she seemed to die symbolically: since she did not remember or could access this child, an icon with two main forms of influence. First, the child could touch her through an experience promoted by trance, essential to re-live the moments in which the Sacred was present and seemed significant, meaningful, and a distinct reference for her. Secondly, the child was also a symbol of a collective mission that would offer her a teleological process for her existence. Therefore, without these two forms of that influence, Claudia felt a strong absence in her life, as if something central had been lost. Her suffering still increased because, despite her problems, engaging in spiritual activities was her way to feel integrated with that mission.

Claudia's case study prominently features essential Trance-Modernity principles. Ethos is not strictly related to the concrete presence of some ethnic or cultural group at particular historical moments (as illustrated by her spiritual guide, a Hindu master). Indeed, she had some ideas about Indian culture and practices related to Western interest in eastern practices since the XIX century (Carvalho, 1994). Nonetheless, from an ethnopsychological perspective (Nathan, 2015; Neubern, 2018), eastern influences are much more fluid than researchers habitually conceive, promoting a conception of Ethos lacking clear boundaries and permeated by polychronic time and diaphanous spaces (Seif, 2019). Ethnopsychologists Miguel Bairrão and Daniela Lemos (2013) bring an extraordinary example from an Umbanda group from Ribeirão Preto, Brazil: it is predominantly inhabited by Indigenous spirits, in contrast with the majority of Umbanda groups in which the spiritual predominance is Afro-Brazilian. This group's cosmology conceives that these Indigenous people died during the Portuguese colonization, which exterminated them. Nevertheless, under Jesus's inspiration, Indigenous spirits worked in this group, intending to help, heal, and guide "white" people, especially those who had been their killers in the past and were now reincarnated so they could evolve. This complex Ethos implicates a Christian value as a central reference, a Kardecist perspective of reincarnation, and Indigenous spirits as protagonists in reframing the tragic events of Indigenous extermination during Portuguese colonization. Here, the spiritual machinery (Nathan, 2014) became a strong instrument for reconstructing historical narratives, especially those permeated by the most striking forms of violence.

The Umbanda group mentioned above, as well as Claudia's experience, yields central ideas on how this reconnection could occur—collectively. Perhaps the first step toward an understanding is their dialogue with traditional knowledges which guard the ancestors' cosmology and many cultural technologies for accessing the spiritual world. The legacy of Ethnopsychology is essential for that process, because many authors (Bairrão & Lemos, 2013; Nathan, 2014; Neubern, 2018) have contributed significantly to describe traditional knowledge *dispositifs*, machinery, and cosmologies (as previously mentioned in this book). From an ethnopsychology perspective, Claudia's experience, as well as Bairrão's report, share many similarities concerning trance induction as a device, allied with traditional knowledge (Umbanda), and cosmology (spirits from Brazilian culture).

Nevertheless, based on an understanding of Trance-Modernity, some questions must be reconsidered through an approximation between traditional knowledges and western science, based on De-sign thinking (Seif, 2013, 2019, 2020a). Initially, traditional knowledge developed a form to investigate a subtle world, which can be verified in different cultures (Martino, 1999; Nathan, 2021). In contrast with western science, especially those related to the Cartesian paradigm, traditional knowledges commonly display particular forms of approaching and understanding firstness processes. Through their *dispositifs* and machineries, their specialists interpolate the invisible world to deal pertinently with the paradox of fabrication *vs.* revelation of beings that emerge from this approach. Spirits, gods, *orixás*, and ancestors inhabited an elusive world while presenting an independence from the specialist's intentions—an independence that can be legitimated by *dispositifs* and the specialist's expertise. To a certain extent, they have significant achievements in letting beings speak and present their intentionalities without losing the condition to verify the legitimacy of that being's expressions. Furthermore, they have the conditions to ascertain if a spirit speaks truth, their role, and their hierarchy—and if these *dispositifs* are correctly applied. However, an attentive reader may ask if western scientists do not do the same, because they, through science's *dispositifs* (such as the laboratory), can create/reveal their beings (such as an electron or a molecule), that can also "speak", that is, provide pertinent answers for the scientists' enunciations (Stengers, 2002).

Cosmology

> *Cosmology is a philosophical branch that tries to explain the origin of the Universe, its forms of organization, and its beings. It can propose ideas concerning Gods, matter, spirits, the human soul, evolution, and the most different relationships between these elements and natural phenomena. As highlighted by* Raposa (1989), *Peirce conferred a central role to the Divine Mind in the Universe and considered evolution through a complex relationship network among laws, existents, and Firstness creative potentialities. In this work, I consider that Peirce's cosmology must be integrated, in some way, with traditional knowledge, especially concerning beings, invisible or not, as proposed by ethnopsychology. It presupposes intentionality from different beings, human or not human, which is essential to understand multiple relations among them.*

The answer to this critical question is still to be constructed, because it touches epistemological barriers that have not yet been overcome, as illustrated mainly by the history of hypnosis (Stengers, 2001, 2002). Nonetheless, to envisage a Trance-Modernity perspective, this answer can be initially thought of in two basic ways. On the one hand, a cosmology (Brioschi, 2016) is necessary to promote intelligibility for the richness, diversity, and complexity that inhabit the universe of firstness, in its multiple forms of expression. Two leading consequences from cosmology can be seen as essential principles for Trance-Modernity. The first is the intelligibility through which this multiple universe can be known in its forms or organizations, habits, laws, and beings, essential for developing coherent *dispositifs* with these characteristics and exigences. Essentially, cosmology is crucial for promoting understandings of how beings speak and of their conditions for dialogue. Thus, when White Feather says, *"We can't allow little Claudia to die"*, one must understand who he is and his intention with this statement. De-sign inquiry (Seif, 2020b) is central to this task, since it implicates the De-signers in their own subjectivity through an imaginary investigative process: they will connect with their own impressions and abductive processes, evoking their own self as a personal universe with inhabitants, which are signs of their Ethos (Neubern, 2016). The De-signer would also work in partnership with Claudia to help her connect with a scene in order to feel and absorb it deeply, within a sheltered context. This therapeutic navigation aims to lead Claudia in her teleologic process, especially concerning her needs and her meaning for life. In synthesis, cosmology is essential to understand the subtle world as a reality, with its characteristics and demands for approach.

Nevertheless, concerning the second point, cosmology, in the sense I adopt here, is not a theory by a single man but a collective construction consolidated over generations. It emerges from human experience and is subject to forms of proof through practice and *dispositifs* that are enhanced to deal more precisely with the subtle world. Placed as a third cultural knowledge (Seif, 2020a), neither in science nor in the humanities, De-sign thinking can have a central role in this collective investigation, connecting different intents for approaching the trance experience. Thus, perceptions, feelings, and designations that emerge from trance experiences are conceived as desirable outcomes because they do not stem from deliberate choices but from unexpected processes that maintain a certain sense of freshness and novelty. De-sign inquiry (Seif, 2019), permeated by that same elusiveness from trance, trigger an organic trait to experiences, marked by systemic comprehension of systematic experiences, in which different scenes, feelings, and images compose a whole by their own organization. Through many moments of dialogue among participants (whether they are human or not), a collective cosmology can emerge and contribute to enhancing *dispositifs*. Therefore, the establishment of recursive links between dialogue, *dispositifs*, and the emergence of beings favors not only an improvement in cosmology but also a development and refinement of social practices related to trance.

These considerations encompass situations concerning Trance-Modernity. In Claudia's case, there is an initial step towards a collective process of cosmogony. In some way, it carries some cosmological elements, especially from Kardecism and

Umbanda, and implicates some level of collectivity, since there was hypnotic practice (scientific knowledge) accessing a spiritual world inhabited by spirits who were socially notorious in Brazil. Claudia's experience is illustrative of early De-sign transcendence of frontiers between western science and traditional knowledge. It was also restricted to her individual therapy, despite her collective process in trance and the consequences for her immediate social circle. Moreover, through a perspective of desirable futures (Seif, 2019), Claudia's case can be converted into a sign of an early construction of trance culture that requires either transcending the divisions between scientific practices and traditional experiences, or an individual process and collective engagement. Both forms of transcendence are intense challenges for trance culture, but they can be faced by incorporating De-sign principles, such as dialogue in social practices.

Nonetheless, these challenges can be thought of, at least initially, through another situation: the absence of cosmology in scientific practices (Brioschi, 2016). Commonly, scientists emphasize theories and methods, neglecting cosmology as a dimension of knowledge that foregrounds their practices. The cartesian paradigm, for example, sustains a universe composed of inert objects and regulated by mechanical and deterministic laws, which are measurable (Gonzalez Rey, 1996). This conflict between scientists' practices and their unacknowledged cosmology can be a source of many disputes, because revealing one's cosmovision beliefs potentially highlights incoherent underlying thoughts by scientists. As we can conclude from Peirce's criticism of mechanicist cosmology (Raposa, 1989), questions such as God, love, feelings, aesthetics, friendship, and destiny (among many others) cannot be well accommodated into a cartesian cosmology, which does not include firstness as reality (Peirce, 1903/1997). In addition, the frequent argument about what is or is not within the scope of science is not enough to solve this problem: the main issue lies in how different realities can coexist in the same universe. As a result, a Trance-Modernity perspective implicates this cohabitation that respects scientific limits but simultaneously requires science to dialogue with these diaphanous universes.

Collective Dispositifs

Trance-Modernity also implicates the construction of a collective device, because the access and consequences of trance experience cannot be restricted to a single person. As occurred during Puységur's (1784/2003) age, a trance culture in which trance becomes a familiar and accessible experience for general people is necessary. Several principles and concepts discussed here favor trance culture, placing this idea as a possible achievement. Erickson (1992), for example, conceives trance as a natural phenomenon that is experienced every day despite most people not recognizing it. Peirce's notion of trance as quale consciousness (CP 6.228) introduces firstness as the prominent category in trance, coherent with some De-sign principles—such as diaphanous spaces and polychronic time (Seif, 2019). Peirce's notion of the self (cited in Colapietro, 1989; Petrilli, 2017) highlights the self's semiotic interpenetration with the world, enabling the idea of a single person as a kind of humanity collective synthesis or hologram (Morin, 2015). Thus, this interpenetration between different dimensions, such as individual vs. social or real vs. imaginary, with time experiences amplified by trance, becomes plausible through De-sign thinking (Seif, 2019) and its critical elements for trance culture.

However, Trance-Modernity presupposes *dispositifs* that intend to implicate people emotionally in a communitarian investigation about subjects of common interest. This common ground by emotions and feelings, or Peircean *commens* (MS 318 L), relates to a kind of firstness attitude presumed collectively, but not always concrete. In some way, that is Erickson's idea of natural trance—except that, in Trance-Modernity, a person accepts trance as a practice either deliberately or emotionally. Being a human-self composed of multiple voices and characters, trance becomes a form to connect and negotiate more vividly with one's world. Monologues, which are the main basis for dialogue basis (CP 6.338), are amplified through trance, more vivid, familiar, and meaningful. If imaginative processes are no longer opposed to reality, but an integrative part of it, sign systems that emerge from trance are conceived through their effective and meaningful actions on a person's life regardless of elusiveness. In contrast with the modern notion of man (Nathan & Stengers, 1999), a possible consequence of this practice is the ego's experience of being accompanied, instead of alone. More importantly, people tend to become more inclined to service and search for an aesthetic ideal, since individuals are no longer dominated by individualistic paradigms. Therefore, without losing their individualities, people can also feel like multiple beings, leading them towards more prudent attitudes toward their numerous sociocultural heritages and connections with the world. Barriers concerning humans, non-humans, and the world are overcome (but not annulled), and subjects such as technology, AI, ecology, Anthropocene, spirituality, economy, and social inequality are no longer discussed from an external view, since they are effectively of collective interest.

The De-signer can take an essential role in the construction of *dispositifs* and in dealing with their answers. From a perspective of presentness, the De-signer can favor a polychronic context, as past and the future meet one another. To be present with somebody in a trance is a Firstness attitude (Neubern, 2023), which supports trance experience and promotes an inquiry process from different periods. In some way, the De-signer meets that collective past, characterized by figures such as ancestors, spirits, and other invisible beings that inhabited an *Ethos*. It implies, on some level, that the De-signer must consider an old formula adopted in many different cultures: trance experience depends on two characters, the person who goes into trance and the specialist who maintains contact with the concrete world (Clément, 2011). Trance experiences can favor risky situations and, as stated by Erickson (1992), people must be protected during this journey, an integrative De-sign principle (Seif, 2019). It also implies a collective dialogue with traditional knowledge, which has commonly enhanced trance technologies for many generations. Thus, as an ethnographer (Martino, 1999), the De-signer's work implies the humble attitude of knowing other universes to learn how a certain knowledge works. These are their own cosmologic references, including communication with invisible beings, the specialist role, the initiation rituals, the technical applications, and mainly an inherent sense of service that is present in their principles. I think the De-signer's role in this inquiry is not limited to translating these principles; instead, they should also make them available to others through dialogue as references that favor collective and intentional appropriations.

Therefore, inquiry into a collective past is closely associated with a teleological perspective, implicating existential meanings (Frankl, 1984). Like Ailton Krenak (2022) defines the idea of an ancestor future, trance *dispositifs* in this investigation are based on an imaginary past but demand a future perspective, characterized by the arrangement between multiple times experiences. However, even if that search is directed towards the past, it cannot be conceived without the future, under the penalty of losing sight of meaning construction. Then, the desirable outcome from this process is the "future memory" (Seif, 2019), in which past dispositions, meetings, teachings, and learnings, especially feelings, desires (*Eros*), and scenes, create a desirable future, a field of experience that anticipates the emergence of the new. Trance *dispositifs* promote the emergence of daydreams that must be lived individually and collectively in order to build a world from aesthetic experiences. Trance-Modernity implies dreams in a broad sense (Kopenawa & Albert, 2015), unopposed to reality but simultaneously an essential influence and component of it. In addition, the dream's aesthetic influence becomes an essential form of worldbuilding which is quite different from the cartesian perspective of control, correlated with domination among nations and the environment. In contrast, as desirable future processes, dreams are related to a dialogical influence that demands connection, an integral respect concerning the world's modes of organization, and a shared construction of ideals.

Consequently, the De-signer's role is also related to the future and its modes of *dispositifs*. That part of this future is already present, as demonstrated by numerous AI studies (Holmes et al., 2019), multiverse works (Linde, 2017), and the intense impact of current technologies in human experiences (Santaella, 2005). Current hypnotic research carries illustrative examples of virtual reality produced through mechanical *dispositifs* leading people to trance (Rosseaux et al., 2021, 2022). The machine in these studies replaces the hypnotist, to produce trance experiences for patients who suffer from anxiety, depression, and chronic pain. By thinking the future through De-sign principles, these studies have relevant contributions because they highlight the barriers overcome between human beings and machines: they are not only intensively connected but also seem to establish a new form of integration. In some way, technology has become part of the human body in such a way that the absence of *dispositifs* could mean losing a limb for some individuals. As Bateson (1972) suggested, the human mind is not limited to the skull but forms a systemic path of information that situates people in the world. As Bateson explained, a blind man with his cane, the ground, objects, and natural elements are perceived by sim through his cane, skin, and other senses; his thoughts compose an information path named mind.

However, the virtual world introduces more complex elements to this notion of the mind, since it creates a new form of reality with its own laws, beings (such as avatars), and modes of organization. Perhaps virtual reality can be compared to the experience of trance, but, while the latter is produced through relationship, experience, and sometimes cultural objects (such as music, sounds, rituals), the former is produced by electronic *dispositifs*. As discussed by Seif (2019), the former can lead to a virtual process, and the former, to a visceral experience, while IA experiences are related to virtual reality, even if these dimensions are not entirely separated amongst them. As a result, a little girl can talk to an avatar or an IA creation to get help with her mathematics homework, and a chronic pain patient can swim into an imaginary sea to change his pain systems. Nonetheless, the situation becomes more complex when machines can produce trance and virtually cohabit with imagination (visceral) and consensual reality (visual). The machine *dispositif* has some level of autonomy: it is not necessarily controlled by a specialist as in trance *dispositifs*—it is only activated by the person with whom it is connected. If the specialist (the hypnotherapist or the shaman) is eliminated, semiotic relational bonds are redirected to machine productions. This dispositive process can create an endless reproduction of images and other signs generated through the mutual influences between machine work and imaginary productions as if two mirrors were placed opposite each other.

Intending to guide the future through a polychronic journey, the De-signer can favor new forms of integration among different *dispositifs* and practices. Despite multiple doubts on this point, the De-signer can promote peaceful cohabitation among different beings originating from the virtual, visual, and visceral spheres that have become growing part of the human experience. The main step is the introduction of wisdom from traditional knowledge, whose trance technology implicates indispensable notions of alterity and collective services for a Trance-Modernity culture. However, human anchorage, as a universal procedure for trance, must be included, because simple reproduction between subjects and machines would be permeated by many risks, propitious for heightened individualism. If AI and other technologies can promote numerous new forms of semiosis, human relationships that occur bodily, emotionally, and collectively are essential for new *dispositifs*, as they must maintain the human bond as a key condition (Binwsanger, 2008), a sign of the past, withe technology as a desirable future. Thus, trance process can be both accompanied by this new specialist, the De-signer, who can access many forms of machine productions from the subject's experience and be emotionally sustained by them through a therapeutic or educational bond. The De-signer must implicate the visceral connection between human beings to create a context of confidence and involvement that considers an individual's needs without abandoning the person to individualistic experiences. This will simultaneously help integrate the virtual world, where navigation is crucial. As expressed in Caetano's song "An Indian," the Indian (an ancestor and sign of the past) will be allied to the most advanced technology (a sign of the future) to transmit an obvious message, an aesthetic ideal.

Therefore, teleology, connected with communitarian senses of belonging, requires the idea of rebirth (Neubern, 2022), essential to integrate various *dispositifs* and practices. The journey toward the future is impossible without reconciling with the past, as well as moving toward the past is doomed without the culture of a desirable future. Claudia's double character during her trance experience highlights important lessons concerning rebirth and the integration between past and future. The little girl is a sign of a fruitful past, when she spontaneously worked in strong affinity with collective spiritual ideals that would disappear in her present, represented by herself in the audience watching those scenes. These numerous memory emergencies during trance may have triggered Claudia's rebirth: she felt renewed by these memories, and opened herself to a new life perspective, or teleology. As in Cristian teachings, Claudia seemed to become a child again, and, consequently, she was reborn. She felt invited to reintegrate the purity of her soul, her spirituality level, and intense desire to serve her neighbors into her new forms of life and thought.

Nonetheless, Trance-Modernity thinking implicates rebirth as a collective principle encompassing people and communities. By using *dispositifs*, meeting with *Ethos*, people can live their own rebirth experiences as a form to place themselves facing an existential future. That becomes possible because firstness experiences become central either to subjects or to their sense of collectivity, through polychronic experiences in which time is not linear (past, present, and future) but prominently circular. Moreover, inspired by Aîlton Krenak (2020), experiences such as Claudia's trance should not be conceived in terms of its utility but simply contemplated as a form of cosmic dance with life. Thus, as contemplation is prominent in comparison to usefulness and results (that are not, however, discarded), Trance-Modernity society is deeply implicated with practices and ideas in which rebirth and renewal are natural and fluid features of reality and not a problem to be controlled. In synthesis, individuals and society maintain something of their roots (*ethos*) through an ancestor's past without the fear of losing their identities and simultaneously leaving themselves in a synechistic navigation toward a desirable future.

In a partial conclusion, Trance-Modernity as a perspective requires *dispositifs* to produce a collective reconnection with *Ethos*. As shown by Peirce (CP 2.536), a common affective ground (*commens*) is necessary, but not only in terms of inquiry—because the intentionality in a Trance-Modernity community is inhabited by an aesthetic ideal that transcends survival and arrives at wisdom contemplation; happiness and love are more important than usefulness (Krenak, 2020). This idea means that technology, with its result-based logic, efficacy, and control, is important, but it must not be the priority in a Trance-Modernity world. It should be dominated by aesthetics and communitarian sense, in contrast with the individualism from current Western societies. Thus, this common ground composed essentially of feelings and other firstness signs does not presuppose the absence of conflict and divergences, because they are necessary for human growth. However, if love is present as teleology, it becomes a sign entire role is to mediate the most different contrasts typical to the human meeting. This common ground, frequently permeated by trance, also favors a crucial epistemological change: firstness signs are assumed as realities, like in traditional societies (Viveiros de Castro, 2018). In reviewing Descartes's affirmation, a De-signer would say, "I feel, so I am," meaning that feelings are not absolute realities but need to be seriously considered despite their powerful integrative influence and their multiple actions upon semiotic processes. They are the main foundation for successive rebirth processes.

The Self and the World

During Claudia's trance, she reported a beautiful scene: ancestors and spirits were with her, and she was simultaneously a protagonist and an audience. She also described memories of her grandparents and their incursions into the forest. In some way, these reports can be well explained via De-sign principles (Seif, 2019), especially by notions such as polychronic time, diaphanous spaces, and dialogue. Nevertheless, based on the idea of quale consciousness experiences as a main principle in Trance-Modernity, many remarks must be made, especially because firstness acquires an ontological *status*. Trance-Modernity principles consider that Claudia's ancestors, her spiritual guides, and these scenes are not only present as imagination but as a form of reality that must be comprehended in greater depth in order to favor new forms of reference for people and communities.

Citizenship and Knowledge

Perhaps the first step in this form of understanding is the flexible conception of self-limits regarding the world. Trance technologies are well-suited for this conception since they promote experiences in which references for reality shift, and many spiritual beings can emerge. Furthermore, Peirce's notion of the self (Colapietro, 1989; Petrilli, 2017) is also another significant contribution because it denies individualist Western ideas, introducing a complex semiotic process of interpenetration between the person and the world, going beyond physic environment and the current time. However, a Trance-Modernity perspective must recover dialogue with traditional knowledges and promote a new form of inquiry, a De-sign inquiry (Seif, 2019) concerning this complex relationship between self and world. Initially, it is necessary to investigate the ways in which sensibility is an epistemological component for traditional forms of inquiry, as human beings feel themselves connected and, more than that, part of the universe they investigate. Through imaginary processes and specific forms of *dispositifs*—some of them including trance –, people from traditional knowledges favor a different form of accessing the world, which can be considered a form of abduction. These practices perhaps can help explain "spells," in which a specialist uses objects from nature with intent to attack or heal somebody, who frequently describes the experience as if some object had been inserted into their body (Nathan, 2021). The same practices can also be useful in understanding situations in which a person can feel an interpenetrative process with the world (Martino, 1999), and obtaining precise information on hunting, fishing, natural disasters, and spiritual revelations. The tragic situation of alcoholism in Indigenous reserves (Brown, 2007) can also find a possible explanation in the cosmology that supports these practices, because their main cosmological principle—*Ethos* closely integrated with Nature—is violently destructed.

De-sign inquiry (Seif, 2020a), then, becomes a dialogical arena where the most different knowledges are welcome. Through trance, many experiences of integration with Nature can emerge, and so can different forms of audiences with whom these experiences can establish dialogical processes without the typical reductionism from Western science (Morin, 1990). A neurologist can be interested in potential neurological correlations in these experiences, but their interest cannot be conceived as the final explicative answer for trance because many other forms of knowledge can also negotiate and promote intelligibility using their specific sign systems. Spiritualists, economists, artists, psychologists, medicals, politicians, anthropologists, and mystical people, among others, can feel themselves invited to dialogue, recognize, and apply their specific *dispositif* techniques with their respective rigor, intending to know more about the signs for which they felt attracted. De-sign is a form of promoting this "knowledge citizenship," as different knowledges are respected and recognized as a possible form of rationality that can be addressed to their different publics. Moreover, as a form of navigation in waters predominantly inhabited by firstness, De-sign gains the *status* of original arena, where different forms of knowledge can have common ground. In some way, this common origin can promote new forms of integration among knowledges, especially considering the possibility of recognizing their differences, and not as a battle arena, in which they frequently struggle (Stengers, 1997). Again, the teleological ideal of love can guide this formation, especially for the protagonist's interrogations concerning their future (what do we want?) and their desirable futures (what do we desire?). A De-sign dialogical arena can be fertile in possible creations, especially concerning questions that are still without answers.

Integration

As the main consequence of this arena of dialogue, Trance-Modernity situates the human self as a semiotic place of collective integration of many dimensions commonly separated since Modernity. Knowledge is not external to human experience, as highlighted by Peirce in his criticism of Cartesian thought (Short, 2009). In contrast with Modernity, Trance-Modernity sustains that these multiple kinds of Knowledge inhabit human experiences and can establish different forms of communication amongst them. Seif's idea of integration is pertinent here (Seif, 2019), because different parts of the human experience, with multiple *phanerons*, cannot remain chaotic processes indefinitely; they demand some form of habit of thinking and acting. The typical amplification of experiences characterized by trance can promote not only a form of thought but especially a way of feeling knowledge, aiming at some level of coherence with them and implicating an aesthetical perspective on life and ethical attitudes for otherness. Therefore, trance *dispositifs* can favor integrative processes relating to thought, feelings, speech, and actions to promote coherence for a specific knowledge and multiple pieces of knowledge that inhabit by the self. Indeed, integration and coherence do not mean the absence of conflict or difference among these different parts of the self, but the possibility of cohabitation and the transcendence of barriers (Seif, 2020b) to create new ideas and perspectives. In this sense, science, religion, arts, law, and poetry become citizens of the same *Polis*, where they can communicate and work together on behalf of the same ideals.

Human beings and Nature are other forms of integration promoted in Trance-Modernity. Traditional knowledge offers an important clue to conceive curious semiosis between concrete natural elements (such as animals, plants, trees, rivers, forests, winds, and lands, among others) and imaginary productions, such as gods and spirits of Nature, commonly achieved through trance, dreams, and divinatory practices. Trance-Modernity follows the same line of thought, including De-sign inquiry (Seif, 2019) as its main foundation. Based on a complex cosmology, imaginary beings are not restricted to what we commonly name "nature" but extend to the most diverse objects produced by human beings (Nathan, 2024). Semiosis, inspired in De-sign inquiry and allied to Ethnopsychology is extremely important in this point because it enables a panoramic perspective of the different signs implicated in the origin of these objects, such as the key-ideas, the specialists, the rituals or *dispositifs*, their message (interpretants), and their role into general cosmology. Perhaps the most immediate consequence of this inquiry is that imaginary processes are not a *chimera*, but a sign related to a broad process with suggestive meanings; and that physical objects and beings are not something to be discharged after being used or explored, but an important link of a broad semiotic chain that frequently contains messages and intentionality. Trance-Modernity presupposes prudence and respect concerning these signs that transcend internal and external limits and animate and inanimate barriers.

Alterity and Intentionality

Nevertheless, the most critical consequence is the change of perspective regarding alterity, which is expanded to include signs and especially imaginary beings. In this sense, *February Man*, Milton Erickson's case study (Erickson & Rossi, 2009), becomes a pertinent point of reflection, especially because of the topics concerning truth and ethics. Many years ago, Erickson received a woman who sought him because she wanted to be a good mother, but she was afraid, as she did not have a prior positive experience with family. She reported that her family was very rich, and her parents did not have time for her; her father was careful and lovely, but he was always busy traveling and working in multiple businesses. Her mother was vapid, interested in social gatherings where she could flaunt her riches. As a result, the girl grew up without parent references; they were never present in important episodes of her life, such as school events. Through complex forms of suggestion, Erickson described a man who was introduced as his father's friend and was present in significant episodes of her life. He introduced himself as *February Man* and always behaved as an emotional support for the girl when she seemed to lack her parental affective presences. This character was Erickson himself, but this information was introduced through an indirect form of suggestion, which would not be registered consciously by the patient, at least at the beginning of treatment. She became a mother and, following Erickson's understanding, she did not seem to feel the emotional absence of her parents as a problem in caring for, transmitting affect, and being present for her sons. Nonetheless, this case study is polemic, especially because Erickson is accused of introducing memories that never happened and a character with whom she never had actual contact. Thus, for many therapists and psychologists, *February Man* was a case of false memories introduced that should merit ethical and professional condemnation despite their therapeutic results.

In contrast, I maintain that these interventions were not ethically reprehensible, especially because memories should not be considered only in terms of their correspondence with actual events. Indeed, criticism against *February Man* is relevant considering numerous abusive situations with false memories that lead to iatrogenic consequences (Loftus & Ketcham, 1994; Hacking, 1995). However, Erickson's approach in this case was based on entirely different principles, which are illustrative to Trance-Modernity. Memories are not a perfect correspondence to reality; since they are a semiotic system traversed by several other influences from personal features as well as social and cultural traits. Many instances of cultural trance (Clément, 2011; Martino, 1999) should be questioned or prohibited because their semiotic production is commonly inhabited by beings that do not have any correspondence with consensual reality. The main issue on this point is whether the experience created from a memory respects some conditions, as explained in Chap. 5, when I discussed extremist movements (Berger, 2018). In Erickson's patient, *February Man* was coherent with her deepest requirement for emotional support, which was essential for her life. It was tailored for her needs, feelings, and uniqueness to promote an emancipatory process from the suffering originated from her parent's emotional absence. As a result, it respected her ecologic systems, family projects, and teleology without inducing her to social or aggressive attitudes toward others, such as her parents or institutions. Moreover, through a polychronic time and diaphanous space perspective (Seif, 2019), the consensual notion of reality was suspended as reality became multiple and flexible. The feeling of presentness that characterizes clinical attitude in hypnotherapy (Neubern, 2023) favors an experience in which time is flexible and multiple, and events are essentially imagination. Therefore, if the *February Man* was not a real man, present in significant moments of her life, he was still a sign of Erickson's therapeutic presence in her life. This would not replace her parents' absence, but supply her with emotional support. Every therapeutic process works with this goal: to supply comfort for absences, introducing emotional experiences when the patient is lacking. However, Erickson seemed to make this more explicit through hypnotic techniques without caring for the consensual and prominent notions of reality. His intervention is allied to Peirce's conduct of life (Atkins, 2016), which considers feelings and instincts over scientific truth based on traditional notions of reality, ethical attitudes, and decisions.

February Man can lead us to consider many contributions to Trance-Modernity thought. In general, it was an interpretant system carefully created by Erickson, who was also a sign system promoting therapeutic changes for his patient. *February Man* was a form tailored by him to enter his patient's self, transcending time and space boundaries and promoting new perspectives (meanings) on reality. Erickson's deliberations were precise, detailed, and developed in order to achieve significant therapeutic results. It is possible, however, to envisage Erickson's intentionality (Deely, 2009; Seif, 2019), which emerged from his experience, his desire to help her as a therapist, and hypnotic use, which is a powerful device for intentional emergences (Neubern, 2022). However, some differences concerning traditional knowledge trance must be traced to analyze possible elements of Trance-Modernity thought. First, *February Man* was Erickson's double, as its actions and discourse concerning the patient were restricted to character construction by himself. Like a theater character, he followed a script created by himself with specific therapeutic goals. Consequently, he had some level of autonomy, but, in general, he repeated his intentions concerning the woman's therapeutic process. Secondly, trance was created under the perspective of a unique universe (Nathan & Stengers, 1999), in which the human being is its own unique thinking power, and other beings, such as spirits, gods, and ancestors, are only fabrications of the human creative mind to give meaning to the universe. Thus, despite the creativity inherent to the character of *February Man*, it was the reproduction of Erickson's geniality that gained life through trance.

Many differences between Erickson's patient and Claudia's case study can be noted, especially concerning *February Man* and the spiritual guide White Feather. Initially, if the former was an individual creation, the latter was a collective one, made and remade for generations and different types of tools from Umbanda and Kardecism. Thus, White Feather would display a more complex script, as he was nourished from different groups, regions, contexts, and ages. As a transgenerational being, White Feather tended to have a richer script than *February Man*'s, because his lines were written and reviewed by many directors (specialists) at different times and in different spaces. As a collective being, it had multiple voices through which it could manifest different versions according to cultural variations in Brazil. Possibly, White Feather's richness in terms of multiple scripts could allow it more autonomy in comparison with *February Man*. Indeed, his autonomy was still more prominent in Claudia's trance, because White Feather was neither created by me through hypnotic suggestion, nor was he mentioned by Claudia during therapist conversations until he appeared during trance. In contrast with *February Man*, White Feather emerged only through Claudia's intentionality and not from deliberateness because none of us wished him into being. In this way, a possible Ethnopsychological explanation can be developed. White Feather was a spiritual being who inhabited a collective machinery, present in Claudia's history and experiences. Because she was under intensive suffering and lived a particular pivotal moment, her search for meaning was connected with this machinery via intentionality and not deliberation, because consciously she refused to accept spiritual ideas. Thus, as trance evoked itself beyond the ego, she was able to accept, at least on some level, the presence of White Feather, who delivered her unexpected messages.

It is important to note that White Feather was more related to Umbanda, which Claudia did not deliberately choose as a religion—she had been Kardecist since her childhood. At this specific moment, although Umbanda is also a religion, a system of thinking strongly rejected by Claudia, it seemed more acceptable to her because it represented a significant contrast with Kardecism. Umbanda was more connected with meaningful subjects for Claudia (such as ecology and traditional peoples, who are commonly marginalized in Brazilian society). On the other hand, Kardecism meant for her the hypocrisy of dominant classes who disregarded legitimate spiritual values. Perhaps these topics should facilitate her intentional search for a kind of spirituality that was more coherent with her values and needs.

Considering the relationship between the self and the world, some topics from these two case studies can illustrate possible Trance-Modernity principles inspired by the notion of De-sign (Seif, 2019). The main topic is alterity, a principle that is expanded to many other beings beyond humans. In general, following traditional knowledges (Krenak, 2022), Trance-Modernity presupposes that natural or physical things are not inanimate entities but living components and intentional inhabitants of our world. This idea not only presupposes a new cosmology, as mentioned, but also introduces the idea of intentionality that permeates semiosis in different systems—it also features in machineries, practices, and *dispositifs*. In revisiting traditional ideas from De-sign (2019, 2020a), intentionality does not assume that a stone, as an individual piece, can think as a human being, but that, as a world object, it is permeated by synechism and evolution that presupposes some intentionality from a superior mind (Raposa, 1989). If signs grow (and a stone is a sign system), they are moved by inherent intentionality traversing different beings and acts upon their evolutionary processes; it is a thirdness process that influences innumerable existents, limited on time without being restricted to them.[3] Therefore, some kind of intentionality emerges from complex interactions between the self and the world: a togetherness (Colapietro, 2014), especially because these interactions are semiotic and produce meaning; this intentionality is a key notion of understanding and approaching this new notion of alterity.

Indeed, deliberateness as present in Erickson's effort to construct *February Man* is an important moment for De-sign inquiry (Seif, 2020b): it can be conceived as an ethical effort toward an aesthetical ideal. The intentionality that emerges from his own ideal of hypnosis, vague as an icon (Raposa, 1989), is essential for De-sign inquiry because it sets an emotional contract with the patient, an incarnated sign of something admirable from hypnotherapy as a human meeting. In synthesis, *February Man* was more a reproduction of Erickson's image; its intentionality should be considered more towards the therapist. The same question—intentionality—is quite different in Claudia's case, since White Feather was an autonomous and collective sign, whose actions were not predictable for the subjects involved, and his message was unexpected for her.

Therefore, if intentionality is closely associated with desirable outcomes and with the emergence of uncommon sense (Seif, 2019), Trance-Modernity requires contexts through which beings' intentionality could emerge and create new

---

[3] It is possible to conceive that traditional knowledges (Martino, 1999) developed a similar perspective because they were spiritualists and presupposed a principle linking all things among them, governed by one/multiple minds or gods.

realities, establishing dialogue with humans. Alterity and intentionality radically change references of external *vs.* internal in trance experiences. De-sign inquiry sustains navigation throughout semiotic chains from Nature to individual trance experiences, bringing the world into the subject. White Feather, for example, had some level of autonomy, as an agent of collective machinery and natural elements; but he was also a sign for this Nature and collectiveness, so his messages were still to be deciphered by Claudia and by those who helped her in this task. Implicit messages from this and other spiritual guides were related to *Ethos*, since the ancestors evoked her intention to continue on her spiritual mission. Nevertheless, the main issue is not only to decipher messages but to deal with these beings as a form of reality. In Trance-Modernity, spiritual beings' ontological dimensions are conceived through a relationship with machinery in terms of intentionality and autonomy— two twin notions that are closely related to alterity. The De-signer, thus, should not only consider the machinery's typical criterion of legitimacy but essentially conceive a complex chain of signs between the spiritual beings and the collectiveness it represents, human or non-human. Spiritual beings are not only imaginary, but have an ontological *status* obtained from the world and from the *dispositifs* utilized to mobilize this world. Natural elements are, then, present through their intentionality, acting deeply into the human self and simultaneously re-linking this self with Nature. It is the same principle from many traditional knowledges worldwide, which relate people to animals and to other natural elements (Nathan & Stengers, 1999).

Alterity and intentionality are closely related to two essential topics for Trance-Modernity. The first of them is the complex idea of truth in trance experiences and the emergence of beings. During a process such as Claudia's, there is a large multiplicity of signs and meaningful productions related to the most different sources, such as ancestry, Claudia's particular history, and the current political scenario, the therapeutic context, trance practice, and my own presence as a therapist, which was also a form of influence and hypnogenesis. Following the maxim of pragmatism, according to which the total number of affirmations can furnish the good idea of an object (Peirce, 1903/1997), many statements could be made from Claudia's experience, especially concerning White Feather. Numerous affirmations by this spiritual guide could have been made by cultural specialists from Umbanda and Kardecism, Claudia's family members, myself, and even spiritual guides through their respective *dispositifs*. However, in a Trance-Modernity context, these affirmations should be made inside a dialogical context (Seif, 2019) through which they could be reflected and assessed under Claudia's teleology as their main guideline. The truth would emerge not following a Modern and objective perspective, but through dialogue, encompassing the multiplicity of signs and meanings from Claudia's experiences. The legitimacy of White Feather as a spiritual being, the correct use of his respective *dispositif*, the pertinence of his actions regarding Claudia's life, my own impressions and interventions, and Claudia's multiple semiotic consequences during and after trance are some facets of this multiple notion of truth that characterizes Trance-Modernity—a truth that can cover elusiveness (visceral), emergent concrete results (visual), and teleologic (virtual) changes related to trance experience.

Moreover, this form of interpellation from the spiritual world implicates the subject of integrity (Seif, 2020a), especially because it can evoke deep dimensions of the self. Trance-Modernity practices can evoke the most different facets of the human self and a central dimension related to a collective and agapistic teleology. If different *dispositifs* can interpolate the most different experiences and spiritual beings, such as healing, spells, blessings, curses, and revelations (Nathan, 2021), there is a main dimension accessed through agapistic intentionality, commonly recognized by traditional knowledges but not by Modern sciences. Sri Aurobindo's criticism of Freud's psychoanalysis is an exemplary illustration (Aurobindo, 1957): psychoanalysis proposed a conception of mind based on the most primitive forms of energy and experiences without considering a *Numinous* dimension for the human self. Despite meaningful exceptions, as Jung (2023) and Frankl (2007), Western prominent trends in psychology followed Freud's idea of conceiving the human self from its animal roots and/or from a materialistic perspective without intellectual space for the *Numinous*, or the spiritual. Nonetheless, Trance-Modernity proposes that intentionality based on Agape is a form of accessing and promoting the *Numinous* dimension (Otto, 2017), like in Claudia's case study. White Feather was a sign system that could evoke her *Numinous* experiences and integrate them into a new system, so they worked as a reference for her personal issues and collective interests. An agapistic teleology would work to promote integrative processes considering love as ideal but without nulling the difference and the specificity of these different forms of experience.

Sri Aurobindo (1852–1950) was a prominent philosopher, politician, and Yogi in India, in the twentieth century. From his childhood to the age of 19, he studied in England, became a profound student of Western culture, languages, and philosophy. When he returned to India, he was implicated in a political movement for India's freedom and imprisoned for two years, accused of terrorist attacks. During a public judgment, no proof was presented against him; he was only charged with writing papers in favor of India's independence. However, in jail, he had many mystic experiences that served as a call to a spiritual mission, leading him to abandon the political movement when he was freed. He developed Integral Yoga, conceiving the multiple parts of the human self that should be governed by superior parts of a certain Divine origin. Many of his disciples came from Western countries for Aurobindo's expertise in Western language and philosophy, so eventually he was asked about Freud's ideas. He considered that Freud's psychoanalysis was an imperfect comprehension of the human self because it uniquely emphasizes the most inferior and primitive dimension of the self without recognizing the superior one (Aurobindo, 1957).

Some essential topics are derived from this consolidative proposal. Perhaps the main question is establishing a difference between spirituality and the meaning adopted here with religion; Trance-Modernity thinking is essentially spiritual. Based on Peirce's philosophy of religion (cited in Raposa, 1989, 2020), *Agape* is the main evolutionary principle that guides or propels semiotic growth in different sign systems, also closely related to synechism. A spiritual life is a life based on the ideals of Agape, which can also include contributions from the most different beings, created from different *dispositifs*, as demonstrated by Ethnopsychology (Nathan, 2014). Thus, a spiritual form of life implicates a sense of integration among beings: they have a common evolutionary ground and grow following the same agapistic principle—love. This understanding is often present among mystics and religious leaders, such as Saint Francis of Assisi or Ramakrishna, but it can go beyond religious boundaries and encompass different knowledges and daily practices. In Trance-Modernity, the sense of neighborhood for spiritual people also becomes familiar for scientists, artists, sportsmen, and common people from quotidian life. However, this principle can gain life through trance *dispositifs*, as it becomes more concrete especially through insertion in invisible works with their own laws and beings, where the De-sign inquiry is central. It is a form of rescuing a sense of enchantment towards the universe, but with semiotic language and understanding that transcend knowledge boundaries and is available to anyone.

Another important consequence is the role of the ego in this integrative process, which requires a De-sign surrender or service to the agapistic ideal. The ego can choose which dimension of the self it must connect to, considering many different forms of experiences that characterize it. A De-sign surrender means that ego should recognize different human necessities and desires and consider their role in human life. Thus, De-sign inquiry can lead people towards the sublime and the grotesque (Seif, 2019, 2020b); more importantly, to experiences that encompass both sorts of feelings. Ludwig Wittgenstein's life trajectory offers a pertinent example: since his youth at the university, he had frequently thought about suicide, a recurring fate in his family. On many occasions, he was approached by professors and colleagues during the night, when he was pacing—expressing his intense anxiety and his suicidal ideas. His genius was, then, accompanied by intense suffering, and many people in this life believed that he would eventually die in a few years. However, he was sent to the war for Austria, voluntarily; in battle, he found time to write one of his most important books, *Tractatus Logicus Philosophicus*, a book on logic which promotes its self-destruction at the end. During this complex journey, he found a unique tome in an old bookstore that seemed crucial and meaningful for him: *The Gospel in Brief*, by Leon Tolstoy. At least as a hypothesis, Tolstoy's book may have established a deep connection with Wittgenstein; more precisely, with his *Numinous* experience. Consequently, the link between his ego and *Numinous* was essential to transform his agony into a symbolic system—a book—so he could reconfigure his suffering into new form of intentionality, that is, a desirable outcome. In other words, instead of choosing death, he wrote a book; or, instead of being inspired by his reactive family legacy, he transformed it into a thirdness process that could outlive him and be accessed and discussed by many people.

Nevertheless, in trance, the ego's choices have different features, because the ego is decentered from its place of command (Neubern, 2016), and other systems or beings become clearly autonomous from it. De-sign thinking is, then, an educative process, because the person must recognize multiple possibilities from different experiences, their risks, and the principle of service, as the ego surrenders itself to agapistic ideals (Seif, 2019) such as *Numinous*, a long trajectory that commonly demands rigorous discipline, as notable in Ramakrishna and Chico Xavier. Nonetheless, despite these two prominent men being inspirational to many as an ideal, they are not necessarily the human model for Trance-Modernity. Common people must also learn how to serve other dimensions, such as *Eros* and *Philos*, even if *Agape* is the ideal. Thus, trance processes become an educative practice in which people need to find gods and demons inside themselves to deal with them as members of an internal community within somebody's personal world. In short, through De-sign education, a person can deal with the "evil" and the "good" and their multiple faces and connections; they are essential for an integrative and coherent process that can avoid Manichean traps that have historically led to different forms of tragedy. This De-sign integrative process, however, should be guided by an agapistic ideal, either to integrate the darkest and most destructive processes or to promote solidarity as the main principle for human relationships.

Collectiveness and Service

The discussion above promotes criticism against the Modern notion of self-made, individualistic man (Nathan & Stengers, 1999). By introducing the idea of an inhabited universe as a form of reality and not only as image production, Trance-Modernity places the human being into an arena of dialogue with many possibilities with the most different forms of beings and intentionality. It criticizes Modern individualism (Dumont, 1983), in which human beings are semiotically isolated from the world, but recognizes, in contrast, that Modern individuality has essential contributions to contemporary societies, such as in human rights, science, and social organizations, among others. In short, it has been a central Western achievement through many centuries, often used as a form of resistance against social and political oppression—and a central pillar for democracy (Dumont, 1983). Therefore, individualism implicates a considerable conflict with collective values because its principles are commonly not coherent with social, communitarian, and ecological needs, as envisaged in tragic economic inequality (Oxfam, 2023). Examples are contemporary wars and genocides (Chomsky, & Polychroniou, 2023), numerous forms of mental disease (Han, 2015), the destruction of the environment and entire ethnic groups (Wallace-Wells, 2020), and different pervasive forms of violence. Based on a straightforward formula, the contemporary age experiences a conflict between "egoism" (fronted by individualism) and solidarity, represented by collective and communitarian perspectives.

Inspired by the De-sign inquiry (Seif, 2019), Trance-Modernity does not offer answers but possible ways of dealing with the conflicts between individualism and collectiveness. Alterity and intentionality are key notions for this inquiry as they invite people to consider otherness, including either humans or non-humans—such as concrete objects and beings from Nature and the invisible world. When inserted in an inhabited and plural semiotic universe (Neubern, 2023), human actions always have consequences because different interlocutors are not inert and lifeless objects, but active entities permeated by systemic intentionality, as explained. Thus, people are constantly invited into a reflexive attitude, an imaginary observer of their own actions in the world, especially concerning their relationships with other entities. Claudia's case study is illustrative because, despite her disbelief, she understood that White Feather and the other spirits were real beings, though their bodies and environment were essentially elusive. Moreover, in addition to demonstrating autonomy, they brought her a powerful message: the death of her inner child would produce negative consequences for her life; its central meanings assumed reality *status* for her. In a Trance-Modern perspective, a person in a similar situation should reflect on their current life to take these beings and their intentionalities seriously before making a decision. As discussed by Krenak (2020), if the world is inhabited by active beings and not by inert objects, human beings cannot use Nature's elements only for their egotistic references. After all their beings are always in an ecologic relationship with us, and thus require recognition and respect.

The balance between *Eros* and *Agape* is another important reference for considering individuality and collectiveness. A brief interpretation of Claudia's case study allows me to conclude that her revolt against Kardecism was basically explained by her deeply wounded *Eros* experience. Her desires, as a woman, friend, medium, professional, and communitarian worker, were intensively attacked by abusive relationships, immoral behaviors, and values that were not coherent with her spiritual values. Thus, for therapeutic reasons, this *Eros* dimension had to be reconnected and lead her back to desire and dreams, with experiences and goals that were essential for her, like sexuality, friendship, professional achievement, personal projects, and healthy social relationships. She felt comfortable, for example, speaking during sessions about men with whom she had some meetings (*amour*), contemplating possible engagements because, in contrast with her religious past, she recognized her sexual and affective needs. She was also engaged in searching for healthy friendships (*Philos*), determined to refuse any abusive bonds she experienced during her trajectory in family or religious groups. Trance with her spiritual guides was also inhabited by *Eros*, especially because it implicated a form of reconnection with Nature in multiple senses, such as with her ancestors, forests, animals, trees, rivers, and people. It was a form of feeding her desires and establishing a concrete link with their social reality. For example, she was able to purchase land near the forest, so she could pursue her ecology projects. She stated that, through this action, she felt more integrated with herself and could contribute to others with good services.

Nonetheless, if *Agape* cannot be conceived without *Eros*, in Trance-Modern thought, the latter would make no sense without the former. Claudia's main conflict was that *Eros* has been repressed and assaulted, so she never could achieve a legitimate *Agape* experience; consequently, many spiritual teachings remained only at ego's level without touching and changing *Numinous* dimensions in the self. Her social ideals also seemed to face many obstacles, which were impossible for her at the time and broadly nourished by the current negativism diffused by the media and by Claudia's previous social circle. Consequently, to achieve her social ideals, reconnecting with *Agape* was mandatory, as the spiritual meeting was promoted by trance into a significant experience. The broad sense of collective ideals come from *Agape* experiences, since these ideals introduce the perspective of *Ethos* and neighborliness with different beings and the Cosmos. At the same time, individual integrity is firstly related to *Eros*, because integrity encompasses recognizing and allowing the expression of the most distinct forms of desires. Then, the human being in Trance-Modernity often navigates between *Eros* and *Agape* concerning his personal integrities, which are related to collective or *transpersonal* aspirations. One's humanity has, at least, a double essence marked by humanity and divinity, as these transit between conflicts, fusions, and dialogue.

The Obvious

Caetano's beautiful song used to introduce this chapter ends with the word *obvious*. The magnificent Indian described there, who came from the stars, expressed *obvious* as his main message without detailing what this obvious message was. In the perspective of Trance-Modernity, the obvious can be meaningful in different senses. Many of Erickson's forms of hypnotic induction (Erickson & Rossi, 1979) were based on the obvious, such as truisms, analogies, and storytelling through which iconicity could exert suggestive powers (Neubern, 2016). Broadly speaking, however, Trance-Modernity deals with a double paradox: the obvious it implicates vagueness, multiple-meaning possibilities, and trance suggestion, evading definition. On the one hand, the obvious is related to a collective contemplation; impressions are constantly renewed. As mentioned, through communitarian practice and thinking, these multiple impressions are not decisive conclusions, instead being preferentially semiotic resources for social bonds to answer a central question for community construction: "What can unify us in our humanity?". Claudia's trance, for example, was appreciated based on the feelings it triggered in people, who could ask and discuss these feelings, their impressions, and how they led them to consider otherness in terms of people, beings, and the world. This form of treating the obvious requires, indeed, a shared teleology that would offer significant references to these dialogical context. As De-signers (Seif, 2019), navigational practices sustain a fluid form of reality, holding a continuity of synechism, albeit in constant change. De-sign thinking (Seif, 2019, 2020a) becomes central in Trance-Modernity's world because people would face the challenge of learning in a world permeated by elusiveness and vagueness, capable of searching for an integrative process.

Finally, the obvious is related to a profound message: we are the world whenever we exert contemplation in a Trance-Modern sense. The self is in the world; it works as an active and creative character to modify many semiotic networks of which it participates (*Umwelt*), as well as the world is into the self through semiotic influence, which is essential for self-development (*Inwelt*). As illustrated in Claudia's trance, there was a form of togetherness (Colapietro, 2014): she was inside that collective world, also penetrated by it and promoting different semiotic processes for her own development. That world was a sign system developed from collective experiences (*Ethos*), and Claudia was the actor and audience in the scene. Nonetheless, Trance-Modernity sustains that individual and collective contemplation (*Lebenswelt*) are forms of hypnogenesis; we not only have ourselves expressed into the world but also have the possibility of promoting our desires for this world. Thus, the *obvious* is either what faces us during contemplation or the relationship in which we can transform this world from our desires and aesthetic ideals. Any readers might ponder that we cannot transform social and physical reality only because we want to—especially considering contemporary challenges related to inequality, peace, and the environment. However, contemplating reality is a form of incarnating our dreams and desires in our own practices in order to begin by transforming the *Inwelt* and sometimes the *Umwelt*, as Claudia tried to do in her environment and social life. *Lebenswelt* is closely related to a desirable future, achieved through a delicate play between the self and the world. Claudia understood that her sons and grandchildren deserved to receive something meaningful to deal with and face the world they would inherit, and this thought was crucial for her to choose health, friendship, and pleasure in her life. She applied to her hypnotherapy a Trance-Modern principle: the desirable future encompasses our love for the next generations, who, despite tragedies, will be receptive to the *obvious* Indian message from the stars.

References

Atkins, R. (2016). *Peirce and the conduct of life. Sentiment and instinct in ethics and religion*. Cambridge University Press.
Aurobindo, S. (1957). *On Yoga*. Pondicherry.
Bairrão, J. F. M., & Lemos, D. (2013). Doença e morte na Umbanda branca: a legião branca Mestre Jesus. *Estudos e Pesquisas em Psicologia, 13*(2), 677–703. https://doi.org/10.12957/epp.2013.8431
Bateson, G. (1972). *Steps to an ecology of mind*. The University of Chicago Press.
Berger, J. M. (2018). *Extremism*. The MIT Press.
Binswanger, L. (2008). Sur la Psychothérapie [On psychotherapy]. In L. Binswanger (Ed.), *Introduction à l'analyse existentielle*. Minuit. (Original work published in 1935).
Brioschi, M. (2016). Hints toward cosmology: The need for cosmology Peirce's philosophy. *SCIO, Revista de Filosofia, 12*, 51–73.
Brown, D. (2007). *Bury my heart at wounded knee. An Indian history of the American West*. Holt Paperback.
Carvalho, J. (1994). O encontro de novas e velhas religiões: Esboço de uma teoria dos estilos de espiritualidade [The meeting of new and old religions: Outline of a theory of styles of spirituality]. In E. A. Moreira & R. Zicnan (Orgs.), *Misticismo e novas religiões* (pp. 67–98). Vozes.

Chomsky, N., & Polychroniou, C. (2023). *The illegitimate authority. Facing the challenges of our time*. Haymarket Books.

Clément, C. (2011). *L'Appel de la Transe* [The Call of the Trance]. Stok.

Colapietro, V. (1989). *Peirce's approach to the self*. Suny.

Colapietro, V. (2014). The ineffable, the individual, and the intelligible: Peircean reflections on the innate ingenuity of the human animal. In V. Romanini & E. Fernandez (Eds.), *Peirce and biosemiotics. A guess at the riddle of life* (pp. 127–150). Springer.

Deely, J. (2009). *Intentionality and semiotics. A Story of Mutual Fecundation*. University of Scranton Press.

Dumont, L. (1983). *Essais sur l'Individualisme. Une perspective anthropologique sur l'idéologie moderne*. [Essays on Individualism. An anthropological Perspective on Modern Ideology]. Seuil.

Erickson, M. (1992). Healing in hypnosis. In E. Rossi, M. Ryan, & F. Sharp (Eds.), *The seminars, workshops, and lectures of Milton Erickson, MD* (Vol. 1). Irvington.

Erickson, M., & Rossi, E. (1979). *Hypnotherapy: An exploratory casebook*. Irvington.

Erickson, M., & Rossi, E. (1980). *The collected papers of Milton Erickson, MD*. Irvington.

Erickson, M., & Rossi, E. (2009). *The February man. Evolving consciousness and identity in hypnotherapy*. Routledge.

Frankl, V. (1984). *Man's search for meaning*. Pocket Books. (Original work published in 1959).

Frankl, V. (2007). *A presença ignorada de Deus* [The ignored presence of God]. Vozes. (Original work published in 1988).

Gonzalez Rey, F. (1996). *Problemas epistemológicos de la Psicología*. Academia.

Hacking, I. (1995). *Rewriting the soul. Multiple personalities and the sciences of memory*. Princeton University Press.

Han, B. (2015). *The burnout society*. Standford Briefs.

Hartshorne, C., & Weiss, P. (1980). *The collected papers of Charles S. Peirce (CP, 8 vol.)*. Harvard University Press.

Holmes, W., Bialik, M., & Fadel, C. (2019). *Artificial intelligence in education. Promises and implications for teaching & learning*. The Center for Curriculum Redesign.

Jung, C. (2023). *The man and his symbols*. Bantman. (Original work published in 1964).

Kopenawa, D., & Albert, B. (2015). A queda do céu. *Palavras de um xamã Yanomami* [The fall of the sky. Words of a Yanomami shaman]. Companhia das Letras.

Krenak, A. (2020). *A vida não é útil* [Life is not useful]. Companhia das Letras.

Krenak, A. (2022). *Futuro ancestral* [Ancestor future]. Companhia das Letras.

Linde, A. (2017). A brief history of the multiverse. *Reports on Progress in Physics, 80*(2), 022001. https://doi.org/10.1088/1361-6633/aa50e4

Loftus, E., & Ketcham, K. (1994). *The myth of repressed memories. False memories and allegations of sexual abuse*. St Martin's Griffin.

Martino, E. (1999). *Le Monde Magique. Parapsychologie, Ethnologie et Histore* [The magical World. Parapsychology, ethnology and history]. Synthélabo. (Original work published in 1944).

Morin, E. (1990). *Science avec conscience* [Science with consciousness]. Seuil.

Morin, E. (2015). *La méthode V. L'humanité de l'humanité. L'identité humaine* [The method V. The humanity of humanity. Human identity]. Points. (Original work published in 2001).

Nathan, T. (2014). *Nous ne sommes pas seuls au monde* [We are not alone in the world]. Seuil. (original work published in 2001).

Nathan, T. (2015). *Quand les dieux sont en guerre* [When the gods are at war]. Synthélabo.

Nathan, T. (2021). *Secrets de thérapeute* [Therapist secrets]. L'Iconoclaste.

Nathan, T. (2024). *Petits objets du quotidien. Ethnomythologie* [Small everyday objects. Ethnomythology]. Le Livre de Poche.

Nathan, T., & Stengers, I. (1999). *Médecins et sorciers* [Doctors and sorcerers]. Synthélabo.

Neubern, M. (2016). Iconicity and complexity in hypnotic communication. *Psicologia: Teoria e Pesquisa, 32*, 1–9. https://doi.org/10.1590/0102-3772e32ne217

Neubern, M. (2018). *Clínicas do transe. Etnopsicologia, hipnose e espiritualidade no Brasil* [Trance clinics. Ethnopsychology, hypnosis and spirituality in Brazil]. Juruá.

Neubern, M. (2022). The role of De-sign and intentionality in understanding hypnosis. In F. Seif (Ed.), *Intentionality and semiotic labyrinths* (pp. 113–126). SSA/Philosophy Documentation Center.

Neubern, M. (2023). Hypnosis, university and democracy: An emancipatory proposal. In M. Neubern & A. Bioy (Eds.), *Hypnosis in academia: Contemporary challenges in research, healthcare and education* (pp. 27–52). Springer.

Neubern, M. (in press). De-sign, renewal, and rebirth: Understanding hypnotic changes in clinical practice. The American Journal of Semiotics.

Otto, R. (2017). *The idea of the Holy*. Pantianos classics. (Original work published in 1917).

Oxfam. (2023). https://www.oxfam.org/en/tags/inequality

Peirce, C. (1903/1997). Pragmatism as a principle and method of right thinking. In P. Turrisi (Ed.), *The 1903 Harvard lectures on pragmatism*. State University of New York Press.

Petrilli, S. (2017). *The self as a sign, the world, and the other*. Routledge.

Puységur, A. M.-J. (1784/2003). Mémoire pour Servir à l'Histoire et à l'Établissement du Magnétisme Animal [Memory to be used for the history and establishment of animal magnetism]. In D. Michaux (Ed.), *Aux Sources de l'Hypnose* (pp. 13–132). Imago.

Raposa, M. (1989). *Peirce's philosophy of religion*. Indiana University Press.

Raposa, M. (2020). *Theosemiotics. Religion, reading, and the gift of meaning*. Fordham University Press.

Robin, R. (1967). *Annotated catalogue of the papers of Charles S. Peirce*. University of Massachusetts Press. (MS Peirce).

Rosseaux, F., et al. (2021). Virtual reality and hypnosis for anxiety and pain management in intensive care units. *European Journal of Anesthesiology, 38*, 1–9.

Rousseaux, F., et al. (2022). Virtual reality hypnosis in the management of pain: Self-reported and neurophysiologic measures in health subjects. *European Journal of Pain, 27*, 148–162. https://doi.org/10.1002/ejp.2045

Santaella, L. (2005). *Corpo e comunicação. Síntese da cultura* [Body and communication. A cultural synthesis]. Paulus.

Seif, F. (2013). Dialogue with Kishtta: A semiotic revelation of the paradox of life and death. *The American Journal of Semiotics, 29*, 101–115. https://doi.org/10.5840/ajs2013291-44

Seif, F. (2019). *De-sing in transmodern world. Envisioning reality beyond absoluteness*. Peter Lang.

Seif, F. (2020a). The role of pragmatism in De-Sign: Persevering through paradoxes of design and semiotics. *Cognition, 21*(1), 112–131.

Seif, F. (2020b). De-sign as a destiny of navigation: The paradox of sustaining boundaries while traversing borders. *The American Journal of Semiotics, 36*(3–4), 179–215.

Short, T. (2009). Peirce's theory of signs. .

Stengers, I. (1997). *La malediction de la tolerance. Cosmopolitiques* 7 [The Curse of tolerance. Cosmopolitics]. Synthélabo.

Stengers, I. (2001). Qu'est-ce que l'hypnose nous oblige à penser? [What does hypnosis force us to think about?]. *Ethnopsy, 3*, 13–68.

Stengers, I. (2002). *Hypnose: Entre Magie et science* [Hypnosis: Between magic and science]. Synthélabo.

Viveiros de Castro, E. (2018). *Metafísicas canibais* [Cannibalistic metaphysics]. Ubu Editora.

Wallace-Wells, D. (2020). *The uninhabitable earth. Life after warming*. Crown.

Index

A
Agape, 10, 13, 14, 48, 54, 56–59, 62, 105, 106, 146, 147, 149, 151, 157–164, 169–180, 182, 184–187, 189–191, 214–218
Amnesia, 13, 56, 58, 74, 76, 103, 123, 152

D
De-sign, 1–14, 17, 23–25, 30, 38, 42, 45–49, 53, 54, 57–67, 69–72, 74, 76–79, 83–87, 90, 95, 96, 101–103, 105, 106, 108, 109, 113–140, 145, 146, 148, 150, 153–155, 158, 159, 164, 171, 172, 174, 177–180, 186, 189–191, 195, 197, 200–204, 207–209, 212, 213, 215–218
Desirable outcomes, 4, 9–10, 12, 14, 24, 44–47, 67, 83–91, 95, 97–99, 101, 104, 106, 108, 109, 130, 133, 137, 140, 148, 149, 154, 156, 164, 172, 180, 181, 201, 204, 212, 215
Dialogue, 2, 3, 7, 12, 25, 30, 35, 41, 47, 74, 77–79, 104, 106, 109, 115–117, 123, 125, 127, 131, 132, 135, 136, 154, 162, 173, 177, 190, 199, 201–204, 207, 208, 213, 216, 218

E
Effectiveness, 4, 12, 17, 43, 46, 53, 66, 83, 84, 91–94, 108–109, 121, 130
Efficacy, 4, 12, 17, 21, 22, 28, 35, 39, 46, 54, 83, 86, 87, 89, 91, 115, 129, 130, 168, 174, 189, 206
Epistemology, 19, 116

Erickson, M., 1, 11–14, 22, 24, 31, 37–47, 49, 87–89, 92–94, 99, 101, 102, 104, 105, 114, 116, 118, 119, 121, 125, 127, 129–133, 151–156, 190, 197, 203, 209–212, 218
Eros, 14, 48, 59, 73, 96, 106, 126, 145–151, 154–156, 164–178, 184, 191, 204, 216–218
Ethnopsychology, 7, 8, 14, 46, 56, 75, 107, 138, 159, 180, 186, 199, 200, 209, 215
Ethos-Rebirth, 14, 195, 199–206

F
Firstness, 5, 7–9, 11, 14, 19, 20, 22, 23, 25, 28, 30, 35–37, 39, 40, 42, 45, 46, 83, 87–89, 95–97, 101, 103, 114, 117, 120, 121, 127, 130, 136, 195, 196, 200–203, 206–208
Freedom *vs.* determinism, 6, 13, 114, 117, 122–128, 139, 140

H
History, 7, 17, 21, 24, 26, 42, 45, 53, 59, 66, 84, 86, 90, 93, 98, 99, 108, 117, 139, 162, 201, 211, 213
Hypnosis, 1–14, 17–49, 53, 54, 56, 58–61, 63, 66, 69, 71, 72, 77–79, 83–100, 102–104, 108, 109, 113–140, 150–154, 195–219
Hypnotherapy, 1, 11, 12, 22, 43, 47, 54, 58, 73, 83, 92, 98, 106, 109, 117, 121–125, 128, 130, 151, 152, 196, 197, 210, 212, 219

I

Integration, 4, 11, 12, 14, 29, 38, 46–49, 61, 66, 83, 95–98, 116, 128, 131–133, 137, 146, 150, 157, 164, 169, 172, 174, 177, 186, 189, 195

Integrity, 29, 48, 64, 69, 84, 95, 102, 106, 147, 151, 172, 196, 197, 214, 218

Intentionality, 4, 12, 13, 48, 49, 58, 72, 76, 87, 88, 92, 95–98, 100, 107, 114, 125, 128, 132, 136, 182, 200, 206, 209–217

L

Love, 3, 9, 13, 14, 18, 48, 54, 56–59, 61, 64, 73, 77, 96, 105, 106, 122, 124, 126, 127, 133, 135, 139, 140, 145–191, 196, 198, 202, 206, 208, 214, 215, 219

M

Madness *vs.* sanity, 114, 117, 128–139

P

Paradoxes, 2, 4, 9, 13, 25, 30, 38, 39, 48, 49, 83, 99, 100, 104, 113–140, 150, 156, 158, 171–173, 188, 190, 200, 218

Partnership, 12, 13, 25, 38, 43, 47, 53, 59, 63, 102, 175, 177, 201

Phenomenological attitudes, 29, 40, 60

Phenomenology, 5, 29

Pornography, 126, 128, 146, 147, 150, 151, 153, 156, 165–178, 184, 185, 189, 191

R

Reality, 1–7, 9–11, 13, 14, 17–49, 59, 60, 65, 73, 77–79, 85, 87–89, 91, 98, 103, 107, 113, 114, 116–121, 124, 129, 140, 146, 149, 150, 152, 158, 159, 188, 191, 195, 196, 201–207, 210, 211, 213, 216–219

S

Semiotics, 2–5, 7–9, 12, 13, 17, 20, 23, 24, 28, 30, 33, 39–43, 45, 49, 53, 58, 59, 62–65, 68, 74–77, 79, 86–89, 93–96, 99–107, 115, 117, 124–126, 128, 130, 132, 136, 137, 146, 153–156, 172, 180, 188–190, 202, 205–210, 212, 213, 215, 217–219

T

Teleology, 3, 4, 20, 42, 48, 106, 114, 116, 117, 121, 129, 133, 156, 174, 205, 206, 210, 213, 214, 218

Traditional knowledge, 7, 21, 25, 71, 100, 196, 199, 200, 202, 203, 205, 207, 209, 211–214

Trance-Modernity, 14, 195–219

www.ingramcontent.com/pod-product-compliance
Lightning Source LLC
Chambersburg PA
CBHW050353270125

20889CB00003BA/98